George Washington

AMERICAN PRESIDENTS REFERENCE SERIES

- *Andrew Jackson*
  Richard E. Ellis

- *Lyndon Baines Johnson*
  Thomas S. Langston

- *Abraham Lincoln*
  Matthew Pinsker

- *Franklin Delano Roosevelt*
  Robert S. McElvaine

- *Theodore Roosevelt*
  Mario R. DiNunzio

- *George Washington*
  Thomas S. Langston
  Michael G. Sherman

- *Woodrow Wilson*
  Kendrick A. Clements
  Eric A. Cheezum

George Washington

THOMAS S. LANGSTON
MICHAEL G. SHERMAN

CQ PRESS

A Division of Congressional Quarterly Inc.
Washington, D.C.

To Taylor
To Alan and Sharon

CQ Press
1255 22nd Street, N.W., Suite 400
Washington, D.C. 20037

(202) 729-1900; toll-free, 1-866-4CQ-PRESS (1-866-427-7737)

www.cqpress.com

Grateful acknowledgment is made to Beacon Press for use of material from *Jefferson's Pillow*, by Roger Wilkins. Copyright 2001 by Roger Wilkins. Reprinted by permission of Beacon Press, Boston. For quoted material, see page 268.

Cover illustration by Talia Greenberg
Design by Karen Doody
Composition by Auburn Associates, Inc., Baltimore, Maryland
Editorial development by the Moschovitis Group, Inc.,
   New York, N.Y.

Printed and bound in the United States of America
07 06 05 04 03   5 4 3 2 1

Library of Congress Cataloging-in-Publication Data

Langston, Thomas S.
   George Washington / Thomas S. Langston, Michael G. Sherman.
      p. cm. — (American presidents reference series)
Includes bibliographical references and index.
   ISBN 1-56802-763-X (hardcover : alk. paper)
      1. Washington, George, 1732-1799. 2. Presidents—United States—Biography. 3. Generals—United States—Biography. 4. United States—History—Revolution, 1775-1783—Sources. 5. United States—Politics and government—1783-1789—Sources. 6. United States—Politics and government—1789-1797—Sources. I. Sherman, Michael G. II. Title. III. Series.
   E312.L27 2003
   973.4'1'092—dc21

                                                        2003010794

Contents

Preface

George Washington shaped the American presidency. The office was, in fact, designed for him.

The state delegates who met in Philadelphia in 1787 to forge a new constitution recognized that, to be effective, a government required an executive officer who possessed dignity, one who was able to balance strength with the acknowledgment that, ultimately, the people ruled. If the executive were too weak, Congress might tyrannize the people with bad laws. If the executive were too strong, Americans would have simply replaced a British king with one born in the colonies.

Everyone at the convention understood that George Washington would be the first to occupy the position of executive. He had lent his immense prestige to the enterprise of making a new constitution by coming to Philadelphia. And he allowed his fellow delegates to designate him unanimously as the presiding officer of the convention. His acceptance of the position signaled his willingness to preside over the new government as well. Secure in the knowledge that the first president would be the man who had won fame in Europe as well as at home by relinquishing command and retiring to his farm after leading the Continental army to victory, the framers, and the voters who ratified the Constitution, accepted the risk inherent in placing one man at the center of the nation's government. Washington had proven he could be trusted with power.

President Washington defined the office that had been crafted for him. He did so with great anxiety, thinking always of the precedents he was establishing for future occupants of the office. He performed the duties of head of state with a mix of republican simplicity and monarchical dignity. To this day, the American president is both a symbol of the nation's commitment to democracy and the closest thing the United States has to a king. As head of government, Washington balanced decisiveness with a now antiquated understanding of the constitutional separation of powers. He never sought to lead Congress in the way that modern presidents do, with persuasive rhetoric, centralized budgets, and the assistance of a large White House staff. He did, however, make full use of the powers of the executive as defined by the Constitution, including the power of the veto and the pardon, and in this way ensured for posterity that these would not be mere paper grants of authority to the nation's presidents.

President Washington also made decisions that defined the nation itself, along with the presidency. He maintained silence as Congress debated Alexander Hamilton's ambitious plans as secretary of the Treasury. Once a bill was placed before him that would establish a central bank, and in the process subordinate state governments to the central government, Washington studied the proposed law and decided to sign it. This bill had momentous consequences for the United States. The central government, not state governments, would exercise the preponderance of influence on the nation's economy. President Washington's use of military force was similarly important. In the Ohio Valley the president's persistent application of force against hostile tribes of Native Americans, who were aided by the British, opened the Northwest to large-scale settlement. In western Pennsylvania the president's use of force against the Whiskey Rebellion upheld the power of the national government to tax its citizens directly and to quell the sort of dissension that had compelled Washington to support the framing of a new constitution in the first place.

George Washington did not, however, enjoy the presidency. He had been truly reluctant to leave retirement to return to the center of national politics when he was called to the Philadelphia Convention, and from there to be the nation's first chief executive. He accepted the challenge dutifully but with regret. He fretted that the fame he had won in battle might be shattered in the bloodless arena of politics. He was right to worry. Washington's insistence in his second term on neutrality in a new war between France and Britain sparked the most extreme criticism he ever endured. The first president was vilified, slandered, libeled, and even reviled by citizens who took to the press, and to the streets, to protest his administration. Nevertheless, Washington persevered, with private anguish but public stoicism. Along with those who protested his actions, he ironically performed one of his greatest services to the nation in these mock battles. Together, Washington, the other members of the government who took sides for or against him, and the everyday citizens who did likewise, showed that the Constitution worked. In the midst of discord the president could make decisions and uphold them until the voters could judge their consequences at the polls. Citizens and their elected leaders could disagree violently with one another without actual violence.

At the end of two terms, during a fortuitous lull in the controversies surrounding America's relations with Europe, Washington retired once more to Mount Vernon, leaving the nation united, prosperous, and at peace.

ORGANIZATION OF THIS BOOK

This book reviews the life and presidency of George Washington. The introduction and chapter 1 provide an overview of the topic and establish the themes of the Washington presidency as national unity and expansion. Chapter 2, on campaigns and elections, details the career of George Washington, politician, from his first campaign for the Virginia House of Burgesses to his selection by the electoral college to continue in the presidency for a second term. Chapter 3 focuses on the major policies of the Washington administration, encompassing among other things his support for the Bank of the United States, the creation of a capital in the District of Columbia, the establishment of a competent regular army and an effective militia, and a foreign policy suitable for a new, militarily weak nation.

Chapter 4, on crises and flashpoints in the administration, focuses on the single overriding issue of Washington's second term: the crisis in America caused by the French Revolution and the consequent war between Britain and France. Chapter 5, on the president's relations with major institutions, covers both the formal institutions created by the Constitution and the two most important informal institutions of American democracy: political parties and the press. Washington's final retirement, the subject of chapter 6, was short and not particularly peaceful. At a time when he would have much preferred to concentrate on agricultural experiments and various pet projects, such as a Potomac River Canal, Washington was called upon by President John Adams to return to command of the American army when the war with France seemed imminent.

Roughly one-half of this book is devoted to primary documents, edited and introduced with headnotes by the authors, and to supplementary material in the appendixes. Appendix A presents brief profiles of the notable figures in the Washington administration. The key events in Washington's life are described in appendix B. Cabinet and other key administration officials are listed in appendix C, along with their terms of office and other information. Finally, appendix D presents detailed presidential election results that cover Washington's two terms in office.

ACKNOWLEDGMENTS

We would like to thank the Moschovitis Group, especially Valerie Tomaselli; Catherine Carter, who undertook the initial editing; and Eleanora von Dehsen, who expertly shepherded the manuscript through successive drafts, ensuring that each new version was not merely different from the one that preceded it but better as well. The authors are indebted to Christopher Anzalone of CQ Press for inviting us to work on this, our second volume in CQ's American Presidents Reference Series, and for providing his detailed commentary on a draft of the manuscript. Belinda Josey, also of CQ Press, ably oversaw production of the book. Freelancer Sabra Bissette Ledent set a high standard as copyeditor, rescuing the authors from factual inconsistencies as well as stylistic blunders. Any errors that remain are, of course, the authors' responsibility. We also are in the debt of the Mount Vernon Ladies' Association for assistance in locating rare documents and for its hospitality in affording one of the authors a private tour of some parts of Mount Vernon not generally open to the public. The Library of Congress's Manuscript Collection is a national treasure, and the archivists there were professional and expert in their help, as were the members of the staff at the Virginia State Historical Society. The David Library of the American Revolution in Washington Crossing, Pennsylvania, was an invaluable resource as well.

Thomas S. Langston
Michael G. Sherman

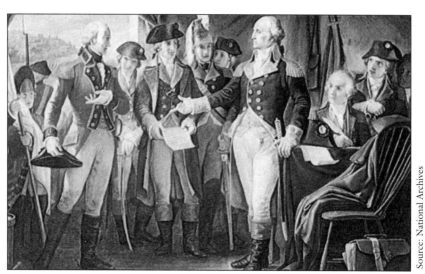

Gen. Lord Charles Cornwallis surrenders to Gen. George Washington following the battle of Yorktown. The painting is by the Italian-born artist Constantino Brumidi, who is best known for his frescoes in the U.S. Capitol.

Introduction

George Washington's place in American political history is unique. As commander in chief of the Continental army during the American War of Independence, he was the first person to command the nation's military, and he was the nation's first president under the Constitution of the United States. He also was extraordinarily self-conscious of being the first to hold these positions. He aimed not merely to succeed for his time, but to establish precedents that would give the new nation the best chance of success in the future. As a result, his career was as remarkable for what he chose *not* to do as for what he did. By wielding power with decisiveness, he held together first the army, then the government. By choosing not to hold onto power longer than was necessary—he voluntarily stepped back into retirement after winning the Revolutionary War and served only two terms as president—he became an icon of democratic self-constraint. By persevering in the lengthy War of Independence, and by proving that democracy need not mutate into tyranny, he became, in the words of his major modern biographer, James Thomas Flexner, the "indispensable man" (Flexner 1974).

Washington's reputation is grounded in his achievements, his character, and his legacy. His reputation is engraved in the image he crafted for himself during his lifetime. Remarkably, that image has survived, with only minor alterations, over a span of two hundred years.

ACHIEVEMENTS

George Washington, Rebel

George Washington commanded the army of the United States under the Articles of Confederation. This force, the Continental army, survived eight years of combat with the British. Washington's army was victorious in few battles, but it denied victory to the British and won often enough to maintain the confidence of the rebellious portion of the population and to inspire the French to come to its assistance. The defeat of the British was remarkable. The British army and navy constituted the strongest military force in the world, and would defeat all national competitors in the succeeding century.

As remarkable as victory in the war was, it was merely the means toward an even more exceptional choice of ends. Washington and his fellow revolutionaries intended to establish not only their independence, but their independence as a republic in which the ordinary adult white yeoman would be the foundation of government. The framers of the Constitution were well aware of the history of republics. None had survived for long, save for a few minor exceptions among the city–states of Greece and the cantons of Switzerland. And no republic had been attempted that would encompass so large a landmass as the thirteen states.

General Washington was not merely the military instrument of the American Revolution; he was himself a leading rebel. In Washington's day, the leading rebels were in most instances the leaders of their communities. Like the shopkeepers and shipowners of Massachusetts, the plantation owners of Virginia such as Washington were personally familiar with the hardships that British colonial policy imposed on American business. Moreover, the socially ambitious members of the provincial gentry throughout the colonies were constantly reminded of the middling status that even the most prominent colonial subjects enjoyed among the upper classes of England.

Perhaps no colonist felt these slights more keenly than George Washington, in whom "the ambition for distinction spun . . . like a dynamo" (Longmore 1988, 1). British policies, as Washington saw things, continually hampered him in his quest for distinction. For example, the king would not permit provincials to hold royal commissions in the army. As commander in chief of the Virginia Regiment, Washington was thus made the formal *inferior* of the lowest-ranking officer in His Majesty's army. The British Parliament would not provide adequate resources for the protection of the colonies against Indian assaults, but dared to tax the colonies for the inadequate level of defense it did provide. And British creditors and merchants treated Washington and other plantation owners with contempt, charging the highest prices for the poorest services.

As a soldier and a planter, Washington came to see that his private concerns were in fact matters of public importance. The colonists were the objects of discrimination. They were being denied the right to fair and equitable treatment by government, which was the right, in theory, of all British subjects. Along with other leading members of his community, Washington debated the proper course of colonial resistance. Meanwhile, he helped to organize and enforce a nonimportation covenant among Virginia planters. And he followed the debate over British policy closely, taking an increasingly radical stance as the moment of separation approached. When it became apparent that the resort to arms was the only recourse left, Washington discreetly put himself forward for the position of commander in chief of the rebel force.

Washington rebelled against what he saw as the despotic policies of a corrupt British government. He was, in this sense, a conservative rebel; he wanted to restore the rights of the British to the British living in the North American provinces. What he helped to accomplish was something more than what he and most other rebels in the colonies sought. Once free of formal ties to Britain, the American nation was free to develop a distinctly American understanding of rights, liberties, and national identity. As a framer of the Constitution and as the first president to serve under the Constitution, Washington moved from being the leader of a rebellion to being the leader of a nation.

George Washington, Nationalist

The American states won independence in the name of freedom from a despotic government. The American government under the Articles of Confederation certainly was not despotic, but was it even a government? George Washington tended to think not. From his position at the head of the army during a war waged under the Articles, Washington had a unique vantage point from which to observe the ill effects of having too weak a government for the states. The army often was not supplied for combat or paid for its services. In peace, would the states simply go their separate ways? Washington hoped not. In his farewell address to the army on November 2, 1783, he remarked with approval on the change made by the war. "Who . . . could imagine, that the most violent local prejudices would cease so soon, and that Men who came from the different parts of the Continent, strongly disposed by the habits of education, to dispise and quarrel with each other, would instantly become but one patriotic band of Brothers?" (Document 1.9).

It was to preserve the possibility of a *national* future for the former British colonies in America that a new Constitution was drafted and submitted to the voting public in 1787. Remarking to a friend that only "popular absurdity and madness" were propelling some people to resist the move to enhance the government's power, Washington expressed his fear that the nation would not last long "without having lodged somewhere a power, which will pervade the whole Union in as energetic a manner as the authority of the State government extends over the several States" (Smith 1980, 21).

Washington presided over the pivotal Constitutional Convention that met in Philadelphia in the summer of 1787. Afterward, he permitted his fellow nationalists such as Alexander Hamilton to use his name in lobbying the public to support the work of the framers. It was inevitable, then, that Washington would become the first president once the new Constitution was ratified and became the law of the land. Indeed, the office was, in a sense, designed with Washington in mind. Those who worried that the powers of the presidency were perhaps too great found courage in the thought that Washington would be the first person to hold the office and exercise those powers. Because he had previously proven his insensibility to the lust for power when he retired to his farm after leading the Continental army to victory, he had the nearly unanimous trust of the citizenry.

As president, Washington undertook important measures that strengthened national unity. Among other things, he persuaded Congress to support a peacetime military establishment and then used the forces to protect frontier settlements and to quell the domestic Whiskey Rebellion. He also established the president's role as chief negotiator in foreign affairs and prevented the United States from going to war against Britain.

President Washington also accomplished a great deal for the nation's new government by getting knocked about in party politics. Washington personally took no comfort in the verbal attacks he was subjected to as president. "The approbation of my country is what I wish," observed Washington, who considered such approval "the highest reward to a feeling mind" (Smith 1993, vii). One can only imagine the president's regret, then, upon reading assertions by fellow Americans such as the following, which appeared in the *Philadelphia Aurora* on December 23, 1796: "If ever a nation was debauched by a man, the American nation has been debauched by WASHINGTON. . . . If ever a nation was deceived by a man, the American nation has been deceived by WASHINGTON. . . . Let the history of the federal government instruct mankind, that the masque of patriotism may be worn to conceal the foulest designs against the liberties of the people" (see Document 5.10).

In retrospect, Washington served his country by allowing himself to become the victim of such personal political invective. The United States has a famously fragmented form of government. If presidents are to lead, they must do more than preside as head of state; they must get into the trenches and engage in political combat. Washington was reluctant to do so, but, buffeted by the most extreme criticisms, he realized he had no choice. He thus made it clear for all who would follow into the White House that the president is a politician after all, and not a king to be held in constant awe.

CHARACTER

What made it possible for Washington to accomplish what he did? His contemporaries found the answer in his character.

Who was George Washington? What manner of man was he? Washington's contemporaries were as eager for the answers to these questions as modern observers are to ones about the private lives of today's public figures. The questions, then, are familiar. But the answers do not come easily.

It is not even known precisely what George Washington looked like. The most accurate likenesses of the man, those that showed his age, did not sell well, leading profit-minded artists to make various "improvements" to Washington's appearance in their paintings (Rasmussen and Tilton 1999, 161, 163). One thing his various portrayals have in common, however, is their depiction of a man in complete control of himself. The tight-lipped, serene, but severe man depicted in the iconic, idealized portrait by Gilbert Stuart is a person who has achieved self-mastery, a character trait highly valued in Washington's time.

In the 1700s a man of honor struggled not to express himself, but to exhibit to others traits held in high esteem. In the words of the English playwright Joseph Addison, who was author of Washington's favorite play, *Cato*, the good man is not "true to self" but "true to others" (McDonald 1992, 55). He is independent of common opinion, but bound by honor to do what is right.

The traits that were most prized at this time were those of the gentleman, including independence from labor and financial pressures, service to the world beyond one's family, and fortitude in adversity. The "ruling passion of the noblest minds" was commonly understood, as Alexander Hamilton famously wrote in *The Federalist Papers* (No. 72), to be a desire for fame (*www.law.ou.edu/hist/federalist*). Glory was a divine gift. A person might share in glory, but could never win it without God's grace. Honor also was highly prized, but it too was not entirely within the power of the individual. One might lose honor through one's actions, but without the right birth it was virtually impossible to place oneself in the upper circles of society where honor bound gentlemen to one another and defined the terms of their service in the world. Fame was different; it could be won. Fame, observed historian Douglass Adair, was for the founding generation "egotism transmuted gloriously into public service" (Adair 1974, 12).

Washington had the good fortune in his lifetime to secure a particularly exalted fame, that reserved, in the words of the first-century Greek biographer Plutarch, for the "lawgiver and the founder of a commonwealth." This type of fame was derived not from thought but from action. Its pursuit was a constant spur to Washington from the time he took command of the Continental army, if not earlier. From that moment on, he appeared in public and in his private correspondence as if he were on a stage in the role of a "character." His stage was the founding of a new republic. His audience was posterity. His role was of necessity improvised, but it was based on the English adulation of the classical tradition, brought back to life in the European Enlightenment. Through his association with his English-educated half-brothers and his noble-born neighbors the Fairfaxes, and through his own extensive reading, Washington absorbed the English regard for virtue and fame. In their fascination with classical models of behavior, in fact, American colonists, especially the elite in Virginia, were more self-consciously English than the English in England (Furtwangler 1987, 70–84).

Like other ambitious men of his time, then, Washington emulated classical heroes. A particular model for Washington was Cato the Younger, the famous defender of the Roman republic against the dictatorial Julius Caesar. Cato's reputation for honesty and his defense of the republic made him an icon of liberty. After Caesar's crushing defeat of pro-republican forces in North Africa where Cato held command in Utica, Cato committed suicide rather than make accommodation with Caesar. No such sacrifice was ever required of Washington, but in stoically persevering through years of war and then through years of verbal assaults as president, Washington meant to remind his audience of his many sacrifices for the nation.

In eagerly retiring to Mount Vernon after the war and after the presidency, Washington consciously followed the example of another classical hero, Cincinnatus, a fifth-century B.C. Roman patriot who, according to legend, put down his plow to assume military command and save Rome from its enemies before hurrying back to a pastoral life. Like Cincinnatus, Washington was a "virtuoso of resignation," because by retiring to private life after holding military supremacy and after serving eight years as president, he demonstrated that he preferred private tranquility to public strife, and thus that when he endured the latter he did so not for himself but for others (Wills 1984, 3).

In his personal life as well, Washington took care to cultivate his public reputation. Voters of Washington's time were as interested in the personal life of the president as voters are today. At the end of the eighteenth century, there was a greater respect for the privacy of public figures, but through newspapers, books, pamphlets, sermons, prints, and engravings, members of the public were offered detailed depictions of their hero's family life and personal habits.

Among voters and their families, Washington was renowned for some personal attributes. He was unusually tall and carried himself somewhat stiffly. To his contemporaries, this gave him the appearance of a natural leader. His horsemanship routinely drew comments. His fellow Virginian Thomas Jefferson thought Washington to be the finest horseman in North America. Washington also was praised for his felicitous relationship with his stepchildren, John "Jack" Custis and Martha "Patsy" Custis, and his step-grandchildren, Eleanor "Nelly" Parke Custis and George Washington Parke Custis. A cultural historian of the revolutionary era observed indeed that Americans during Washington's lifetime "praised the nonmilitary dimensions of Washington more than his martial side" (Kenneth Silverman, quoted by Higginbotham 2001, 141–164).

Thousands of Washington's countrymen also made personal pilgrimages to the home of their hero. Mount Vernon was, as Washington wrote to his mother even before assuming the presidency, somewhat comparable to a "well-resorted tavern, as scarcely any strangers who are going from north to south, or from south to north do not spend a day or two at it" (Rasmussen and Tilton 1999, 183). Even before he became a truly national hero, Colonel and Mrs. Washington entertained about two thousand guests at their plantation from 1768 to 1775.

LEGACY

Because of his numerous virtues and the tremendous importance he placed on being *seen* as virtuous, Washington is an irresistible target for the satire of contemporary observers. His legacy, however, goes considerably beyond the stuffed-shirt image on the American dollar bill. It is not just the portrait of Washington that continues unchanged; two centuries after Washington's death the United States bears a striking resemblance to the republic over which Washington presided.

The presidency is still, as it was in 1789, at the symbolic and substantive center of the federal government. In part, the remarkable continuity of not just the presidency, but also the government of which it is a part, is Washington's legacy. If Washington had acted differently as president, or if he had declined the burden of the presidency altogether, it is conceivable that the American experiment in republicanism might have gotten off to a far different start. Washington might, for example, have revealed himself to be what his detractors insisted he was: a would-be king in republican clothing. He might in that case have usurped the warmaking powers of Congress and dragged the nation into another war with Britain. He also might have remained in office for life. Had he, for a contrary example, lost his nerve while president, he might have turned decision-making power over to his cabinet, encouraged association between the executive and legislative branches, and transformed the presidency into a parliamentary executive. The reality is simpler: Washington left a legacy of executive independence and pragmatic neutrality in foreign affairs. His service to his country was an inspiration that helped to unite the nation as it expanded, and it was not equaled for generations.

George Washington was a bibliophile. When he died, he left a library of almost a thousand books and pamphlets on a wide range of subjects, "all systematically arranged in order for reference," according to J. M. Toner, M.D., *Some Account of George Washington's Library and Manuscript Records, etc., etc.* (Washington, D.C.: Government Printing Office, 1894), 75. Not surprisingly, the first president also left behind an enormous collection of correspondence and journals, with some texts rewritten and edited by Washington himself to correct grammatical errors and to improve their legibility for posterity. The papers of Washington have been collected and published in the following sources, frequently cited throughout this volume:

- Donald Jackson, ed., and Dorothy Twohig, assoc. ed., *The Diaries of George Washington*, 6 vols. (Charlottesville: University Press of Virginia, 1976–1979).
- W. W. Abbot, ed.; Dorothy Twohig, assoc. ed.; and Philander D. Chase, Beverly H. Runge, and Frederick Hall Schmidt, ass't eds., *The Papers of George Washington, Colonial Series,* 10 vols. (Charlottesville: University Press of Virginia, 1983–1995).
- W. W. Abbot and Dorothy Twohig, eds.; Philander D. Chase and Beverly H. Runge, assoc. eds.; and Beverly S. Kirsch and Debra B. Kesler, ass't eds., *The Papers of George Washington. Confederation Series,* 6 vols. (Charlottesville: University Press of Virginia, 1992–1997).
- Dorothy Twohig, ed., *The Papers of George Washington. Presidential Series,* 11 vols. to date (Charlottesville: University Press of Virginia, 1987–2002).
- Dorothy Twohig, ed.; Philander D. Chase, sr. assoc. ed.; Beverly H. Runge, assoc. ed.; Frank E. Grizzard Jr., et al., ass't eds., *The Papers of George Washington, Retirement Series,* 4 vols. (Charlottesville: University Press of Virginia, 1998–1999).
- Philander D. Chase, ed., *The Papers of George Washington, Revolutionary War Series,* 12 vols. to date (Charlottesville: University Press of Virginia, 1985–2002).
- John C. Fitzpatrick, ed., *The Writings of George Washington from the Original Manuscript Sources, 1745–1799,* 37 vols. (Washington, D.C.: Government Printing Office, 1931–1944).

The University of Virginia's Papers of George Washington series (*gwpapers. virginia.edu/index.html*) is not yet complete because of the voluminous correspondence that Washington maintained during the American War of Independence.

James Thomas Flexner is Washington's major modern biographer. His four-volume biography, published in Boston by Little, Brown, consists of *George Washington, The Forge of Experience, 1732–1775* (1965); *George Washington in the American Revolution, 1775–1783* (1968); *George Washington and the New Nation, 1783–1793* (1970); and *George Washington, Anguish and Farewell, 1793–1799* (1972). The most complete biography is still Douglas Southall Freeman's *George Washington: A Biography* (completed by J. A. Carroll and M. W. Ashworth), 7 vols. (New York: Scribner's, 1948–1957).

Mason Locke "Parson" Weems's idolatrous and best-selling *Life of Washington,* first published months after Washington's death and kept in print for years afterward, is available today with primary documents and an introduction by Peter S. Onuf (Armonk, N.Y.: M. E. Sharpe, 1996). A landmark in the more modern, debunking tradition is W. E. Woodward, *George Washington: The Image and the Man* (New York: Boni and Liveright, 1926). According to Woodward, not only did Washington see to it that a farm girl was lashed for hiding his clothes while he was swimming, but, as a general, he conveyed pessimism that prolonged the war by discouraging enlistments.

Objective, single-volume biographies of Washington include: Flexner, *Washington: The Indispensable Man* (Boston: Little, Brown, 1974); J. R. Alden, *George Washington: A Biography* (Baton Rouge: Louisiana State University Press, 1984); and Willard Sterne Randall, *George Washington: A Life* (New York: Henry, Holt, 1997).

Biographical studies concentrating on Washington's character include the following essays: Forrest McDonald, "Washington, Cato, and Honor: A Model for Revolutionary Leadership," in *American Models of Revolutionary Leadership,* ed. Daniel K. Elazar and Ellis Katz (Lanham, Md.: University Press of America, 1992), 43–58; Dorothy Twohig, "The Making of George Washington," in *George Washington and the Virginia Backcountry,* ed. Warren Hofstra (Madison, Wis.: Madison House, 1998), 3–34; Don Higginbotham, "George Washington and Revolutionary Asceticism," in *George Washington Reconsidered,* ed. Don Higginbotham (Charlottesville: University Press of Virginia, 2001), 141–164; and, in the same volume, two essays by W. W. Abbot, "An Uncommon Awareness of Self, The Papers of George Washington" and "George Washington, the

West, and the Union." Also see Douglass Adair, "Fame and the Found-ing Fathers," in *Fame and the Founding Fathers,* ed. Trevor Colbourn (New York: Norton, for the Institute of Early American History and Cul-ture in Williamsburg, Virginia, 1974), 27–52.

Books on the same subject include: Garry Wills, *Cincinnatus: George Washington and the Enlightenment* (Garden City, N.Y.: Doubleday, 1984); Richard Brookhiser, *Founding Father: Rediscovering George Washington* (New York: Free Press, 1996); and Paul K. Longmore, *The Invention of George Washington* (Berkeley: University of California Press, 1988), which is richly detailed and insightful.

The image of Washington is the subject of a number of books, includ-ing: Barry Schwartz, *George Washington: The Making of an American Sym-bol* (New York: Free Press, 1987); Kenneth L. Cope, *George Washington in and as Culture* (New York: AMS Press, 2001); and Barbara J. Mitnick, gen. ed., *George Washington, American Symbol* (Stony Brook, N.Y.: Hud-son Hills Press, 1999).

Washington's centrality to American nationalism is discussed in Liah Greenfeld, *Nationalism: Five Roads to Modernity* (Cambridge, Mass.: Har-vard University Press, 1992); Page Smith, *The Shaping of America, a Peo-ple's History of the Young Republic,* Vol. 3 (New York: Penguin, 1980); Susan-Mary Grant, "Making History: Myth and the Construction of American Nationhood," in *Myths and Nationhood,* ed. Geoffrey Hosking and George Schopflin (New York: Routledge, 1997), 88–106; and Ken-neth Silverman, *A Cultural History of the American Revolution: Paint-ing, Music, Literature and the Theatre in the Colonies and the United States, from the Treaty of Paris to the Inauguration of George Washington, 1763–1789* (New York: Crowell, 1976).

Washington's physical appearance and his portrayal by artists are stud-ied in the immensely useful book by William M. S. Rasmussen and Robert S. Tilton, *George Washington: The Man behind the Myths* (Charlottesville: University Press of Virginia, 1999).

A delegate to the Constitutional Convention signs the document while George Washington looks on.

CHAPTER ONE

A Biographical Sketch

George Washington was born on February 11, 1732, near the Potomac River in Westmoreland County, Virginia. When, twenty years later, the Julian calendar was replaced with the Georgian, Washington's birthday became February 22. His father, Augustine, was a member of one of the elite families of the area. In keeping with the family's social status, the Washington home had four large rooms downstairs, each with a fireplace, and bedrooms above. Augustine, who operated several sizable plantations, was an ambitious businessman. He engaged in land speculation, mining, and even light manufacturing in an effort to acquire sufficient wealth to pass an independent estate (that is, self-sustaining and not shared with a brother beneficiary) on to at least the oldest sons. With his first wife, Jane Butler Washington, he had two male heirs, Lawrence and Augustine Jr. After Jane's death, he married Mary Ball, who produced George and five younger siblings (Betty, Samuel, John Augustine, Charles, and Mildred).

When George was eleven years old, his father died. In accordance with Augustine Washington's wishes, his property passed principally to his three oldest sons. His first-born son, Lawrence, was confirmed as master of the finest of the estates, Little Hunting Creek, along the Potomac. Augustine Jr. inherited Pope's Farm. George was to receive title to Ferry Farm when he reached sixteen years of age, or maturity. George's younger brothers would be on their own in the bustle to acquire land and position.

The elite families of Virginia sent their male children to England for a secondary education. Afterward, the children would either matriculate in one of the small but respectable collegiate establishments in the colonies, remain in England to study at Oxford or Cambridge University, or return to Virginia to pursue their adult calling. George's older half-brothers had followed this pattern, attending the Appleby School outside of London. With the death of the family patriarch, such expenses were out of the question for George and his younger siblings. He was tutored at home. His teachers stressed practical education, leaving George self-consciously deficient in the liberal arts as an adult. John Adams churlishly wrote of the first president that it was "past dispute" that Washington "was too illiterate, unread, unlearned for his station and reputation" (Flexner 1965, 23).

Washington's education may not have been extensive, but it was suited to his position. He learned the rudiments of mathematics and how to apply them. He studied business practices essential to the operation of a plantation. To teach the boy the principles by which a man of his class was expected to behave in the world, one of George's tutors required him to copy out a laborious list of 110 "Rules of Civility" (Document 1.1). These rules reflect the importance that educated Virginians placed on decorum, self-restraint, and knowing one's place in a hierarchical society.

SOCIAL APPRENTICESHIP

George's half-brother Lawrence was particularly fond of George and helped to mentor the boy once their father died. In Lawrence, Washington had a model of gentlemanly achievement of a high order to emulate.

Lawrence first distinguished himself as a soldier. In 1740 he sailed with four hundred other Virginians in Adm. Edward Vernon's failed expedition against Cartagena, a Spanish Caribbean stronghold off the coast of Colombia. In this imperial fighting, which the British termed the War of the Austrian Succession but patriotic colonists called King George's War, Lawrence carried a royal commission. The expedition to the Caribbean was a source of bitterness between many colonists and the British. The British were unimpressed with the run of colonial soldiers; the colonial soldiers thought their British officers were uncaring and insulting. For Lawrence and other well-placed colonists, however, to serve with a royal commission in one of the wars of His Majesty, the King of England, was a great honor. In fact,

Augustine Washington rewarded Lawrence for his service in this expedition with the title to his finest plantation, Little Hunting Creek, which Lawrence renamed Mount Vernon after his commanding officer.

Three years later, Lawrence further advanced his social standing by marrying into one of the most prominent families in the colonies. His bride was Anne Fairfax, the daughter of William Fairfax. William was the agent in Virginia of Thomas, Sixth Lord of Fairfax. An earlier holder of the title, Lord of Fairfax, had been granted a five-million-acre tract in Virginia in 1649. After being educated at Oxford and living the life of a courtier in England, the contemporary lord set up residence in Virginia to oversee the management of his extensive holdings. His agent and cousin, William, was, from 1743 on, father-in-law to Lawrence and an esteemed and kindly patron to George.

Young George Washington spent much of his time in residence at his brother's estate. And while sleeping under his brother's roof, George also seems to have passed a considerable amount of time at the Fairfax estate, Belvoir. Some years later, in a letter of advice to his younger brother John Augustine Washington, George wrote, "Live in harmony and good fellowship with the family at Belvoir, as it is in their power to be very serviceable upon many occasions to us as young beginners: I would advise your visiting often as one step towards the rest, if any more is necessary, your own good sense will sufficient dictate" (Rasmussen and Tilton 1999, 20). In 1774 the Fairfaxes, having inherited a manor in England, put Belvoir's furnishings up for sale. George Washington, by that time the owner of Mount Vernon, managed the sale and purchased many of the finer pieces for himself. The apprentice had become the master. But before that could happen, George had to make his way in the world of Virginia gentlemen. Not truly wealthy by inheritance and lacking a superior education, the young man turned naturally to land acquisition and soldiering as avenues to distinction.

George first sought to emulate Lawrence by joining the Royal Navy. George, however, was only fourteen years of age at the time, and his mother was alarmed at the idea. Mary Ball Washington consulted her half-brother in England for his advice. His response, "I think he had better be put apprentice to a tinker," summed up her feelings and the writer's disdain for tinkers (Rasmussen and Tilton 1999, 17). George would find his way into the military soon enough, but first he headed west to survey Fairfax property and to acquire frontier land for himself.

When George was sixteen, he assisted in a survey of the western boundaries of the Fairfax property. His Fairfax contemporary, George William Fairfax (eldest son of William Fairfax), was in charge of the expedition. This was the beginning of Washington's lifelong passion with the West. Though he found the people in the western settlements coarse as "a parcel of Dogs," he was a sensible and ambitious young man (Rasmussen and Tilton 1999, 33). As such, he well understood that the surest path to riches for a man such as himself was through the purchase of large tracts of virgin land.

From 1748 to 1752 Washington practiced his first profession, surveying. In doing so, he had the critical assistance of the Fairfaxes, who gave him assignments and acquired for him the position of official surveyor of Culpeper County. In the process, Washington earned a handsome salary, purchased thousands of acres of land in the Shenandoah Valley, and gained valuable familiarity with a region of Virginia that was under military threat from the French.

When Lawrence became ill from a severe case of tuberculosis, George traveled with him in 1751 to Barbados, where it was thought the climate might benefit Lawrence's condition. (This was to be George's only trip outside of the American mainland, and the source of rumors that he was the father of the illegitimate-born Alexander Hamilton.) On his return trip to Virginia, George stopped in Williamsburg to introduce himself to the royal governor, Robert Dinwiddie. Lawrence held the post of adjutant general of the Virginia militia, and he apparently intended for George to "inherit" the position. Upon Lawrence's death in 1752, the governor and his council chose to break up the enormous colony for military purposes into districts. The younger Washington was appointed adjutant for the southern district, and given the rank of major and a salary of one hundred pounds. Washington had just taken the first step in his military career.

FOR KING AND COUNTRY

Alarmed at French settlement of the Ohio Valley, Governor Dinwiddie urged the powerful Board of Trade in Britain to take action. The response from London was forceful. Send an emissary to the French, wrote King George II, to "require of them peaceably to depart." Should they refuse, proclaimed the king, "we do strictly command and charge you to drive them out by force of arms" (Flexner 1965, 54). Major Washington volunteered to deliver the king's warning.

In 1753 Washington, an Indian interpreter, a guide, and four attendants set out across the mountains to find first the Indians, then the French. Washington won a renewal of friendship on behalf of the British government with the Indian leader Half King before heading to Fort Le Boeuf, located in present-day Waterford, Pennsylvania.

The French commander received Washington stiffly, telling him that he had wasted his time, because any decisions about French policy were to be made in France, or French Canada. The point of Washington's trip, though, was not merely to deliver a letter, but to demonstrate British resolve, collect intelligence, and discuss the situation with Indian leaders.

In this first military mission for his sovereign, Washington was found to have performed admirably. As a result, he came to the attention of leading men in the colonies and Britain. His appointment as emissary was in fact reported in the *Gentleman's Magazine,* a leading journal for the educated public of the English-speaking world, published in London. Dinwiddie, wishing to raise awareness of French designs upon the frontier, published Major Washington's diary of the trip. The Virginia House of Burgesses awarded Washington fifty pounds as a token of its gratitude.

Adhering to the king's letter, Governor Dinwiddie followed the threat with action. Again, Washington assumed a leading role. Dinwiddie was authorized by the Crown to call out Virginia's militia for the expedition, but the local burgesses would not consent to appropriate enough money to equip and mobilize a sufficient force. In response, Dinwiddie decided to form a volunteer army called the Virginia Regiment. To mobilize this force, the governor promised to compensate the volunteers with land. They would share the 200,000 acres that Dinwiddie and other leading men controlled through a speculative venture, the Ohio Company (Lawrence Washington had been a founder of the Ohio Company when George Washington was but a teenager). The commander of the regiment would merit 10 percent of this land. Thus the military mission to force the French from land claimed by the colonies would provide George not only with the opportunity for military glory, but also with the opportunity to acquire a true fortune in land.

Washington took command of the regiment after the untimely death of the more experienced man at first assigned to lead the expedition. Two military disasters then followed for the British, but not, ironically, for Washington. First, there was what came to be known as the Jumonville Affair. Coming upon a detachment of French troops led by a French officer, Coulon de Jumonville, Washington and his three-hundred-man "army" opened fire. In fifteen minutes, Washington's force killed ten of the enemy, including Jumonville, and took twenty-two prisoners. Unfortunately, the French officers who survived, and the French press afterward, insisted that Washington had attacked a diplomatic party on a mission much like the one he had undertaken the year before.

Shortly after the battle, Washington's force and the several hundred remaining French soldiers sought to maneuver to advantage. In case of attack, Washington, by now a colonel, ordered his soldiers to build "a small palisaded fort" which he called Fort Necessity, located near present-day Farmington, Pennsylvania (Flexner 1965, 93). Half King, who had joined with Washington's army on this occasion, considered the fort's defensive value "trifling," but Washington declined to heed the advice of a "savage" (Flexner 1965, 94). When the French forces found Washington's regiment, they attacked. Washington lost one-third of his force in a day-long barrage of musket fire. The terms of surrender signed by the colonel acknowledged, in French, the "assassination" of Coulon de Jumonville.

Remarkably, Washington escaped fault for both the Jumonville Affair and the disaster at Fort Necessity. Dinwiddie and most British in the colonies agreed with Washington that the French could not possibly have been on a diplomatic mission. The French force was larger than that needed for a purely diplomatic objective, and Jumonville and his troops had been discovered by Washington's Indian allies in a remote location, where they appeared to be interested in surprising, not conversing with, the British. As for the massacre at Fort Necessity, the burgesses ordered that thanks be given to Colonel Washington and others "for their late gallant and brave Behavior in the Defense of their Country" (Rasmussen and Tilton 1999, 55).

In Washington's third mission for his "country" of Virginia, he served as a volunteer aide to Maj. Gen. Edward Braddock, an English officer who arrived in 1755 with 1,400 Redcoats to give greater force to the effort to expel the French from the Ohio Valley. Braddock's army was ambushed by the French, and Braddock himself killed. The British regulars sent with Braddock to carry the fight ran in retreat, headlong into lines of sturdy colonial volunteers, according to the version of events favored in Virginia.

Ironically, although his colonial status made him apparently immune to criticism from fellow Americans, Washington throughout his career chafed at the distinction between colonial and British officers. At this time in his life, Washington saw himself through British, not American, eyes, and under British policy, a general with a colonial commission was outranked by even a lowly lieutenant with a royal commission. For a self-consciously proud member of the Virginia gentry like George Washington, this was a grave matter. In building Fort Necessity, for example, Colonel Washington had been forced to work alongside and, in many respects under, a captain of British regulars. When the lower-ranking British captain refused to order his troops to assist in the manual labor of constructing the fort, Washington ordered his own troops to a new location. Only the threat of impending battle against a larger French force had compelled Washington back to Fort Necessity.

After Braddock's defeat, the Virginia Regiment was reinstated, and Washington spent another three years as its commander. Washington's frustration with British discrimination against colonial officers grew even fiercer during this time, as did his skill and maturity as a commander. Meanwhile, the government of Virginia was holding him accountable for the safety of Virginia settlers, yet it refused to provide adequate resources for Washington to accomplish that task. As long as the French were present, Native Americans along the frontier were emboldened to resist with force the incursions of Virginians into their lands. Washington built forts, pleaded with civilian authorities for greater resources, and struggled with low morale and high rates of desertion.

During his years of duty in the West, Washington developed a greater feeling for its white inhabitants. Of the frontier families, Washington wrote: "I SEE their situation, KNOW their danger, and participate in their SUFFERINGS; without having it in my power to give them further relief, than uncertain promises" (Rasmussen and Tilton 1999, 65). In 1757 William Pitt accepted the leadership of the British cabinet. Previously, the British government had been virtually paralyzed by indecision following reversals in the global struggle with France. Pitt's confidence and popularity gave him unrivaled power for a time in British politics, and he poured personnel and money into the struggle for empire, sending six thousand new soldiers to the colonies. At last faced with a British force equal to British threats, the French simply abandoned their positions in the disputed territory in the fall of the next year, without the climactic encounter for which Washington had prepared his troops. As the French left, Washington's military service to the Crown came to an end.

WASHINGTON'S FIRST RETIREMENT

Although Washington had achieved fame as a military commander, had a reputation in the colonies as a brave and experienced militia leader, and was even discussed on occasion by the leading figures of Britain and France, his inability to secure a royal commission deeply wounded his pride. Ironically, it may have been Washington's own actions in the Jumonville Affair that caused the king to proclaim the rigid and discriminatory proscription against royal commissions for colonists that Washington so bitterly opposed. Washington was not, however, interested in military service as an end in itself, any more than he was interested in surveying for the opportunity it afforded to travel in the West. Washington's eyes were turned during this period of his life toward the east, toward his home in tidewater Virginia and Britain beyond the sea.

To cement his status as a gentleman planter, Washington needed a proper wife. Lawrence had, again, set the standard for his younger brother by marrying into the Fairfax family. Washington was enamored of a Fairfax, but could not act upon his affection. The lady, Sally Fairfax, was the wife of George's friend and contemporary George William Fairfax. While professing in coy missives his love to Sally (see Document 1.2), Colonel Washington made quick work of the courtship of the widow Custis, proposing on his third visit to her home. They wed on January 6, 1759.

Martha Dandridge Custis had inherited plantations in five Virginia counties. Upon her husband's death, her wealth and that of her two children, John "Jack" Custis and Martha "Patsy" Custis, elevated her to the ranks of the first families of Virginia. Through his marriage to Martha, George came into possession of fifteen thousand acres of farmland; two hundred slaves; and cash, stock, and mortgages valued at 100,000 pounds. In addition, he could now claim the twenty thousand acres of frontier land that had been promised to him as his share of veterans' bounty land. Western lands were a source of constant trouble for the landowner because of squatters, conflicting deeds, and other problems endemic to "real estate development" in a wilderness, but those same lands made up a considerable portion of Washington's wealth. He would add to them continually, so that by 1789 he owned a half-million acres of western land (McDonald 1979, 154).

Washington spent the better part of the two decades after his marriage leading the life of a country gentleman on his estate of Mount Vernon. He had, as such, several passions and numerous duties. Washington was renowned, for example, as a horseman. As a young man, he had been a favorite companion of Lord Fairfax because of his skills in the hunt. Washington continued to "ride to the hounds" as an independent gentleman in his own right. In addition, Washington was an avid agriculturalist. He ordered from London numerous works on farming and studied them carefully. His diary records experiments in implementing the latest theories on crop rotation, the seeding of grains, and the proper management of his working estate.

As for Washington's house at Mount Vernon, that was both a passion and a duty. As a gentleman in the English fashion, it was essential that Washington reside on a proper country estate. In 1761 Washington inherited from his brother's widow a spacious one-story house. In the year before his retirement from the Virginia Regiment, Washington undertook a substantial renovation, doubling the size of the house. The expansion was intended to accommodate not only Washington's new family, but his many visitors as well.

Washington was seldom if ever alone in his mansion. He and Martha entertained approximately two thousand guests from 1768 to 1775. Many stayed for extended periods. The retired colonel also made several excursions to the west to evict squatters from his lands, and otherwise to pursue his lifelong interest in profiting from western lands through land sales and leasing to tenants. At home in Virginia, Washington carried on a voluminous correspondence and attended to the duties of a gentleman. In Washington's case, these included serving as trustee of the town of Alexandria and as a representative to the Virginia House of Burgesses, at first representing a frontier district whose inhabitants he had protected from Indian raids associated with the Seven Years' War. He also was a member of the vestry of the local Anglican church. The vestry, the lay governing body of the parish, took care of the church building, maintained records, and hired and fired the ministers of the parish.Washington's life was not, however, entirely without difficulties.

For him, debt was a way of life, as it was for most of his neighbors. Land-rich but often cash-poor, Washington sought continually to diminish his indebtedness to the London agents or "factors" who traded his crops on the European market and purchased for his estate the latest in English fineries. Being so far from his market, however, Washington found it difficult to control his own affairs. In addition, British policy alienated Washington and his fellow colonists. Just as he felt he had been hampered in the military by an English contempt for men born in the colonies, Washington "began to relate his personal frustrations" as a planter "to a larger problem, the developing constitutional and political crisis between the mother country and the colonies" (Longmore 1988, 73).

Washington's own Fairfax County was a hotbed of revolutionary discontent against British policy. Washington took a leading role in mobilizing Virginians against well-known offenses to the colonies such as the Stamp Act and the Townshend Duties. Although Washington denounced the licentious Boston Tea Party, he was a founder of the Nonimportation Association of Virginia (see Document 1.3). Members of the association agreed not to purchase taxed British goods. As a member of the Virginia House of Burgesses, by this time representing his home seat, Washington helped to draft the Fairfax County Resolves of 1774, the year before he took command of the Continental army (see Document 1.4). The resolves forcefully expressed the grievances of the colonies. The colonists must, Washington reasoned, "assert our Rights, or Submit to every Imposition that can be heap'd upon us; till custom and use, will make us as tame, & abject Slaves, as the Blacks we Rule over with such arbitrary Sway" (Document 1.5).

WAR

Washington was a delegate to both Continental Congresses, formed to address colonial grievances. At the second, in 1775, he appeared in the uniform of the Virginia Regiment, not so subtly advertising his availability for command of the army that would have to be raised to give substance to the resolves and the declarations of the angry colonists. Despite his yearning for the fame that might be won at the head of a revolutionary army, Washington was sensibly anxious about the undertaking. "From the day I enter upon the command of the American armies," Washington once told his fellow Virginia patriot Patrick Henry, "I date my fall, and the ruin of my reputation" (Rasmussen and Tilton 1999, 112).

In the late winter of 1775, American rebels and the British government came into open conflict in the Massachusetts colony. With the British sending in reinforcements and the colonies sending volunteers to help the rebels, the Continental Congress put Washington formally in command of the Continental army, which at first consisted of the some seventeen thousand men who had come to the aid of the residents of Boston. He took command on the Cambridge Commons on July 3, 1775.

The American War of Independence was lengthy and costly. The shooting war lasted until 1781. The Treaty of Paris that concluded the war was ratified by Congress on April 15, 1783. In November of that year the British at last left New York City. In fact, the war was the second longest in American history; only the war in Vietnam was longer. And it was second only to the Civil War in its lethality, measured in terms of war-related deaths as a percentage of the population. Its duration and deadliness were hard for the Americans to bear, because the war was fought on their soil and by their own citizens. The British, of course, had no need to fear American invasion, and relied heavily on mercenaries from various German principalities.

Though time often appeared to be on the side of the British, the Americans enjoyed advantages of demography, geography, and ideology. The colonies experienced tremendous population growth in the latter half of the 1700s, almost closing what had been a large gap between the population of the colonies and that of the mother country. The population explosion stemmed from declining mortality, a young marriage age, large-scale food production, and a wave of immigration from Ulster and Scotland. The total non-Indian population of colonial North America (including the then-French territories) increased from approximately 1.3 million in 1750 to somewhere between 2.3 and 2.6 million in 1775 (Meinig 1986, 288).

Because of the geographic fragmentation of the United States, the British were unable to defeat the Americans by pursuing victory over a capital city. There was no city in the colonies of comparable value to an enemy as London or Paris. The wealth, power, and resources of the colonies were spread among thirteen states, each with a capital of its own. Moreover, the states were spread over a considerable distance, further complicating the military problem of the British.

Ideology also was important to American success in that leading members of the British Parliament, and even the British army and navy, considered the Americans to be the carriers of "an emerging Whig political culture with which they had considerable sympathy" (Phillips 1999, 295). The British Whigs, a faction within British politics, were dedicated to reforming the monarchy and Parliament. As a result, many of them sympathized with the rebels in the colonies, and looked up to Washington and other leading members of the founding generation. The British general Sir William Howe and his brother Lord Richard Howe, vice admiral and commander in chief in North America, were themselves prominent in Whig politics in Britain. At the opening of the American War of Independence, Sir Howe and his fellow British officers in North America took their time before fully engaging the Americans in battle. Perhaps this was merely caution, but to some it seemed more than that. "He [Sir Howe] is one of us and will do the Americans no harm," one Whig leader was reported as commenting in Britain (Phillips 1999, 294).

Nevertheless, victory for Washington's troops came only with the greatest of difficulties. Fortunately, a British disaster outside Boston gave Washington a full year to prepare his army for battle. At the misnamed Battle of Bunker Hill, British commanders launched frontal assaults on entrenched positions. They knew better, but looked on the American soldiers as unworthy adversaries to whom the rules of warfare need not be applied. The colonists, "hordes of peasants armed with old muskets and fowling pieces" in British eyes, had, after all, dug in on the wrong hill. They had set up their defenses on Breed's Hill, because it was closer to Boston, even though Bunker Hill was higher and therefore tactically the superior location. At the end of the day, June 17, 1775, British dead and wounded numbered more than 1,000, to 411 for the Americans. Howe, who was reluctant to conquer the Americans in any event, would not engage the American army in battle for another year.

From 1776 to 1778 the major engagements of the war took place in the northern states. General Howe, after evacuating Boston in March 1776, concentrated his forces on Staten Island, New York. After seeing his army humiliated at Long Island, Harlem Heights, and other locations in the environs of New York City, Washington escaped with what remained of his army by retreating across New Jersey toward Pennsylvania.

In one of the most celebrated victories in American warfare, General Washington saved the revolutionary cause from being extinguished militarily by organizing and leading a raid on Hessian forces at Trenton, New Jersey, on December 26, 1776 (see Document 1.6). The raid across the

Delaware River was a desperate measure. Washington was faced with the prospect of losing almost his entire army at the end of the year when the typical soldier's term of enlistment would expire. In New Jersey, the British occupied themselves in pacifying the countryside. Thousands of New Jersey militiamen swore allegiance to the Loyalist cause and were pardoned for their treason. While the bulk of the British army retreated to winter quarters, detachments of Hessians and British soldiers were posted in the countryside to protect the presumably pro-British citizens against Washington's soldiers and rebellious neighbors. The post closest to Washington, garrisoned by several thousand Hessians, was in Trenton.

Washington divided his force into thirds, which would cross at different points and surround the objective. Because of the extreme weather, only the 2,400 men directly under Washington's command made it across the partially frozen river. The Hessians "were to laugh away as ridiculous" a sentry's report of Washington's advancing force (Flexner 1974, 95). Washington's troops lost not a single soldier in the battle, and they captured nine hundred prisoners. After this victory, half of Washington's troops reenlisted.

Washington's personal leadership of his men had not been sufficient to prevent infamous retreats in the fighting around New York City, but his determination at Trenton boosted his status with his soldiers considerably. Shortly after the victory at Trenton, Washington on horseback led his men as they advanced against a British line of fire. According to Flexner (1974, 97), this was "the first time that Washington's troops had, in open combat, made a British line break." At the Battle of Monmouth on June 28, 1778, Washington again placed himself at the head of an American line on the verge of breaking into retreat, and he rallied American soldiers to continue fighting.

After his experiences in New York, Washington studiously avoided pitting his army against the bulk of the British force. The single exception, until the war's conclusion at Yorktown, was in September 1777. On that occasion, Washington, compelled by the symbolic importance of the capital city, attempted at least a defense. His loss outside of Philadelphia, at Brandywine Creek, was offset in October by a rebel victory in the Battle of Saratoga, in which American general Horatio Gates defeated British general John Burgoyne.

Washington's critics in the Continental Congress did not always understand his reluctance to fight, but the commander in chief had good reason not to risk his army. "It is our arms, not defenceless towns, they have to subdue," Washington recognized (Millett and Maslowski 1994, 70). By keeping the Continental army in the field, Washington prolonged the war and avoided defeat. A long war was a grave hardship for the Americans, but it also gave them their best chance at winning international support and dividing British opinion. In enduring a long and defensive-minded war, the American army was held together by its personal loyalty to Washington.

Washington may have been preeminent in the Continental army by war's end, but he was never without rivals and critics. For example, the Pennsylvania legislature complained to the commander that by settling in for the winter of 1777–1778 outside of Philadelphia rather than in the city itself, Washington had left the capital unprotected. Washington reminded the state's elected leaders that "it is a much easier and less distressing thing to draw remonstrances in a comfortable room by a good fireside than to occupy a cold, bleak hill and sleep under frost and snow without clothes or blankets," but that he nonetheless "from (his) soul (felt) pity for those miseries which it is neither in my power to relieve or prevent" (Flexner 1974, 111).

To win, the Americans had to survive. To win, the British had to conquer. After significant exertions in and around Boston, New York City, and Philadelphia, and through Canada and upstate New York, the British were failing. In response, the French took the opportunity in June 1778 to side openly with the Americans. The next year, Spain too declared itself at war with Britain. And in 1780 Holland joined in against Britain as well. Because Britain was now engaged in another costly global war, it shifted its focus in the colonies to those in the South such as North and South Carolina and Georgia. Assuming that the southern colonies were the most loyal, the British believed they might be able to defeat the Americans in the South with the least expenditure of resources. In the end, the southern theater became the site of guerrilla warfare between Loyalist and "partisan" militias.

When the opportunity for a decisive battle at last presented itself in Pennsylvania, Washington hurried his troops to Yorktown. There, on October 19, 1781, a combined French-American naval and ground force compelled the surrender of Maj. Gen. Charles Cornwallis. The British still had sizable forces in North America with which to carry on the fight, but given Britain's complex and burdensome imperial pressures, the costs of continued fighting seemed to be outweighed by the benefits of a nego-tiated peace. A year later, on November 30, 1782, the Treaty of Paris for-mally brought hostilities to a close. On April 15, 1783, Congress ratified the treaty that ended the war.

While Congress deliberated treaty ratification, Washington maintained a remnant of the Continental army at Newburgh, New York. The army would be disbanded only when Congress accepted the treaty. Washing-ton had no cause for concern about the status of negotiations over the Treaty of Paris. He did, however, share with all of his fellow officers a grave concern about Congress's seeming inability or disinclination to pay its soldiers and officers their promised wages. The officers also were anx-ious about their pensions, which some members of Congress now appeared inclined not to fund.

In early March 1983 a group of officers at the army's headquarters at Newburgh attempted to take matters into their own hands, circulat-ing anonymous papers throughout camp calling for a general assembly of the officers to discuss what action to take on the men's many griev-ances (see Document 1.7). Leaders among the disgruntled officers decided that Maj. Gen. Alexander McDougall and two colonels should deliver to Congress a petition warning of dire consequences should the civilians not do justice to their army. Rash nationalists in Congress actu-ally encouraged the protesting officers to sharpen the threatened use of force. If the more timid members of Congress could be sufficiently frightened, they would at last support nationalist plans to strengthen the government so that it might raise sufficient funds to pay its soldiers what they were owed. Gen. Horatio Gates and his aides, resentful of Wash-ington's command, lobbied their fellow officers in Newburgh to demand action from Congress and to "suspect the man who would advise to more moderation and longer forbearance" (Kohn 1986, 88).

The man who would advise to more moderation was, of course, Wash-ington. In cooling the passions of his fellow officers and quelling the threat that the Revolutionary War would end with a military assault on civilian government, Washington demonstrated again his commitment to the Revolution as an ideological cause. He issued a general order in which he disapproved of the anonymous letters being circulated in camp. Nevertheless, he called on the officers to assemble four days later to dis-cuss McDougall's latest report from Congress. Washington's order closed by directing the "senior officer in Rank present" at the meeting to issue to Washington a report, suggesting that Washington himself would not attend (Allen 1988, 214).

On the appointed day, March 15, 1783, Washington surprised Gates and the others by his attendance. Before they had occasion to conduct any other business, Washington addressed the assembly (see Document 1.8). In an angry tone, he warned them against "the man who wishes, under any specious pretences, to overturn the liberties of our country, and who wickedly attempts to open the flood gates of civil discord, & deluge our rising empire in blood." He assured them, moreover, of his faith in Congress's determination to make good on its pledges to the army.

While delivering his written remarks, Washington paused to put on his spectacles, which few of the officers had ever seen him wear. "Unaffectedly, the tall general murmured that he had grown gray in the service of his country and now found himself growing blind" (Kohn 1986, 89). Washington's dramatic gesture disrupted the cool anger of the assemblage. Some of the officers openly wept. Washington then left, and the remaining officers disassembled after passing resolutions condemning the threat of civil war and expressing their "unshaken confidence" in Congress (Kohn 1986, 89).

In truth, Washington was no more enamored of Congress under the Articles of Confederation than the would-be coup plotters. Washington had enjoyed a unique vantage point during the Revolution. As the sole commander in chief, carrying out the orders of a national government that itself had no single person in command, Washington had ample occasion to lament the problems that could arise from parochialism and timidity. The Articles of Confederation, he knew, provided each state with an incentive to let the others sacrifice for the common good. "The contest among the different states," he complained at one point during the war, "is not which shall do most for the common cause, but which shall do least" (Phelps 1993, 57). As he waited for the order to disband his army, Washington looked back on the struggle and observed in a letter to Alexander Hamilton in March 1783, "No man perhaps has felt the bad effects of it [our present Confederation] more sensibly. . . . More than half the perplexities I have experienced in the course of my command, and almost the whole of the difficulties and distress of the Army have their origin here" (Allen 1988, 230). Washington exited the war a convinced, if cautious, nationalist (Phelps 1993, 53).

When he formally relinquished command, Washington met with his "family" of subordinate officers at Fraunces Tavern in Manhattan. Overcome with emotion, he was unable to speak but rather embraced his fellow generals one by one as he took their leave. Washington did, however, leave a verbal legacy, in his "Farewell Orders," issued on November 2, 1783 (Document 1.9), and his "Circular to the States," issued in June 1783 (Fitzpatrick, 1931–1944, 26:483–496).

The circular was Washington's last official communication to the leaders of the state governments. In it, he demonstrated how the experience of the war had influenced his thinking. Speaking in behalf of the nationalist cause, Washington identified the "present crisis" of the nation as arising from a weak national government, and he urged the civilian leaders of the states to overcome local prejudice as had the soldiers and officers of the army. The stakes could not be higher, Washington pointed out, because America's citizens had been "placed in the most enviable condition, as the sole Lords and Proprietors of a vast Tract of Continent . . . peculiarly designated by Providence for the display of human greatness and felicity." Now, the world was watching to see what the Americans would do with their freedom. If the free people of America did not continue to live "free and happy, the fault will be intirely their own." If the states could not rise above their petty jealousies, Washington warned, the federation would fall. Such an outcome would prove the Revolution just concluded not a blessing but "a curse, not to the present age alone, for with our fate will the destiny of unborn Millions be involved."

WASHINGTON'S SECOND RETIREMENT

Despite his worries that the nation's hard-won independence might be lost without strength in the national government, Washington was intent on returning to Mount Vernon after the war. The victorious general knew that the world was watching to see what he would do after leading his army to its surprise victory. King George III himself asked the American painter Benjamin West for his opinion on the general's next move. To West's reply that he was likely to return to Mount Vernon, the monarch observed, "If he does that, he will be the greatest man in the world" (Ferling 2000, 272). It was to lay claim to such accolades, and to complete his enactment of the life of the heroic Cincinnatus (see Introduction), that Washington angrily rebuked a young newspaper correspondent who dared to suggest in May 1782 that Washington take command of the government himself rather than returning to his plow. "[I]f you have any regard for your Country, concern for yourself or posterity, or respect for me," Washington replied, "banish these thoughts" (Ward 1999, 160). After relinquishing his commission before Congress, Washington returned to Mount Vernon, arriving Christmas Eve 1783.

At home once more, Washington settled into the patterns of gentlemanly life. He and Martha were again the guardians of two Custis children, this time two of Martha's grandchildren from her first marriage— George Washington Parke Custis, called Washington, and Eleanor "Nelly" Parke Custis. The Washingtons also were once again hosts to a great number of visitors, some who came by invitation and many who appeared unannounced. As he had throughout his adult life, Washington maintained a voluminous correspondence. To assist him with his letters and with other chores, Washington hired a secretary, Tobias Lear, who remained in his employ into Washington's presidency.

Washington also resumed his practice of devoting considerable time to improvements to the mansion and to agricultural experiments, including developing a pattern of crop rotation and crop selection that would yield profitable crops over the long term. Overall, he continued to develop the self-sufficiency of Mount Vernon and endeavored, with no success, to lessen his dependence on slave labor. Finally, Washington watched over his western lands, though he relinquished any claim to the bounty lands Congress had promised to veterans of the Revolutionary War.

Meanwhile, Washington had the time and occasion to worry in his second retirement about public as well as private concerns. For example, he sometimes bored visitors to Mount Vernon with facts and figures aimed at demonstrating the superiority of his cherished Potomac River Canal project over other proposed routes for inland navigation. He dreamed of a day when a series of canals might link farmers to their markets wherever the farmers lived in the settled parts of the states. Because the success of the Potomac Canal project would depend on cooperation among the states, Washington took the lead in assembling delegates from several states to discuss how the states might best promote and regulate such business ventures. Washington had an abiding anxiety that the canal would never be built without a central government strong enough to overcome state jealousies.

Although Washington hoped for a quick resolution of certain small matters on a national basis, such as settling border disputes in the area of his proposed canal, he did not anticipate rapid reform of the national government as a whole. Washington believed that the residents of the states had to "feel" the effects of a weak federal government before they could "see" the necessity of strengthening it (Flexner 1974, 198). But Washington continued to hope that he would be able to remain out of the political fray. Entering politics, he realized, would risk the ruin of his reputation. Nevertheless, Washington's resolve to lend his immense prestige to the cause of reforming the government strengthened in response to a series of events in the 1780s that demonstrated the weakness of the national government under the Articles of Confederation.

The most prominent crisis of the decade was Shays's Rebellion, a debtors' uprising in western Massachusetts in 1786. Shays, a veteran of the Revolutionary War, raised and trained a private militia, which set out to close the state courts to prevent them from foreclosing on bankrupt farms. Washington, like many other social and economic conservatives in the United States, was alarmed. "What, gracious God, is man!" Washington wrote to his friend and wartime compatriot Henry Knox, "that there should be such inconstancy and perfidiousness in his conduct?" (Phelps 1993, 86–87). Why did the government not act against the rebellious farmers with force? By permitting lawlessness, Washington added in the same letter to Knox, the United States risked making republicanism "contemptible" in the eyes of America's "English foes." "What stronger evidence can be given of the want of energy in our governments," Washington observed to his fellow Virginian James Madison, "than these disorders?" (Flexner 1970, 101).

Even after Shays's Rebellion, Washington hesitated to leave his retirement. For almost six months, writes one analyst of Washington's role in framing the new government, he "played the reluctant bridegroom" (Phelps 1993, 93). His "suitors" knew he was in earnest only when he left for the Constitutional Convention in Philadelphia in the summer of 1787 as a delegate from Virginia. Washington's very presence was an important victory for the convention organizers. He was one of North America's only two world-renowned men, the other being Benjamin Franklin (Wills 1984, 158, 195–196). Because Washington's reputation was without parallel as a stalwart of American independence, his participation would deflect criticism that the framers were undermining the work of the founders. On the first day of the convention, Franklin intended therefore to nominate Washington to preside (Jackson and Twohig 1979, 5:162). But because Franklin was ill, the honor fell to Robert Morris. A ballot then revealed Washington to be the unanimous choice of the convention.

As president of the Constitutional Convention, Washington felt constrained by his office from taking part in the deliberations. He spoke from the floor only once, apologizing for his breach of propriety, to endorse an amendment to reduce the number of persons that each member of the proposed House of Representatives was to represent. But because much of the work of the delegates was done through the parliamentary device of the Committee of the Whole, Washington was more active in Philadelphia than is commonly believed. When the delegates sat as the Committee of the Whole, Washington handed the gavel to another delegate, who presided as committee chairman. Washington then took a seat with the other delegates from Virginia. As a member of the Virginia delegation, Washington voted on an equal basis with the other state delegates in determining how their state would cast its single ballot. In that setting, Washington voted in favor of a strong executive, supporting a motion that the president's powers be concentrated in a single executive officer, that the president be removable by Congress only through impeachment, and that the president be eligible for reelection.

Although Washington remained above the fray of convention politics by refraining, with a single exception, from voicing his opinions during the convention's deliberations, he was not neutral about the Constitution. He may not have spoken or written directly in its favor during the lengthy, state-by-state struggle for ratification, but he did permit his name to be used by federalists in their debate literature. Washington's support, though indirect, was pivotal. "Be assured," James Monroe wrote to Thomas Jefferson, "his influence carried this government" (Flexner 1974, 211).

FIRST PRESIDENT

Having demonstrated that he could be trusted with power, Washington's fellow citizens naturally looked to him to be the first to wield the authority of the American chief executive. After his agreement to serve, in early 1789 the electoral college unanimously elected Washington president of the new nation. In that office, Washington intended to place the presidency on a firm, but constitutionally constrained, foundation. As president, he was acutely aware of the precedents that he set. "Few who are not philosophical spectators," he wrote at the outset of his first term, "can realize the difficult and delicate part which a man in my situation has to act. . . . In our progress toward political happiness my station is new; and, if I may use the expression, I walk on untrodden ground. There is scarcely any part of my conduct which may not hereafter be drawn into precedent" (Landy and Milkis 2000, 23).

Washington took the oath of office at Federal Hall in New York City, the temporary capital, on April 30, 1789. In his inaugural address, he reminded the assembled members of Congress of what was at stake in the American "experiment" (see Document 1.10). "[T]he preservation of the sacred fire of liberty and the destiny of the republican model of government are justly considered as *deeply*, perhaps as *finally staked*" on that experiment.

Washington did not believe that a strong national government required that he, as president, step over the boundaries of the separation of powers. Washington's respect for these boundaries is illustrated famously in "the slightly ludicrous case of the unopened packet" (Phelps 1989, 266). In December 1790 Washington received a packet of papers from the French government addressed to "The President and Members of the American Congress." Rather than opening the envelope himself, Washington submitted a written question to Congress: who should open the packet? The Senate authorized the president to undertake the task and to report to Congress if the contents of the packet warranted its attention.

Washington did not even believe he should represent the people. That was the job of Congress. Nor did he intend to lead Congress. Congress was to make laws as it saw fit, though the president might recommend matters for its consideration. Despite these ideas about executive deference to the legislature, Washington did *not* believe in a weak presidency.

To begin with, he believed in and superbly performed the important task of consolidating the nation by embodying the people symbolically. This kingly function made the president self-conscious as he groped his way to an acceptable republican understanding of how a head of state might behave. Just two days after his inauguration, the president was already frustrated that he had no time to *be* president, because he was constantly attending to the visitors who came often with no actual business to conduct, but merely to bask in the glow of the nation's symbolic head. Washington therefore published in New York newspapers a notice that the executive would be available to receive "visits of compliment" from two to three o'clock in the afternoon on Tuesdays and Fridays (McDonald 1974, 26). After receiving complaints about these too-limited "office hours," the president amended his plan. Anyone respectably dressed would now be able to see the president at his or her choice of weekly receptions—a levee for gentlemen on one day and a tea on another day for men and women, hosted by the president's wife (the term *first lady* had yet to be coined), but with her husband always in attendance (see Document 1.11). Moreover, the president and Martha Washington would host a series of dinners at their residence every Thursday afternoon at four o'clock for government officials, especially members of Congress, and their wives. To avoid any hint of partisanship or favoritism, guests would be invited by rotation, with no attempt made to gather persons by reference to their political positions.

Not everyone who wished to see the president, of course, could come to New York or, once the capital had been relocated in 1790, Philadelphia. To allow himself to be seen by as many people as possible, the president adapted to his own purposes the monarchical tradition of the procession. From October 15 to November 13, 1789, the president toured New England, except Rhode Island, which had not yet ratified the Constitution.

In Boston a squabble over protocol erupted. John Hancock, governor of Massachusetts, wished the chief executive to visit and dine with *him,* thus symbolically acknowledging the supremacy within the Union of each individual state. Washington let it be known that this was unacceptable; Hancock would first have to pay a courtesy call on the president in his rooms in Boston. They would then go jointly to Hancock's residence or anywhere else, the superior dignity of the Union having been established. Even a feigned illness by Hancock could not budge the president from his insistence on this point of honor to the Constitution.

Two years later, again while Congress was in adjournment, Washington toured the southern states, this time in spring. Washington had never been south of Virginia, and was interested to make the journey for his own edification, as well as for its value in promoting the unity of the new nation.

Though Washington tried, it was impossible to strike a balance between familiarity and ostentation that would please everyone. Ten days prior to the second inaugural, the capital was the site of numerous "birthnight balls" to celebrate Washington's sixty-second birthday. The Jeffersonian paper, the *National Gazette,* announced that these balls were a "monarchical farce." The public had "passed over the absurdities of levees and every species of royal pomp and parade" owing to their affection for Washington, but it was time now for the people to protest "with the manliness of freemen who are resolved not to erect a funeral pyre for their liberties" (Flexner 1972, 13).

Washington's conception of the presidency was not, however, strictly ceremonial and passive. By assembling a cabinet of leading figures and struggling to forge consensus among them on the leading issues of his administration, the president made it clear that the chief executive would not merely "preside" over the executive branch of government, but would direct it. This approach was in keeping with Alexander Hamilton's arguments in *The Federalist Papers* on behalf of an energetic executive who would be, in essence, the chief operating officer of the government.

Washington gave life, moreover, to the president's veto power when he struck down two bills during his eight years in office (see Chapter 5). The first would have allocated seats in the House of Representatives in a manner that Washington thought would violate the Constitution's strict rules on the ratio of representatives to citizens. In vetoing this bill, Washington asserted for the president a duty to protect the Constitution against unconstitutional acts of Congress. Only after Washington's two terms ended did the Supreme Court claim for itself the right to "constitutional review" in *Marbury v. Madison* (1803). Even after that momentous case, early presidents continued to follow Washington's lead in acting as chief magistrate, protecting the nation from unlawful laws.

The second statute that Washington vetoed would have reduced the military to such an extent that the settlers on the frontier would have been left without adequate assistance in Indian warfare. In his "oft-overlooked second veto," Washington claimed for the president a responsibility to protect the nation against bad laws, even if those laws were constitutional (Phelps 1989, 268). Ironically, this veto was so extraordinary for its time—in the suggestion that the president should play a major role in negotiating with Congress over good policy—that it established no precedent.

Washington also established the president's role in personally select-ing the members of the nation's highest judicial body, the Supreme Court. The president selected John Jay of New York as the first chief jus-tice, after Jay expressed his preference for that position rather than becoming secretary of state. At first, the Court, which acts primarily as an appeals court, had no important work to do, because the appeal process is a lengthy one. The Court's members therefore occupied them-selves largely by riding circuit, sitting with other federal judges at the first level of the federal appellate process, and the circuit courts. The president therefore had little business to attend to before the Court, though he regularly consulted Chief Justice Jay for political and policy advice on issues, including, but going far beyond, judicial matters (see Chapter 5).

Throughout his presidency, Washington pursued an especially vigor-ous approach toward issues of military affairs and foreign policy. Through control of the military and the nation's diplomacy, Washing-ton established perhaps his most significant precedent—that of the pres-ident as guardian of the nation. During Washington's terms, the nation was threatened primarily on two fronts. First, there was the issue of inter-nal rebellion. When an antitax revolt in western Pennsylvania became violent in 1794, Washington ordered a militia force from the states to assemble in the capital. In a literal interpretation of the commander-in-chief clause, he then led the columns of soldiers as they marched to quell the Whiskey Rebellion (see Chapter 3). Second, there was the continual threat that the United States might find itself involved in the wars of Europe, even though at this stage in its development its strength was only minimal.

In the Ohio Valley, British emissaries encouraged Indian assaults on encroaching settlers. Washington understood that the danger to Amer-ican citizens in the wilderness was posed not only by Native Americans, but also by the British. The Treaty of Paris had ended one war, but it had not ended the threat of another war with Britain, nor had it established control of the North American continent west of the lines of American settlement. It had not even forced the removal of the British from fron-tier forts on American soil. At roughly the same time that Washington utilized the state militia in response to the Whiskey Rebellion, he ordered the nation's regular army into action along the frontier. After great dif-ficulty and a humiliating defeat for the Americans, on August 20, 1794,

Maj. Gen. Anthony Wayne at last won a decisive victory in the Ohio Valley at the Battle of Fallen Timbers.

As the military historian Russell Weigley notes, Wayne's expedition and the army's march into Pennsylvania were in response to events and "not an expression of anything that can be called a general national military policy or strategy" (Weigley 1973, 42). Precisely because the United States lacked the means for a settled military policy, Washington expended the greatest effort during his presidency in defense of American neutrality in the conflicts between Britain and France.

Indeed, he promoted his policy of neutrality while trying to maintain consensus within his government. Despite their common abhorrence of political parties, Washington and his leading cabinet members, Secretary of Treasury Alexander Hamilton and Secretary of State Thomas Jefferson, became embroiled in partisan conflict. The basic line of cleavage between the Hamiltonians and Jeffersonians was support for the president's neutrality policy. The pro-British Hamiltonians favored the president's policy; the pro-French Jeffersonians disputed the president's authority to decide the nation's foreign policy. In the end, President Washington's policy of neutrality was upheld during his term of office, despite the best efforts of his opponents to undo his actions and undermine his authority.

As Washington's second term neared its end, he began to prepare a valedictory address that would explain and justify his actions as president (Document 1.12). Several themes in what has become known as the Farewell Address stand out. First, Washington emphasized his dependence on the people. Addressing his countrymen, Washington wished it "always be remembered to your praise . . . that . . . the constancy of your support was the essential prop of the efforts, and a guarantee of the plans by which they were effected." This, Washington said, was an idea he would carry to his grave. Second, Washington reminded his audience of his untiring efforts to promote national unity. "The name of American, which belongs to you, in your national capacity," Washington wrote, "must always exalt the just pride of Patriotism, more than any appellation derived from local discriminations."

In addition, Washington issued several famous warnings in his Farewell Address. The nation should be cautious, he wrote, to maintain a just respect for the importance of religion as a bulwark of national morality. In a section of his message devoted to threats to national unity and prosperity, Washington broached the threat of immorality. Morality, along with religion, Washington asserted, are "indispensable supports" to "political prosperity." Washington conceded that for persons with "minds of peculiar structure," a "refined education" alone might provide the foundation for morality. For the great mass of humanity, however, Washington observed that it is fruitless to expect moral behavior "in exclusion of religious principle."

The nation also should be wary of political factions and "the Spirit of Party, generally." Factions, in the eyes of Washington and most other leading citizens of his time, were instruments of small and enterprising minorities determined to substitute "the will of a party" for the "delegated will of the Nation." The dangers of factions had been made clear, Washington believed, in the furious conflict over his administration's foreign policy. Rather than review that conflict, Washington drew from it certain principles. "The Nation," he wrote, "which indulges towards another an habitual hatred, or an habitual fondness, is in some degree a slave. It is a slave to its animosity or to its affection, either of which is sufficient to lead it astray from its duty and its interest."

Because European states have a "set of primary interests," they "must be engaged in frequent controversies." Americans have no cause to "implicate [them]selves, by artificial ties, in the ordinary vicissitudes" of European politics. The time is near, Washington concluded, when the United States will be sufficiently strong to "defy material injury from external annoyance," and "choose peace or war, as our interest guided by our justice shall Counsel." Until such strength is achieved, the policy of the United States must of necessity be defensive as well as neutral. The nation should steer clear of "permanent alliances," trusting "to temporary alliances for extraordinary emergencies."

FINAL RETIREMENT

Near the end of his Farewell Address, Washington articulated his vision of his final retirement. "I anticipate with pleasing expectation . . . ," he wrote, "the sweet enjoyment of partaking, in the midst of my fellow Citizens, the benign influence of good Laws under a free Government . . . and the happy reward, as I trust, of our mutual cares, labours and dangers." Public life, in Washington's view, was subordinate to private life. A gentleman had a duty to play as influential a role in the public life of his community as his talents permitted. For the greatest service, the reward might be a very public fame. But the ultimate object for which sacrifice was required, and fame earned, was the enjoyment of domestic felicity.

Sadly for Washington, then, much of his time and energy during the fall of 1798, the last full year of his life, were consumed with the possibility of war with France. He was called upon once again to take command of the American military when it appeared that war was imminent. The fact that war was averted should not hide the value of Washington's final military service, "because the prospect of the battle-hardened and inspirational general once again in command was an effective means to rally the troops and citizenry and thereby to dissuade the French from taking action" (Rasmussen and Tilton 1999, 248). On other public fronts, Washington maintained his interest in the Potomac River Canal project, the establishment of a national university and a national military academy, and the new capital city, which Washington, out of modesty, could not bring himself to call by its proper name, Washington, D.C.

In his final retirement, Washington also had the satisfaction of guiding into adulthood the two Custis grandchildren who had been raised at Mount Vernon. Washington formally adopted Nelly so that he could give her away in marriage in 1799. At first, Washington had considerable difficulty with his grandson, Washington. The young man "means well," the retired president wrote to a friend, "but has not the resolution to act well" (Rasmussen and Tilton 1999, 250). After several vain attempts to motivate him into success at various colleges, the elder Washington found a position for his namesake in a cavalry unit to be commanded by Nelly's new husband.

Washington also spent much time entertaining the many visitors to Mount Vernon, keeping up with his correspondence, and overseeing the operations of his plantation. On December 10, 1799, he laid down in detail his plans for the coming year's planting and estate operations. Four days later, George Washington died at Mount Vernon after a painful but brief illness.

BIBLIOGRAPHIC ESSAY

James Thomas Flexner's standard biography covers the first president's entire life. Cited in this chapter are Flexner's *Washington: The Indispensable Man* (1974); *George Washington, the Forge of Experience, 1732–1775* (1965); and *George Washington and the New Nation, 1783–1793* (1970), all published in Boston by Little, Brown. William M. S. Rasmussen and Robert S. Tilton's *George Washington: The Man Behind the Myths* (Charlottesville: University Press of Virginia, 1999) is both rigorous and visually compelling. Paul K. Longmore's *The Invention of George Washington* (Berkeley: University of California Press, 1988) contains details that conventional biographies of Washington sometimes miss. Many major documents are collected in W. B. Allen, ed., *George Washington: A Collection* (Indianapolis: Liberty Classics, 1988). An outstanding source on early American geography is D. W. Meinig, *The Shaping of America: A Geographical Perspective on 500 Years of History,* Vol. 1, *Atlantic America, 1492–1800* (New Haven: Yale University Press, 1986). John Ferling's *Setting the World Ablaze: Washington, Adams, Jefferson and the American Revolution* (New York: Oxford University Press, 2000) is an illuminating group biography.

On Washington in the backcountry of his native Virginia, see: Warren R. Hofstra, ed., *George Washington and the Virginia Backcountry* (Madison, Wis.: Madison House, 1998), especially the articles by Hofstra on Washington's relationship with the settlers of the Shenandoah Valley, by J. Frederick Fausz on Washington and the Indians, by Philander D. Chase on Washington's career as a surveyor, and by John E. Ferling on Washington's leadership of the Virginia Regiment. Still relevant is Charles H. Ambler's *George Washington and the West* (Chapel Hill: University of North Carolina Press, 1936).

A standard source on U.S. military history, including the Revolutionary War, is Allan R. Millett and Peter Maslowski's *For the Common Defense: A Military History of the United States of America,* rev. and expanded ed. (New York: Free Press, 1994). Also see Ian Barnes, ed., and Charles Royster, consultant ed., *The Historical Atlas of the American Revolution* (New York: Routledge, 2000). On Washington as a strategist, see Russell F. Weigley, *The American Way of War: A History of United States Military Strategy and Policy* (Bloomington: Indiana University Press, 1973). Living up to its title is Richard H. Kohn's "The Inside History of the Newburgh Conspiracy: America and the Coup d'Etat," in *The Military in America: From the Colonial Era to the Present,* rev. ed., ed. Peter Karsten (New York: Free Press, 1986). In *The Cousins' Wars: Religion, Politics and the Triumph of Anglo-America* (New York: Basic Books, 1999), Kevin Phillips argues that the British were handicapped in the war by the sympathy of leading British generals for the American cause. On the Continental army and the relationship of the army to civilian society, consult James Kirby Martin and

Mark Edward Lender, *A Respectable Army: The Military Origins of the Republic, 1763–1789* (Arlington Heights, Ill.: Harlan Davidson, 1982); Charles Patrick Neimeyer, *America Goes to War: A Social History of the Continental Army* (New York: New York University Press, 1996); and Harry M. Ward, *The War for Independence and the Transformation of American Society* (London: University College of London, 1999).

In the *Presidency of George Washington* (Lawrence: University Press of Kansas, 1974), Forrest McDonald stresses the role in Washington's administration of Alexander Hamilton. On Washington's partnership with another revolutionary companion, see Stuart Leibiger, *Founding Friendship: George Washington, James Madison and the Creation of the American Republic* (Charlottesville: University Press of Virginia, 1999). Glenn A. Phelps explores the precedents set by President Washington in "George Washington: Precedent Setter," in *Inventing the American Presidency,* ed. Thomas E. Cronin (Lawrence: University Press of Kansas, 1989), 259–281, which is cited here, and which is elaborated on in Phelps, *George Washington and American Constitutionalism* (Lawrence: University Press of Kansas, 1993). On George Washington as a presidential "great," see Marc Landy and Sidney M. Milkis, *Presidential Greatness* (Lawrence: University Press of Kansas, 2000).

Document 1.1   "Rules of Civility & Decent Behaviour In Company and Conversation"

George Washington's formal education took place at home and at a small school operated by John Hobby near Fredericksburg, Virginia. From Hobby and from tutors Washington learned how to keep accounts, execute contracts, and mind his manners. His 218-page "School Exercise Book" contains meticulously copied lessons and practice problems. The final ten pages of the book contain 110 copied maxims entitled "Rules of Civility & Decent Behaviour In Company and Conversation." Washington's character throughout his life is so accurately embodied by the "Rules" that many biographers have placed significant importance on them.

[Ferry Farm, c. 1744]

1st Every Action done in Company, ought to be with Some Sign of Respect, to those that are Present.

2d When in Company, put not your Hands to any Part of the Body, not usualy Discovered.

3d Shew Nothing to your Freind that may affright him.

4 In the Presence of Others Sing not to yourself with a humming Noise, nor Drum with your Fingers or Feet.

5th If You Cough, Sneeze, Sigh, or Yawn, do it not Loud but Privately; and Speak not in your Yawning, but put Your handkercheif or Hand before your face and turn aside.

6th Sleep not when others Speak, Sit not when others stand, Speak not when you Should hold your Peace, walk not on when others Stop.

7th Put not off your Cloths in the presence of Others, nor go out your Chamber half Drest.

8th At Play and at Fire its Good manners to Give Place to the last Commer, and affect not to Speak Louder than Ordinary.

9th Spit not in the Fire, nor Stoop low before it neither Put your Hands into the Flames to warm them, nor Set your Feet upon the Fire especially if there be meat before it.

10th When you Sit down, Keep your Feet firm and Even, without putting one on the other or Crossing them. . . .

105th Be not Angry at Table whatever happens & if you have reason to be so, Shew it not but on a Chearfull Countenance especially if there be Strangers for Good Humour makes one Dish of Meat a Feas[t].

106th Set not yourself at the upper of the Table but if it Be your Due or that the Master of the house will have it So, Contend not, least you Should Trouble the Company.

107th If others talk at Table be attentive but talk not with Meat in your Mouth.

108th When you Speak of God or his Atributes, let it be Seriously & [wt.] Reverence. Honour & Obey your Natural Parents altho they be Poor.

109th Let your Recreations be Manfull not Sinfull.

110th Labour to keep alive in your Breast that Little Spark of Ce[les]tial fire Called Conscience.

Finis

Source: John Rhodehamel, ed., *Writings /George Washington* (New York: Library of America, 1997), 3–10.

Document 1.2   Washington to Sarah "Sally" Cary Fairfax, September 12, 1758

Four months before his marriage to Martha Custis, Washington wrote to William Fairfax's wife, Sarah "Sally" Cary Fairfax, with whom he was infatuated his entire life. Most biographers doubt that George and Sally ever consummated their relationship.

Dear Madam,

Yesterday I was honourd with your short, but very agreable favour of the first Instt. How joyfully I catch at the happy occasion of renewing a Corrispondance which I feard was disrelishd on your part, I leave to time, that never failing Expositor of All things.—and to a Monitor equally as faithful in my own Breast, to Testifie. In silence I now express my Joy.—Silence which in some cases—I wish the present—speaks more Intelligably than the sweetest Eloquence.

If you allow that any honour can be derivd from my opposition to Our present System of management, you destroy the merit of it entirely in me by attributing my anxiety to the annimating propsect of possessing Mrs. Custis. When—I—need not name it.—guess yourself.—Shoud not my own Honour, and Country's welfare be the excitement? Tis true, I profess myself a Votary of Love—I acknowledge that a Lady is in the Case—and further I confess, that this Lady is known to you.—Yes Madam, as well as she is to one, who is too sensible of her Charms to deny the Power, whose Influence he feels and must ever submit to, I feel the force of her amiable beauties in the recollection of a thousand tender passages that I coud wish to obliterate, till I am bid to revive them.—but experience alas! sadly reminds me how Impossible this is.—and evinces a Destiny, which has the Sovereign controul of our Actions—not to be resisted by the strongest efforts of Human Nature.

You have drawn me my dear Madam, or rather I have drawn myself, into an honest confession of a simple Fact—misconstrue not my meaning—'tis obvious—doubt it not, nor expose it,—the World has no business to know the object of my Love, declard in this manner to—you when I want to conceal it—One thing, above all things in this World I wish to know, and only one person of your Acquaintance can solve me that, or guess my meaning.—but adiue to this, till happier times, if I ever shall see them.—the hours at present are melancholy dull.—neither the rugged Toils of War, nor the gentler conflict of A—B—s is in my choice.—I dare believe you are as happy as you say—I wish I was happy also—Mirth, good Humour, ease of Mind and.—what else? Cannot fail to render you so; and consummate your Wishes. . . , be assured that I am Dr Madam with the most unfeigned regard, Yr Most Obedient & Most Obligd Hble Servt

Source: John Rhodehamel, ed., *Writings /George Washington* (New York: Library of America, 1997), 96–98.

Document 1.3   Washington to Bryan Fairfax, July 4, 1774

George Washington befriended Bryan Fairfax, the younger brother of George Fairfax, during his time at the family estate. They maintained frequent correspondence and were lifelong friends despite differing political views. In a letter to Washington on July 3, 1774, Fairfax explained that he would not stand for election in Virginia while his fellow citizens seemed intent on violent measures. Washington replied the next day.

Dear Sir,

John has just delivered to me your favor of yesterday, which I shall be obliged to answer in a more concise manner, than I could wish, as I am very much engaged in raising one of the additions to my house, which I think (perhaps it is fancy) goes on better whilst I am present, than in my absence from the workmen. . . .

As to your political sentiments, I would heartily join you in them, so far as relates to a humble and dutiful petition to the throne, provided there was the most distant hope of success. But have we not tried this already? Have we not addressed the Lords, and remonstrated to the Commons? And to what end? Did they deign to look at our petitions? Does it not appear, as clear as the sun in its meridian brightness, that there is a regular, systematic plan formed to fix the right and practice of taxation upon us? Does not the uniform conduct of Parliament for some years past confirm this? Do not all the debates, especially those just brought to us, in the House of Commons on the side of government, expressly declare that America must be taxed in aid of the British funds, and that she has no longer resources within herself? Is there any thing to be expected from petitioning after this? Is not the attack upon the liberty and property of the people of Boston, before restitution of the loss to the India Company was demanded, a plain and self-evident proof of what they are aiming at? Do not the subsequent bills (now I dare say acts), for depriving the Massachusetts Bay of its charter, and for transporting offenders into other colonies or to Great Britain for trial, where it is impossible from the nature of the thing that justice can be obtained, convince us that the administration is determined to stick at nothing to carry its point? Ought we not, then, to put our virtue and fortitude to the severest test?

With you I think it a folly to attempt more than we can execute, as that will not only bring disgrace upon us, but weaken our cause; yet I think we may do more than is generally believed, in respect to the non-importation scheme. As to the withholding of our remittances, that is another point, in which I own I have my doubts on several accounts, but principally on that of justice; for I think, whilst we are accusing others of injustice, we should be just ourselves; and how this can be, whilst we owe a considerable debt, and refuse payment of it to Great Britain, is to me inconceivable. Nothing but the last extremity, I think, can justify it. Whether this is now come, is the question.

I began with telling you, that I was to write a short letter. My paper informs me I have done otherwise. I shall hope to see you tomorrow, at the meeting of the county in Alexandria, when these points are to be considered. I am, dear Sir, your most obedient and humble servant.

Source: Beverly H. Runge, ed., *The Papers of George Washington. Colonial Series,* Vol. 10, *March 1774–June 1775* (Charlottesville: University Press of Virginia, 1995), 109–110.

Document 1.4   Washington to Bryan Fairfax, July 20, 1774

The elected leadership of Fairfax County continued to meet and to deliberate on resolutions expressive of their grievances even after issuing the Fairfax Resolves or Fairfax Resolutions of 1773. Unable to attend, Bryan Fairfax sent a letter to George Washington to be read on his behalf. Washington replied on July 20, invoking the doctrine of natural justice by claiming that Britain's tyrannical policies and the enforcement of those policies usurped the rights and liberties of the colonists.

Dear Sir,

Your Letter of the 17th was not presented to me till after the Resolution's (which were adjudg'd advisable for this county to come to) had been revis'd, alterd, & corrected in the Committee; nor till we had gone into a general Meeting in the Court House, and my attention necessarily call'd every moment to the business that was before it; I did however upon receipt of it (in that hurry & bustle) hastily run it over, and handed it round to the Gentlemen on the Bench, of which there were many; but as no person present seem'd in the least disposed to adopt your Sentiments—as there appeard a perfect satisfaction, & acquiescence to the measures propos'd (except from a Mr Williamson, who was for adopting your advise litterally, without obtaining a Second voice on his Side)—and as the Gentlemen to whom the Letter was shown, advis'd me not to have it read, as it was not like to make a Convert, & repugnant (some of them thought) to the very principle we were contending for, I forebore to offer it otherwise than in the manner abovementioned, which I shall be sorry for, if it gives you any dissatisfaction in not having your Sentiments read to the County at large, instead of communicating them to the first People in it, by offering them the Letter in the manner I did.

That I differ very widely from you, in respect to the mode of obtaining a repeal of the Acts so much, & so justly complaind of, I shall not hesitate to acknowledge; & that this difference in opinion may, probably, proceed from the different Construction's we put upon the Conduct, & Intention of the Ministry, may also be true; But as I see nothing on the one hand, to induce a belief that the Parliament would embrace a favourable oppertunity of Repealing Acts which they go on with great rapidity to pass, in order to enforce their Tyrannical System; and on the other, observe, or think I observe, that Government is pursuing a regular Plan at the expence of Law & justice, to overthrow our Constitutional Rights & liberties, how can I expect any redress from a Measure which hath been ineffectually tryd already—For Sir what is it we are contending against? Is it against paying the duty of 3d. pr lb. on Tea because burthensome? No, it is the Right only, we have all along disputed, & to this end we have already Petitiond his Majesty in as humble, & dutiful a manner as Subjects could do; nay more, we applied to the House of Lords, & House of Commons in their different Legislative Capacities setting forth that, as Englishmen, we could not be deprivd of this essential, & valuable part of our Constitution; If then (as the Fact really is it is against the Right of Taxation we now do), & (as I before said) all along have contended, why should they suppose an exertion of this power would be less obnoxious now, than formerly? and what reasons have we to believe that, they would make a Second attempt whilst the same Sentiments fill'd the Breast of every American, if they did not intend to inforce it if possible? The conduct of the Boston People could not justify the rigour of their Measures, unless their had been a requisition of payment & refusal of it; nor did that measure require an Act to deprive the Governmt of Massachusets Bay of their Charter; or to exempt Offenders from tryal in the place, where Offences were Committed, as there was not, nor could not be, a single Instance produced to manifest the necessity of it—Are not all these things self evident proofs of a fixed & uniform Plan to Tax us? If we want further proofs, does not all the Debates in the House of Commons serve to confirm this? and hath not Genl Gage's Conduct since his arrival (in Stopping the Address of his Council, & Publishing a Proclamation more becoming a Turkish Bashaw than an English Govr & declaring it Treason to associate in any manner by which the Commerce of Great Britain is to be affected) exhibited unexampled Testimony of the most despotick System of Tyranny that ever was practiced in a free Government. In short what further proofs are wanting to satisfy one of the design's of the Ministry than their own Acts; which are uniform, & plainly tending to the same point—nay, if I mistake not, avowedly to fix the Right of Taxation—what hope then from Petitioning, when they tell us that now, or never, is the time to fix the matter—shall we after this whine & cry for releif, when we have already tried it in vain?, or shall we supinely sit, and see one Provence after another fall a Sacrafice to Despotism? If I was in any doubt as to the Right wch the Parliament of Great Britain had to Tax us without our Consents, I should most heartily coincide with you in opinion, that to Petition, & petition only, is the proper method to apply for relief; because we should then be asking a favour, & not claiming a Right wch by the Law of Nature & our Constitution we are, in my opinion, indubitably entitled to; I should even think it criminal to go further than this, under such an Idea; but none such I have, I think the Parliament of Great Britain hath no more Right to put their hands into my Pocket, without my consent, than I have to put my hands into your's, for money; and this being already urged to them in a firm, but decent manner by all the Colonies, what reason is there to expect any thing from their justice?

As to the Resolution for addressing the Throne, I own to you Sir I think the whole might as well have been expung'd; I expect nothing from the measure; nor shd my voice have accompanied it, if the non-Importation Scheme was intended to be Retarded by it; for I am convinc'd, as much as I am of my Existance, that there is no relief for us but in their distress; & I think, at least I hope, that there is publick Virtue enough left among us to deny ourselves every thing but the bare necessaries of Life to accomplish this end—this we have a Right to do, & no power upon Earth can compel us to do otherwise, till they have first reducd us to the most abject state of Slavery that ever was designd for Mankind. The Stopping our Exports would, no doubt, be a shorter Cut than the other, to effect this purpose, but if we owe Money to Great Britain, nothing but the last necessity can justify the Non-payment of it; and therefore, I have great doubts upon this head, & wish to see the other method, which is legal, & will facilitate these payments, first tried.

I cannot conclude, without expressing some concern that I should differ so widely in Sentiments from you in a matter of such great Moment, & general Import; & should much distrust my own judgment upon the occasion, if my Nature did not recoil at the thought of Submitting to Measures which I think Subversive of every thing that I ought to hold dear and valuable—and did I not find, at the sametime, that the voice of Mankind is with me. I must appologize for sending you so rough a sketch of my thoughts upon your Letter. when I look'd back and saw the length of my own, I could not, as I am also a good deal hurried at this time, bear the thoughts of making off a fair Copy. I am Dr Sir Yr Most Obedt Humble Servt

Go: Washington

Source: Beverly H. Runge, ed., *The Papers of George Washington. Colonial Series,* Vol. 10, *March 1774–June 1775* (Charlottesville: University Press of Virginia, 1995), 128–131.

Document 1.5   Washington to Bryan Fairfax, August 24, 1774

In this letter to his lifelong friend Bryan Fairfax, Washington declares that the time for action against Great Britain has arrived. He likens the British oppression of America to the American treatment of colonial slaves, warning that unless the colonists assert their liberty, they will suffer the continued diminution of their rights.

Dear Sir

. . . [A]n Innate Spirit of freedom first told me, that the Measures which Administration hath for sometime been, and now are, most violently pursuing, are repugnant to every principle of natural justice; whilst much abler heads than my own, hath fully convinced me that it is not only repugnant to natural Right, but Subversive of the Laws & Constitution of Great Britain itself; in the Establishment of which some of the best Blood in the Kingdom hath been Spilt; Satisfied then that the Acts of a British Parliament are no longer Govern'd by the Principles of justice—that it is trampling upon the Valuable Rights of American's, confirmd to them by Charter, & the Constitution they themselves boast of; & convinc'd beyond the smallest doubt, that these Measures are the result of deliberation; & attempted to be carried into Execution by the hand of Power is it a time to trifle, or risk our Cause upon Petitions which with difficulty obtain access, and afterwards are thrown by with the utmost contempt—or should we, because heretofore unsuspicious of design and then unwilling to enter into disputes with the Mother Country go on to bear more, and forbear to innumerate our just causes of Complaint—For my own part, I shall not undertake to say where the Line between Great Britain and the Colonies should be drawn, but I am clearly of opinion that one ought to be drawn; & our Rights clearly ascertaind. I could wish, I own, that the dispute had been left to Posterity to determine, but the Crisis is arrivd when we must assert our Rights, or Submit to every Imposition that can be heap'd upon us; till custom and use, will make us as tame, & abject Slaves, as the Blacks we Rule over with such arbitrary Sway.

I intended to have wrote no more than an apology for not writing, but find I am Insensibly running into a length I did not expect, & therefore shall conclude with remarking, that if you disavow the Right of Parliament to Tax us (unrepresented as we are) we only differ in respect to the mode of opposition; and this difference principally arises from your belief that they (the Parliament I mean) want a Decent oppertunity to Repeal the Acts; whilst I am as fully convinc'd, as I am of my existance, that there has been a regular Systematick Plan formd, to enforce them; and that nothing but Unanimity in the Colonies (a stroke they did not expect) and firmness can prevent it. . . .

Source: Beverly H. Runge, ed., The Papers of George Washington. Colonial Series, Vol. 10, March 1774–June 1775 (Charlottesville: University Press of Virginia, 1995), 154–156.

Document 1.6   Washington to Brig. Gen. Alexander McDougall, December 28, 1776

The Battle of Trenton was a turning point in the Revolutionary War. Washington describes his success in a letter to Brig. Gen. Alexander McDougall. Lt. Ranald S. McDougall, the prisoner mentioned at the end of this letter, was released shortly after the Princeton victory.

I have yours of the 27th and am sorry that Affairs bore so bad an Aspect in your Quarter at that time. But I hope that the late Success at Trenton on the 26th and the Consequence of it, will change the face of Matters not only there but every where else. I crossed over to Jersey the Evening of the 25th about 9 miles above Trenton with upwards of 2000 Men and attacked three Regiments of Hessians consisting of fifteen hundred Men about 8 o'Clock next Morning. Our Men pushed on with such Rapidity that they soon carried four pieces of Cannon out of Six, Surrounded the Enemy and obliged 30 Officers and 886 privates to lay down their Arms without firing a Shot. Our Loss was only two Officers and two or three privates wounded. The Enemy had between 20 and 30 killed.

We should have made the whole of them prisoners, could Genl. Ewing have passed the Delaware at Trenton and got in their Rear, but the ice prevented him. I am informed that Count Donnop with the remainder of the Army below Trenton, decamped immediately upon this News, and is on his march towards South Amboy. Generals Mifflin, Ewing and Cadwallader have already passed over to Jersey with a Capital Force and I shall follow with the Continental Regiments as soon as they have recovered from the late Fatigue which was indeed very great.

I hope you, Sir, Genl. Maxwell to whom I have wrote, Colo. Vose, Colo. Ford and every Gentleman who is well affected will exert themselves in encouraging the Militia and assuring them that nothing is wanting, but for them to lend a hand, and driving the Enemy from the whole province of Jersey Pray watch the motions of the Enemy, and if they incline to retreat or advance, harass their Rear and Flanks But at all Events endeavour to collect a Body of men to be ready to join me, or act otherwise as occasion may be.

Your son was mentioned among the first of our prisoners that I demanded in Exchange, but Genl. Howe (or Mr. Loring in his Absence) Sent out others than those I demanded. I have remonstrated to him upon this head and have assured him that I will send in no more prisoners till he sends out the paroles of the Officers taken in Canada.

I am dear Sir
Your most obt Servt
G. Washington

Source: John C. Fitzpatrick, ed., *The Writings of George Washington from the Original Manuscript Sources, 1745–1799,* 39 vols. (Washington, D.C.: Government Printing Office, 1931–1944), 6:448–449.

Document 1.7   Anonymous Letter to the Officers of the Army at Newburgh, New York, March 12, 1783

In the winter of 1783 frustrated officers housed at military headquarters in Newburgh, New York, grew increasingly impatient with Congress's inability to meet the military payroll. On March 12 an anonymous officer distributed the following letter to his fellow officers.

Gentlemen,

A FELLOW-SOLDIER, whose interest and affections bind him strongly to you; whose past sufferings have been as great, and whose future fortune may be as desperate as yours—would beg leave to address you. Age has its claims, and rank is not without its pretensions to advise; but though unsupported by both, he flatters himself that the plain language of sincerity and experience, will neither be unheard nor unregarded. Like many of you, he loved private life, and left it with regret. He left it, determined to retire from the field with the necessity that called him to it, and not till then; not till the enemies of his country, the slaves of power, and the hirelings of injustice, were compelled to abandon their schemes, and acknowledge America as terrible in arms as she had been humble in remonstrance.

With this object in view, he has long shared in your toils, and mingled in your dangers; he has felt the cold hand of poverty without a murmur, and has seen the insolence of wealth without a sigh. But, too much under the direction of his wishes, and sometimes weal enough to mistake desire for opinion, he has, till lately, very lately, believed in the justice of his country. . . .

But faith has its limits, as well as temper. . . .

Have you not, more than once, suggested your wishes, and made known your wants to Congress? Wants and wishes which gratitude and policy should have anticipated, rather than evaded. And have you not lately, in the meek language of entreating memorial, begged from their justice, what you would no longer expect from their favour? How have you been answered? Let the letter which you are called to consider to-morrow, make reply.

If this, then, be your treatment, while the swords you wear are necessary for the defence of America, what have you to expect from peace, when your voice shall sink, and your strength dissipate by division?

When these very swords, the instruments and companions of your glory, shall be taken from your sides, and no remaining mark of military distinction left, but your wants, infirmities, and scars! Can you then consent to be the only sufferers by this revolution, and retiring from the field, grow old in poverty, wretchedness, and contempt? Can you consent to wade through the vile mire of dependency, and owe the miserable remnant of that life to charity, which has hitherto been spent in honour?—if you can, go—and carry with you the jest of tories, and the scorn of whigs—the ridicule, and what is worse, the pity of the world! Go, starve, and be forgotten!

But if your spirit should revolt at this; if you have sense enough to discover, and spirit enough to oppose tyranny, under whatever garb it may assume; whether it be the plain coat of republicanism, or the splendid robe of royalty; if you have yet learned to discriminate between a people and a cause, between men and principles—awake!—attend to your situation, and redress yourselves. If the present moment be lost, every future effort is in vain; and your threats then will be as empty as your entreaties now.

I would advise you, therefore, to come to some final opinion, upon what you can bear, and what you will suffer. If your determination be in any proportion to your wrongs, carry your appeal from the justice to the fears of government—change the milk and water style of your last memorial; assume a bolder tone—decent, but lively—spirited and determined; and suspect the man who would advise to more moderation and longer forbearance. . . ,

[T]he army has its alternative. If peace, that nothing shall separate you from your arms but death; if war, that courting the auspices and inviting the directions of your illustrious leader, you will retire to some unsettled country, smile in your turn, and 'mock when their fear cometh on.' . . .

[Anonymous]

Source: David Ramsay, *The Life of George Washington, Commander in Chief of the Armies of the United States, in the War which Established Their Independence; and First President of the United States* (Baltimore: Cushing and Jewett, 1818), 163–166.

Document 1.8   Washington to the Officers of the Army at Newburgh, March 15, 1783

By mid-March 1783 the potential of an army mutiny was clear. Washington interceded, canceled an unauthorized gathering of officers, and scheduled a sanctioned meeting of the officer corps instead. When Washington entered the meeting, he was greeted with open hostility from some of his own officers. After Washington's address to the officers, they passed resolutions of gratitude to Washington and loyalty to civilian authority.

Gentlemen,

By an anonymous summons, an attempt has been made to convene you together? How inconsistent with the rules of propriety!—how unmilitary!—and how subversive of all order and discipline, let the good sense of the army decide.

   In the moment of this summons, another anonymous production was sent into circulation; addressed more to the feelings of passions, than to the reason & judgment of the army.—The author of the piece, is entitled to much credit for the goodness of his pen:—and I could wish he had as much credit for the rectitude of his heart—for, as men we see thro' different optics, and are induced by the reflecting faculties of the mind, to use different means to attain the same end:—the author of the address, should have had more charity, than to mark for suspicion, the man who should recommend moderation and longer forbearance—or, in other words, who should not think as he thinks, and act as he advises.—But he had another plan in view, in which candor and liberality of sentiment, regard to justice, and love of country, have no part, and he was right, to insinuate the darkest suspicion, to effect the blackest designs.

That the address is drawn with great art, and is designed to answer the most insidious purposes.—That it is calculated to impress the mind, with an idea of premeditated injustice in the sovereign power of the United States, and rouse all those resentments which must unavoidably flow from such a belief.—That the secret mover of this scheme (whoever he may be) intended to take advantage of the passions, while they were warmed by the recollection of mind which is so necessary to give dignity & stability to measures, is rendered too obvious, by the mode of conducting the business to need other proof than a reference to the proceeding.

Thus much, gentlemen, I have thought it incumbent on me to observe to you, to shew upon what principles I opposed the irregular and hasty meeting which was proposed to have been held on Tuesday last:—and not because I wanted a disposition to give you every opportunity, consistent with your own honor, and the dignity of the army, to make known your grievances.—If my conduct heretofore, has not evinced to you, that I have been a faithful friend to the army, my declaration of it at this time would be equally unavailing & improper.—But as I was among the first who embarked in the cause of our common country—As I have never left your side one moment, but when called from you, on public duty—As I have been the constant companion & witness of your distresses, and not among the last to feel, & acknowledge your merits—As I have ever considered my own military reputation as inseperably connected with that of the army—As my Heart has ever expanded with joy, when I have heard its praises—and my indignation has arisen, when the mouth of detraction has been opened against it—it can scarcely be supposed, at this late stage of the war, that I am indifferent to its interests.

But—how are they to be promoted? The way is plain, says the anonymous addresser—If war continues, remove into the unsettled country—there establish yourselves, and leave an ungrateful country to defend itself—But who are they to defend?—Our wives, our children, our farms, and other property which we leave behind us.—or—in this state of hostile seperation, are we to take the two first (the latter cannot be removed)—to perish in a wilderness, with hunger cold & nakedness?—If peace takes place, never sheath your sword says he until you have obtained full and ample justice—This dreadful alternative, of either deserting our country in the extremest hour of her distress, or turning our arms against it, (which is the apparent object, unless Congress can be compelled into instant compliance) has something so shocking in it, that humanity revolts at the idea.

My God! What can this writer have in view, by recommending such measures? ? Can he be a friend to the army?—Can he be a friend to this country?—Rather is he not an insidious foe?—Some emissary, perhaps, from New York, plotting the ruin of both, by sowing the seeds of discord & seperation between the civil & military powers of the continent?—And what compliment does he pay to our understandings, when he recommends measures in either alternative, impracticable in their nature?

But here, gentlemen, I will drop the curtain;—and because it would be as imprudent in me to assign my reasons for this opinion, as it would be insulting to your conception, to suppose you stood in need of them.—A moment's reflection will convince every dispassionate mind of the physical impossibility of carrying either proposal into execution.

There might, gentlemen, be an impropriety in my taking notice, in this address to you, of an anonymous production—but the manner in which that performance has been introduced to the army—the effect it was intended to have, together with some other circumstances, will amply justify my observations on the tendency of that writing.—With respect to the advice given by the author—to suspect the man, who shall recommend moderate measures and longer forbearance—I spurn it—as every man, who regards that liberty, & reveres that justice for which we contend, undoubtedly must—for if men are to be precluded from offering their sentiments on a matter, which may involve the most serious and alarming consequences, that can invite the consideration of Mankind; reason is of no use to us—the freedom of speech may be taken away—and, dumb & silent we may be led, like sheep, to the slaughter.

I cannot, in justice to my own belief, & what I have great reason to conceive is the intention of Congress, conclude this address, without giving it as my decided opinion; that that honourable body, entertain exalted sentiments of the services of the army;—and, from a full conviction of its merits & sufferings, will do it complete justice:—That their endeavors, to discover & establish funds for this purpose, have been unwearied, and will not cease, till they have succeeded, I have succeeded, I have not a doubt. But, like all other large bodies, where there is a variety of different interests to reconcile, their deliberations are slow. Why then should we distrust them?—and, in consequence of that distrust, adopt measures, which may cast a shade over that glory which, has been so justly acquired; and tarnish the reputation of an army which is celebrated thro' all Europe, for its fortitude and patriotism?—and for what is this done?—to bring the object we seek for nearer?—No!—most certainly, in my opinion, it will cast it at a greater distance.—

For myself (and I take no merit in giving the assurance, being induced to it from principles of gratitude, veracity & Justice)—a grateful sense of the confidence you have ever placed in me—a recollection of the cheerful assistance, & prompt obedience I have experienced from you, under every vicisitude of fortune,—and the sincere affection I feel for an army I have so long had the honor to command, will oblige me to declare, in this public & solemn manner, that, in the attainment of compleat justice for all your toils & dangers, and in the gratification of every wish, so far as may be done consistently with the great duty I owe my country, and those powers we are bound to respect, you may freely command my services to the utmost of my abilities.

While I give you these assurances, and pledge my self in the most unequivocal manner, to exert whatever ability I am possessed of, in your favor—let me entreat you, gentlemen, on your part, not to take any measures, which, viewed in the calm light of reason, will lessen the dignity, & sully the glory you have hitherto maintained—let me request you to rely on the plighted faith of your country, and place a full confidence in the purity of the intentions of Congress; that, previous to your dissolution as an Army they will cause all your accounts to be fairly liquidated, as directed in their resolutions, which were published to you two days ago—and that they will adopt the most effectual measures in their power, to render ample justice to you, for your faithful and meritorious Services.—And let me conjure you, in the name of our common country—as you value your own sacred honor—as you respect the rights of humanity; as you regard the military & national character of America, to express your utmost horror & detestation of the man who wishes, under any specious pretences, to overturn the liberties of our country, & who wickedly attempts to open the flood gates of civil discord, & deluge our rising empire in blood.

By thus determining—& thus acting, you will pursue the plain & direct road to the attainment of your wishes.—You will defeat the insidious designs of our enemies, who are compelled to resort from open force to secret artifice.—You will give one more distinguished proof of unexampled patriotism & patient virtue, rising superior to the pressure of the most complicated sufferings;—And you will, by the dignity of your conduct, afford occasion for posterity to say, when speaking of the glorious example you have exhibited to mankind, had this day been wanting, the world has never seen the last stage of perfection to which human nature is capable of attaining.

Source: David Ramsay, *The Life of George Washington, Commander in Chief of the Armies of the United States, in the War which Established Their Independence; and First President of the United States* (Baltimore: Cushing and Jewett, 1818), 167–173.

Document 1.9   Washington's Farewell Orders to the Armies of the United States, November 2, 1783

Washington resigned his military post after learning that the Treaty of Paris had been signed. Satisfied that his officers and soldiers would receive fair compensation, Washington retired for a second time to Mount Vernon. He distributed the following farewell orders to the Continental army on November 2, 1783. In them he urges his comrades to become good citizens and to aid their fellow citizens in strengthening the federal government.

The United States in Congress assembled, after giving the most honorable testimony to the Merits of the Federal Armies, and presenting them with the thanks of their Country for their long, eminent and faithful Services, having thought proper, by their Proclamation bearing date the 18th day of October last, to discharge such part of the Troops as were engaged for the War, and to permit the Officers on Furlough to retire from Service from and after tomorrow, which Proclamation having been communicated in the public papers for the information and government of all concerned; it only remains for the Commander in Chief to address himself once more, and that for the last time, to the Armies of the United States (however widely dispersed the Individuals who composed them may be) and to bid them an affectionate—a long farewell. . . .

A contemplation of the compleat attainment (at a period earlier than could have been expected) of the object for which we contended, against so formidable a power, cannot but inspire us with astonishment and gratitude—The disadvantageous circumstances on our part, under which the War was undertaken, can never be forgotten—The singular interpositions of Providence in our feeble condition were such, as could scarcely escape the attention of the most unobserving—where the unparalleled perseverance of the Armies of the United States, through almost every possible suffering and discouragement, for the space of eight long years was little short of a standing Miracle.

It is not the meaning nor within the compass of this Address, to detail the hardships peculiarly incident to our Service, or to discribe the distresses which in several instances have resulted from the extremes of hunger and nakedness, combined with the rigors of an inclement season. Nor is it necessary to dwell on the dark side of our past affairs. Every American Officer and Soldier must now console himself for any unpleasant circumstances which may have occurred, by a recollection of the uncommon scenes in which he has been called to act, no inglorious part; and the astonishing Events of which he has been a witness—Events which have seldom, if ever before, taken place on the stage of human action, nor can they probably ever happen again. For who has before seen a disciplined Army formed at once from such raw Materials? Who that was not a witness could imagine, that the most violent local prejudices would cease so soon, and that Men who came from the different parts of the Continent, strongly disposed by the habits of education, to dispise and quarrel with each other, would instantly become but one patriotic band of Brothers? Or who that was not on the spot can trace the steps by which such a wonderful Revolution has been effected, and such a glorious period put to all our Warlike toils?

It is universally acknowledged that the enlarged prospect of happiness, opened by the confirmation of our Independence and Sovereignty, almost exceeds the power of description. And shall not the brave Men who have contributed so essentially to these inestimable acquisitions, retiring victorious from the Field of War, to the Field of Agriculture, participate in all the blessings which have been obtained? In such a Republic, who will exclude them from the rights of Citizens and the fruits of their labours? In such a Country so happily circumstanced the persuits of Commerce and the cultivation of the Soil, will unfold to industry the certain road to competence. To those hardy Soldiers, who are actuated by the spirit of adventure, the Fisheries will afford ample and profitable employment, and the extensive and fertile Regions of the West will yield a most happy Asylum to those, who, fond of domestic enjoyment are seeking for personal independence. Nor is it possible to conceive that any one of the United States will prefer a National Bankrupcy and a dissolution of the Union, to a compliance with the requisitions of Congress and the payment of its just debts—so that the Officers and Soldiers may expect considerable assistance in recommencing their civil occupations from the sums due to them from the Public, which must and will most inevitably be paid.

In order to effect this desirable purpose, and to remove the prejudices which may have taken possession of the Minds of any of the good People of the States, it is earnestly recommended to all the Troops that with strong attachments to the Union, they should carry with them into civil Society the most conciliating dispositions; and that they should prove themselves not less virtuous and usefull as Citizens, than they have been persevering and victorious as Soldiers. What tho' there should be some envious Individuals who are unwilling to pay the Debt the public has contracted, or to yield the tribute due to Merit, yet let such unworthy treatment produce no invective, or any instance of intemperate conduct, let it be remembered that the unbiased voice of the Free Citizens of the United States has promised the just reward, and given the merited applause, let it be known and remembered that the reputation of the Federal Armies is established beyond the reach of Malevolence, and let a conciousness of their achievements and fame, still incite the Men who composed them to honorable Actions; under the persuasion that the private virtues of economy, prudence and industry, will not be less amiable in civil life, than the more splendid qualities of valour, perseverence and enterprise, were in the Field: Every one may rest assured that much, very much of the future happiness of the Officers and Men, will depend upon the wise and manly conduct which shall be adopted by them, when they are mingled with the great body of the Community. And altho', the General has so frequently given it as his opinion in the most public and explicit manner, that unless the principles of the Federal Government were properly supported, and the Powers of the Union encreased, the honor, dignity and justice of the Nation would be lost for ever; yet he cannot help repeating on this occasion, so interesting a sentiment, and leaving it as his last injunction to every Officer and every Soldier, who may view the subject in the same serious point of light, to add his best endeavours to those of his worthy fellow Citizens towards effecting these great and valuable purposes, on which our very existence as a Nation so materially depends.

The Commander in Chief conceives little is now wanting to enable the Soldier to change the Military character into that of the Citizen, but that steady and decent tenor of behaviour which has generally distinguished, not only the Army under his immediate Command, but the different Detachments and seperate Armies, through the course of the War; from their good sense and prudence he anticipates the happiest consequences; And while he congratulates them on the glorious occasion which renders their Services in the Field no longer necessary, he wishes to express the strong obligations he feels himself under, for the assistance he has received from every Class—and in every instance. He presents his thanks in the most serious and affectionate manner to the General Officers, as well for their Counsel on many interesting occasions, as for their ardor in promoting the success of the plans he had adopted—To the Commandants of Regiments and Corps, and to the other Officers for their great Zeal and attention in carrying his orders promptly into execution—To the Staff for their alacrity and exactness in performing the duties of their several Departments—And to the Non-commissioned officers and private Soldiers, for their extraordinary patience in suffering, as well as their invincible fortitude in Action—To the various branches of the Army, the General takes this last and solemn oppertunity of professing his inviolable attachment & friendship—He wishes more than bare professions were in his power, that he was really able to be usefull to them all in future life; He flatters himself however, they will do him the justice to believe, that whatever could with propriety be attempted by him, has been done. And being now to conclude these his last public Orders, to take his ultimate leave, in a short time, of the Military Character, and to bid a final adieu to the Armies he has so long had the honor to Command—he can only again offer in their behalf his recommendations to their grateful Country, and his prayers to the God of Armies. May ample justice be done them here, and may the choicest of Heaven's favors both here and hereafter attend those, who under the divine auspices have secured innumerable blessings for others: With these Wishes, and this benediction, the Commander in Chief is about to retire from service—The Curtain of seperation will soon be drawn—and the Military Scene to him will be closed for ever.

Source: "Rocky Hill 2d Novr 1783 Genl Washington's Farewell Orders to the Armies of the United States," November 2, 1783, Draft Copy. Washington Papers, Library of Congress, Washington, D.C.

Document 1.10   First Inaugural Address, April 30, 1789

On April 16, 1789, George Washington recorded the following thoughts in his diary. "About ten o'clock I bade adieu to Mount Vernon, to private life, and to domestic felicity; and with a mind oppressed with more anxious and painful sensations than I have words to express, set out for New York . . . , with the best dispositions to render service to my country in obedience to its call, but with less hope of answering its expectations" (Rhodehamel 1997, 730).

Two weeks later, Robert R. Livingston, chancellor of the state of New York, administered the oath of office outside the Senate chamber in New York. After taking the oath, Washington entered the chamber and delivered his first message as president of the United States.

Fellow-Citizens of the Senate and of the House of Representatives: Among the vicissitudes incident to life no event could have filled me with greater anxieties than that of which the notification was transmitted by your order, and received on the 14th day of the present month. On the one hand, I was summoned by my Country, whose voice I can never hear but with veneration and love, from a retreat which I had chosen with the fondest predilection, and, in my flattering hopes, with an immutable decision, as the asylum of my declining years—a retreat which was rendered every day more necessary as well as more dear to me by the addition of habit to inclination, and of frequent interruptions in my health to the gradual waste committed on it by time. On the other hand, the magnitude and difficulty of the trust to which the voice of my country called me, being sufficient to awaken in the wisest and most experienced of her citizens a distrustful scrutiny into his qualifications, could not but overwhelm with despondence one who (inheriting inferior endowments from nature and unpracticed in the duties of civil administration) ought to be peculiarly conscious of his own deficiencies. In this conflict of emotions all I dare aver is that it has been my faithful study to collect my duty from a just appreciation of every circumstance by which it might be affected. All I dare hope is that if, in executing this task, I have been too much swayed by a grateful remembrance of former instances, or by an affectionate sensibility to this transcendent proof of the confidence of my fellow-citizens, and have thence too little consulted my incapacity as well as disinclination for the weighty and untried cares before me, my error will be palliated by the motives which mislead me, and its consequences be judged by my country with some share of the partiality in which they originated.

Such being the impressions under which I have, in obedience to the public summons, repaired to the present station, it would be peculiarly improper to omit in this first official act my fervent supplications to that Almighty Being who rules over the universe, who presides in the councils of nations, and whose providential aids can supply every human defect, that His benediction may consecrate to the liberties and happiness of the people of the United States a Government instituted by themselves for these essential purposes, and may enable every instrument employed in its administration to execute with success the functions allotted to his charge. In tendering this homage to the Great Author of every public and private good, I assure myself that it expresses your sentiments not less than my own, nor those of my fellow-citizens at large less than either. No people can be bound to acknowledge and adore the Invisible Hand which conducts the affairs of men more than those of the United States. Every step by which they have advanced to the character of an independent nation seems to have been distinguished by some token of providential agency; and in the important revolution just accomplished in the system of their united government the tranquil deliberations and voluntary consent of so many distinct communities from which the event has resulted can not be compared with the means by which most governments have been established without some return of pious gratitude, along with an humble anticipation of the future blessings which the past seem to presage. These reflections, arising out of the present crisis, have forced themselves too strongly on my mind to be suppressed. You will join with me, I trust, in thinking that there are none under the influence of which the proceedings of a new and free government can more auspiciously commence.

By the article establishing the executive department it is made the duty of the President "to recommend to your consideration such measures as he shall judge necessary and expedient." The circumstances under which I now meet you will acquit me from entering into that subject further than to refer to the great constitutional charter under which you are assembled, and which, in defining your powers, designates the objects to which your attention is to be given. It will be more consistent with those circumstances, and far more congenial with the feelings which actuate me, to substitute, in place of a recommendation of particular measures, the tribute that is due to the talents, the rectitude, and the patriotism which adorn the characters selected to devise and adopt them. In these honorable qualifications I behold the surest pledges that as on one side no local prejudices or attachments, no separate views nor party animosities, will misdirect the comprehensive and equal eye which ought to watch over this great assemblage of communities and interests, so, on another, that the foundation of our national policy will be laid in the pure and immutable principles of private morality, and the preeminence of free government be exemplified by all the attributes which can win the affections of its citizens and command the respect of the world. I dwell on this prospect with every satisfaction which an ardent love for my country can inspire, since there is no truth more thoroughly established than that there exists in the economy and course of nature an indissoluble union between virtue and happiness; between duty and advantage; between the genuine maxims of an honest and magnanimous policy and the solid rewards of public prosperity and felicity; since we ought to be no less persuaded that the propitious smiles of Heaven can never be expected on a nation that disregards the eternal rules of order and right which Heaven itself has ordained; and since the preservation of the sacred fire of liberty and the destiny of the republican model of government are justly considered, perhaps, as deeply, as finally, staked on the experiment entrusted to the hands of the American people.

Besides the ordinary objects submitted to your care, it will remain with your judgment to decide how far an exercise of the occasional power delegated by the fifth article of the Constitution is rendered expedient at the present juncture by the nature of objections which have been urged against the system, or by the degree of inquietude which has given birth to them. Instead of undertaking particular recommendations on this subject, in which I could be guided by no lights derived from official opportunities, I shall again give way to my entire confidence in your discernment and pursuit of the public good; for I assure myself that whilst you carefully avoid every alteration which might endanger the benefits of an united and effective government, or which ought to await the future lessons of experience, a reverence for the characteristic rights of freemen and a regard for the public harmony will sufficiently influence your deliberations on the question how far the former can be impregnably fortified or the latter be safely and advantageously promoted.

To the foregoing observations I have one to add, which will be most properly addressed to the House of Representatives. It concerns myself, and will therefore be as brief as possible. When I was first honored with a call into the service of my country, then on the eve of an arduous struggle for its liberties, the light in which I contemplated my duty required that I should renounce every pecuniary compensation. From this resolution I have in no instance departed; and being still under the impressions which produced it, I must decline as inapplicable to myself any share in the personal emoluments which may be indispensably included in a permanent provision for the executive department, and must accordingly pray that the pecuniary estimates for the station in which I am placed may during my continuance in it be limited to such actual expenditures as the public good may be thought to require.

Having thus imparted to you my sentiments as they have been awakened by the occasion which brings us together, I shall take my present leave; but not without resorting once more to the benign Parent of the Human Race in humble supplication that, since He has been pleased to favor the American people with opportunities for deliberating in perfect tranquillity, and dispositions for deciding with unparalleled unanimity on a form of government for the security of their union and the advancement of their happiness, so His divine blessing may be equally conspicuous in the enlarged views, the temperate consultations, and the wise measures on which the success of this Government must depend.

Source: Avalon Project, Yale Law School *(www.yale.edu/lawweb/avalon/presiden/inaug/wash1.htm).*

Document 1.11   Abigail Adams to Mary Cranch, January 5, 1790

Abigail Adams was the wife of John Adams, the second president of the United States and vice president under Washington. She frequently corresponded with her older sister, Mary Cranch. This letter details the New Year's celebrations Abigail attended in 1790. She includes a description of her interaction with President Washington as well as an overall description of his character.

MY DEAR SISTER:

I begin my Letter with the congratulations of the season, to you and all my other Friends & for many happy returns in succeeding years. The New Years day in this state, & particularly in this city is celebrated with every mark of pleasure and satisfaction. The shops and publick offices are shut. There is not any market upon this day, but every person laying aside Business devote[s] the day to the social purpose of visiting & receiving visits. . . . The V.P. visited the President & then returnd home to receive His Friends. In the Evening I attended the drawing Room, it being Mrs. W[ashington']s publick day. It was as much crowded as a Birth Night at St. James, and with company as Briliantly drest, diamonds & great hoops excepted. My station is always at the right hand of Mrs. W.; through want of knowing what is right I find it sometimes occupied, but on such an occasion the President never fails of seeing that it is relinquished for me, and having removed Ladies several times, they have now learnt to rise & give it to me, but this between our selves, as *all distinction* you know is unpopular. Yet this same P[resident] has so happy a faculty of appearing to accommodate & yet carrying his point, that if he was not really one of the best intentioned men in the world he might be a very dangerous one. He is polite with dignity, affable without familiarity, distant without Haughtyness, Grave without Austerity, Modest, wise & Good. These are traits in his Character which peculiarly fit him for the exalted station he holds, and God Grant that he may Hold it with the same applause & universal satisfaction for many many years, as it is my firm opinion that no other man could rule over this great peopl & consolidate them into one mighty Empire but He who is set over us.

Source: Stewart Mitchell, ed., *New Letters of Abigail Adams, 1788–1801* (Boston: Houghton Mifflin, 1947), 34–35.

Document 1.12   Farewell Address, September 19, 1796

Washington never actually delivered his Farewell Address; instead, he chose to publish it in the Philadelphia newspaper American Daily Advertiser *on September 19, 1796. The editor ran it without editorial commentary, with a simple title, "To the PEOPLE of the United States, Friends and fellow citizens." In this famous document Washington affirms his dependence on the public and his optimism about the future of the United States. Despite his optimism, he cautions his fellow Americans about several dangers to unity and prosperity: the "spirit of party" and "permanent alliances" with foreign nations.*

The period for a new election of a Citizen, to Administer the Executive government of the United States, being not far distant, and the time actually arrived, when your thoughts must be employed in designating the person, who is to be cloathed with that important trust, it appears to me proper, especially as it may conduce to a more distinct expression of the public voice, that I should now apprise you of the resolution I have formed, to decline being considered among the number of those, out of whom a choice is to be made.

I beg you, at the same time, to do me the justice to be assured, that this resolution has not been taken, without a strict regard to all the considerations appertaining to the relation, which binds a dutiful Citizen to his country—and that, in withdrawing the tender of service which silence in my Situation might imply, I am influenced by no diminution of zeal for your future interest, no deficiency of grateful respect for your past kindness; but am supported by a full conviction that the step is compatible with both.

The acceptance of, & continuance hitherto in, the Office to which your Suffrages have twice called me, have been a uniform sacrifice of inclination to the opinion of duty, and to a deference for what appeared to be your desire. I constantly hoped, that it would have been much earlier in my power, consistently with motives, which I was not at liberty to disregard, to return to that retirement, from which I had been reluctantly drawn. The strength of my inclination to do this, previous to the last Election, had even led to the preparation of an address to declare it to you; but mature reflection on the then perplexed & critical posture of our Affairs with foreign nations, and the unanimous advice of persons entitled to my confidence, impelled me to abandon the idea.

I rejoice, that the state of your concerns, external as well as internal, no longer renders the pursuit of inclination incompatible with the sentiment of duty, or propriety; & am persuaded whatever partiality may be retained for my services, that in the present circumstances of our country, you will not disapprove my determination to retire.

The impressions, with which, I first undertook the arduous trust, were explained on the proper occasion. In the discharge of this trust, I will only say, that I have, with good intentions, contributed towards the Organization and Administration of the government, the best exertions of which a very fallible judgment was capable. Not unconscious, in the outset, of the inferiority of my qualifications, experience in my own eyes, perhaps still more in the eyes of others, has strengthned the motives to diffidence of myself; and every day the encreasing weight of years admonishes me more and more, that the shade of retirement is as necessary to me as it will be welcome. Satisfied that if any circumstances have given peculiar value to my services, they were temporary, I have the consolation to believe, that while choice and prudence invite me to quit the political scene, patriotizm does not forbid it.

In looking forward to the moment, which is intended to terminate the career of my public life, my feelings do not permit me to suspend the deep acknowledgment of that debt of gratitude wch I owe to my beloved country, for the many honors it has conferred upon me; still more for the stedfast confidence with which it has supported me; and for the opportunities I have thence enjoyed of manifesting my inviolable attachment, by services faithful & persevering, though in usefulness unequal to my zeal. If benefits have resulted to our country from these services, let it always be remembered to your praise, and as an instructive example in our annals, that, under circumstances in which the Passions agitated in every direction were liable to mislead, amidst appearances sometimes dubious, vicissitudes of fortune often discouraging, in situations in which not unfrequently want of Success has countenanced the spirit of criticism, the constancy of your support was the essential prop of the efforts, and a guarantee of the plans by which they were effected. Profoundly penetrated with this idea, I shall carry it with me to my grave, as a strong incitement to unceasing vows that Heaven may continue to you the choicest tokens of its beneficence—that your Union & brotherly affection may be perpetual—that the free constitution, which is the work of your hands, may be sacredly maintained—that its Administration in every department may be stamped with wisdom and Virtue—that, in fine, the happiness of the people of these States, under the auspices of liberty, may be made complete, by so careful a preservation and so prudent a use of this blessing as will acquire to them the glory of recommending it to the applause, the affection—and adoption of every nation which is yet a stranger to it.

Here, perhaps, I ought to stop. But a solicitude for your welfare, which cannot end but with my life, and the apprehension of danger, natural to that solicitude, urge me on an occasion like the present, to offer to your solemn contemplation, and to recommend to your frequent review, some sentiments; which are the result of much reflection, of no inconsiderable observation, and which appear to me all important to the permanency of your felicity as a People. These will be offered to you with the more freedom as you can only see in them the disinterested warnings of a parting friend, who can possibly have no personal motive to biass his counsel. Nor can I forget, as an encouragement to it, your endulgent reception of my sentiments on a former and not dissimilar occasion.

Interwoven as is the love of liberty with every ligament of your hearts, no recommendation of mine is necessary to fortify or confirm the Attachment.

The Unity of Government which constitutes you one people is also now dear to you. It is justly so; for it is a main Pillar in the Edifice of your real independence, the support of your tranquility at home; your peace abroad; of your safety; of your prosperity; of that very Liberty which you so highly prize. But as it is easy to foresee, that from different causes & from different quarters, much pains will be taken, many artifices employed, to weaken in your minds the conviction of this truth; as this is the point in your political fortress against which the batteries of internal & external enemies will be most constantly and actively (though often covertly & insidiously) directed, it is of infinite moment, that you should properly estimate the immense value of your national Union to your collective & individual happiness; that you should cherish a cordial, habitual & immoveable attachment to it; accustoming yourselves to think and speak of it as of the Palladium of your political safety and prosperity; watching for its preservation with jealous anxiety; discountenancing whatever may suggest even a suspicion that it can in any event be abandoned, and indignantly frowning upon the first dawning of every attempt to alienate any portion of our Country from the rest, or to enfeeble the sacred ties which now link together the various parts.

For this you have every inducement of sympathy and interest. Citizens by birth or choice, of a common country, that country has a right to concentrate your affections. The name of American, which belongs to you, in your national capacity, must always exalt the just pride of Patriotism, more than any appellation derived from local discriminations. With slight shades of difference, you have the same Religeon, Manners, Habits & political Principles. You have in a common cause fought & triumphed together—The independence & liberty you possess are the work of joint councils, and joint efforts—of common dangers, sufferings and successes.

But these considerations, however powerfully they address themselves to your sensibility are greatly outweighed by those which apply more immediately to your Interest. Here every portion of our country finds the most commanding motives for carefully guarding & preserving the Union of the whole.

The North, in an unrestrained intercourse with the South, protected by the equal Laws of a common government, finds in the productions of the latter, great additional resources of Maratime & commercial enterprise and—precious materials of manufacturing industry. The South in the same Intercourse, benefitting by the Agency of the North, sees its agriculture grow & its commerce expand. Turning partly into its own channels the seamen of the North, it finds its particular navigation envigorated; and while it contributes, in different ways, to nourish & increase the general mass of the National navigation, it looks forward to the protection of a Maratime strength, to which itself is unequally adapted. The East, in a like intercourse with the West, already finds, and in the progressive improvement of interior communications, by land & water, will more & more find a valuable vent for the commodities which it brings from abroad, or manufactures at home. The West derives from the East supplies requisite to its growth & comfort—and what is perhaps of still greater consequence, it must of necessity owe the Secure enjoyment of indispensable outlets for its own productions to the weight, influence, and the future maritime strength of the Atlantic side of the Union, directed by an indissoluble community of Interest as one Nation. Any other tenure by which the West can hold this essential advantage, whether derived from its own seperate strength, or from an apostate & unnatural connection with any foreign Power, must be intrinsically precarious.

While then every part of our country thus feels an immediate & particular Interest in Union, all the parts combined cannot fail to find in the united mass of means & efforts greater strength, greater resource, proportionably greater security from external danger, a less frequent interruption of their Peace by foreign Nations; and, what is of inestimable value! they must derive from Union an exemption from those broils and Wars between themselves, which so frequently afflict neighbouring countries, not tied together by the same government; which their own rivalships alone would be sufficient to produce, but which opposite foreign alliances, attachments & intriegues would stimulate & imbitter. Hence

likewise they will avoid the necessity of those overgrown Military establishments, which under any form of Government are inauspicious to liberty, and which are to be regarded as particularly hostile to Republican
Liberty: In this sense it is, that your union ought to be considered as a
main prop of your liberty, and that the love of the one ought to endear
to you the preservation of the other.

These considerations speak a persuasive language to every reflecting
& virtuous mind, and exhibit the continuance of the Union as a primary
object of Patriotic desire. Is there a doubt, whether a common government can embrace so large a sphere? Let experience solve it. To listen to
mere speculation in such a case were criminal. We are authorized to hope
that a proper organization of the whole, with the auxiliary agency of governments for the respective Subdivisions, will afford a happy issue to the
experiment. 'Tis well worth a fair and full experiment. With such powerful and obvious motives to Union, affecting all parts of our country,
while experience shall not have demonstrated its impracticability, there
will always be reason, to distrust the patriotism of those, who in any quarter may endeavor to weaken its bands.

In contemplating the causes wch may disturb our Union, it occurs as
matter of serious concern, that any ground should have been furnished
for characterizing parties by Geographical discriminations—Northern
and Southern—Atlantic and Western; whence designing men may
endeavour to excite a belief that there is a real difference of local interests and views. One of the expedients of Party to acquire influence, within
particular districts, is to misrepresent the opinions & aims of other Districts. You cannot shield yourselves too much against the jealousies &
heart burnings which spring from these misrepresentations. They tend
to render Alien to each other those who ought to be bound together
by fraternal Affection. The Inhabitants of our Western country have lately
had a useful lesson on this head. They have Seen, in the Negociation by
the Executive, and in the unanimous ratification by the Senate, of the
Treaty with Spain, and in the universal satisfaction at that event,
throughout the United States, a decisive proof how unfounded were the
suspicions propagated among them of a policy in the General Government and in the Atlantic States unfriendly to their Interests in regard to
the Mississippi. They have been witnesses to the formation of two
Treaties, that with G: Britain and that with Spain, which secure to them
every thing they could desire, in respect to our Foreign relations, towards

confirming their prosperity. Will it not be their wisdom to rely for the preservation of these advantages on the Union by wch they were procured? Will they not henceforth be deaf to those Advisers, if such there are, who would sever them from their Brethren and connect them with Aliens?

To the efficacy and permanency of Your Union, a Government for the whole is indispensable. No Alliances however strict between the parts can be an adequate substitute. They must inevitably experience the infractions & interruptions which all Alliances in all times have experienced. Sensible of this momentous truth, you have improved upon your first essay, by the adoption of a Constitution of Government, better calculated than your former for an intimate Union, and for the efficacious management of your common concerns. This government, the offspring of our own choice uninfluenced and unawed, adopted upon full investigation & mature deliberation, completely free in its principles, in the distribution of its powers, uniting security with energy, and containing within itself a provision for its own amendment, has a just claim to your confidence and your support. Respect for its authority, compliance with its Laws, acquiescence in its measures, are duties enjoined by the fundamental maxims of true Liberty. The basis of our political Systems is the right of the people to make and to alter their Constitutions of Government. But the Constitution which at any time exists, 'till changed by an explicit and authentic act of the whole People, is sacredly obligatory upon all. The very idea of the power and the right of the People to establish Government presupposes the duty of every Individual to obey the established Government.

All obstructions to the execution of the Laws, all combinations and Associations, under whatever plausible character, with the real design to direct, controul, counteract, or awe the regular deliberation and action of the Constituted authorities are distructive of this fundamental principle and of fatal tendency. They serve to Organize faction, to give it an artificial and extraordinary force—to put in the place of the delegated will of the Nation, the will of a party; often a small but artful and enterprizing minority of the Community; and, according to the alternate triumphs of different parties, to make the public Administration the Mirror of the ill concerted and incongruous projects of faction, rather than the Organ of consistent and wholesome plans digested by common councils and modefied by mutual interests. However combinations or

Associations of the above description may now & then answer popular ends, they are likely, in the course of time and things, to become potent engines, by which cunning, ambitious and unprincipled men will be enabled to subvert the Power of the People, & to usurp for themselves the reins of Government; destroying afterwards the very engines which have lifted them to unjust dominion.

Towards the preservation of your Government and the permanency of your present happy state, it is requisite, not only that you steadily discountenance irregular oppositions to its acknowledged authority, but also that you resist with care the spirit of innovation upon its principles however specious the pretexts. One method of assault may be to effect, in the forms of the Constitution, alterations which will impair the energy of the system, and thus to undermine what cannot be directly overthrown. In all the changes to which you may be invited, remember that time and habit are at least as necessary to fix the true character of Governments, as of other human institutions—that experience is the surest standard, by which to test the real tendency of the existing Constitution of a Country—that facility in changes upon the credit of mere hypotheses & opinion exposes to perpetual change, from the endless variety of hypotheses and opinion: and remember, especially, that for the efficient management of your common interests, in a country so extensive as ours, a Government of as much vigour as is consistent with the perfect security of Liberty is indispensable—Liberty itself will find in such a Government, with powers properly distributed and adjusted, its surest Guardian. It is indeed little else than a name, where the Government is too feeble to withstand the enterprises of faction, to confine each member of the Society within the limits prescribed by the laws & to maintain all in the secure & tranquil enjoyment of the rights of person & property.

I have already intimated to you the danger of Parties in the State, with particular reference to the founding of them on Geographical discriminations. Let me now take a more comprehensive view, & warn you in the most solemn manner against the baneful effects of the Spirit of Party, generally.

This Spirit, unfortunately, is inseperable from our nature, having its root in the strongest passions of the human Mind. It exists under different shapes in all Governments, more or less stifled, controuled, or repressed; but in those of the popular form it is seen in its greatest rankness and is truly their worst enemy.

The alternate domination of one faction over another, sharpened by the spirit of revenge natural to party dissention, which in different ages & countries has perpetrated the most horrid enormities, is itself a frightful despotism. But this leads at length to a more formal and permanent despotism. The disorders & miseries, which result, gradually incline the minds of men to seek security & repose in the absolute power of an Individual: and sooner or later the chief of some prevailing faction more able or more fortunate than his competitors, turns this disposition to the purposes of his own elevation, on the ruins of Public Liberty.

Without looking forward to an extremity of this kind (which nevertheless ought not to be entirely out of sight) the common & continual mischiefs of the spirit of Party are sufficient to make it the interest and the duty of a wise People to discourage and restrain it.

It serves always to distract the Public Councils and enfeeble the Public Administration. It agitates the Community with ill founded Jealousies and false alarms, kindles the animosity of one part against another, foments occasionally riot & insurrection. It opens the door to foreign influence & corruption, which find a facilitated access to the government itself through the channels of party passions. Thus the policy and the will of one country, are subjected to the policy and will of another.

There is an opinion that parties in free countries are useful checks upon the Administration of the Government and serve to keep alive the spirit of Liberty. This within certain limits is probably true—and in Governments of a Monarchical cast Patriotism may look with endulgence, if not with favour, upon the spirit of party. But in those of the popular character, in Governments purely elective, it is a spirit not to be encouraged. From their natural tendency, it is certain there will always be enough of that spirit for every salutary purpose. And there being constant danger of excess, the effort ought to be, by force of public opinion, to mitigate & assuage it. A fire not to be quenched; it demands a uniform vigilance to prevent its bursting into a flame, lest instead of warming it should consume.

It is important, likewise, that the habits of thinking in a free Country should inspire caution in those entrusted with its Administration, to confine themselves within their respective Constitutional Spheres; avoiding in the exercise of the Powers of one department to encroach upon another. The spirit of encroachment tends to consolidate the powers of all the departments in one, and thus to create whatever the form of government, a real despotism. A just estimate of that love of power, and proneness to abuse it, which predominates in the human heart, is sufficient to satisfy us of the truth of this position. The necessity of reciprocal checks in the exercise of political power; by dividing and distributing it into different depositories, & constituting each the Guardian of the Public Weal against invasions by the others, has been evinced by experiments ancient & modern; some of them in our country & under our own eyes. To preserve them must be as necessary as to institute them. If in the opinion of the People, the distribution or modification of the Constitutional powers be in any particular wrong, let it be corrected by an amendment in the way which the Constitution designates. But let there be no change by usurpation; for though this, in one instance, may be the instrument of good, it is the customary weapon by which free governments are destroyed. The precedent must always greatly overbalance in permanent evil any partial or transient benefit which the use can at any time yield.

Of all the dispositions and habits which lead to political prosperity, Religion and morality are indispensable supports. In vain would that man claim the tribute of Patriotism, who should labour to subvert these great Pillars of human happiness, these firmest props of the duties of Men & citizens. The mere Politican, equally with the pious man ought to respect & to cherish them. A volume could not trace all their connections with private & public felicity. Let it simply be asked where is the security for property, for reputation, for life, if the sense of religious obligation desert the Oaths, which are the instruments of investigation in Courts of Justice? And let us with caution indulge the supposition, that morality can be maintained without religion. Whatever may be conceded to the influence of refined education on minds of peculiar structure—reason & experience both forbid us to expect that National morality can prevail in exclusion of religious principle.

'Tis substantially true, that virtue or morality is a necessary spring of popular government. The rule indeed extends with more or less force to every species of Free Government. Who that is a sincere friend to it, can look with indifference upon attempts to shake the foundation of the fabric.

Promote then as an object of primary importance, Institutions for the general diffusion of knowledge. In proportion as the structure of a government gives force to public opinion, it is essential that public opinion should be enlightened.

As a very important source of strength & security, cherish public credit. One method of preserving it is to use it as sparingly as possible: avoiding occasions of expence by cultivating peace, but remembering also that timely disbursements to prepare for danger frequently prevent much greater disbursements to repel it—avoiding likewise the accumulation of debt, not only by shunning occasions of expence, but by vigorous exertions in time of Peace to discharge the Debts which unavoidable wars may have occasioned, not ungenerously throwing upon posterity the burthen which we ourselves ought to bear. The execution of these maxims belongs to your Representatives, but it is necessary that public opinion should cooperate. To facilitate to them the performance of their duty, it is essential that you should practically bear in mind, that towards the payment of debts there must be Revenue—that to have Revenue there must be taxes—that no taxes can be devised which are not more or less inconvenient & unpleasant—that the intrinsic embarrassment inseperable from the Selection of the proper objects (which is always a choice of difficulties) ought to be a decisive motive for a candid construction of the Conduct of the Government in making it, and for a spirit of acquiescence in the measures for obtaining Revenue which the public exigencies may at any time dictate.

Observe good faith & justice towds all Nations. Cultivate peace & harmony with all—Religion & morality enjoin this conduct; and can it be that good policy does not equally enjoin it? It will be worthy of a free, enlightened, and, at no distant period, a great Nation, to give to mankind the magnanimous and too novel example of a People always guided by an exalted justice & benevolence. Who can doubt that in the course of time and things the fruits of such a plan would richly repay any temporary advantages wch might be lost by a steady adherence to it? Can it be, that Providence has not connected the permanent felicity of a Nation with its virtue? The experiment, at least, is recommended by every sentiment which ennobles human Nature. Alas! is it rendered impossible by its vices?

In the execution of such a plan nothing is more essential than that permanent inveterate antipathies against particular Nations and passionate attachments for others should be excluded; and that in place of them just & amicable feelings towards all should be cultivated. The Nation, which indulges towards another an habitual hatred, or an habitual fondness, is in some degree a slave. It is a slave to its animosity or to its affection, either of which is sufficient to lead it astray from its duty and its interest. Antipathy in one Nation against another—disposes each more readily to offer insult and injury, to lay hold of slight causes of umbrage, and to be haughty and intractable, when accidental or trifling occasions of dispute occur. Hence frequent collisions, obstinate envenomed and bloody contests. The Nation, prompted by ill will & resentment sometimes impels to War the Government, contrary to the best calculations of policy. The Government sometimes participates in the national propensity, and adopts through passion what reason would reject; at other times, it makes the animosity of the Nation subservient to projects of hostility instigated by pride, ambition and other sinister & pernicious motives. The peace often, sometimes perhaps the Liberty, of Nations has been the victim.

So likewise, a passionate attachment of one Nation for another produces a variety of evils. Sympathy for the favourite nation, facilitating the illusion of an imaginary common interest, in cases where no real common interest exists, and infusing into one the enmities of the other, betrays the former into a participation in the quarrels & Wars of the latter, without adequate inducement or justification: It leads also to concessions to the favourite Nation of priviledges denied to others, which is apt doubly to injure the Nation making the concessions—by unnecessarily parting with what ought to have been retained—& by exciting jealousy, ill will, and a disposition to retaliate, in the parties from whom equal priviledges are withheld: And it gives to ambitious, corrupted, or deluded citizens (who devote themselves to the favourite Nation) facility to betray, or sacrifice the interests of their own country, without odium, sometimes even with popularity; gilding with the appearances of a virtuous sense of obligation a commendable deference for public opinion, or a laudable zeal for public good, the base or foolish compliances of ambition corruption or infatuation.

As avenues to foreign influence in innumerable ways, such attachments are particularly alarming to the truly enlightened and independent Patriot. How many opportunities do they afford to tamper with domestic factions, to practice the arts of seduction, to mislead public opinion, to influence or awe the public Councils! Such an attachment of a small or weak, towards a great & powerful Nation, dooms the former to be the satellite of the latter.

Against the insidious wiles of foreign influence, (I conjure you to believe me, fellow citizens) the jealousy of a free people ought to be constantly awake; since history and experience prove that foreign influence is one of the most baneful foes of Republican Government. But that jealousy to be useful must be impartial; else it becomes the instrument of the very influence to be avoided, instead of a defence against it. Excessive partiality for one foreign nation and excessive dislike of another, cause those whom they actuate to see danger only on one side, and serve to veil and even second the arts of influence on the other. Real Patriots, who may resist the intriegues of the favourite, are liable to become suspected and odious; while its tools and dupes usurp the applause & confidence of the people, to surender their interests.

The Great rule of conduct for us, in regard to foreign Nations is in extending our comercial relations to have with them as little political connection as possible. So far as we have already formed engagements let them be fulfilled, with perfect good faith. Here let us stop.

Europe has a set of primary interests, which to us have none, or a very remote relation. Hence she must be engaged in frequent controversies, the causes of which are essentially foreign to our concerns. Hence therefore it must be unwise in us to implicate ourselves, by artificial ties, in the ordinary vicissitudes of her politics, or the ordinary combinations & collisions of her friendships, or enmities.

Our detached & distant situation invites and enables us to pursue a different course. If we remain one People, under an efficient government, the period is not far off, when we may defy material injury from external annoyance; when we may take such an attitude as will cause the neutrality we may at any time resolve upon to be scrupulously respected; when belligerent nations, under the impossibility of making acquisitions upon us, will not lightly hazard the giving us provocation; when we may choose peace or War, as our interest guided by justice shall Counsel.

Why forego the advantages of so peculiar a situation? Why quit our own to stand upon foreign ground? Why, by interweaving our destiny with that of any part of Europe, entangle our peace and prosperity in the toils of European Ambition, Rivalship, Interest, Humour or Caprice?

'Tis our true policy to steer clear of permanent Alliances, with any portion of the foreign World—So far, I mean, as we are now at liberty to do it—for let me not be understood as capable of patronising infidility to existing engagements, (I hold the maxim no less applicable to public than to private affairs, that honesty is always the best policy)—I repeat it therefore, Let those engagements be observed in their genuine sense. But in my opinion, it is unnecessary and would be unwise to extend them.

Taking care always to keep ourselves, by suitable establishments, on a respectably defensive posture, we may safely trust to temporary alliances for extraordinary emergencies.

Harmony, liberal intercourse with all Nations, are recommended by policy, humanity and interest. But even our Commercial policy should hold an equal and impartial hand: neither seeking nor granting exclusive favours or preferences; consulting the natural course of things; diffusing & deversifying by gentle means the streams of Commerce, but forcing nothing; establishing with Powers so disposed—in order to give to trade a stable course, to define the rights of our Merchants, and to enable the Government to support them—conventional rules of intercourse; the best that present circumstances and mutual opinion will permit, but temporary, & liable to be from time to time abandoned or varied, as experience and circumstances shall dictate; constantly keeping in view, that 'tis folly in one Nation to look for disinterested favors from another—that it must pay with a portion of its Independence for whatever it may accept under that character—that by such acceptance, it may place itself in the condition of having given equivalents for nominal favours and yet of being reproached with ingratitude for not giving more. There can be no greater error than to expect, or calculate upon real favours from Nation to Nation. 'Tis an illusion which experience must cure, which a just pride ought to discard.

In offering to you, my Countrymen, these counsels of an old and affectionate friend, I dare not hope they will make the strong and lasting impression, I could wish—that they will controul the usual current of the passions, or prevent our Nation from running the course which has hitherto marked the Destiny of Nations: But if I may even flatter myself, that they may be productive of some partial benefit, some occasional good; that they may now & then recur to moderate the fury of party spirit, to warn against the mischiefs of foreign Intriegue, to guard against the Impostures of pretended patriotism—this hope will be a full recompence for the solicitude for your welfare, by which they have been dictated.

How far in the discharge of my Official duties, I have been guided by the principles which have been delineated, the public Records and other evidences of my conduct must witness to You and to the world. To myself, the assurance of my own conscience is, that I have at least believed myself to be guided by them.

In relation to the still subsisting War in Europe, my Proclamation of the 22d of April 1793 is the index to my Plan. Sanctioned by your approving voice and by that of Your Representatives in both Houses of Congress, the spirit of that measure has continually governed me; uninfluenced by any attempts to deter or divert me from it.

After deliberate examination with the aid of the best lights I could obtain I was well satisfied that our Country, under all the circumstances of the case, had a right to take, and was bound in duty and interest, to take a Neutral position. Having taken it, I determined, as far as should depend upon me, to maintain it, with moderation, perseverence & firmness. The considerations, which respect the right to hold this conduct, it is not necessary on this occasion to detail. I will only observe, that according to my understanding of the matter, that right, so far from being denied by any of the Belligerent Powers has been virtually admitted by all.

The duty of holding a neutral conduct may be inferred, without any thing more, from the obligation which justice and humanity impose on every Nation, in cases in which it is free to act, to maintain inviolate the relations of Peace and amity towards other Nations.

The inducements of interest for observing that conduct will best be referred to your own reflections & experience. With me, a predominant motive has been to endeavour to gain time to our country to settle & mature its yet recent institutions, and to progress without interruption, to that degree of strength & consistency, which is necessary to give it, humanly speaking, the command of its own fortunes.

Though in reviewing the incidents of my Administration, I am unconscious of intentional error—I am nevertheless too sensible of my defects not to think it probable that I may have committed many errors. Whatever they may be I fervently beseech the Almighty to avert or mitigate the evils to which they may tend. I shall also carry with me the hope that my Country will never cease to view them with indulgence; and that after forty five years of my life dedicated to its Service, with an upright zeal, the faults of incompetent abilities will be consigned to oblivion, as myself must soon be to the Mansions of rest.

Relying on its kindness in this as in other things, and actuated by that fervent love towards it, which is so natural to a Man, who views in it the native soil of himself and his progenitors for several Generations; I anticipate with pleasing expectation that retreat, in which I promise myself to realize, without alloy, the sweet enjoyment of partaking, in the midst of my fellow Citizens, the benign influence of good Laws under a free Government—the ever favourite object of my heart, and the happy reward, as I trust, of our mutual cares, labours and dangers.

G. Washington, United States, September 7, 1796

Source: George Washington, "Farewell Address," September 19, 1796, Final Copy. Washington Papers, Library of Congress, Washington, D.C.

LIVINGSTON ST.CLAIR. OTIS KNOX SHERMAN WASHINGTON STEUBEN ADAMS

INAUGURATION OF WASHINGTON.

From the original Painting by Chappel, in the possession of the Publishers.

Johnson, Fry & Co. Publishers, New York.

Campaigns and Elections

T hat George Washington would be chosen to serve as the nation's first chief executive was taken for granted in the framing of the Constitution and in the debate over its ratification. Indeed, his unanimous selection by the electoral college was perhaps the least surprising outcome of any of the nation's presidential elections. Because he did not campaign for office in preparation for either of his two terms as president, his selection more resembled a coronation than a presidential contest. Yet despite the uniqueness of Washington's claim on the presidency, he was not naive when it came to campaigns and elections. After all, as a young man he had served fifteen years in the Virginia House of Burgesses.

HOUSE OF BURGESSES

In colonial Virginia, only members of the elite were chosen for inclusion in the government. George Washington, an affluent planter of Fairfax County, was undeniably of that class eligible for positions of leadership. As a typical man of his station, he could expect certain community offices to come his way. He was, for example, a justice of the county court—a position from which he dispensed justice in simple disputes between residents of Fairfax County. As a member of the vestry of his Anglican parish from 1763 to 1774, Washington and other elected members of the vestry were responsible for hiring the church's rector and building and maintaining a house of worship. As a trustee for the town of Alexandria, he was expected to promote the development of the town and facilitate the nascent city's relationship with the colony's governing bodies. Yet these duties were seldom onerous. Washington attended fewer than half of the vestry meetings held during his tenure on that body, and he went to his first meeting of the Alexandria trustees four years after his election. Men of somewhat higher station—the most affluent and well-born planters, such as his neighbors the Fairfaxes—might be commissioned by the king himself, after nomination by the governor, to serve on the governor's council, a prestigious and powerful institution made up of a dozen men who advised the governor, sat as the colony's highest court, and served as the upper body of the Virginia Assembly, or colonial legislature. But Washington was not so well born that he could rely on preferment alone to lead him into the colonial government. His path lay instead through election to the House of Burgesses, the lower body of the legislature.

Burgess is now merely a historic term, but, according to the 2002 edition of the *Oxford English Dictionary,* for centuries it referred to "an inhabitant of a borough; strictly, one possessing full municipal rights; a citizen, freeman of a borough." Its more specific meaning in eighteenth-century Britain was "the member of parliament for a borough, corporate town, or university." In Virginia and some of the other American colonies, burgesses were "the representatives sent by the towns to the legislative body," called the House of Burgesses. In Virginia, each community was entitled to send two elected representatives to the House. Elections were irregular, depending in part on the pleasure of the governor, who had power to dissolve the House and call for elections to seat a new one whenever he saw fit to do so.

Only male "freeholders" could vote for a burgess. It was English custom, as stated in William Blackstone's *Commentaries on the Laws of England* (published in England from 1765 to 1769 and available a few years later in the colonies), to exclude from suffrage "such persons as are in so mean a situation as to be esteemed to have no will of their own" (Williamson 1960, 11). This concept was so widespread that when the Continental Congress appealed to Britain, it did so naturally in the terms of aggrieved freeholders: "Why should not the freeholders of America enjoy the same rights enjoyed by the freeholders of Great Britain?"

(Williamson 1960, 19). But how much property was enough for a man to be esteemed to have a will of his own?

Virginia's requirement reflected its diversity: one hundred acres of unsettled land or twenty-five improved acres. Under this standard, about half of white male Virginians twenty-one years or older were probably eligible to vote. A man cast his ballot by publicly stating his preference in the presence of the candidates or their representatives, election officials, and as many other voters as happened to be in the range of hearing when the voter made his way to the front of the voting line.

Although only freeholders could vote, elections were broadly inclusive of the white male residents of Virginia's counties. It was common practice at the county level to include all white male residents in political assemblies, though only freeholders were expected to share in deliberations. On election day, residents and their families were welcome at the parties that candidates customarily hosted for all comers. Refreshments, especially rum punch, were expected, as was a buffet and some form of entertainment, such as a fiddler. The popular reference to the practice of electioneering in Virginia, "swilling the planters with bumbo," suggested the carnival atmosphere of election day (Troy 1991, 9).

In 1762 the legislature passed a campaign reform act that made it unlawful for a candidate to give any voter "any money, meat, drink, entertainment, or provisions, or make any present, gift, reward, or entertainment, or any promise, agreement, obligation or engagement" except "in his usual and ordinary course of hospitality in his own house." The reform, however, had little practical effect (Freeman 1951, 120–121). Politics was, after all, a form of cultural expression in the colonies, and in Virginia that meant politics expressed the bonds among neighbors of differing classes. If the most ambitious men of the better sort desired the support of their social inferiors, the least they could do in return was to host a party.

CANDIDATE FOR THE HOUSE OF BURGESSES

George Washington first announced his interest in becoming a burgess in 1755. A friend, John Carlyle, discussed with Washington a bill then pending in the House to split Fairfax County, making room for two more representatives. Carlyle, older and more prosperous than Washington, asked his young friend whether he might like the position. Washington, fearful that Carlyle was jesting, made no reply, but did ask one of his brothers to make quiet inquiries about his prospects in Fairfax County. The results of this informal stealth poll were not encouraging, so Washington made no efforts on his own behalf.

Later that year, however, Washington entered himself in the contest for burgess in Frederick County, the seat of his military command. That year, Gov. Robert Dinwiddie had brought the Virginia Regiment back into existence, and had granted Washington its command. Colonel Washington strove for the next three years to protect the frontier settlers of the Shenandoah Valley against hostile Indians and a sometimes apathetic and stingy colonial government. In addition to being the man most responsible for the physical security of Frederick County, located in the heart of the Shenandoah Valley over the Blue Ridge Mountains from Mount Vernon, Washington was a landowner in the county. Despite his clear interest in winning his first election for the House of Burgesses, the candidate himself seems not to have taken an active part in the campaign. His friends presented his name, but "as they had made no previous canvass, they could not muster many votes for him" (Freeman 1948, 147). Washington, nevertheless, carefully made a record of all who had declared for him.

On election day, Washington was, in any event, not even on the frontier in Frederick County, but on leave, lobbying the Virginia Assembly. During his leave, Washington also spent time campaigning for his friend, George William Fairfax, who was a candidate for the House of Burgesses from Fairfax County.

While soliciting votes for Fairfax, Washington lost his temper in a dispute over the relative merits of the candidates, and thereby provoked a supporter of another candidate, who struck Washington with a club, knocking him to the ground. The other man, William Payne, feared that a duel might ensue, but when Washington called upon him through an intermediary to meet the next day, it was to apologize.

From 1755 through 1758, Washington struggled to defend Virginia's settlers in Frederick County and elsewhere. He suffered crippling rates of desertion and insufficient support from the Assembly. Meanwhile, he cultivated sympathetic burgesses and councilors and remonstrated sometimes angrily with Gov. Dinwiddie. Critics of Washington even whispered that he had fabricated stories of hostile Indians merely to gain more money and men from the government. Others carped about his aristocratic lifestyle, which included taking fencing lessons on the frontier, and about the allegedly pretentious and immoral behavior of the officers generally. His supporters, by contrast, including most of the leading men of the Shenandoah Valley, praised Washington's willingness to sacrifice on behalf of even the most backward regions of Virginia and urged him to again seek a seat in the House of Burgesses.

In 1758 Washington did so, launching in the same year both a political campaign and his last military campaign on behalf of Virginia and the British Crown. That year, the British government, feeling new urgency in its global contest with the French, at last sent a sizable force to the colonies. Virginia's government had reorganized its colonial force as a consequence. In the reorganization, Washington gave up sole command of the undersized and poorly supported Virginia Regiment, but took command in Frederick County of one of two newly formed regiments that enjoyed the full backing of the British Empire. While not preparing his soldiers for a final push to remove the French from British-claimed territory, Washington politicked by defending the political and commercial interests of Virginia against the claims of neighboring Pennsylvania. The British objective was to project their force across the mountains and to attack Fort Duquesne (on the site of present-day Pittsburgh). For this purpose, Virginians urged use of the same route taken by the ill-fated general Edward Braddock in the summer of 1755. Pennsylvanians recommended creating a new route, which would be shorter and more accessible to forage. Washington pushed Virginia's case so hard that he was upbraided by his commander, Gen. John Forbes, for "weakness" in attachment to his native colony, "having never heard from any Pennsylvania person one word" (Randall 1997, 186). In the end, Washington may have lost the battle for the road (the path through Pennsylvania is now incorporated into the Pennsylvania Turnpike), but he gained in his reputation as a Virginian.

Washington's status as a politician was made official in his political success of July 1758 in Frederick County (see Document 2.1). He ran in that election as part of an informal two-man team against the frontier county's incumbents. A friend of Washington's, Col. Thomas Byran Martin, had recently inherited Greenway Court in Frederick County from Lord Fairfax. Martin targeted his campaign against a local man, Hugh West, leaving Washington to challenge the other incumbent, militia officer Thomas Swearingen. Washington had had tense relations with the militia and was, moreover, not present to canvass for votes. He was stationed at Fort Cumberland on the Potomac, and his superiors rejected his request for what might be termed "political leave." Lord Fairfax himself worried that Washington would be "very hard pushed" in the election (Freeman 1948, 2:318). James Wood of Frederick County and John Carlyle and George William Fairfax of Fairfax County campaigned in his stead (see Document 2.2), and a fellow officer, Lt. Charles Smith, arranged for the usual campaign refreshments and entertainment (see Document 2.3). The result was election for Washington, at twenty-six years of age.

Washington took his seat in the House of Burgesses on February 22, 1759, next to his friend George William Fairfax. In 1758 he had concluded (or so he believed) his military career, had married, and had expanded Mount Vernon. Now he was beginning service in the House of Burgesses, where he would serve for the next fifteen years, moving his seat to Fairfax County at the first opportunity, which turned out to be 1765.

Washington's tenure in the House began auspiciously. Speaker John Robinson, who knew Washington well from their work together on military affairs, appointed the new burgess to one of the two standing committees of the body, the Committee of Propositions and Grievances. On the third day of the session, Washington was asked to stand while Robinson read aloud a resolution of thanks to Washington for his services in the recently concluded battle against the French in the Virginia wilderness. The resolution, naturally, passed without dissent. Washington's fame did not, however, make him a person of influence in the legislature. Though unanimously acclaimed by his peers, he was not one of the inner circle of men who "were accustomed to determining in private the action they later called on their colleagues to take" (Freeman 1951, 362).

In part, Washington's low influence during his early political years stemmed from his irregular attendance. Williamsburg, the colonial capital, was a considerable distance from Frederick County and a four days' ride from Mount Vernon. If little county business was to be addressed, and if no personal business compelled him to Williamsburg, Washington often as not absented himself from the sessions of the House of Burgesses. Thus on the day in 1768 when the burgesses first took up Massachusetts's Circular Letter protesting the Stamp Act, Washington recorded in his diary: "Catched a fox after three hours chase" (Randall 1997, 234). Because no formal or informal record of the work of the legislature was kept, it is impossible to know how Washington's fulfillment of his legislative duties compared with the norm. It is known that the freeholders of first Frederick and then Fairfax County had apparently little reason for complaint. Washington was reelected each time he stood as a candidate for office.

THE BURGESS IS ELECTED
TO HELP MAKE A REVOLUTION

As a member of the House of Burgesses, Washington had the opportunity to deliberate with other colonial leaders, such as George Mason and Richard Henry Lee, on the imperial crisis that had begun to influence Virginia's relations with Britain in the 1760s. "The first even mildly prominent role Washington" played in the revolutionary cause was as an elected representative of his home county, when he spoke out in 1769 in support of an agreement on the nonimportation of British goods (Flexner 1965, 314). As the crisis worsened, Washington's presence at Williamsburg became more constant, as did his resolve in behalf of the rights of English colonists. Through election to a series of extralegal assemblies, Washington was placed in a position to be asked to take command of the Continental army in 1775.

The first step from burgess to commander in chief was taken in 1774. In that year, the House took up the Coercive Acts, Britain's harsh response to the Boston Tea Party. Because it passed a resolution of fasting and mourning, the governor of Virginia, Lord Dunmore, dissolved the House of Burgesses. The House nevertheless continued to meet in a local tavern. In their tavern deliberations, the burgesses passed resolutions to form a nonimportation association, whose members promised not to purchase taxed British goods. They also passed resolutions instructing counties to take up the issues before the colonies and to elect delegates to a statewide convention.

In Fairfax County, the freemen and other residents met as requested, with Washington presiding, and passed various resolutions or resolves. At the same time, the Fairfax voters elected Washington to attend the August 1774 Virginia Convention. At that convention, Washington was elected as one of seven delegates from Virginia to the First Continental Congress in Philadelphia. In the balloting, he stood third among fourteen for whom votes were counted. This, in the opinion of historian

Douglas Southall Freeman, was "the decisive step in the rise of George Washington as a continental leader." "Suppose," Freeman suggests, "he had stood eighth on the list and had not gone to the First Continental Congress—could he have had the opportunity that came to him the next year?" (Freeman 1951, after 373).

At Philadelphia, Washington's growing stature was confirmed. When five of Virginia's seven delegates departed to return either to their homes or to Williamsburg for the new session of the House of Burgesses, four of them gave their proxies to Washington. Meanwhile, back in Virginia militia companies from throughout the colony were meeting to assess the situation. Many of them approved resolutions electing Washington their commander should the militia be called to war. The next year, the burgesses themselves elected Washington to represent Virginia at the second and decisive Continental Congress. In this, the final pre-presidential contest of ballots in which Washington took part, he received the second highest number of votes, and the greatest distinction he ever earned in the Virginia Assembly. In that Congress, Washington was selected commander in chief of the revolutionary army.

A PLAN FOR PRESIDENTIAL SELECTION

After the American Revolution and a period of retirement, George Washington reentered politics through his election to represent Virginia at the Constitutional Convention of 1787. By this time, Washington's eminence had become his preeminence. Any assemblage of freeholders anywhere in the colonies would likely have chosen him to represent them in framing a new government, if they had had the choice. Similarly, once the new government was set in motion, it was taken for granted that Washington would be the first chief executive, if he would consent to take the position. For this reason, and because of the nature of the presidency as it was first conceived, Washington's presidential campaigns and elections were unlike those of any other president.

Washington "won" the presidency in the Revolutionary War; he did not have to win it again in either 1789 or 1792. Something similar might be said of other war heroes turned presidents, such as Zachary Taylor, Ulysses S. Grant, and Dwight D. Eisenhower. But those men were all intimately involved in a partisan struggle for the presidency unimaginable to the antiparty framers. Moreover, among heroes turned president, only Washington was placed in office before the development of mass-based parties and before universal white male suffrage.

The framers of the Constitution intended the presidency to remain an office not out of sight of, but certainly not under the thumb of, the mass public. Nevertheless, the modern presidency and the modern presidential campaign, featuring appeals to the very masses the framers intended to keep out of presidential politics, emerged from within the framework established for George Washington. Because of Washington, the framers designed a presidency with the potential to be transformed into a modern, democratic office.

The presidency as designed in 1787 enjoyed a national electoral base independent of Congress. Unlike many governors at the time, the president was not forced to share power with a "council of revision." Such a council, as debated in 1787, would have given the president but one vote in a body responsible for exercising the veto power. The other council members would have been federal judges and justices and heads of executive departments. The singularity of the executive and the independence of the position from Congress are the two basic features of the office responsible for its elasticity. These features ensure that modern presidents have the ability to respond for the nation in times of crisis. But today these features also open the presidency to criticism that it is driven excessively by public opinion, that it is, in fact, a "plebiscitary" office (see Lowi 1985). The framers took the risk of making the presidency potentially a fount of great democratic power, because they were certain that Washington at least would not abuse the power of the office.

"It is no exaggeration to say," historian Forrest McDonald observed, "that Americans were willing to venture the experiment with a single, national republican chief executive only because of their unreserved trust in George Washington" (McDonald 1994, 209). In an oft-cited letter from the time, Pierce Butler, a South Carolina delegate to the Constitutional Convention and the one most responsible for the final design of the electoral college, wrote to a family member in England: "*entre nous,* I do not believe they [the executive powers] would have been so great, had not many of the members cast their eyes toward General Washington as President; and shaped their Ideas of the Powers to be given a President, by their opinions of his Virtue" (Thach 1969, 65).

The electoral college was the work of a Committee of Unfinished Business, which issued a report to the Committee of the Whole on September

4, 1787. The Committee of Unfinished Business proposed that the president be given a power base independent of the national legislature, but not directly dependent on the opinion of the nation's freeholders. Presidential electors were to be chosen in each state, in any way that a state's government desired. Each state would select as many electors, or "delegates," as that state had representatives in Congress. The electors would never meet as the electoral college, but would meet in their respective states to cast ballots. Each elector would cast two ballots for two different persons, one of whom had to be from a state other than the elector's. The votes would be transmitted to the presiding officer of the Senate. The winner, should he have a majority of the total ballots cast, would be president; the runner-up would be vice president. The Committee of the Whole decided that in the event no majority winner emerged, the House of Representatives would select the president from among the top candidates, voting by state, with each state having one vote.

The electoral college was cumbersome, but it neatly solved a number of problems. By leaving presidential selection to electors chosen democratically in each state, the framers ensured that the nation's freeholders would be the *indirect* point of reference for a president. By preventing the electors from meeting together, the framers discouraged bargaining for the nation's highest office. By granting to each state the same proportion of power in the choice of a president that it enjoyed in Congress, the framers mirrored in presidential selection the compromise in representation between small and large states that was a cornerstone of constitutional design. By requiring a majority for election, the framers guaranteed that whoever might be selected president would have considerable support from throughout the nation.

There were, of course, problems with this design. How could a candidate win majority support without the aid of political parties? All the framers knew for certain was that one man had won such universal acclaim for his service to his country that he could claim widespread support without the efforts in his behalf of a party. But after Washington, could a majority sentiment be formed for a candidate without the action of a political party to urge its members to unite behind one of presumably many plausible contenders? Some experts, such as Richard Pious, have doubted this so much that they have speculated that the framers intended the normal selection method to lead to the "backup," letting the House decide (Pious 1979, 28). Also, once systematic differences of opinion emerged, the failure to separate presidential and vice presidential ballots became problematic. This problem was addressed by constitutional amendment after the election of 1800, in which the House had to break a tie between Thomas Jefferson and Aaron Burr. Everyone knew that the votes for Jefferson were supposed to be presidential votes, those for Burr vice presidential. But Burr was within his constitutional rights to insist that he had as much claim as Jefferson to the presidency. The more enduring problem, that of attaining a majority in the electoral college, was addressed informally by the creation of stable two-party competition. These innovations would come later, after George Washington's retirement and death. In the first two presidential selections, the electoral college performed precisely as it was intended.

His Elective Majesty

The last Congress under the Articles of Confederation fixed the dates for the selection of Washington as the first president. Under the Constitution, the president was to be elected indirectly by electors chosen in any way that a state's government desired. Electors were to be selected on the first Wednesday in January 1789; they would cast ballots on the first Wednesday in February. The newly elected Congress would assemble on the first Wednesday of March, count the ballots for president and vice president, and announce that George Washington was elected president. Alexander Hamilton's energetic correspondence campaign ensured that John Adams received enough votes to secure the vice presidency, but not so many votes as to suggest that Washington had any rivals for the affection of the electors.

Washington's presence actually inhibited the development of presidential campaign politics. Only when he was no longer a candidate did the nation's politicians begin to establish precedents for presidential campaigning. There was, however, at least one sense in which the supporters of the president needed to campaign to place Washington at the head of the executive branch; they had to persuade him to accept the job.

Washington was anxious, as ever, about his reputation and his hard-won fame. After all, he had retired, and he feared that if he came out of retirement to accept the presidency, some people might accuse him of inconsistency and even ambition (Troy 1991, 10). Washington's friends, especially Alexander Hamilton, weighed in with arguments in correspondence to Mount Vernon. "It is to little purpose," Hamilton wrote, "to have *introduced* a system, if the weightiest influence is not given to its firm *establishment*, in the outset" (Cunliffe 1971, 210). Washington had acquiesced already, Hamilton reminded him, to attend the Constitutional Convention itself, where, of course, he had been selected to preside. But he had been hesitant to do even that for the same reasons that he was now reluctant to preside over the government. But once having made the first step, it would be unseemly not to take the second. "It would," Hamilton wrote, "be inglorious in such a situation not to hazard the glory however great previously acquired" (Cunliffe 1971, 210). If Washington did not consent to be selected president, he would see his fame diminished rather than preserved. There was, then, no choice, though the decision was nevertheless difficult for Washington, who wrote in October 1788 to Hamilton of his "gloom" about the situation (see Document 2.4), and elsewhere compared the sensation of waiting for official word of his election to a condemned man waiting to be escorted to the gallows.

Congress, scheduled to convene in New York on March 4, 1789, at last gained a quorum on April 6. The first act of the Senate was to count the ballots for president and vice president. As anticipated, Washington ascended to the presidency without opposition being recorded in the official count (see Appendix D.1). That the outcome was unanimous was all the more impressive in light of the diversity of processes whereby the states had chosen their electoral college delegates (see Appendix D.2). A delegation was sent to Mount Vernon to relay news of his election to Washington. While awaiting the presence of a quorum, Washington worried over the apparent "listlessness" of Congress. He was peeved that so many members took their time showing up for the new government.

Meanwhile, Washington put his private affairs in order. The most pressing personal matter was to pay off some debts. Though he would be paid a considerable salary as president ($25,000, at a time when an artisan in New York City might make 1 percent of that amount), Washington foresaw that his expenses as president were likely to exceed even this amount. He requested that Congress pay his actual expenses rather than a salary, but his request was denied, making it all the more important for him to do what he could to pay off old debts before incurring new ones. Although Washington presumably was a good credit risk despite his constant indebtedness, he found it difficult to arrange financing, even when he appealed to "the most monied man" of his acquaintance, who turned him down. Finally, a wealthy man from Alexandria extended Washington a loan, with interest. Nevertheless, before setting off for New York Washington had to appeal to his new patron for an additional hundred pounds to finance his journey to the nation's temporary capital (Flexner 1970, 171).

On his way, Washington stopped many times to accept salutations from well-wishers. As would be the custom throughout the entire next century, the president-elect was not expected to speak to the people about pressing issues of policy or politics, but merely to allow himself to be seen. While Washington made his way northward, the Senate and House debated how to address the president. The House, being the only body in the national government with a direct electoral link to the citizenry, determined that the president should be styled simply the "President." Most senators thought this too common an appellation, because there were, as one senator noted in debate, "presidents of Fire Companies and of a Cricket Club" (McDonald 1994, 213). The Senate considered numerous options, including "His Most Benign Highness," "Serene Highness," "Elective Majesty," "His Excellency," "Elective Highness," and the favorite of John Adams, "His Highness the President of the United States and Protector of the Rights of the Same" (McDonald 1994, 213).

Even once Washington arrived in New York, the Senate continued to debate titles. This gave Washington an opportunity to weigh in unofficially. At a dinner party with several members of the new government, he asked the Speaker of the House, Gen. John Muhlenberg of Pennsylvania, "Well, General Muhlenberg, what do you think of the title of High Mightiness?" "Why, General," replied the newly elected Speaker, "if we were certain that the office would always be held by men as large as yourself or my friend Wyncoop [a rotund politician from Pennsylvania, also present at the party], it would be appropriate enough; but if by chance a President as small as my opposite neighbor should be elected, it would be ridiculous" (Griswold 1854, 153). Washington was not amused. "High Mightiness" was the title applied to stadtholders (elected provincial executive officers) in the Dutch Republic, and Washington apparently felt it appropriate for the new American republic.

In the end, the House refused to accede to the Senate's desire for a more elevated title than "President," and thus on the last day of April

1789 George Washington was inaugurated as the first president of the United States. His inauguration nevertheless mixed regal and democratic themes. The day began with church bells calling the citizens and the thousands of "tourists" in town to assemble for prayer. Then a procession marched to the president's temporary home, Number 3 Cherry Street, at a distance from the most fashionable residences, but large and ample. The procession featured military companies in elaborate uniforms, including some in clothing imitative of the guard of Frederick the Great. After the militia companies came the sheriff of New York City and County; a committee of senators; a committee of House members; secretary ad interim for foreign affairs, John Jay; the secretary-elect of the War Department, Henry Knox; the chancellor of the state of New York, Robert Livingston; and various distinguished citizens. Washington took his place in the procession, between the representatives of the Senate and the House. In a cream-colored carriage pulled by six horses, the president-elect was escorted by this assemblage to the site of his inauguration.

Washington took the oath of office, as prescribed in the Constitution, on the balcony of Federal Hall, in view of the thousands of cheering onlookers. Because the Supreme Court had not yet been assembled, Chancellor Livingston of New York administered the oath. (Under British custom, the chief administrator of the courts bore the title lord chancellor. Livingston was the first chancellor of New York.) After swearing the oath, to which he added the words "So help me, God," Washington bent down to kiss the Bible on which he had rested his hand (Bowen 1889). Immediately afterward, Washington delivered his inaugural address (Document 1.10) in the Senate chamber, with both houses present. In a democratic touch, Washington, always studied in his dress, wore a suit of homespun brown cloth with eagle buttons, stockings, a wig, and a dress sword. During his twenty-minute speech, Washington trembled and was oftentimes barely audible. His audience interpreted the president's demeanor as expressive of humility and reverence, and the speech was well received.

This part of the inaugural ceremony was patterned after the opening of each new session of Parliament in Britain, where the monarch appeared in person in the chamber of the upper body and made a brief speech. Each house completed the ritual by fashioning a formal reply to His Majesty. For Washington's inaugural, the House and Senate did the same, which gave the Senate yet another opportunity to debate just how regal its treatment of the executive should be. (Should its reply refer to Washington's "most gracious speech," as Parliament replied to the "most gracious speech" of the king? After considerable deliberation, the adjective "gracious" was dropped.) The Senate's and the president's desire to set proper and deferential precedents led the president to then thank the Senate for its appreciation of the president's remarks. The Senate followed up with a note expressing its gratitude of the president's gratitude of its thanks. Washington replied with yet another note. At last the Senate capitulated, allowing Washington to have the last word in "this escalating process of mutual appreciation" (Maas 2001, 17).

After his address, Washington, members of Congress, and assorted luminaries attended an Episcopal service at St. Paul's Chapel before the president retired to his house for dinner in the company of a select group of government leaders. In the evening, Washington got back in his carriage, pulled now by only four horses. (The carriage was pulled by a full complement of six horses only when transporting Washington on official business to Federal Hall.) The president put in appearances at several receptions and again allowed himself to be seen. "I have seen him!" reported an excited young woman in town from Boston. "I never saw a human being that looked so great and noble as he does" (Griswold 1854, 138). At night, there were fireworks and "illuminations," painted transparencies lit from behind by candlelight or gas flames. These panels were hung over windows of public and private buildings throughout the town. Though there was much festivity, there were no balls on the night of the first inaugural, because of the absence in town of Mrs. Washington, who had not yet arrived from Mount Vernon.

STANDING FOR REELECTION

After his first term, President Washington longed for retirement, and he had no lack of reasons to decline a second term. He was sixty years old, and his memory was in decline—or so he believed. He also realized it was important not to die in office so that America might demonstrate to itself and to Europe that it had accepted the principle of peaceful, *elective* change in government. Moreover, though the Constitution provided for the assumption of presidential duties by the vice president upon the death of the incumbent, it was unclear whether a vice president assuming duties under such conditions would merely serve as the acting president or would assume the full range of presidential duties as if he had been placed in the presidential office by ballot. Whatever the case, it would be best not to put the question to a test so early in the government's history. Finally, the government was in a crisis over foreign relations, leading many government leaders and others to urge Washington to remain in office until the crisis passed.

Even in late 1792 it was apparent that the regions of the country and their nascent political parties were not yet irrevocably committed to government under the Constitution. By taking sides in the renewed warfare between France and Britain, which would deepen over the next four years, the factions and regions within the new nation might yet pull the nation apart and render its Constitution moot. Thomas Jefferson and Alexander Hamilton, the leaders of the collection of notables who would develop into the first political parties, could agree on few things at this time, but they both wanted the president to continue in office.

"North and South will hang together," Jefferson told Washington, "if they have you to hang upon" (Schlesinger 1971, 48). Hamilton added that the "affairs of the national government are not yet firmly established," and that Washington need not fear that the electoral college would resent his standing once again for office. Hamilton in fact assured the president that, as in the first election, he could expect a unanimous or near unanimous vote. Although there could be electors who would vote against the president "if they durst follow their inclinations," Hamilton speculated, they will not dare to do so, being "restrained by an apprehension of public resentment" (Schlesinger 1971, 51). Washington's confidante, Eliza Powell, added that if Washington did not remain in office, observers would say that "ambition has been the moving spring of your acts" and that, once criticized, "you would take no further risks" for your country (Troy 1991, 11).

Washington indicated his willingness to serve by not declining to do so before electors were chosen in the states. This was the extent of the second presidential campaign.

In 1792, by Congress's choice, electors were selected earlier, within thirty-four days of the first Wednesday in December, the date for electors in this election to cast their ballots. As before, though there was no uniform method for choosing electors in the various states, and though there was no bargaining or politicking for votes, the vote for Washington was unanimous (see Appendixes D.3 and D.4). Those opposed to the president dared not vote against him. Instead, they took aim at his administration through the vice presidency. John Adams was nevertheless returned to office as well, though by a smaller margin of victory than in his first election. In a half-serious outburst against his fate, the vice president commented upon his reelection, "Damn 'em, damn 'em, damn 'em! You see that an elective government will not do!" (Boller 1985, 6).

Washington's cabinet was divided over the proper tone of a second inaugural. The president, pleased at the "pretty respectable vote" he had commanded (see Document 2.5), nevertheless looked with dread upon commencing work anew in the midst of internecine warfare within his own executive "family." Washington ultimately decided to dispense with virtually all pomp and celebration. After a brief ceremony in the Senate chamber, he delivered a perfunctory address and retired to his private residence.

CONCLUSION

In 1796 Washington could have decided to stand for election a third time. Although he had suffered the greatest insults of his life during his second term, he was still the cornerstone of American nationalism, and was guaranteed the support, if grudging in some instances, of virtually all electors, like in 1792 and 1789. He declined.

Even though Washington chose to retire after two terms, there is no reason to believe that he intended thereby to establish a two-term tradition. After all, Washington sincerely desired to leave office after his first term. Moreover, in a letter to the Marquis de Lafayette at the time of the adoption of the Constitution, Washington defended the indefinite reeligibility of the president prescribed by the Constitution (Phelps 1993, 106). Nevertheless, Washington's decision to retire for a final time came to be interpreted as a check against dynastic ambition in the presidency. The power of this "precedent" was demonstrated forcefully over a hundred years later when Theodore Roosevelt promised that if elected to the presidency in 1904, he would not run for reelection in 1908. He considered, he said, his nearly four full years as president, upon the death of William McKinley in 1901, tantamount to a first term. In making this promise, he cited the supposed example of George Washington. Washington was unlike all presidential contenders from John Adams on in that he was the only man who won the presidency by *standing* as opposed to *running* for office. Washington was like all the other presidential aspirants, though, in having to contend with the ironies of the presidential office. Presidents are not kings, but they are the closest thing to kings the American government has ever devised, and winning the presidency usually depends on commanding the respect and even the awe of the multitudes.

BIBLIOGRAPHIC ESSAY

Douglas Southall Freeman's biographies contain exceptionally detailed information. On Washington's elections to the House of Burgesses and the presidency, Freeman's volumes are still the best first source to turn to, especially *George Washington: A Biography*, Vol. 2, *Young Washington* (New York: Scribner's, 1948), and Vol. 3, *Planter and Patriot* (1951). Also see James Thomas Flexner, *George Washington and the New Nation, 1783–1793* (Boston: Little, Brown, 1970), and *George Washington: Anguish and Farewell, 1793–1799* (1972); as well as Willard Sterne Randall, *George Washington, A Life* (New York: Henry Holt, 1997). The archives on the House of Burgesses at the Virginia State Library were consulted on several details, including the date of Washington's movement of his district from Frederick County to Fairfax County.

On the deliberations that led to the creation of the presidency under the Constitution, a standard source is Charles C. Thach Jr., *The Creation of the Presidency, 1775–1789: A Study in Constitutional History* (New York: Da Capo Press, 1969), which is a republication of Series 40, No. 4, of the Johns Hopkins University Studies in Historical and Political Science (1922). Also see Forrest McDonald, *The American Presidency: An Intellectual History* (Lawrence: University Press of Kansas, 1994). For comprehensive information on balloting in the first two presidential elections, see Marcus Cunliffe, "Elections of 1789 and 1792," in *History of American Presidential Elections, 1789–1969,* ed. Arthur M. Schlesinger Jr. (New York: McGraw Hill, 1971), 3–58, including an appendix of relevant correspondence from the time. Also see Eugene H. Roseboom, *A History of Presidential Elections, From George Washington to Richard M. Nixon* (New York: Macmillan, 1970). Chilton Williamson, *American Suffrage: From Property to Democracy, 1760–1860* (Princeton: Princeton University Press, 1960), surveys voting requirements in the states at the time of Washington's elections to the House of Burgesses as well as the presidency.

The inauguration of 1789 is described in detail in Rufus Wilmot Griswold, *The Republican Court, or American Society in the Days of Washington* (New York: D. Appleton, 1854). Some of the precedents that Washington established in his inauguration are covered in the breezy but worthwhile essay by David E. Maas, "The Founding Father of the American Presidency," in *George Washington In and As Culture,* ed. Kevin L. Cope (New York: AMS Press, 2001), 11–24. Paul F. Boller Jr., *Presidential Campaigns* (New York: Oxford University Press, 1985), provides expert commentary with humorous anecdotes. Gil Troy, *See How They Ran: The Changing Role of the Presidential Candidate* (New York: Free Press, 1991), puts the Washington noncampaigns in the context of the transition from deferential to democratic norms in presidential politics.

Finally, Theodore J. Lowi, *The Personal President: Power Invested, Promise Unfulfilled* (Ithaca: Cornell University Press, 1985), chronicles and critiques the transformation of the presidency into a plebiscitary office.

Document 2.1   Charles Smith to Washington, July 24, 1758

The Virginia House of Burgesses was the first democratic body in North America. Established in 1619, it represented the citizenry of the colony's towns and villages and governed in association with the governor and the Governor's Council, an appointed body. The electorate was composed of "freeholders," a group of adult white male property owners. To vote, a freeholder would enter the county courthouse where the candidates or their surrogates would be seated at a table. In the presence of the sheriff and senior justices of the county court, the voter would announce his selection aloud. Military obligations kept Washington from being present during the election, so a fellow officer, Lt. Charles Smith, informed Washington of his success in a "Dear Burgess" letter.

Dr Burgis

I have the Happiness to Inform You Your Friends have been Very Sincere so that were Carried by a Number of Votes more than any Candidate, as by the Number under Certifyed. Colo: James Wood Sat on the Bench, and Represented Your Honour, and was Carried round the Town with General applause, Huzawing Colo. Washington, pray Excuse my haste. I am

Entertaining Your and my Friends, and am with Due Regard Your Most Humble Servt.

Charles Smith

P.S. The representatives that Sat up were as Followeth and Number of Votes Viz.

Your Honour	307
Colo. Martin	240
Captn Swearingen	45
Hugh West	199
	791—the half is 395

This is the True State of the Ellection.

Source: Beverly H. Runge, ed., *The Papers of George Washington, Colonial Series,* Vol. 5, *March 1774–June 1775* (Charlottesville: University Press of Virginia, 1995), 323.

Document 2.2   Washington to Col. James Wood, July 28, 1758

Because Washington was unable to leave his post as commander in chief of the Virginia military, he asked several friends to greet the voters of Frederick County on his behalf. James Wood, a prominent citizen who founded the town of Winchester, the seat of Frederick County, served as one of Washington's surrogates. Wood's presence indicated Washington's endorsement by what Virginians called the "better sort" and voters today might call "the establishment." Wood greeted the freeholders and reminded everyone of what they already knew, that the regimental commander was busy defending their very lives in the French and Indian War.

My Dear Colonel

If thanks flowing from a heart replete with joy and Gratitude can in any Measure compensate for the fatigue anxiety & Pain you had at my Election be assurd you have them. Tis a poor, but I am convinced welcome tribute to a generous Mind—such, I believe yours to be.

How I shall thank Mrs Wood for her favourable wishes? And how acknowledge my Sense of Obligations to the People in General for their choice of me I am at a loss to resolve on—but why—can I do it more effectually than by making there Interests (as it really is) my own and doing every thing that lyes in my little Power for the Honr and welfare of the County—I think not—and my best endeavours they may always Command—I promise this now, when promises may be regarded—before they might pass as words of Course.

I am extreme thankly to you & my other friends for entertaining the Freeholder in my name—I hope no exception were taken to any that voted against me but that all were alike treated and all had enough it is what I much desird—my only fear is that you spent with too sparing a hand.

I don't like to touch upon our Publick Affairs the Prospect is overspread by too many ill to give a favourable Acct. I will therefore say little—but yet say this, that backwardness appears in all things but the approach of Winter—that joggs on apace.

Source: Beverly H. Runge, ed., *The Papers of George Washington, Colonial Series,* Vol. 5, *March 1774–June 1775* (Charlottesville: University Press of Virginia, 1995), 349.

Document 2.3   Charles Smith to Washington, July 26, 1758

In his absence, George Washington charged Charles Smith and Henry Heth, prominent citizens supporting Washington's candidacy, with the responsibility of entertaining voters, their families, and other residents of the county in town for the festival-like atmosphere of a colonial election day. Smith and Heth organized an elegant "treat," a party for all comers with copious amounts of liquor. This letter includes receipts for the hundreds of gallons of rum, wine, and cider purchased. It was sent to Washington two days after the election.

Sr

I have this Day Discharged the Expences on acct of Ellection, as by the Enclosed accts. I have Sent an acct of The proceedings by Express, also I have Sent Your two horses By Colo. John Carlyle, who is to receive them at Your quarter and Take them down to Your Place according to Your Order. The Small Pox has not Spread in Town as yet, but the Flux is Very bad in the fort, there has been two of the old Regiament Dead, and five of the New, Since Your departure. I am but weack in the Garrison, as by my weekly return to You will appear, I have Sent You a True Copy of the Poll whereby You will be a Compitent Judge of Your Friends. Your Friend Joseph Carroll whom I employ'd To take the Poll as one of the Clerks Desires to be remembered to you. Pray Sir Excuse hast, as I am your sincear friend, and Humble Servt

Chs Smith

Enclosure I
Account with Henry Brinker
July the 24[–25], 1758
    Corl George Washington Dr To Henry Brinkler one the Acct of the Election.
    To Thirtey Galls. of Strong Beer at 8d. _r Galln _01 Recd the above Acct of Lieut. Charles Smith one the Acct of Corl George Washington

Samuel Chinowitz
July 25, 1758
Test
Robt Fox

Enclosure II
Account with John Funk
July 24th. 1758

Colo. George Washington Dr. to John Funk	£ S. D.
To 131/2 Galls. of Wine @ 10/	6.15.0
To 31/2 pts. of Brandy @ 1/3	0.4–4½
To 13 Galls. Bear @ 1/3 3	0.16.3
To 8 Qts. Cyder Royl. @ 1/6	0.12.0
To Punch	0.3.9
	£ 8.11.4 1/2

    Fort Loudoun, July the 26th
    Receivd. of Leut. Chs. Smith the above Accot. in the Behalf of Colo. George Washington
perr me,

John Funk
Test
Joseph Carroll

Enclosure III
Account with Henry Heth
July the 24[–26]th 1758
George Washington Esqr. Commander of the. First Virginia Regiament
Dr

To 40, Gallons of Rum Punch @ 3/6 perr Galn	7.0.0
To 15, Gallons of Wine @ 10/0 perr Galln	7.10.0
To Dinner for Your Friends	3.0.0
	£ 17.10. 0

Fort Loudoun, July the 26th
Received of Lieut. Charles Smith the above acct. in Behalf of Colo.
George Washington
perr me
Henry Heth
Test
Joseph Carroll

Enclosure IV
Account with Alexander Woodrow
Winchester 1758, July 24
Dr. Colo. George Washington By order of Lieut. Chas. Smith to Alexr
Woodrow
For 1 hhd & 1 Barrell of Punch

consisting of 26 Gals. best Barbadoes

Rum 5/,	6.10.0
& 12 ½ Pds. S. Refd. Sugar 1/6	0.18.9
To 6 Gallons best Madiera Wine of Mr Thos Lemen 10.	3.0.0
	£10.8.9

Recd. of Lieut. Charles Smith Ten Pounds Eight Shills. and nine pence in full of the Above Accot.

Alexr Woodrow
Test
Joseph Carroll

Source: Transcribed from original document in Library of Congress, Manuscript Collection. Also available in: Beverly H. Runge, ed., *The Papers of George Washington, Colonial Series,* Vol. 5, *March 1774–June 1775* (Charlottesville: University Press of Virginia, 1995), 331–334.

Document 2.4   Washington to Alexander Hamilton, October 3, 1788

Alexander Hamilton implored George Washington to serve as the nation's first president in a September 1788 letter in which he said, "I am clearly of opinion that the crisis which brought you again into public view left you no alternative but to comply (the Constitutional Convention)—and I am equally clear in the opinion that you are by that act pledged *to take a part in the execution of the government. I am not less convinced that the impression of this necessity of your filling the station in question is so universal that you run no risk of any uncandid imputation, by submitting to it" (Twohig 1987, 23). Hamilton went on to warn Washington that without his leadership an unsuccessful president could take office and undermine trust in the new government. The following letter is Washington's reply.*

Mount Vernon, October 3d. 1788

In acknowledging the receipt of your candid and kind letter by the last Post; little more is incumbent upon me, than to thank you sincerely for the frankness with which you communicated your sentiments, and to assure you that the same manly tone of intercourse will always be more than barely wellcome, Indeed it will be highly acceptable to me. I am particularly glad, in the present instance; you have dealt thus freely and like a friend. Although I could not help observing from several publications and letters that my name had been sometimes spoken of, and that it was possible the *Contingency* which is the subject of your letter might happen; yet I thought it best to maintain a guarded silence and to [seek] the *counsel* of my best friends (which I certainly hold in the highest estimation) rather than to hazard an imputation unfriendly to the delicacy of my feelings. For, situated as I am, I could hardly bring the question into the slightest discussion, or ask an opinion even in the most confidential manner; without betraying, in my Judgement, some impropriety of conduct, or without feeling an apprehension that a premature display of anxiety, might be construed into a vain-glorious desire of pushing myself into notice as a Candidate. Now, if I am not grossly deceived in myself, I should unfeignedly rejoice, in case the Electors, by giving their votes in favor of some other person, would save me from the dreaded Dilemma of being forced to accept or refuse. If that may not be—I am, in the next place, earnestly desirous of searching out the truth, and of knowing whether there does not exist a probability that the government would be just as happily and effectually carried into execution, without my aid, as with it. I am *truly* solicitous to obtain all the previous information which the circumstances will afford, and to determine (when the determination can with propriety be no longer postponed) according to the principles of right reason, and the dictates of clear conscience; without too great a reference to the unforeseen consequences, which may affect my person or reputation. Untill that period, I may fairly hold myself open to conviction—though I allow your sentiments to have the weight in them; and I shall not pass by your arguments without giving them as dispassionate a consideration, as I can possibly bestow upon them.

In taking a survey of the subject in whatever point of light I have been able to place it; I will not suppress the acknowledgment, my Dr. Sir that I have always felt a kind of gloom upon my mind, as often as I have been taught to expect, I might, and perhaps must ere long be called to make a decision. You will, I am well assured, believe the assertion (though I have little expectation it would gain credit from those who are less acquainted with me) that if I should receive the appointment and if I should be prevailed upon to accept it; the acceptance would be attended with more diffidence and reluctance than ever I experienced before in my life. It would be, however, with a fixed and sole determination of lending whatever assistance might be in my power to promote the public weal, in hopes that at a convenient and an early period, my services might be dispensed with, and that I might be permitted once more to retire—to pass an unclouded evening, after the stormy day of life, in the bosom of domestic tranquility.

But why these anticipations? If the friends to the Constitution conceive that my administering the government will be a means of its acceleration and strength, is it not probable that the adversaries of it may entertain the same ideas and of course make it an object of opposition? That many of this description will become Electors, I can have no doubt of; any more than that their opposition will extend to any character who (from whatever cause) would be likely to thwart their measures. It might be impolite in them to make this declaration *previous* to the Election, but I shall be out in my conjectures if they do not act conformably thereto—and from that the seeming moderation by which they appear to be actuated at present is neither more nor less than a finesse to lull and deceive. Their plan of opposition systemised, and a regular intercourse, I have much reason to believe between the Leaders of it in the several States is formed to render it more effectual.

Source: Dorothy Twohig, ed., *The Papers of George Washington, Presidential Series,* Vol. 1, *September 1788–March 1789* (Charlottesville: University Press of Virginia, 1987), 31–33.

Document 2.5   Washington to Gov. Henry Lee, January 20, 1793

Washington was not eager to serve a second term as president. In this letter to Henry Lee, a longtime friend and the governor of Virginia, Washington describes his hesitancy about a second term—a hesitancy born of political and personal concerns.

Dear Sir,

I have been favored with your letter of the 6th instant, congratulatory on my re-election to the Chair of Government. A mind must be insensible indeed, not to be gratefully impressed by so distinguished, & honorable a testimony of public approbation & confidence: and, as I suffered my name to be contemplated on this occasion, it is more than probable that I should, for a moment, have experienced chagreen if my re-election had not been by a pretty respectable vote. But to say I feel pleasure from the prospect of commencing another tour of duty, would be a departure from truth; for however it might savour of Affectation in the opinion of the world (who by the bye can only guess at my sentimts as it never has been troubled with them) my particular, & confidential friends well know, that it was after a long and painful conflict in my own breast, that I was withheld (by considerations which are not necessary to mention) from requesting, in time, that no votes might be thrown away upon me; it being my fixed determination to return to the walks of private life, at the end of my term.

I am sorry to be informed by your letter, that death has snatched from us my old acquaintance & friend Colo. Bassett. The manner of it, adds to the regret. We shall all follow; some sooner & some later; & from accounts, my poor Nephew is likely to be amongst the first.

Mrs Washington joins me in wishing you the return of many new & happy years. With very great esteem & regard I am always Your Affecte Servt

Go: Washington

Source: John C. Fitzpatrick, ed., *The Writings of George Washington from the Original Manuscript Sources, 1745–1799,* 39 vols. (Washington, D.C.: Government Printing Office, 1931–1944), 32:309–310.

Illustration of "Bank of the United States, in Third Street [Philadelphia]"

CHAPTER THREE

Administration Policies

T he overriding policy of the Washington presidency was to promote the young nation. This policy involved enhancing the nation's political unity. The states were not, after all, *fated* to be united. They had proclaimed their unity and had acted in concert to secure their independence. More recently, they had placed their union on a potentially firm foundation by ratifying the Constitution and entrusting the presidency to George Washington. The nation's central government was, however, untested. Under Washington, it would have to prove itself capable of acting as a government: levying and collecting taxes far from the capital; peaceably resolving disputes among its constituent states; and protecting the lives, liberties, and property of its citizens from threats, both domestic and foreign. If the new government could not do these things and more, Washington might be the last as well as the first president under the Constitution of 1787.

In looking down the road, Washington hoped that his economic, financial, educational, and military policies would efface the prejudices of the different regions of the nation. He knew as well that his actions as president would establish precedents that might shape the governance of the nation far into the future. "Many things which appear of little importance in themselves and at the beginning," he observed, "may have great and durable consequences from their having been established at the commencement of a new general government" (Degregorio 1993, 9).

He was determined to set sound precedents that would enable future executives to keep the United States united in fact, not just in name.

As if uniting the nation under its new government were not work enough for one presidency, the nation-building imperative required more. The task of government at this time was not only to preserve the Union, but to expand it. The nation whose government Washington presided over from 1789 to 1797 was growing fast and moving westward. This expansion placed remarkable strains on the government—strains that Washington wrestled with in policymaking. Unity and growth were the themes of the presidential policies of George Washington.

POLICIES FOR UNITY

As president, Washington promoted unity by asserting the independence and national responsibility of the executive within the national government (see Chapter 5) and by supporting policies that enhanced the national government's power and that drew the nation together by bonds of common interest.

Finance

The president did not seek to lead Congress. He did, however, decide when to support the heads of his executive departments as they worked with members of Congress to craft legislation within their areas of responsibility. One of the most important areas of government policy in the early United States was financial reform. In this area, Washington relied heavily on the talents and energy of his secretary of the Treasury, Alexander Hamilton.

Debt Redemption. When Washington assumed the presidency, the national government was carrying a foreign debt of $10 million. It was behind in interest payments alone by over $1.5 million. No one knew the total amount of money that the government owed its own citizens. Under the Articles of Confederation, the Continental army and other agencies of the government had issued numerous certificates of indebtedness (essentially IOUs) when, for example, requisitioning supplies or in lieu of pay to soldiers. Hamilton estimated the amount at $27 million. If the nation was to be treated with respect by foreign countries and if it wished its own citizens to place confidence in its government, these debts would have to be paid.

Hamilton wanted the government to accept the burden of repaying these debts as well as those the state governments had incurred. This was a high-stakes gamble on the ability of the national government, in its infancy, to assert its primacy over the states. If it failed, Hamilton's plan would betray not the strength but the feebleness of the national government. To succeed, the national government would have to develop the will and capacity to move beyond traditional revenue sources.

Customs duties were the government's principal source of revenue in the early days of the Republic, bringing in roughly $4.5 million in 1791 and $6.5 million in 1796. At the time, the revenue and expenditures of the national government were hovering at about $8–$10 million a year. (The Treasury oversaw a budget surplus throughout the Washington administration.) The government also raised money through sales of public lands and postal fees. Therefore, to move beyond these traditional revenue sources the U.S. government would have to impose taxes on its citizens.

Internal taxation was not expected to raise great sums. Indeed, Washington's administration typically took in from internal taxation sums equivalent to less than 10 percent of the funds raised from tariffs. Still, the internal tax revenues were considerably more than the amounts collected annually from land sales and postage combined. Moreover, Hamilton and his allies saw a value to internal taxation that could not be glimpsed in a ledger book. By collecting taxes from its own citizens, the new government would demonstrate its power. By assuring leading citizens of Philadelphia and New York of the government's willingness to do whatever was necessary to fund its debts, the national government would unite the wealthy and powerful behind the government and, in particular, the executive branch. Finally, by resorting to internal taxation the government would prove the nation's credit worthiness to foreign lenders.

What sort of taxes could the government impose on its citizenry to pay off its debts and those of the states? There would be no individual income tax in the United States until the Civil War. The early government relied instead on excise taxes on certain categories of domestic products that were manufactured in abundance and widely distributed. Whiskey fit both requirements. Later during Washington's administration, taxes were extended to snuff, loaf sugar, and carriages.

In addition to excise taxes, Hamilton's plan called for the sale of new government bonds. Newly issued government bonds sold abroad would fund the foreign debt, and bonds sold at home would help to fund the domestic debt. Both old and new bonds would be redeemable at face value. With the promise of full payment by the government whenever the bond holder requested, these certificates of indebtedness would circulate throughout the economy as currency, thereby expanding the nation's financial resources by increasing its "money supply." (The nation would not have a uniform currency until after the Civil War.)

Hamilton's plan seemed immoderate and elitist to James Madison, who led the struggle against it in the House of Representatives. If the national government was to assume states' debts, Madison argued, it must out of fairness do so with discrimination. *Discrimination* was the term used to describe a policy whereby the government would give the current bond holder only a portion of the bond's value; the rest would be paid to the person or persons who originally purchased the certificate. But this approach, insisted Hamilton, was against the letter of the law. The certificates themselves stipulated that the documents were "bearer bonds," payable in full to their owner. Moreover, it would be impossible to implement Madison's plan fully, and expensive and cumbersome to implement it even in part.

Nevertheless, Hamilton's plan remained odious to Madison and his backers, because it would reward the speculators in "paper money" who had accumulated massive quantities of the IOUs the government had issued over the years since independence had been declared. These certificates had typically been bought from those to whom they had been issued for pennies on the dollar. Publicly, Hamilton argued fairness in defense; it was a free market, and those who sold did so for what they considered a fair price. Privately, he and his allies in high finance had an additional line of reasoning. First, it was necessary and proper for money to be concentrated in the hands of the wealthy; they were the ones who knew what to do with it. They would invest in new enterprises, thus providing benefits that would trickle down to the benefit of all. Second, the moneyed class would be of great importance to the future of the nation. Whosoever they allied with stood to gain in power as the wealthy gained in riches. Hamilton wanted therefore to ally the wealthiest citizens of the nation with the national government and, in particular, the executive. If creditors recognized they could expect to "receive their dues" from the national government, they would support it (Flexner 1970, 243).

In 1790 the Senate endorsed Hamilton's plan (see Document 3.1). The House, through the efforts of Madison as well as others, accepted a portion of the plan, but rejected assumption of states' debts. Hamilton was certain that without assumption the states with the most to gain from assumption would rebel and perhaps even secede. The result could be disunion. Hamilton asked Secretary of State Thomas Jefferson for help.

Jefferson was not in favor of Hamilton's plan, but he was not unyieldingly opposed to it. In fact, as minister to France under the Articles of Confederation, he had assured bankers in nearby Holland that assumption would eventually become the policy of the government. Later, however, Jefferson regretted his part in the arrangement, because he thought Hamilton's plan overcentralized power and gave Hamilton too great an influence in the government. But in 1790 it was Jefferson who brought together the major antagonists in the financial battle.

Over dinner at Jefferson's house, Hamilton and Madison worked out a famous bargain. Madison would not change his own vote, but he would change the votes of others. In return, the capital would be moved to the South. Pennsylvania's representatives, in consolation, would be guaranteed the opportunity to host the government for ten years.

Washington himself took no part in the famous bargain. He admitted in retrospect that he had harbored great anxiety over the debt and residency issues as "questions of the most delicate and interesting nature . . . more in danger of having convulsed the government itself than any other points" (Washington to Marquis de la Luzerne, August 10, 1790, Fitzpatrick 1931–1944, 31:84). But Washington, believing that a president had no authority to intervene in the deliberative process of the legislature, kept his silence during the debate. He was, however, greatly pleased with the results, and it soon became clear that he backed both Hamilton's plan for debt redemption and the bargain that had led to its approval by Congress.

Several years later, in an addendum to his sixth annual address to Congress (November 19, 1794), Washington exhorted the House of Representatives to complete its work on redeeming the public debt. The "time which has elapsed since the commencement of our fiscal measures," he pointed out, "has developed our pecuniary resources so as to open the way for a definite plan for the redemption of the public debt." To finish the task would bring benefit to the nation and gratitude from "our constituents." "Indeed, whatsoever is unfinished of our system of public credit can not be benefited by procrastination; and as far as may be practicable we ought to place that credit on grounds which can not be disturbed, and to prevent that progressive accumulation of debt which must ultimately endanger all governments" (Richardson 1897, 159).

The First Bank of the United States.   Hamilton also argued for establishment of a national bank. The bank was to be modeled on the Bank of England, a privately owned but publicly controlled institution. In the U.S. model, one-fifth of the bank's stock would be held by the government. The bank would be the government's repository for tax receipts; it would make loans to the states, the national government, and private businesses; and shares of its stock would be valued throughout the country and abroad and would circulate in an open secondary market. In addition, the bank would help the nation by acting as the government's fiscal agent in transactions such as the sale of new government bonds.

Curiously, the plan for the bank, unlike the plan for the national government's assumption of states' debts, caused little complaint at first. It was in retrospect, in the words of the Jeffersonian opposition, "one of those sly and subtle movements which marched silently to its object: the vices of it were at first not palpable" (Flexner 1970, 279). Madison devoted only one day to arguing against it in the House.

The president also heard out Madison and asked both Madison and Hamilton to prepare written arguments on the issue. Madison argued that the Constitution gave the government no authority to create a bank. Hamilton argued that the bank was a necessity, and that the Constitution would be meaningless if it were interpreted so as to prevent the government from doing things essential to the success of the nation. Jefferson disagreed with Hamilton on the necessity of a bank, but did not think it proper for the president to overrule the legislature. In the end, Washington signed the bank bill. He came to see the adoption of Hamilton's plan for a central bank as a bulwark of unity. Indeed, he wrote glowingly of the bank to his friend, the financier and presidential special envoy Gouverneur Morris: "In my late tour through the southern States, I experienced great satisfaction in seeing the good effects of the general Government in that part of the Union" (Fitzpatrick 1931–1944, 31:328–329). Especially gratifying to the people of the South, observed the president, was the rapidity with which subscriptions to the Bank of the United States were filled. "In two hours after the books were opened by the Commissioners the whole number of shares were taken up, and 4000 more applied for than were allowed by the Institution."

Under the bank's charter of 1791, the secretary of the Treasury was empowered to inspect the affairs of the Bank at any time and the government was permitted to subscribe to one-fifth of its stock. For the duration of Washington's administration, the Bank operated in a salutary fashion, making nonspeculative loans to the government and to private enterprises. Like the Federal Reserve system of today, the Bank forced sound banking practices on sometimes reluctant state institutions by refusing to credit their notes if they departed from minimal banking standards.

The "Residency" Question.   The "residency" question was every bit as contentious in the early government as the nation's plan for payment of its war debts. In fact, the selection of a capital was the first highly divisive issue debated in Congress's first session. Partisans of Philadelphia maneuvered to have their city named at least a temporary capital, certain as they were that once in residence in North America's only respectable urban center, the nation's elected leadership would give up all thought of moving elsewhere. Southerners pointed to the contribution Virginia had made to the Revolution, and argued for a site near the home of the most famous Virginian of them all. Northerners and westerners ridiculed the alleged "paradise of the Potowmack" and searched for a compromise spot, perhaps in western Pennsylvania along the Susquehanna River (see Document 3.2).

Under the terms of the bargain for the creation of a sound financial system, the federal government's residency would be established permanently in the upper South. Exactly where would be left to the president himself. Washington had been characteristically careful during the congressional debate over the issue not to reveal his preference. In fact, he wrote nothing on the subject until Congress had acted. Nevertheless, it was assumed, correctly, that the president preferred a site along the Potomac. Thus Congress's action amounted to an agreement to settle the Federal City at some point not distant from Mount Vernon. Sen. William Maclay of Pennsylvania, a frequent critic of the president, wrote in his journal that the president "had a great influence in this business" (Maclay 1890, 328–329).

The bill for "establishing the temporary and permanent seat of the government of the United States" was passed by Congress in 1790 (see Document 3.3). The law empowered the president to select the site and to appoint three commissioners to supervise its development. French military engineer Maj. Charles Pierre L'Enfant, who had pressed his services on Washington, was selected to plan the city. He was to report to the commissioners.

Throughout his presidency, Washington made it a habit to combine trips to Mount Vernon with visits to the site of the Federal City. He took a hand in every aspect of the work there, including surveying, financing, and architectural design. Because of constant friction between the commissioners and L'Enfant, the president also immersed himself in various legal and political skirmishes over issues such as L'Enfant's authority to demolish private residences in the Federal City (see Documents 3.4 and 3.5).

Washington viewed L'Enfant as a man possessed of great talent but excessive zeal. He even chastised the major in one letter for his "precipitate conduct" (see Document 3.5). L'Enfant's heavy-handed management and his refusal to heed the directions of the commissioners led finally to his resignation after a year, but in that brief time he laid out the plan that shapes Washington, D.C., to this day.

Slavery

Well before assuming office, Washington had come to believe that slavery debased both master and slave. "No man living," Washington wrote in 1786, "wishes more sincerely than I do to see the abolition" of slavery (Flexner 1972, 121). It should, he believed, be eliminated by "slow, sure, and imperceptible degrees." While president, Washington even conceived a plan by which he hoped to free his own slaves. The scheme was to rent all his farms, except "Mansion House Farm," to skilled immigrant farmers. With the proceeds from the rental of his farms, he would pay the costs associated with manumission, such as the care in perpetuity of those freed slaves too infirm or old to work. As part of the rental agreement, the new tenants would be required to hire on the former slaves as laborers. For want of takers, the plan failed.

As president, however, Washington took pains to keep his private views and plans out of the public's sight, because he thought that abolitionism would dissolve the Union if not kept off the government's agenda. In 1790 Benjamin Franklin signed his name to a memorial presented to Congress demanding that the legislature do all within its power to promote the abolition of slavery. A special committee of the House responded to this petition, citing the Constitution's proscription against abolition of the slave trade before 1808 (Article I, Section 9).

Washington maintained official silence on the work of this committee. When a leading abolitionist lobbied the president personally, the chief executive replied that "as it was a matter which might come before me for official decision I was not inclined to express any sentimts. on the merits of the question before this should happen." Privately, Washington expressed annoyance at the abolitionist movement, termed the Franklin memorial "mal-apropos," and applauded Congress's action in seeing it "put to sleep" (Hirschfeld 1997, 184–185).

Education

Although Washington shied away from establishing an administration policy on slavery, he was not similarly reticent about education. The passions associated with education were not so great, and the vested interests not so overwhelming or divisive. Washington's policy for education was clear. There should be a great national university, and the government should pay for it. But his success at promoting this policy was minor at best.

Perhaps forgetting that he would have followed his brothers to England for education himself had his father not died when George was just a boy, the president observed to a friend once that it had "always been a source of regret" to see young Americans cross the Atlantic for their education. In his mature years, Washington came to believe that American youth acquired "habits of dissipation and extravagance" in Europe and were taught "principles unfriendly to the rights of man" before having the opportunity to form "correct ideas of the blessings of the country they leave" (Flexner 1972, 199).

Washington was not opposed to university education, simply to university education of American men in Europe. Yet European faculties were vastly superior to those of the "seminaries of learning" established in some of the states. The "funds upon which [those seminaries, such as Harvard and William and Mary] rest," he observed in his final annual address to Congress on December 7, 1796, were simply too small for them to have progressed far beyond the ability to offer remedial instruction (Richardson 1897, 194). The solution, he was certain, was for the government to establish a national university. By 1796 Washington had already called on Congress to consider this project numerous times, but because "the desirableness" of the institution seemed to increase over time, he simply had to take advantage of this last opportunity to commend it to the legislature.

The benefit to the nation, Washington argued, would be great, because such an institution would help with "the assimilation of the principles, opinions, and manners of our countrymen by the common education of a portion of our youth from every quarter" (Richardson 1897, 194). "The more homogeneous our citizens can be made in these particular," the executive reminded the legislators, "the greater will be our prospect of permanent union."

The government, however, remained unmoved. After all, many of the leading members of the early American government were alumni of those lesser "seminaries" that the first president thought deficient. For example, 44 percent of the cabinet and major diplomatic appointees of the Washington and Adams administrations were graduates of Harvard, Yale, or Princeton; only 13 percent had, like Washington, never been to college (Purvis 1995, 219). Washington's commitment to this project spurred him, nevertheless, to direct in his will that shares of stock in his beloved Potomac Canal Company be given upon his death for "the endowment of a university to be established in the Federal District provided that some well-digested plan be achieved before 1800" (Flexner 1972, 199). No plan, well-digested or otherwise, was made before 1800.

Before his death, however, an opportunity did arise for the president to make a different but complementary bequest of stock in the James River Canal. Those shares had been given to Washington by the state of Virginia after the Revolution, but he asked the Virginia legislature whether it would consent for him to return the stock so it could be used to endow the university he sought. The sentiment of Virginia's government was mixed. Most of the leading men of Virginia were closer in thought to Thomas Jefferson than Washington. They were skeptical of cities and of explicitly nationalist institutions. They preferred, they said, to locate the proposed university in the "upper country." Washington acceded to the wishes of the state. He changed his will to reflect the agreed-upon plan, and left the money to found Liberty Hall, which is today Washington and Lee University.

POLICIES FOR GROWTH

Unity was necessary but hardly sufficient to achieve Washington's aspirations for his presidency. The United States in 1789 was a collection of rapidly growing but thinly settled entities. Most of the population still lived within a short stretch of shoreline. The geographic core of the nation was centered about New York, its first political capital, and Philadelphia, its first financial capital. Outside the core lay what geographers would term the "national domain, the remainder of the area actually colonized and controlled by American settlers" (Meinig 1986, 404–405). The domain was split about evenly between territories encompassing and prohibiting slavery. Outside the domain was a "protectorate," in which the authority of the national government was continually tested.

The American protectorate included all the land northwest of the Ohio River and east of the Mississippi, and in the South an immense area reaching from Nashville in the center of the country to Natchez, in the Mississippi Territory near New Orleans, and from that point reaching eastward through the pines and swamps of the Florida panhandle. These territories, like the remainder of the continent in later years, were physically incorporated into the nation "by a series of congressional acts, warfare, and intimidation" (Meinig 1986, 404–405). The envelopment of the protectorate into the body of the United States was a process that began before Washington assumed the presidency and continued long after his time in office. As the nation grew, the core shifted, and the domain and protectorate grew and moved westward as well. Eventually, the protectorate was successfully colonized all the way to the Pacific, and it turned into domain.

During this lengthy process, Washington's eight years in office were important in adding military force to government claims. The new government might pass as many resolutions as it cared to, announcing its right to occupy the lands to the west once claimed by its former colonial parent, but without force, those claims would remain ineffective. Britain still possessed a valuable colony to the north of the United States. (The name "Canada" was officially adopted by the British in early 1791. From the British victory in the French and Indian War until that time, the colony was simply referred to as "British North America.") From their strategic location in the Great Lakes region, the British still sent troops to garrison forts on land that by treaty had been ceded to the United States at the close of the War of Independence. American claims also were in conflict in the West with the imperial ambitions of Spain and France, and with the historic tenancy of numerous Native American nations.

Overall, by pursuing policies for a strong military, the defeat of hostile Indians, the addition of new states to the Union, and a respite from warfare with the European powers whose North American empires encircled the United States, Washington promoted the physical expansion of the United States.

Military Policy: A Standing Army to Open the Northwest to Settlement

As the outgoing commander of the Continental army, Washington had issued in 1783 what he thought was a restrained and practical report calling for a peacetime force of 2,631 professional officers and soldiers, supplemented by a nationalized militia. Instead, Congress authorized the First American Regiment, a force of 700 citizen soldiers, or militiamen, to be loaned to the federal government for one-year enlistments. Although the Confederation Congress allocated 40 percent of its budget to the army, the amount was so meager that offensive operations against hostile Indians were banned in the Ohio Valley for want of men (Perret 1989, 71, 77). The postwar army was enlarged incrementally under the Articles of Confederation, but pro-army leaders such as Washington had a difficult time convincing military skeptics such as Thomas Jefferson that the benefit of a standing army outweighed its potential cost. After all, a standing army not only was expensive, but also had historically often been the ruin of republican government.

Under mounting pressure from settlers at war with Indians, and by means of the government's mechanism for taxation and military organization established in the Constitution, the military was at last enlarged and reorganized. The task of military reform was not completed, however, in time to save the American army from two humiliating defeats during Washington's presidency.

In their first year in their respective offices, Secretary of War Henry Knox advised President Washington of the government's dilemma. Twenty or more white settlers were being killed each month by Indians in skirmishes and raids in the Ohio River Valley. The "Indians, being the prior occupants, possess the right of soil" in much of the territory, Knox advised Washington (Perret 1989, 82). The United States might take the land through legal purchase, treaty, or "conquest in a just war," but the United States had only a small army.

Washington, with the consent of Congress, pursued negotiations while making limited military preparations. Civilian agents of the government, working from within the Department of War, encouraged Indians to farm, offering free tools and instruction. Despite such efforts, Washington reported to Congress in 1790, in his second annual message, that Indian "depredations" were causing the "sacrifice" of a "number of valuable citizens . . . some of them under circumstances peculiarly shocking" (Richardson 1897, 74). "[T]he aggressors should be made sensible that the Government of the Union is not less capable of punishing their crimes than it is disposed to respect their rights and reward their attachments" (Document 3.6). Washington utilized the powers of the Constitution and a recently enacted law of Congress to call forth the militia of several states, combine it with the small band of regular soldiers that a wary Congress had authorized, and send them into battle.

A Continental army veteran, Brig. Gen. Josiah Harmar, was ordered to lead these forces on a punitive expedition against the Shawnee, Cherokee, and Wabash Indians of Ohio. His force consisted of about 1,200 militiamen and only 400 army regulars. Washington knew that Harmar's army was hardly worthy of the name, being undersized and overly reliant on militia. In a letter to his secretary of war, the president unburdened himself of his anxieties while awaiting news of Harmar's expedition. "I expected *little* from the moment I heard he was a *drunkard*. I expected *less* as soon as I heard that on *this account* no confidence was reposed in him by the people of the Western Country. And I gave up *all hope* of Success, as soon as I heard that there were disputes with *him* about command" (Washington to Henry Knox, November 19, 1790, in Fitzpatrick 1931–1944, 31:156–157).

Washington's foreboding proved to be justified. Harmar fragmented his small force and was ambushed. The militia, many of whose members had enrolled principally for free passage to the frontier, ran in retreat. The regulars stood their ground but took devastating casualties. Secretary of War Knox wrote to Harmar to say that "[i]t would be deficiency of candor on my part were I to say your conduct is approved by the President of the United States, or the public" and to recommend that Harmar request a court of inquiry to examine his conduct. In this inquiry, Harmar was eventually exonerated, but testimony prejudicial to his reputation and that of the army received a wide hearing (Document 3.7).

Washington then turned to plans for a second expedition. In preparation, a historic compromise was reached between government members, led by the president, who wanted a larger army composed almost entirely of regular soldiers enlisted for multiyear terms, and those who wanted the government to rely in war as well as in peace on short-term militia. The regular army was doubled in size, and "levies" were authorized—that is, short-term volunteers were enrolled from the states but placed under regular army discipline for the duration of their service. These levies, as the troops themselves were known, represented a compromise between regulars and common militia. "Such volunteers were to provide the bulk of American wartime forces," notes a historian of the American military, "for more than a century to come" (Perret 1989, 83).

The first effort of the enlarged and reorganized U.S. Army was, however, even more disastrous than Harmar's effort had been. The army was put under the command of another aging veteran of the Revolutionary War, Maj. Gen. Arthur St. Clair. His troops, moving out in August 1791, proceeded slowly, stopping to build forts along the way. Like Harmar, St. Clair failed to send out regular scouting patrols, nor was he vigilant in camp. As a result, a group of Indians led by Little Turtle of the Miamis and Blue Jacket of the Shawnees was able to attack St. Clair's men while they were huddled around their morning campfires. In an even fight, two-thirds of St. Clair's men were killed, wounded, or taken prisoner. It was the greatest victory Indians would ever achieved over U.S. troops.

Washington and Knox liked St. Clair, whose reputation was untarnished. Moreover, he was regular, if less than zealous, in his orders and disciplined in his leadership. At least this time, the militia did not run in retreat through the ranks of the regulars. Back in Washington, St. Clair's defeat was forgiven, in the words of Knox, as "one of those incidents which sometimes happen in human affairs, which could not, under existing circumstances, have been prevented" (Henry Knox to Arthur St. Clair, December 23, 1791, in Smith 1882, 275–276).

St. Clair's defeat nevertheless added weight to the administration's persistent pleas to Congress to improve the military. Therefore, Congress at last overcame the widespread fear of a large standing army and an overly powerful national government and gave Washington's administration almost all it asked for in military policy.

Reorganized along the lines recommended by Washington's old ally from the Revolutionary War, Baron Friedrich von Steuben, the army was authorized to enlist men for three-year terms. Named the Legion of the United States, it was authorized at a strength of 5,414, with new categories of officers, including adjutant and inspector, and new categories of enlistees, such as saddler and sergeant major (Heitman 1903, 1:81, 2:560–562).

Maj. Gen. "Mad" Anthony Wayne was placed in charge of an expeditionary army of 2,000 regulars and 1,500 levies, most of the latter mounted riflemen from Kentucky. In 1794, at the site of St. Clair's defeat, Wayne repelled an attack by Indian warriors. He then headed north to assault a fort on the Maumee River, at present-day Toledo, Ohio, that had been built by the British and that they still claimed a right to occupy. Wayne's Legion defeated there a mixed force of Canadian militia and Indians in the battle of Fallen Timbers. General Wayne later reported his victory to the secretary of war with unrestrained pride (see Document 3.8). In 1795 several Indian nations ceded to the United States half of Ohio and much of Indiana in the Treaty of Greenville (see Document 3.9). The British at last pulled back into Canada.

Military Policy: An Adequate Militia to Smash Dissent against Federal Law

At the same time that the regular army was reorganized, the militia was reorganized, on paper at least, in the Uniform Militia Act of 1792. Washington himself labored over the bill before sending it to Knox for transmittal to Congress. The act made all "free able-bodied white male citizens" eighteen to forty-five years of age members of the militia, and called on the states to be rigorous in militia drill and instruction. But the act proved to be utopian in its very title, and many years would pass before the militia was transformed into a National Guard under effective and uniform military discipline. Still, the militia was historically the force that English-speaking communities turned to for protection against domestic disturbances, and it was the militia that President Washington called on in his second term to enforce the government's controversial internal taxation.

To redeem its debts, the nation needed new revenue sources. As a result, excise taxes were placed on whiskey, whether imported or domestic. Whiskey was taxed not because it was sinful (and a tax would discourage its use), but because it was a plentiful, easily transportable, easily stored commodity of roughly constant value. It was frequently used in payment of debts as a sort of frontier currency.

The tax on whiskey was unpopular and difficult to enforce. In his third annual message to Congress in late 1791, Washington alluded diplomatically to the difficulties encountered in the government's efforts at taxation. "The novelty," Washington stated, "of the tax in a considerable part of the United States and a misconception of some of its provisions have given occasion in particular places to some degree of discontent" (Richardson 1897, 97). Protests against the tax continued. In 1792 Washington rather feebly issued a proclamation "to exhort all persons whom it may concern to refrain and desist from all unlawful combinations and proceedings whatsoever having for object or tending to obstruct the operation of the laws aforesaid" (Richardson 1897, 117).

By 1794 protests against the tax had reached the proportions of an internal rebellion. In that year, armed men in western Pennsylvania attacked a U.S. marshal and burned down the home and office of a U.S. revenue inspector. The government's agents took their testimony of frontier conditions to an associate justice of the Supreme Court, James Wilson, who notified the president that in the far west of Pennsylvania the law was opposed and "execution thereof obstructed by combinations too powerful to be suppressed by the ordinary course of judicial proceedings or by the powers vested in the marshals of by that act" (see Document 3.10).

Washington called on four states to enroll 15,000 militia for federal service. At first, calls for volunteers went unheeded, and Maryland, Virginia, and Pennsylvania had to impose a limited draft to raise the required troops. As news of the regular army's triumph in the Northwest spread, however, and as Washington himself made personal visits to the militia to inspire them, fear increased in the frontier settlements.

Putting down the Whiskey Rebellion was of enormous importance to the first president. In a literal reading of the commander-in-chief clause (Article II, Section 2) of the Constitution, he personally led the troops to their jumping-off place beyond the mountains of Pennsylvania. On September 25, 1794, Washington issued a proclamation announcing with satisfaction that a force "adequate to the exigency is already in motion" to points of assembly (see Document 3.11). Then he and Secretary of the Treasury Alexander Hamilton, who had authored the tax that provoked the revolt and who harbored as yet unsatisfied ambitions of military leadership, rode to Carlisle, Pennsylvania, to review the troops raised from that state. Next, they went to Fort Cumberland, the site of Washington's headquarters during much of the French and Indian War. At Fort Cumberland, the troops of Pennsylvania were met by the soldiers of Maryland and Virginia. From that point, Washington led the army over the mountains. For his personal use, he ordered that whiskey, in place of the more traditional rum, be included in his supplies.

While Washington marched the militia from the east over three hundred miles of rugged terrain, several thousand people in the frontier area fled into Indian country, into Canada, and into the Spanish protectorate. When the army crossed the mountains, hundreds were compelled to swear loyalty oaths to the Constitution and the government. Scores of rioters were taken into custody, handed over to civilian authorities, and made to stand trial.

After the dissension had been broken, President Washington devoted almost all of his sixth annual message to Congress in November 1794 to the Whiskey Rebellion (see Document 3.12). Two rebels were eventually convicted and sentenced to death. On July 10, 1795, President Washington made the first use of the presidential pardon power to rescue these two men from punishment and restore them to their communities (see Document 3.13).

The dual success of Washington's military policy in 1794—against Indians and the British in the Northwest and against internal dissension in the West—gave a tremendous boost to the nation. To begin with, thousands of the men who had marched across the mountains to fight the Indians and overawe the frontiersmen simply stayed and settled the area. Moreover, the success of these soldiers against the enemies of the government made way for thousands more settlers. Overall, then, President Washington's policy of military strength enabled the government to prosecute its claims and defend its interests as it expanded physically across its colonial sphere, its "protectorate."

In 1796 Democratic-Republicans in Congress abolished the Legion and reorganized the army. This step may have been a victory for the military skeptics in the Democratic-Republican faction, but it was a victory for the Federalists as well. A *standing army* would survive into peacetime. "The 1796 legislation irrevocably committed the nation to the maintenance of a frontier constabulary that spearheaded western expansion for the next century" (Millett and Maslowski 1994, 99).

In naval policy, Washington pursued less dramatic but significant innovations that also contributed force to the government's leadership of an expanding nation. During his administration, Congress permitted the president to establish four arsenals, primarily for the navy, and a Corps of Artillerists and Engineers to garrison coastal fortifications. Also, Congress authorized the executive in 1794 to build six heavily armed frigates, which were to be the nation's first warships. The frigates were intended to meet an emergency need—to protect U.S. commerce from pirates of the Barbary states of Algiers, Morocco, Tunis, and Tripoli. Once a treaty with Algiers, the strongest of the pirating nations, was signed in 1796, Washington asked Congress for guidance about the navy's construction program. It authorized the executive to complete the three frigates, including the USS *Constitution* (known later as "Old Ironsides") on which actual construction had already begun.

Indian Policy

Washington viewed Native Americans as did probably most other white Americans of his day—as an "unenlightened race" whose happiness depended on the conduct of the U.S. government (Richardson 1897, 97). It would therefore be "honorable to the national character" for the United States to pursue toward the Indians "a system corresponding with the mild principles of religion and philanthropy." In practice, this meant Washington favored "rational experiments . . . for imparting to them the blessings of civilization as may from time to time suit their condition" and urged Congress to establish a uniform and impartial policy for "alienating their lands."

Whether whites and Indians could ever live in peace within the same land was, to Washington, an open question. To promote the possibility, he urged Indians to take up the plow, and urged Congress to take up measures to improve the honesty of commerce with Indian tribes (see Document 3.14). In his fifth annual message to Congress in 1793, Washington observed that "next to a rigorous execution of justice on the violators of peace . . . the establishment of commerce with the Indian nation in behalf of the United States is most likely to conciliate their attachment" (Richardson 1897, 133). Indeed, the government itself should seek uniform trade with the Indians. It could guarantee a market for Indian products, and sell farm implements and other goods to the Indians at prices that would allow it to be "reimbursed only." Congress, however, was slow to act. Thus in Washington's seventh annual message to Congress in 1795 he returned to the topic in the concluding paragraph of that address: "To enforce upon the Indians the observance of justice it is indispensable that there shall be competent means of rendering justice to them. If these means can be devised by the wisdom of Congress . . . I should not hesitate to entertain a strong hope of rendering our tranquility permanent." If Congress could find the means of doing the Indians justice, Washington added, he foresaw "the probability even of their civilization" (Richardson 1897, 177).

In the Southwest, President Washington gave expression to his generally pacific Indian policy when he stepped into a conflict between Georgia frontier families, the state government, and the Indians. Georgia had sought to open the territory between the Mississippi and the Yazoo Rivers to white settlers. The Georgia legislature therefore took it upon itself to sell to speculators in 1790 over fifteen million acres of land that it did not truly own because the federal government had ceded to the Choctaws, Cherokees, and Chickasaws much of the disputed land, which was, in any event, also claimed by Spain. The president was alarmed by this turn of events. He desired no war with Spain, and held a sincere, although ineffectual, sentiment in favor of honest dealing with Native Americans (see Document 3.15).

In response to the situation, Washington issued a proclamation in 1790 forbidding settlement in the disputed region, and his administration negotiated a new treaty, the Treaty of New York, with a leader of one of the Creek Confederacy. In this agreement, the government returned to its Indian inhabitants a large portion of land that Georgia had claimed the right to sell to settlers. When presenting the treaty to the Senate, Washington assured its members that Georgia and the speculators in western land, if not pleased, had at least every reason to be pleased, because the treaty contained "a regular, full, and definitive relinquishment" of Creek claims to the most valuable part of the disputed land (Richardson 1897, 70). By contrast, Washington described the territory ceded to the Indians as "generally barren, sunken, and unfit for cultivation" though "of the highest importance" to the Creeks as a winter hunting ground.

In the course of these negotiations, Washington set a precedent in favor of executive predominance in the negotiation of treaties. He personally went to the Senate chambers in Federal Hall with Secretary of War Henry Knox for the "advice" of that chamber on the proper position to take with regard to the Creek Indians. The senators were reluctant to advise the president without having had the opportunity to deliberate among themselves on the issues the president put before them. When Senator Maclay urged that the issue be sent to committee, the president complained that "this defeats every purpose of my coming here" (Randall 1997, 461). When leaving the chambers after a second day of inconclusive talks, Washington exclaimed that he "would be damned" if he ever went to the Senate again. From that time on, the Senate would typically be asked to ratify treaties once negotiated, not to help shape them in the first place.

Policy for New States

The population of the United States grew by 35 percent during the 1790s. Fortunately for the Americans, the federal form of government was well suited to a growing population. When the Constitution went into effect, only eleven states were members of the Union. North Carolina and Rhode Island, the last of the original thirteen states to ratify the new plan of government, joined during the first year of Washington's presidency.

Washington faced a more complicated issue when it came to adding states carved from territory claimed by one or more of the original states. Article IV, Section 3, of the Constitution stipulates that "no new State shall be formed or erected within the jurisdiction of any other State; nor any State be formed by the junction of two or more States, or parts of States, without the consent of the legislatures of the States concerned as well as the Congress." The original states had by and large relinquished their rather fanciful claims on western lands even before the ratification of the new Constitution, and in some cases before victory in the War of Independence. Once New Hampshire and New York gave up their claims in the area of Vermont, it opened the way for the addition to the Union of the first new state. Influential Vermonters had long resented New York's and New Hampshire's pretensions to dominion, but they did not necessarily favor statehood. Some leading families of Vermont envisioned a special relationship with Britain in order to preserve commercial access to the St. Lawrence Seaway (Meinig 1986, 349). As the new nation prospered, however, sentiment coalesced around joining the United States. Thus the "independent republic of Vermont" joined the Union as the fourteenth state on March 4, 1791.

Kentucky's admission to the Union the next year was even more uncertain than Vermont's. There was considerable sentiment in the area, formally a part of Virginia, for independence or perhaps alliance with Spain. The federal government's ineptness under the Articles and its military haplessness in the early Washington administration gave Kentucky residents little faith in the national government. Spanish diplomats worked publicly to persuade American settlers to cross the Mississippi into Spanish North America. Spanish spies worked with American adventurers to foment rebellion against U.S. authority on the "American" side of the river (see Document 3.16).

The "Spanish Conspiracy" did not unduly alarm the president. Like most American statesmen of his day, he considered Spain a weak threat to the United States, and hoped that the steady growth of the government and its powers would in time align settlers in the Southwest with the nation out of sheer interest if not patriotism. Intrigues to dissociate Kentucky from the United States continued until local conventions overwhelmingly backed statehood, which was arranged in 1792. In that year, Kentucky was simultaneously granted independence from Virginia and admission to the United States.

In Washington's final year in office, 1796, one more state (the sixteenth) was added to the Union. Under the Articles of Confederation, Congress had organized the Northwest Territory in 1787. The Northwest Ordinance established an orderly process for the formation of new states from formally claimed U.S. territories. The first state to be added to the Union in this way was Tennessee, on June 1, 1796.

FOREIGN POLICY

In his first annual address to Congress in 1789, Washington requested that body's assent to his conduct of foreign affairs. "The interests of the United States," Washington observed, "require that our intercourse with other nations should be facilitated by such provisions as will enable me to fulfill my duty in that respect in the manner which circumstances may render most conducive to the public good" (Richardson 1897, 58). Washington went on during his eight years as president to claim the pre-eminent role in the conduct of foreign affairs for the chief executive. At times, the president had to defend his claim against determined opponents in Congress and the press. The president's effort to keep the nation neutral during the European-wide war that began after the French Revolution caused considerable controversy over the executive's power to set foreign policy, and led to the greatest crisis of his presidency (see Chapter 4). At times during his second term, it seemed that Washington might lose hold of foreign affairs and be forced to surrender his favored policy of neutrality. Ultimately, however, he prevailed, and set forth in his Farewell Address (see Document 1.12) what he hoped would be principles of the conduct of foreign policy for the nation's foreseeable future. "Observe good faith and justice toward all nations. Cultivate peace and harmony with all." Such conduct, Washington intoned, is surely enjoined by morality and religion, and what morality and religion enjoin must be good policy. Moreover, it would, the president noted, be a remarkable, indeed novel, thing for the nation to set an example for the world of benevolence and magnanimity in its foreign relations.

To implement a policy of magnanimity and benevolence, the nation would have to harbor no "inveterate antipathies against particular nations and passionate attachments for others." "How many opportunities do they [such attachments and antipathies] afford to tamper with domestic factions, to practice the arts of seduction, to mislead public opinion, to influence or awe the public councils!" Finally, Washington pointed out the underlying principle to be followed by the United States in relations with foreign nations: "in extending our commercial relations to have with them as little *political* connection as possible."

Washington's Farewell Address was an emotional document. Nowhere else in Washington's public papers from his presidency did he positively plead with his countrymen that they heed his advice. That in leaving office Washington should be so passionate about an impassionate foreign policy is understandable in light of the president's difficult experience in the conduct of the nation's foreign policy toward the European powers (see Chapter 4).

BIBLIOGRAPHIC ESSAY

The correspondence of the president from this period is to be found in John C. Fitzpatrick, ed., *The Writings of George Washington from the Original Manuscript Sources, 1745–1799,* 39 vols. (Washington, D.C.: Government Printing Office, 1931–1944). James D. Richardson, comp., *Messages and Papers of the Presidents,* 20 vols. (New York: Bureau of National Literature, 1897), conveniently offers in volume 1 a collection of the president's official documents. Richardson's encyclopedic indexes in volumes 19 and 20 also are highly useful.

Standard biographies cover the policies of the Washington administration in detail, including those by James Thomas Flexner: *George Washington and the New Nation* (Boston: Little, Brown, 1970); *George Washington:*

Anguish and Farewell (1972); and *Washington: The Indispensable Man* (1974). Also see Willard Sterne Randall, *George Washington: A Life* (New York: Henry Holt, 1997). The semibiographical work by Forrest McDonald, *The American Presidency: An Intellectual History* (Lawrence: University Press of Kansas, 1995), is also worth consulting for information on presidential policies of the Washington administration.

A very concise guide to the Constitution is that by Floyd G. Cullop, *The Constitution of the United States: An Introduction, Revised and Updated* (New York: Mentor, 1984). An excellent source of historical data on the early American government is that by Thomas L. Purvis, ed., *Revolutionary America, 1763–1800* (New York: Facts on File, 1995).

On the life of L'Enfant, the most recent source is unfortunately more than fifty years old: Hans Paul Caemmerer, *The Life of Pierre Charles L'Enfant, Planner of the City Beautiful, the City of Washington* (Washington, D.C.: National Republic Publishing, 1950). James Sterling Young, *The Washington Community, 1800–1828* (New York: Harvest, 1966), analyzes L'Enfant's design and how it shaped as well as reflected the behavior of early members of the government.

The design of the capital is but one topic in the impressive geographic history of the United States by D. W. Meinig, *The Shaping of America: A Geographical Perspective on 500 Years of History,* Vol. 1, *Atlantic America, 1492–1800* (New Haven: Yale University Press, 1986).

On the military history of the early Republic, see: Allan R. Millett and Peter Maslowski, *For the Common Defense: A Military History of the United States of America,* rev. and expanded (New York: Free Press, 1994), which is the single best one-volume history of the U.S. military in war and peace. Also see Geoffrey Perret, *A Country Made by War* (New York: Vintage, 1989), which covers much of the same ground but with a less scholarly treatment; and two specialized books: Edward M. Coffman, *The Old Army: A Portrait of the American Army in Peacetime, 1784–1898* (New York: Oxford University Press, 1986); and Francis Paul Prucha, *The Sword of the Republican, The United States Army on the Frontier, 1783–1846* (London: Collier-Macmillan, 1969). Wiley Sword, *President Washington's Indian War: The Struggle for the Old Northwest, 1790–1795* (Norman: University of Oklahoma Press, 1985), covers in detail the three expeditions that Washington sent to the Northwest. Richard Kohn, a leading military historian, presents a detailed account of Washington's role in the creation of a sound military policy in *Eagle and Sword: The Federalists and the*

Creation of the Military Establishment in America, 1783–1802 (New York: Free Press, 1975).

Document 3.1   Assuming the States' War Debts
This report of a special committee of the U.S. Senate served as the foundation for the funding bill passed on August 4, 1790. The report's language was formal and technical, but its meaning was revolutionary: the enormous war debts of the states were to be assumed by the federal government, which would redeem certificates of indebtedness from the various states "upon the same terms as in respect to the loans which may be proposed concerning the domestic debt of the United States" as a whole.

In Senate, July the 12th, 1790;

WHEREAS a provision for the debt of the respective States by the United States, would be greatly conducive to an orderly, economical and effectual arrangement of the public finances—would tend to an equal distribution of burthens among the citizens of the several States—would promote more general justice to the different classes of public creditors, and would serve to give stability to public credit: And whereas the said debts having been essentially contracted in the prosecution of the late war, it is just that such provision should be made.

Resolved, That a loan be proposed, to the amount of twenty-one million of dollars, and that subscriptions to the said loan be received at the same times and places, by the same persons, and upon the same terms as in respect to the loans which may be proposed concerning the domestic debt of the United States, subject to the exceptions and qualifications hereafter mentioned.—And the sums which shall be subscribed to the said loan, shall be payable in the principal and interest of the certificates or notes, which, prior to the first day of January last, were issued by the respective States, as acknowledgements or evidences of debts by them respectively owing, and which shall appear by oath or affirmation (as the case may be) to have been the property of an individual or individuals, or body politic, other than a State, on the said first day of January last.—Provided, that no greater sum shall be received in the certificates of any State, than as follows—That is to say,

	Dollars.
In those of New-Hampshire,	300,000
In those of Massachusetts,	4,000,000
In those of Rhode-Island and Providence Plantations,	200,000
In those of Connecticut,	1,600,000
In those of New-York,	1,200,000
In those of New-Jersey,	800,000
In those of Pennsylvania,	2,200,000
In those of Delaware,	200,000
In those of Maryland,	800,000
In those of Virginia,	3,200,000
In those of North-Carolina,	2,200,000
In those of South-Carolina,	4,000,000
In those of Georgia,	300,000
	21,00,000

And provided that no such certificate shall be received which from the tenor thereof or from any public record, act or document, shall appear or can be ascertained to have been issued for any purpose other than compensations and expenditures for services or supplies towards the prosecution of the late war, and the defence of the United States, or of some part thereof during the same.

Resolved, That the interest upon the certificates which shall be received in payment of the sums subscribed towards the said loan, shall be computed to the last day of the year one thousand seven hundred and ninety-one inclusively; and the interest upon the stock which shall be created by virtue of the said loan, shall commence or begin to accrue on the first day of the year one thousand seven hundred and ninety-two, and shall be payable quarter yearly, at the same time, and in like manner as the interest on the stock to be created by virtue of the loan that may be proposed in the domestick debt of the United States.

Resolved, That if the whole of the sum allowed to be subscribed in the debt or certificates of any State, as aforesaid, shall not be subscribed within the time for that purpose limited, such State shall be entitled to receive, and shall receive from the United States, at the rate of four per centum per annum, upon so much of the said sum as shall not have been so subscribed, in trust for the non subscribing creditors of such State; to be paid in like manner as the interest on the stock which may be created by virtue of the said loan, and to continue until there shall be a settlement of accounts between the United States and the individual States; and in case a balance shall then appear in favor of such State, until provision shall be made for the said balance.

But as certain States have respectively issued their own certificates, in exchange for those of the United States, whereby it might happen that interest might be twice payable on the same sums:

Resolved, That the payment of interest, whether to States or to individuals, in respect to the debt of any State, by which such exchange shall have been made, shall be suspended, until it shall appear to the satisfaction of the Secretary of the Treasury, that certificates issued for that purpose, by such State, have been re-exchanged or redeemed, or until those which shall not have been re-exchanged or redeemed, shall be surrendered to the United States.

And it is further,

Resolved, That the faith of the United States be, and the same is hereby pledged to make like provision for the payment of interest on the amount of the stock arising from subscriptions to the said loan, with the provision which shall be made touching the loan that may be proposed in the domestic debt of the United States; and so much of the debt of each State as shall be subscribed to the said loan, shall be a charge against such State, in account with the United States.

Source: Senate Committee Report, 1st Cong., 2d sess., July 12, 1790.

Document 3.2   Anonymous Public Letter, September 6, 1789

Selecting a location for the capital city was the first highly divisive issue debated before Congress. Some members feared that the factionalism bred by this issue could threaten the integrity of the new government before it was in full operation. The letter reproduced here was written anonymously by a Massachusetts congressman on September 6, 1789, and was printed one week later in the Salem-Mercury *newspaper.*

The perplexing and unseasonable subject of a permanent residence for Congress, has engrossed our attention for three days past, and we have not as yet come to an [illegible] on the question. Some time since, when an assignment for taking up this business was in contemplation, the whole of the eastern members pressed a postponement in order to accomplish the necessary business for putting the government into complete operation; but this was rejected by our southern brethren, from a fond persuasion that there existed between them & the Pennsylvania members so good an understanding, as by giving to Philadelphia the temporary residence of Congress, they should in concert be able to effect its permanent residence on the Potowmack. Being thus circumstanced, we were compelled to consult together, & be prepared to meet what was our ardent wish to avoid [illegible], and came forward with a proposition for fixing the temporary residence in this city, & the permanent residence on the east bank of Susquehanna: This proposition, founded, as we conceived, upon national and accommodating principles, has broken up the plan which first gave rise to this business, and left the advocates for the paradise of the Potowmack chagrined & disappointed and who in turn have become the supplicants for a postponement, to prevent the doors being ever shut against them for again renewing the attempt of their favourite object. For my own part, I believe it would have been hapy, if this Constitution had never held up the idea of a permanent residence, but had left it to have lighted upon the spot which, time and experience should have directed: But in as mach as a permanent residential fever prevails in those States where there is any probability Congress may finally rest, I think we shall be ever tormented with this contentious question, until it is ultimately decided on, and taking things as they are, perhaps sooner the better—at least after the government is in full operation.

Source: Salem Mercury, September 15, 1789. Transcribed from original document at the Library of Congress.

Document 3.3   Establishing the Seat of the Federal Government

Article I, Section 8, of the U.S. Constitution states that Congress has the power "to exercise exclusive Legislation in all Cases whatsoever, over such District (not exceeding ten Miles square) as may, by Cession of particular States, and the Acceptance of Congress, become the Seat of the Government of the United States." On July 16, 1790, the new government made use of this authority and overcame the first of two highly divisive issues that threatened the Union.

An Act for establishing the temporary and permanent Seat of the Government of the United States.

SECTION 1. Be it enacted by the Senate and House of Representatives of the United States of America in Congress assembled, That a district of territory, not exceeding ten miles square, to be located as here-after directed on the River Potomac at some place between the mouths of the Eastern branch and Connogochegue be, and the same is hereby accepted for the permanent Seat of the Government of the United States. Provided nevertheless, that the operation of the laws of the State within such district shall not be affected by this acceptance, until the time fixed for the removal of the government thereto, and until Congress shall otherwise by law provide.

SEC. 2. And be it further enacted, That the President of the United States be authorized to appoint, and by supplying vacancies happening from refusals to act or other causes, to keep in appointment as long as may be necessary, three Commissioners, who, or any two of whom, shall, under the direction of the President, survey, and by proper metes and bounds define and limit a district of territory, under the limitations above mentioned; and the district so defined, limited and located, shall be deemed the district accepted by this act, for the permanent seat of the government of the United States.

SEC. 3. And be it [further] enacted, That the said commissioners, or any two of them, shall have power to purchase or accept such quantity of land on the eastern side of the said River, within the said district, as the President shall deem proper for the use of the United States, and according to such plans as the President shall approve, the said commissioners, or any two of them, shall, prior to the first Monday in December, in the year one thousand eight hundred, provide suitable buildings for the accommodation of Congress, and of the President, and for the public Offices of the government of the United States.

SEC. 4. And be it [further] enacted, That for defraying the expense of such purchases and buildings, the President of the United States be authorized and requested to accept grants of money.

SEC. 5. And be it [further] enacted, That prior to the first Monday in December next, all offices attached to the seat of the government of the United States, shall be removed to, and until the said first Monday in December, in the year one thousand eight hundred, shall remain at the

City of Philadelphia, in the State of Pennsylvania, at which place the Session of Congress next ensuing the present shall be held.

SEC. 6. And be it [further] enacted, That on the said first Monday in December, in the year one thousand eight hundred, the seat of the government of the United States shall, by virtue of this Act, be transferred to the district and place aforesaid. And all Offices attached to the said seat of government, shall accordingly be removed thereto by their respective holders, and shall, after the said day, cease to be exercised elsewhere; and that the necessary expense of such removal shall be defrayed out of the duties on imposts and tonnage, of which a sufficient sum is hereby appropriated.

Approved, July 16, 1790.

Source: Act of July 16, 1790, Chapter 28, 1st Cong., 2d sess. Printed by authority of Congress in: Richard Peters, ed., The Public Statutes at Large of the United States of America, from the Organization of the Government in 1789, to March 3, 1845, Vol. 1 (Boston: Charles C. Little and James Brown, 1845), 130.

Document 3.4   Washington to Daniel Carroll, November 28, 1791

Daniel Carroll of Duddington, the nephew of Daniel Carroll of Rock Creek, one of the three commissioners for the creation of the Federal City, owned more land in the capital city than any other person. After he began construction of a home on one of his parcels of land, Maj. Pierre Charles L'Enfant decided to situate the Capitol at the same location and informed Carroll that his house must be demolished. Carroll took his protest to the president. This is Washington's reply.

Sir: Your letter of the 21st. came to my hands on thursday afternoon. By the Post of next morning I was unable to answer it; and this is the first opportunity that has offered since by wch. it cd. be done.

It would have been better, and given me more satisfaction if you had made your appeal to the Commissioners; to whom all matters respecting the Federal district and City are now committed; but as you have made it to me, I must furnish you with my opinion; and reasons for it.

First then, permit me to regret, and I do it sincerely, that the dispute between the public and yourself is brought to the point, at which it now stands. But what practicable relief remains for you? I see none. You say yourself if the House is a nuisance you agree to its being pulled down. a simple fact decides the question upon your own principles. viz. is the whole, or part of it in the Street? If the answer is in the affirmative, it is unquestionably a nuisance. 1st., because the Street is injured by it; 2dly., because the regulations are infringed; and 3dly., which indeed may be considered as the primary reason, because the original compact is violated.

You add, that other Houses have fallen in the Streets and are suffered to remain: but does it follow from hence that they are to continue in the Streets? and is there not a wide difference between a House built, and a house building? the first has already incurred all the expence that is necessary to make it habitable; therefore the public will have no more, perhaps not so much, to pay for it 3, 5, or 7 years hence as now; and the possessor may enjoy the benefit of it in the interim: but would that be the case with a House not covered in, and which, to make inhabitable, will require a considerable additional expence? Who is to bear this expence when a removal (for a House never will be suffered to obstruct a Street, and a principal street too) takes place? Would you not complain more 5, or even 7 years hence at being obliged to pull down your new building after having incurred (at your own expence) a large additional sum in the completion, than to do it now when the Walls only are up? The answer in my opinion is plain; but, in the present state of the building, under the existing circumstances, as there appears to have been some misconception between Majr. L'Enfant and you in this business; I am inclined, in behalf of the public, to offer you the choice of two alternatives: first, to arrest and pull down the building in its present state, and raise it to the same height next Spring, if it is your desire, agreeably to the regulations wch. have been established without any expence to you; or, 2dly. to permit you to finish it at your own cost, and occupy it 6 years from the present date; at which period it must be removed, with no other allowance from the public than a valuation for the Walls in the present state of them. I am etc.

Source: John C. Fitzpatrick, ed., *The Writings of George Washington from the Original Manuscript Sources, 1745–1799,* 39 vols. (Washington, D.C.: Government Printing Office, 1931–1944), 31:429–430.

Document 3.5   Washington to Pierre Charles L'Enfant, December 2, 1791

On November 25, 1791, the commissioners wrote George Washington with urgent news. L'Enfant had dispensed with all legal formalities and simply demolished the home of Daniel Carroll of Duddington. The president responded to the commissioners, claiming his innocence in the matter and hinting that the major may have overestimated his indispensability. "His value to us," the president commented, "has its limits" (Washington to the Commissioners for the District of Columbia, December 1, 1791, in Mastromarino and Warren 2000, 242). In this letter to L'Enfant, the president places the urban planner on notice.

Dear Sir:

I have received with sincere concern the information from yourself as well as others, that you have proceeded to demolish the house of Mr. Carroll of Duddington, against his consent, and without authority from the Commissioners or any other person. In this you have laid yourself open to the Laws, and in a Country where they will have their course. To their animadversion will belong the present case. In future I must strictly enjoin you to touch no man's property without his consent, or the previous order of the Commissioners. I wished you to be employed in the arrangements of the Federal City: I still wish it: but only on condition that you tend to, some of which, perhaps, may be unknown to you; Commissioners (to whom by law the business is entrusted, and who stands between you and the President of the United States) to the laws of the land, and to the rights of its citizens. Your precipitate conduct will, it is to be apprehended, give serious alarm and produce disagreeable consequences. Having the beauty, and regularity of your Plan only in view, you pursue it as if every person, and thing was obliged to yield to it; whereas the Commissioners have many circumstances to attend to, some of which, perhaps, may be unknown to you; which evinces in a strong point of view the propriety, the neccessity and even the safety of your acting by their directions. I have said, and I repeat it to you again, that it is my firm belief that the Gentlemen now in Office have favorable dispositions towards you, and in all things reasonable and proper, will receive, and give full weight to your opinions; and ascribing to your Zeal the mistakes that have happened, I persuade myself, under this explanation of matters, that nothing in future will intervene to disturb the harmony which ought to prevail in so interesting a work. With sincere esteem etc.

Source: John C. Fitzpatrick, ed., *The Writings of George Washington from the Original Manuscript Sources, 1745–1799,* 39 vols. (Washington, D.C.: Government Printing Office, 1931–1944), 31:434–435.

Document 3.6   Second Annual Address, December 8, 1790

President Washington reported to Congress in this address his pleasure at the recently approved legislation for the assumption of states' debts. He also communicated to the House and Senate the good news that Kentucky's accession to the Union was imminent, "in case the requisite sanction of Congress be added." Two lengthy paragraphs in this address are devoted to the less happy situation the nation faced in the vast territory to the northwest of the Ohio River. In this document, Washington dared not mention the British threat in the region. If he had done so and then failed to defeat the British-allied Indians in the region, he would only have underscored the weakness of his government.

Fellow-Citizens of the Senate and House of Representatives:

In meeting you again I feel much satisfaction in being able to repeat my congratulations on the favorable prospects which continue to distinguish our public affairs. The abundant fruits of another year have blessed our country with plenty and with the means of a flourishing commerce. The progress of public credit is witnessed by a considerable rise of American stock abroad as well as at home, and the revenues allotted for this and other national purposes have been productive beyond the calculations by which they were regulated. This latter circumstance is the more pleasing, as it is not only a proof of the fertility of our resources, but as it assures us of a further increase of the national respectability and credit, and, let me add, as it bears an honorable testimony to the patriotism and integrity of the mercantile and marine part of our citizens. The punctuality of the former in discharging their engagements has been exemplary.

In conformity to the powers vested in me by acts of the last session, a loan of 3,000,000 florins, toward which some provisional measures had previously taken place, has been completed in Holland. As well the celerity with which it has been filled as the nature of the terms (considering the more than ordinary demand for borrowing created by the situation of Europe) give a reasonable hope that the further execution of those powers may proceed with advantage and success. The Secretary of the Treasury has my directions to communicate such further particulars as may be requisite for more precise information.

Since your last session I have received communications by which it appears that the district of Kentucky, at present a part of Virginia, has concurred in certain propositions contained in a law of that State, in consequence of which the district is to become a distinct member of the Union, in case the requisite sanction of Congress be added. For this sanction application is now made. I shall cause the papers on this very important transaction be laid before you. The liberality and harmony with which the parties, and the sentiments of warm attachment to the Union and its present Government expressed by our fellow-citizens of Kentucky can not fail to add an affectionate concern for their particular welfare to the great national impressions under which you will decide on the case submitted to you.

It has been heretofore known to Congress that frequent incursions have been made on our frontier settlements by certain banditti of Indians from the northwest side of the Ohio. These, with some of the tribes dwelling on and near the Wabash, have of late been particularly active in their depredations, and being emboldened by the impunity of their crimes and aided by such parts of the neighboring tribes as could be seduced to join in their hostilities or afford them a retreat for their prisoners and plunder, they have, instead of listening to the humane invitations and overtures made on the part of the United States, renewed their violences with fresh alacrity and greater effect. The lives of a number of valuable citizens have thus been sacrificed, and some of them under circumstances peculiarly shocking, whilst others have been carried into a deplorable captivity.

These aggravated provocations rendered it essential to the safety of the Western settlements that the aggressors should be made sensible that the Government of the Union is not less capable of punishing their crimes than it is disposed to respect their rights and reward their attachments. As this object could not be effected by defensive measures, it became necessary to put in force the act which empowers the President to call out the militia for the protection of the frontiers, and I have accordingly authorized an expedition in which the regular troops in that quarter are combined with such drafts of militia as were deemed sufficient. The event of the measure is yet unknown to me. The Secretary of War is directed to lay before you a statement of the information on which it is founded, as well as an estimate of the expense with which it will be attended.

The disturbed situation of Europe, and particularly the critical posture of the great maritime powers, whilst it ought to make us the more thankful for the general peace and security enjoyed by the United States, reminds us at the same time of the circumspection with which it becomes us to preserve these blessings. It requires also that we should not overlook the tendency of a war, and even of preparations for a war, among the nations most concerned in active commerce with this country to abridge the means, and thereby at least enhance the price, of transporting its valuable productions to their proper markets. I recommend it to your serious reflections how far and in what mode it may be expedient to guard against embarrassments from these contingencies by such encouragements to our own navigation as will render our commerce and agriculture less dependent on foreign bottoms, which may fail us in the very moments most interesting to both of these great objects. Our fisheries and the transportation of our own produce offer us abundant means for guarding ourselves against this evil.

Your attention seems to be not less due to that particular branch of our trade which belongs to the Mediterranean. So many circumstances unite in rendering the present state of it distressful to us that you will not think any deliberations misemployed which may lead to its relief and protection. . . .

Go. Washington

Source: James D. Richardson, comp., Messages and Papers of the Presidents, 20 vols. (New York: Bureau of National Literature, 1897), 1:73–75.

Document 3.7   Brig. Gen. Josiah Harmar's Treatment of the Miami Indians

In 1790 Brig. Gen. Josiah Harmar, a lifelong military officer, was directed to punish bands of raiding Indians and establish military bases on the Ohio frontier. To the satisfaction of his government, Harmar's troops burned villages and destroyed 20,000 bushels of corn. In doing so, however, the Americans encountered resistance that forced them to retreat on October 22 to Fort Washington (Cincinnati). Under the leadership of Little Turtle, chief of the

Miami tribe, a group of Indians carried out a devastating ambush that killed forty-eight soldiers and two officers of Harmar's meager force. This account of the expedition was related by Capt. Joseph Asheton to a court of inquiry. Two key points addressed in this document are Harmar's fragmentation of his force and the lack of discipline of the militiamen.

Captain Asheton being sworn, deposed—That the organization of General Harmar's army was a source of trouble and difficulty, arising from disputes among the militia officers for precedency; but when effected, was in all its parts systematical . . . the motives which influenced the detachments of the 14th, 19th, and 21st October, could only be accounted for by the General himself: but he supposed, that the detachment under Col. Hardin, was sent in consequence of information gained from a prisoner taken on the morning of the 13th, and from a Frenchman employed as a guide. . . . "On the morning of the 18th, I mounted guard in front of the encampmed. In the course of that day, I was informed that a detachment of 300 men was ordered out under Colonel Trotter, with three days provision, with order to scour the country; but they returned the same evening to camp, without effecting any thing. Colonel Hardin, disgusted at the conduct of Colonel Trotter, and anxious to retrieve the lost honour of his countrymen, solicited the same command, which was granted. He marched on the morning of the 19th, while he was yet on guard, and was defeated the same day by the Indians." He could not say what influenced the General to send out a detachment on the 21st, but he observed that the Indians were flushed with success in the action of the 19th.—That it had become necessary to give them a sudden check, in order to prevent the army from being harassed on its return; and that if this was the General's intention, he was fully persuaded it had its desired effect. . . .The detachment marched in three columns, the federal troops in the centre, at the head of which he was posted, with Major Wyllys and Colonel Hardin in his front—the militia formed the columns to the right and left. From several delays, occasioned by the militia's halting, they did not reach the banks of the Omee till some time after sun rise. The spies then discovered the enemy, and reported to Major Wyllys, who halted the federal troops, and moved the militia on some distance in front, where he gave his orders and plan of attack to the several commanding officers of the corps. . . . After the attack commenced, the troops were by no means to separate, but were to embody, or that battalions to support each other as circumstances required. From the disposition it appeared evidence, that it was the intention of Major Wyllys to surround the enemy, and that if Colonel Hall, who had gained his ground undiscovered, had not wantonly disobeyed his orders, by firing on a single Indian, the surprise must have been complete. The Indians then fled with precipitation, the battalions of militia pursuing in different directions. Major Fontaine made a charge upon a small party of Savages; he fell in the first fire, and his troops dispersed. The federal troops who were then left unsupported, became an easy sacrifice to much the largest party of Indians that had been seen that day. It was his opinion that the misfortunes of that day, were owing to the separation of the troops, and disobedience of orders. . . . He was convinced that the detachment, if it had been kept embodied, was sufficient to have answered the fullest expectations of the General, and needed no support; but that he was informed a battalion under Major Ray, was ordered out for that purpose.

Question. By the Court. Is it your opinion, that if the General had ordered the army back, that the militia would have gone?

Answer. I do not think they would.

Source: *The Proceedings of a Court of Enquiry, Held at the Special Request of Brigadier General Josiah Harmar, to Investigate His Conduct, as Commanding Officer of the Expedition Against the Miami Indians, 1790: The same having been transmitted to Major General St. Clair, to the Secretary of the United States, for the Department of War* (Philadelphia: John Fenno, 1791), 19–20.

Document 3.8   Maj. Gen. Anthony Wayne to Secretary of War Henry Knox, August 28, 1794

After two failed expeditions to the Northwest Territory, President Washington turned to Maj. Gen. Anthony Wayne, a Revolutionary War officer with a distinguished military record. Wayne succeeded St. Clair as commander in chief of the army. Heeding Washington's advice, Wayne relied heavily on scouts to prevent an ambush. On August 20, 1794, he won a decisive victory in the Battle of Fallen Timbers.

Sir: It's with infinite pleasure that I now announce to you the brilliant success of the Federal army under my Command in a General action with the combined force of the Hostile Indians & a considerable number of the

Volunteers & Militia of Detroit on the 20th Instant, on the banks of the Miamis, in the vicinity of the British post & Garrison at the foot of the rapids.

The army advanced from this place on the 15th & arrived at Roche de Bout, on the 18th. The 19th we were employed in making a temporary post for the reception of our stores & baggage, & in reconnoitring the position of the enemy who were encamped behind a thick brushy wood and the British Fort. [The "temporary post" was Fort Deposit.]

At 8. Oclock on the morning of the 20th the army again advanced in Columns agreeably to the standing order of March—the legion on the right, its right flank cover'd by the Miamis, One Brigade of Mounted Volunteers on the left, under Brigr General Todd, & the other in the rear under Brigr Genl Barbee, a select Battalion of Mounted Volunteers moved in front of the Legion commanded by Major Price, who was directed to keep sufficiently advanced, so as to give timely notice for the troops to form in case of Action.

It being yet undetermined whether the Indians wou'd decide on peace or war:

After advancing about Five miles, Major Price's corps received so severe a fire from the enemy, who were secreted in the woods & high grass, as to compel them to retreat.

The Legion was immediately formed in two lines principally in a close thick wood which extended for miles on our left & for a very considerable distance in front; the ground being cover'd with old fallen timber probably occasioned by a tornado, which render'd it impracticable for the Cavalry to act with effect, & afforded the enemy the most favorable covert for their mode of warfare these savages were formed in three lines within supporting distance of each other & extending near two miles at right angles with the River. I soon discover'd from the weight of the fire, & and extent of their Lines that the enemy were in full force in front in possession of their favorite ground & endeavoring to turn our left flank, I therefore gave orders for the second line to advance and support the first, and directed Major Genl Scott to gain & turn the right flank of the savages with the whole of the Mounted Volunteers by a circuitous route, at the same time I ordered the front line to advance & charge with trailed arms & rouse the Indians from their coverts at the point of the bayonet, & when up to deliver a close & well directed fire on their backs followed by a br[i]sk charge, so as not to give time to load again. I also order'd Captain Mis

Campbell who commanded the Legionary Cavalry to turn the left flank of the Enemy next the river & which afforded a favorable field for that corps to act in.

All those orders were obeyed with spirit & promptitude, but such was the impetuosity of the charge by the first line of Infantry—that the Indians & Canadian Militia & Volunteers were drove from all their Coverts in so short a time, that altho every possible exertion was used by the Officers of the second line of the Legion, & by Generals Scott, Todd & Barbee of the Mounted Volunteers, to gain their proper position's but part of each cou'd get up in season to participate in the Action; the enemy being drove in the course of One hour, more than two miles thro' the thick woods already mentioned, by less than one half their Numbers, from Every account the Enemy amounted to two thousand combatants, the troops actually engaged against them were short of nine hundred; [author's note: The handwriting is illegible; the best guess is "this horde of"] Savages with their allies abandoned themselves to flight & dispersed with terror & dismay, leaving our victorious army in full & quiet possession of the field of battle, which terminated under the influence of the Guns of the British garrison, as you will observe by the enclosed correspondence between Major Campbell the Commandant & myself upon the Occasion.

The bravery & conduct of every officer belonging to the Army from the generals down to the ensigns, merit my highest approbation. . . .

Enclosed is a particular return of the killed & Wounded—the loss of the Enemy was more that [author's note: than] double to that of the Federal army—the woods were strewed for a considerable distance with the dead bodies of Indians & their white auxiliaries, the latter armed with British Muskets & bayonets.

After remaining three days & nights on the banks of the Miamis in front of the Field of battle during which time all the Houses & Corn fields were consumed & destroyed for a considerable distance both above & below Fort Miamis, as well as within pistol shot of the Garrison who were compelled to remain tacit spectators to this general devastation & Conflagration, among which were the Houses stores & property of Colo Mckee the British Indian Agent & principal stimulator of the war now existing between the United States & the savages.

The army returned to this place on the 27th by easy marches laying waste the Villages & Corn fields for about Fifty miles on eachs side of the Miamis. . . .

Under those Impressions I have the honor to be Your Most Obt & very Huml Sert.

Anty Wayne

Source: Anthony Wayne, *A Name in Arms: Soldier, Diplomat, Defender of Expansion Westward of a Nation, The Wayne-Knox-Pickering-McHenry Correspondence,* trans. and ed. Richard C. Knopf (Pittsburgh: University of Pittsburgh Press, 1960), 351–355.

Document 3.9   Treaty of Greenville, August 3, 1795

After the Battle of Fallen Timbers, Maj. Gen. Anthony Wayne proceeded to burn several Indian villages and crop fields to prevent the Native Americans from returning to the American frontier. Defeated and demoralized, those northwest of the Ohio River acquiesced to the expansionist policy of the Americans. In Article 4 of this treaty, the United States asserts a willingness to respect new boundaries beyond which American settlers would penetrate at their own risk. In reality, the treaty "decisively opened for development" the upper half of the American West and "ended Indian hope of holding the Americans to the Ohio River" (Meinig 1986, 354).

A treaty of peace between the United States of America, and the tribes of Indians called the Wyandots, Delawares, Shawanees, Ottawas, Chippewas, Pattawatimas, Miamis, Eel Rivers, Weas, Kickapoos, Piankeshaws, and Kaskaskias.

To put an end to a destructive war, to settle all controversies, and to restore harmony and friendly intercourse between the said United States and Indian tribes, Anthony Wayne, major general commanding the army of the United States, and sole commissioner for the good purposes above mentioned, and the said tribes of Indians, by their sachems, chiefs, and warriors, met together at Greenville, the head quarters of the said army, have agreed on the following articles, which, when ratified by the President, with the advice and consent of the Senate of the United States, shall be binding on them and the said Indian tribes.

Art. 1: Henceforth all hostilities shall cease; peace is hereby established, and shall be perpetual; and a friendly intercourse shall take place between the said United States and Indian tribes.

Art. 2: All prisoners shall, on both sides, be restored. The Indians, prisoners to the United States, shall be immediately set at liberty. The people of the United States, still remaining prisoners among the Indians, shall be delivered up in ninety days from the date hereof, to the general or commanding officer at Greenville, fort Wayne, or fort Defiance; and ten chiefs of the said tribes shall remain at Greenville as hostages, until the delivery of the prisoners shall be effected. . . .

Art. 4: In consideration of the peace now established, and of the cessions and relinquishments of lands made in the preceding article by the said tribes of Indians, and to manifest the liberality of the United States, as the great means of rendering this peace strong and perpetual, the United States relinquish their claims to all other Indian lands northward of the river Ohio, eastward of the Mississippi, and westward and southward of the Great Lakes and the waters, uniting them, according to the boundary line agreed on by the United States and the King of Great Britain, in the treaty of peace made between them in the year 1783. . . .

And for the same considerations and with the same views as above mentioned, the United States now deliver to the said Indian tribes a quantity of goods to the value of twenty thousand dollars, the receipt whereof they do hereby acknowledge; and henceforward every year, forever, the United States will deliver, at some convenient place northward of the river Ohio, like useful goods, suited to the circumstances of the Indians, of the value of nine thousand five hundred dollars; reckoning that value at the first cost of the goods in the city or place in the United States where they shall be procured. The tribes to which those goods are to be annually delivered, and the proportions in which they are to be delivered, are the following:

1st. To the Wyandots, the amount of one thousand dollars.

2nd. To the Delawares, the amount of one thousand dollars.

3rd. To the Shawanees, the amount of one thousand dollars.

4th. To the Miamis, the amount of one thousand dollars.

5th. To the Ottawas, the amount of one thousand dollars.

6th. To the Chippewas, the amount of one thousand dollars.

7th. To the Pattawatimas, the amount of one thousand dollars, and

8th. To the Kickapoo, Wea, Eel River, Piankeshaw, and Kaskaskia tribes, the amount of five hundred dollars each.

Provided, that if either of the said tribes shall hereafter, at an annual delivery of their share of the goods aforesaid, desire that a part of their annuity should be furnished in domestic animals, implements of husbandry, and other utensils convenient for them, and in compensation to useful artificers who may reside with or near them, and be employed for their benefit, the same shall, at the subsequent annual deliveries, be furnished accordingly.

Art. 5: To prevent any misunderstanding about the Indian lands relinquished by the United States in the fourth article, it is now explicitly declared, that the meaning of that relinquishment is this: the Indian tribes who have a right to those lands, are quietly to enjoy them, hunting, planting, and dwelling thereon, so long as they please, without any molestation from the United States; but when those tribes, or any of them, shall be disposed to sell their lands, or any part of them, they are to be sold only to the United States; and until such sale, the United States will protect all the said Indian tribes in the quiet enjoyment of their lands against all citizens of the United States, and against all other white persons who intrude upon the same. And the said Indian tribes again acknowledge themselves to be under the protection of the said United States, and no other power whatever.

Art. 6: If any citizen of the United States, or any other white person or persons, shall presume to settle upon the lands now relinquished by the United States, such citizen or other person shall be out of the protection of the United States; and the Indian tribe, on whose land the settlement shall be made, may drive off the settler, or punish him in such manner as they shall think fit; and because such settlements, made without the consent of the United States, will be injurious to them as well as to the Indians, the United States shall be at liberty to break them up, and remove and punish the settlers as they shall think proper, and so effect that protection of the Indian lands herein before stipulated.

Art. 7: The said tribes of Indians, parties to this treaty, shall be at liberty to hunt within the territory and lands which they have now ceded to the United States, without hindrance or molestation, so long as they demean themselves peaceably, and offer no injury to the people of the United States.

Art. 8: Trade shall be opened with the said Indian tribes; and they do hereby respectively engage to afford protection to such persons, with their property, as shall be duly licensed to reside among them for the purpose of trade; and to their agents and servants; but no person shall be permitted to reside among them for the purpose of trade; and to their agents and servants; but no person shall be permitted to reside at any of their towns or hunting camps, as a trader, who is not furnished with a license for that purpose, under the hand and seal of the superintendent of the department northwest of the Ohio, or such other person as the President of the United States shall authorize to grant such licenses; to the end, that the said Indians may not be imposed on in their trade. And if any licensed trader shall abuse his privilege by unfair dealing, upon complaint and proof thereof, his license shall be taken from him, and he shall be further punished according to the laws of the United States. And if any person shall intrude himself as a trader, without such license, the said Indians shall take and bring him before the superintendent, or his deputy, to be dealt with according to law. And to prevent impositions by forged licenses, the said Indians shall, at least once a year, give information to the superintendent, or his deputies, on the names of the traders residing among them.

Art. 9: Lest the firm peace and friendship now established, should be interrupted by the misconduct of individuals, the United States, and the said Indian tribes agree, that for injuries done by individuals on either side, no private revenge or retaliation shall take place; but instead thereof, complaint shall be made by the party injured, to the other: by the said Indian tribes or any of them, to the President of the United States, or the superintendent by him appointed; and by the superintendent or other person appointed by the President, to the principal chiefs of the said Indian tribes, or of the tribe to which the offender belongs; and such prudent measures shall then be taken as shall be necessary to preserve the said peace and friendship unbroken, until the legislature (or great council) of the United States, shall make other equitable provision in the case, to the satisfaction of both parties. Should any Indian tribes meditate a war against the United States, or either of them, and the same shall come to the knowledge of the before mentioned tribes, or either of them, they do hereby engage to give immediate notice thereof to the general, or officer commanding the troops of the United States, at the nearest post.

And should any tribe, with hostile intentions against the United States, or either of them, attempt to pass through their country, they will endeavor to prevent the same, and in like manner give information of such attempt, to the general, or officer commanding, as soon as possible, that all causes of mistrust and suspicion may be avoided between them and the United States. In like manner, the United States shall give notice to the said Indian tribes of any harm that may be meditated against them, or either of them, that shall come to their knowledge; and do all in their power to hinder and prevent the same, that the friendship between them may be uninterrupted.

Art. 10: All other treaties heretofore made between the United States, and the said Indian tribes, or any of them, since the treaty of 1783, between the United States and Great Britain, that come within the purview of this treaty, shall henceforth cease and become void.

In testimony whereof, the said Anthony Wayne, and the sachems and war chiefs of the before mentioned nations and tribes of Indians, have hereunto set their hands and affixed their seals. Done at Greenville, in the territory of the United States northwest of the river Ohio, on the third day of August, one thousand seven hundred and ninety five. . . .

Source: Avalon Project, Yale Law School (*www.yale.edu/lawweb/avalon/greenvil. htm*).

Document 3.10   Washington on the Whiskey Rebellion, August 7, 1794

Under the Articles of Confederation, the national government had demonstrated fatal weakness when it failed to respond to a 1786 rebellion in western Massachusetts led by Daniel Shays. His "troops" pillaged militia storehouses and took possession of state courts. When protest against the federal excise tax on whiskey erupted into violent rebellion in the summer of 1794, Washington was determined that this time the government's response would be forceful. At the same time, as this proclamation demonstrates, Washington was at pains to justify any use of force he might decide on as fully warranted by events and sustained by congressional and constitutional law.

A PROCLAMATION

Whereas combinations to defeat the execution of the laws laying duties upon spirits distilled within the United States and upon stills have from the time of the commencement of those laws existed in some of the western parts of Pennsylvania.

And whereas, the said combinations, proceeding in a manner subversive equally of the just authority of government and of the rights of individuals, have hitherto effected their dangerous and criminal purpose by the influence of certain irregular meetings whose proceedings have tended to encourage and uphold the spirit of opposition by misrepresentations of the laws calculated to render them odious; by endeavors to deter those who might be so disposed from accepting offices under them through fear of public resentment and of injury to person and property, and to compel those who had accepted such offices by actual violence to surrender or forbear the execution of them; by circulation vindictive menaces against all those who should otherwise, directly or indirectly, aid in the execution of the said laws, or who, yielding to the dictates of conscience and to a sense of obligation, should themselves comply therewith; by actually injuring and destroying the property of persons who were understood to have so complied; by inflicting cruel and humiliating punishments upon private citizens for no other cause than that of appearing to be the friends of the laws; by intercepting the public officers on the highways, abusing, assaulting, and otherwise ill treating them; by going into their houses in the night, gaining admittance by force, taking away their papers, and committing other outrages, employing for these unwarrantable purposes the agency of armed banditti disguised in such manner as for the most part to escape discovery;

And whereas, the endeavors of the legislature to obviate objections to the said laws by lowering the duties and by other alterations conducive to the convenience of those whom they immediately affect (though they have given satisfaction in other quarters), and the endeavors of the executive officers to conciliate a compliance with the laws by explanations, by forbearance, and even by particular accommodations founded on the suggestion of local considerations, have been disappointed of their effect by the machinations of persons whose industry to excite resistance has increased with every appearance of a disposition among the people to relax in their opposition and to acquiesce in the laws, insomuch that many persons in the said western parts of Pennsylvania have at length been hardy enough to perpetrate acts, which I am advised amount to treason, being overt acts of levying war against the United States, the said persons having on the 16th and 17th of July last past proceeded in arms (on the second day amounting to several hundreds) to the house of John Neville, inspector of the revenue for the fourth survey of the district of Pennsylvania; having repeatedly attacked the said house with the persons therein, wounding some of them; having seized David Lenox, marshal of the district of Pennsylvania, who previous thereto had been fired upon while in the execution of his duty by a party of armed men, detaining him for some time prisoner, till, for the preservation of his life and the obtaining of his liberty, he found it necessary to enter into stipulations to forbear the execution of certain official duties touching processes issuing out of a court of the United States; and having finally obliged the said inspector of the revenue and the said marshal from considerations of personal safety to fly from that part of the country, in order, by a circuitous route, to proceed to the seat of government, avowing as the motives of these outrageous proceedings an intention to prevent by force of arms the execution of the said laws, to oblige the said inspector of the revenue to renounce his said office, to withstand by open violence the lawful authority of the government of the United States, and to compel thereby an alteration in the measures of the legislature and a repeal of the laws aforesaid;

And whereas, by a law of the United States entitled "An act to provide for calling forth the militia to execute the laws of the Union, suppress insurrections, and repel invasions," it is enacted that whenever the laws of the United States shall be opposed or the execution thereof obstructed in any state by combinations too powerful to be suppressed by the ordinary course of judicial proceedings or by the powers vested in the marshals by that act, the same being notified by an associate justice or the district judge, it shall be lawful for the President of the United States to call forth the militia of such state to suppress such combinations and to cause the laws to be duly executed. And if the militia of a state, when such combinations may happen, shall refuse or be insufficient to suppress the same, it shall be lawful for the President, if the legislature of the United States shall not be in session, to call forth and employ such numbers of the militia of any other state or states most convenient thereto as may be necessary; and the use of the militia so to be called forth may be continued, if necessary, until the expiration of thirty days after the commencement of the ensuing session; Provided always, that, whenever it may be necessary in the judgment of the President to use the military force hereby directed to be called forth, the President shall forthwith, and previous thereto, by proclamation, command such insurgents to disperse and retire peaceably to their respective abodes within a limited time;

And whereas, James Wilson, an associate justice, on the 4th instant, by writing under his hand, did from evidence which had been laid before him notify to me that "in the counties of Washington and Allegany, in Pennsylvania, laws of the United States are opposed and the execution thereof obstructed by combinations too powerful to be suppressed by the ordinary course of judicial proceedings or by the powers vested in the marshal of that district";

And whereas, it is in my judgment necessary under the circumstances of the case to take measures for calling forth the militia in order to suppress the combinations aforesaid, and to cause the laws to be duly executed; and I have accordingly determined so to do, feeling the deepest regret for the occasion, but withal the most solemn conviction that the essential interests of the Union demand it, that the very existence of government and the fundamental principles of social order are materially involved in the issue, and that the patriotism and firmness of all good citizens are seriously called upon, as occasions may require, to aid in the effectual suppression of so fatal a spirit;

Therefore, and in pursuance of the proviso above recited, I, George Washington, President of the United States, do hereby command all persons, being insurgents, as aforesaid, and all others whom it may concern, on or before the 1st day of September next to disperse and retire peaceably to their respective abodes. And I do moreover warn all persons whomsoever against aiding, abetting, or comforting the perpetrators of the aforesaid treasonable acts; and do require all officers and other citizens, according to their respective duties and the laws of the land, to exert their utmost endeavors to prevent and suppress such dangerous proceedings.

In testimony whereof I have caused the seal of the United States of America to be affixed to these presents, and signed the same with my hand. Done at the city of Philadelphia the seventh day of August, one thousand seven hundred and ninety-four, and of the independence of the United States of America the nineteenth.

G. WASHINGTON,
By the President,
Edm. Randolph

Source: Claypoole's Daily Advertiser, August 11, 1794, Library of Congress, Washington, D.C.

Document 3.11   Washington's Proclamation of September 25, 1794
Because the president's previous proclamation (Document 3.10) was ignored, he at last set in motion a force of militiamen to assert federal supremacy beyond the mountains.

A PROCLAMATION

Whereas from a hope that the combinations against the Constitution and laws of the United States in certain of the western counties of Pennsylvania would yield to time and reflection I thought it sufficient in the first instance rather to take measures for calling forth the militia than immediately to embody them, but the moment is now come when the overtures of forgiveness, with no other condition than a submission to law, have been only partially accepted; when every form of conciliation not inconsistent with the being of Government has been adopted without effect; when the well-disposed in those counties are unable by their influence and example to reclaim the wicked from their fury, and are compelled to associate in their own defense; when the proffered lenity has been perversely misinterpreted into an apprehension that the citizens will march with reluctance; when the opportunity of examining the serious consequences of a treasonable opposition has been employed in propagating principles of anarchy, endeavoring through emissaries to alienate the friends of order from its support, and inviting its enemies to perpetrate similar acts of insurrection; when it is manifest that violence would continue to be exercised upon every attempt to enforce the laws; when, therefore, Government is set at defiance, the contest being whether a small portion of the United States shall dictate to the whole Union, and, at the expense of those who desire peace, indulge a desperate ambition:

Now, therefore, I, George Washington, President of the United States, in obedience to that high and irresistible duty consigned to me by the Constitution "to take care that the laws be faithfully executed," deploring that the American name should be sullied by the outrages of citizens on their own Government, commiserating such as remain obstinate from delusion, but resolved, in perfect reliance on that gracious Providence which so signally displays its goodness towards this country, to reduce the refractory to a due subordination to the law, do hereby declare and make known that, with a satisfaction which can be equaled only by the merits of the militia summoned into service from the States of New Jersey, Pennsylvania, Maryland, and Virginia, I have received intelligence of their patriotic alacrity in obeying the call of the present, though painful, yet commanding necessity; that a force which, according to every reasonable expectation, is adequate to the exigency is already in motion to the scene of disaffection; that those who have confided or shall confide in the protection of Government shall meet full succor under the standard and from the arms of the United States; that those who, having offended against the laws, have since entitled themselves to indemnity will be treated with the most liberal good faith if they shall not have forfeited their claim by any subsequent conduct, and that instructions are given accordingly.

And I do moreover exhort all individuals, officers, and bodies of men to contemplate with abhorrence the measures leading directly or indirectly to those crimes which produce this resort to military coercion; to check in their respective spheres the efforts of misguided or designing men to substitute their misrepresentation in the place of truth and their discontents in the place of stable government, and to call to mind that, as the people of the United States have been permitted, under the Divine favor, in perfect freedom, after solemn deliberation, and in an enlightened age, to elect their own government, so will their gratitude for this inestimable blessing be best distinguished by firm exertions to maintain the Constitution and the laws.

And, lastly, I again warn all persons whomsoever and wheresoever not to abet, aid, or comfort the insurgents aforesaid, as they will answer the contrary at their peril; and I do also require all officers and other citizens, according to their several duties, as far as may be in their power, to bring under the cognizance of the laws all offenders in the premises.

In testimony whereof I have caused the seal of the United States of America to be affixed to these presents, and signed the same with my hand.

Done at the city of Philadelphia, the 25th day of September, 1794, and of the Independence of the United States of America the nineteenth.

G. Washington
By the President:

Source: Annals of Congress, 3d Cong., 1st sess., 1413–1415.

Document 3.12   Sixth Annual Address, November 19, 1794

The Whiskey Rebellion was not to Washington the tragicomedy it is sometimes portrayed as having been. Rather, it represented "crimes which reached the very existence of social order." When the militia army marched to quell the disturbance, Washington took personal command of the troops. Washington

knew that he was breaking with his own tradition by devoting so much atten-
tion in an annual address to a single issue, but he thought that events justi-
fied his decision. "I shall be more prolix in my speech to Congress," he fore-
warned John Jay, "on the commencement and progress of this insurrection,
than is usual in such an instrument, or, than I should have been, on any other
occasion: but, as numbers (at home and abroad) will hear of the insurrection,
and will read the speech, that may know nothing of the documents to which
it might refer, I conceived, it would be better to encounter the charge of pro-
lixity, by giving a cursory detail of facts . . . than to let it go naked into the
world, to be dressed up according to the fancy or the inclination of the read-
ers, or the policy of our enemies" (Washington to John Jay, November 1[–5],
1794, in Allen 1988, 604).

Fellow-Citizens of the Senate and of the House of Representatives:

When we call to mind the gracious indulgence of Heaven by which the American people became a nation; when we survey the general prosperity of our country, and look forward to the riches, power, and happiness to which it seems destined, with the deepest regret do I announce to you that during your recess some of the citizens of the United States have been found capable of an insurrection. It is due, however, to the character of our Government and to its stability, which can not be shaken by the enemies of order, freely to unfold the course of this event.

During the session of the year 1790 it was expedient to exercise the legislative power granted by the Constitution of the United States "to lay and collect excises." In a majority of the States scarcely an objection was heard to this mode of taxation. In some, indeed, alarms were at first conceived, until they were banished by reason and patriotism. In the four western counties of Pennsylvania a prejudice, fostered and imbittered by the artifice of men who labored for an ascendancy over the will of others by the guidance of their passions, produced symptoms of riot and violence. It is well known that Congress did not hesitate to examine the complaints which were presented, and to relieve them as far as justice dictated or general convenience would permit. But the impression which this moderation made on the discontented did not correspond with what it deserved. The arts of delusion were no longer confined to the efforts of designing individuals. The very forbearance to press prosecutions was misinterpreted into a fear of urging the execution of the laws, and associations of men began to denounce threats against officers employed. From a belief that by a more formal concert their operation might be defeated, certain self-created society assumed the tone of condemnation. Hence, while the greater part of Pennsylvania itself were conforming themselves to the acts of excise, a few counties were resolved to frustrate them. It was now perceived that every expectation from the tenderness which had been hitherto pursued was unavailing, and that further delay could only create an opinion of impotency or irresolution in the Government. Legal process was therefore delivered to the marshal against the rioters and delinquent distillers.

No sooner was he understood to be engaged in this duty than the vengeance of armed men was aimed at *his* person and the person and property of the inspector of the revenue. They fired upon the marshal, arrested him, and detained him for some time as a prisoner. He was obliged, by the jeopardy of his life, to renounce the service of other process on the west side of the Allegheny Mountain, and a deputation was afterward sent to him to demand a surrender of that which he *had* served. A numerous body repeatedly attacked the house of the inspector, seized his papers of office, and finally destroyed by fire his buildings and whatsoever they contained. Both of these officers, from a just regard to their safety, fled to the seat of Government, it being avowed that the motives to such outrages were to compel the resignation of the inspector, to withstand by force of arms the authority of the United States, and thereby to extort a repeal of the laws of excise and an alteration in the conduct of Government.

Upon the testimony of these facts an associate justice of the Supreme Court of the United States notified to me that "in the counties of Washington and Allegheny, in Pennsylvania, laws of the United States were opposed, and the execution thereof obstructed, by combinations too powerful to be suppressed by the ordinary course of judicial proceedings or by the powers vested in the marshal of that district." On this call, momentous in the extreme, I sought and weighed what might best subdue the crisis. On the one hand the judiciary was pronounced to be stripped of its capacity to enforce the laws; crimes which reached the very existence of social order were perpetrated without control; the friends of Government were insulted, abused, and overawed into silence or an apparent acquiescence; and to yield to the treasonable fury of so small a portion of the United States would be to violate the fundamental principle of our Constitution, which enjoins that the will of the majority shall prevail. On the other, to array citizen against citizen, to publish the dishonor of such excesses, to encounter the expense and other embarrassments of so distant an expedition, were steps too delicate, too closely interwoven with many affecting considerations, to be lightly adopted. I postponed, therefore, the summoning the militia immediately into the field, but I required them to be held in readiness, that if my anxious endeavors to reclaim the deluded and to convince the malignant of their danger should be fruitless, military force might be prepared to act before the season should be too far advanced.

My proclamation of the 7th of August last was accordingly issued, and accompanied by the appointment of commissioners, who were charged to repair to the scene of insurrection. They were authorized to confer with any bodies of men or individuals. They were instructed to be candid and explicit in stating the sensations which had been excited in the Executive, and his earnest wish to avoid a resort to coercion; to represent, however, that, without submission, coercion *must* be the resort; but to invite them, at the same time, to return to the demeanor of faithful citizens, by such accommodations as lay within the sphere of Executive power. Pardon, too, was tendered to them by the Government of the United States and that of Pennsylvania, upon no other condition than a satisfactory assurance of obedience to the laws.

Although the report of the commissioners marks their firmness and abilities, and must unite all virtuous men, by shewing that the means of conciliation have been exhausted, all of those who had committed or abetted the tumults did not subscribe the mild form which was proposed as the atonement, and the indications of a peaceable temper were neither sufficiently general nor conclusive to recommend or warrant the further suspension of the march of the militia.

Thus the painful alternative could not be discarded. I ordered the militia to march, after once more admonishing the insurgents in my proclamation of the 25th of September last.

It was a task too difficult to ascertain with precision the lowest degree of force competent to the quelling of the insurrection. From a respect, indeed, to economy and the ease of my fellow-citizens belonging to the militia, it would have gratified me to accomplish such an estimate. My very reluctance to ascribe too much importance to the opposition, had its extent been accurately seen, would have been a decided inducement to the smallest efficient numbers. In this uncertainty, therefore, I put into motion 15,000 men, as being an army which, according to all human calculation, would be prompt and adequate in every view, and might, perhaps, by rendering resistance desperate, prevent the effusion of blood. Quotas had been assigned to the States of New Jersey, Pennsylvania, Maryland, and Virginia, the governor of Pennsylvania having declared on this occasion an opinion which justified a requisition to the other States.

As commander in chief of the militia when called into the actual service of the United States, I have visited the places of general rendezvous to obtain more exact information and to direct a plan for ulterior movements. Had there been room for a persuasion that the laws were secure from obstruction; that the civil magistrate was able to bring to justice such of the most culpable as have not embraced the proffered terms of amnesty, and may be deemed fit objects of example; that the friends to peace and good government were not in need of that aid and countenance which they ought always to receive, and, I trust, ever will receive, against the vicious and turbulent, I should have caught with avidity the opportunity of restoring the militia to their families and homes. But succeeding intelligence has tended to manifest the necessity of what has been done, it being now confessed by those who were not inclined to exaggerate the ill conduct of the insurgents that their malevolence was not pointed merely to a particular law, but that a spirit inimical to all order has actuated many of the offenders. If the state of things had afforded reason for the continuance of my presence with the army, it would not have been withholden. But every appearance assuring such an issue as will redound to the reputation and strength of the United States, I have judged it most proper to resume my duties at the seat of Government, leaving the chief command with the governor of Virginia. . . .

While there is cause to lament that occurrences of this nature should have disgraced the name or interrupted the tranquility of any part of our community, or should have diverted to a new application any portion of the public resources, there are not wanting real and substantial consolations for the misfortune. It has demonstrated that our prosperity rests on solid foundations, by furnishing an additional proof that my fellow citizens understand the true principles of government and liberty; that they feel their inseparable union; that notwithstanding all the devices which have been used to sway them from their interest and duty, they are now as ready to maintain the authority of the laws against licentious invasions as they were able to defend their rights against usurpation. It has been a spectacle displaying to the highest advantage the value of republican government to behold the most and the least wealthy of our citizens standing in the same ranks as private soldiers, preeminently distinguished by being the army of the Constitution—undeterred by a march of 300 miles over rugged mountains, by the approach of an inclement season, or by any other discouragement. Nor ought I to omit to acknowledge the efficacious and patriotic cooperation which I have experienced from the chief magistrates of the States to which my requisitions have been addressed.

To every description of citizens, indeed, let praise be given. But let them preserve in their affectionate vigilance over that precious depository of American happiness, the Constitution of the United States. Let them cherish it, too, for the sake of those who, from every clime, are daily seeking a dwelling in our land. And when in the calm moments of reflection they shall have retraced the origin and progress of the insurrection, let them determine whether it has not been fomented by combinations of men who, careless of consequences and disregarding the unerring truth that those who rouse can not always appease a civil convulsion, have disseminated, from an ignorance or perversion of facts, suspicions, jealousies, and accusations of the whole Government.

Having thus fulfilled the engagement which I took when I entered into office, "to the best of my ability to preserve, protect, and defend the Constitution of the United States," on you, gentlemen, and the people by whom you are deputed, I rely for support. . . .

Go. Washington

Source: James D. Richardson, comp., *Messages and Papers of the Presidents,* 20 vols. (New York: Bureau of National Literature, 1897), 1:154–160.

Document 3.13   The First Presidential Pardon, July 10, 1795

President Washington made the first use of the power of presidential pardon to restore to their communities two men who had been sentenced to death for their part in the Whiskey Rebellion.

Whereas the commissioners appointed by the President of the United States to confer with the citizens in the western counties of Pennsylvania during the late insurrection which prevailed therein, by their act and agreement bearing date the 2d day of September last, in pursuance of the powers in them vested, did promise and engage that, if assurances of submission to the laws of the United States should be bona fide given by the citizens resident in the fourth survey of Pennsylvania, in the manner and within the time in the said act and agreement specified, a general pardon should be granted on the 10th day of July the next ensuing of all treasons and other indictable offenses against the United States committed within the said survey before the 22d day of August last, excluding therefrom, nevertheless, every person who should refuse or neglect to subscribe such assurance and engagement in manner aforesaid, or who should after such subscription violate the same, or willfully obstruct or attempt to obstruct the execution of the acts for raising a revenue on distilled spirits and stills, or be aiding or abetting therein; and

Whereas I have since thought proper to extend the said pardon to all persons guilty of the said treasons, misprisions of treasons, or otherwise concerned in the late insurrection within the survey aforesaid who have not since been indicted or convicted thereof, or of any other offense against the United States:

Therefore be it known that I, George Washington, President of the said United States, have granted, and by these presents do grant, a full, free, and entire pardon to all persons (excepting as is hereinafter excepted) of all treasons, misprisions of treason, and other indictable offenses against the United States committed within the fourth survey of Pennsylvania before the said 22d day of August last past, excepting and excluding therefrom, nevertheless, every person who refused or neglected to give and subscribe the said assurances in the manner aforesaid (or having subscribed hath violated the same) and now standeth indicted or convicted of any treason, misprision of treason, or other offense against the said United States, hereby remitting and releasing unto all persons, except as before excepted, all penalties incurred, or supposed to be incurred, for or on account of the premises.

In testimony whereof I have hereunto set my hand and caused the seal of the United States to be affixed, this 10th day of July, A.D. 1795, and the twentieth year of the Independence of the said United States.

Go. Washington

Source: James D. Richardson, comp., *Messages and Papers of the Presidents,* 20 vols. (New York: Bureau of National Literature, 1897), 1:173.

Document 3.14   Talk to the Cherokee Nation, August 29, 1796

Shortly before retiring a final time to his farm, President Washington made an emotional appeal to the leaders of the Cherokee nation and, through the distribution of his "talk" (actually a printed message conveyed to the Cherokees by the government's agent to the Cherokees), to all North American Indians to devote themselves to farming and to peaceable coexistence with white (and black) Americans.

Beloved Cherokees:

Many years have passed since the White people came to America. In that long space of time many good men have considered how the condition of the Indian natives of the country might be improved; and many attempts have been made to effect it. But, as we see at this day, all these attempts have been nearly fruitless. I also have thought much on this subject, and anxiously wished that the various Indian tribes, as well as their neighbours, the White people, might enjoy in abundance all the good things which make life comfortable and happy. I have considered how this could be done; and have discovered but one path that could lead them to that desirable situation. In this path I wish all the Indian nations to walk. From the information received concerning you, my beloved Cherokees, I am inclined to hope that you are prepared to take this path and disposed to pursue it. It may seem a little difficult to enter; but if you make the attempt, you will find every obstacle easy to be removed. . . .

Beloved Cherokees, You now find that the game with which your woods once abounded, are growing scarce; and you know when you cannot meet a deer or other game to kill, that you must remain hungry; you know also when you get no skins by hunting, that the traders will give you neither powder nor cloathing; and you know that without other implements for tilling the ground than the hoe, you will continue to raise only scanty crops of corn. Hence you are sometimes exposed to suffer much from hunger and cold; and as the game are lessening in numbers more and more, these sufferings will increase. And how are you to provide against them? Listen to my words and you will know.

My beloved Cherokees, Some among you are already experiencing the advantage of keeping cattle and hogs: let all keep them and increase their numbers, and you will ever have a plenty of meet. To these add sheep, and they will give you cloathing as well as food. Your lands are good and of great extent. By proper management you can raise live stock not only for your own wants, but to sell to the White people. By using the plow you can vastly increase your crops of corn. You can also grow wheat, (which makes the best bread) as well as other useful grain. To these you will easily add flax and cotton, which you may dispose of to the White people, or have it made up by your own women into cloathing for yourselves. Your wives and daughters can soon learn to spin and weave; and to make this certain, I have directed Mr. Dinsmoor [US Government Indian Agent in the Southwest Territory], to procure all the necessary apparatus for spinning and weaving, and to hire a woman to teach the use of them. He will also procure some plows and other implements of husbandry, with which to begin the improved cultivation of the ground which I recommend, and employ a fit person to shew you how they are to be used. I have further directed him to procure some cattle and sheep for the most prudent and industrious men, who shall be willing to exert themselves in tilling the ground and raising those useful animals. He is often to talk with you on these subjects, and give you all necessary information to promote your success. I must therefore desire you to listen to him; and to follow his advice. I appointed him to dwell among you as the Agent of the United States, because I judged him to be a faithful man, ready to obey my instructions and to do you good.

But the cares of the United States are not confined to your single nation. . . . For which reason other agents are appointed; and for the four southern nations there will be a general or principal agent. . . . His whole time will be employed in contriving how to do you good, and you will therefore act wisely to follow his advice.

Beloved Cherokees, What I have recommended to you I am myself going to do. After a few more moons are passed I shall leave the great town and retire to my farm. There I shall attend to the means of increasing my cattle, sheep and other useful animals; to the growing of corn, wheat, and other grain, and to the employing of women in spinning and weaving; all which I have recommended to you, that you may be as comfortable and happy as plenty of food, clothing and other good things can make you.

Beloved Cherokees, When I have retired to my farm I shall hear of you; and it will give me great pleasure to know that you have taken my advice, and are walking in the path which I have described. But before I retire, I shall speak to my beloved man, the Secretary of War, to get prepared some medals, to be given to such Cherokees as by following my advice shall best deserve them. . . .

Beloved Cherokees, The advice I here give you is important as it regards your nation; but still more important as the event of the experiment made with you may determine the lot of many nations. If it succeeds, the beloved men of the United States will be encouraged to give the same assistance to all the Indian tribes within their boundaries. But if it should fail, they may think it vain to make any further attempts to better the condition of any Indian tribe; for the richness of the soil and mildness of the air render your country highly favorable for the practice of what I have recommended. . . .

I now send my best wishes to the Cherokees, and pray the Great spirit to preserve them.

Source: W. B. Allen, comp., *George Washington: A Collection* (Indianapolis: Liberty Classics, 1988), 645–648.

Document 3.15   Presidential Proclamation, December 12, 1792

Amid a resurgence of violence in 1792 between American settlers on the frontier and Native Americans, Washington maintained his policy of achieving peace through negotiations and enforcing the boundaries of existing treaties. In this presidential proclamation, he demands that those who destroyed an Indian village be brought to justice. The $500 reward he offered was never claimed.

By the President of the United States

Whereas I have received authentic information that certain lawless and wicked persons of the western frontier in the State of Georgia did lately invade, burn, and destroy a town belonging to the Cherokee Nation, although in amity with the United States, and put to death several Indians of that nation; and

Whereas such outrageous conduct not only violates the rights of humanity, but also endangers the public peace, and it highly becomes the honor and good faith of the United States to pursue all legal means for the punishment of those atrocious offenders:

I have therefore thought fit to issue this my proclamation, hereby exhorting all the citizens of the United States and requiring all the officers thereof, according to their respective stations, to use their utmost endeavors to apprehend and bring those offenders to justice. And I do moreover offer a reward of $500 for each and every of the above-named persons who shall be so apprehended and brought to justice and shall be proved to have assumed or exercised any command or authority among the perpetrators of the crimes aforesaid at the time of committing the same.

In testimony whereof I have caused the seal of the United States to be affixed to these presents, and signed the same with my hand.

Done at the city of Philadelphia, the 12th day of December, A.D. 1792, and of the Independence of the United States the Seventeenth.

Go WASHINGTON,
By the President:
TH: JEFFERSON.

Source: National Gazette, December 15, 1792.

Document 3.16   Presidential Proclamation, March 19, 1791

In the Southwest, the eventual statehood of unceded Indian lands was never certain. There was, as in the Northwest, considerable resistance from resident Indian tribes against American encroachments. Spain controlled navigation of the Mississippi River and held colonial title to the Louisiana Territory. In addition, military adventurers dreamed of using force to establish an independent, Spanish-aligned republic in the region. One such person was James O'Fallon, agent general and attorney for the Yazoo Land Company, which had made a purchase of dubious legality of five million acres of frontier land. During the winter of 1789 and 1790, O'Fallon raised a volunteer army and wrote to the Spanish governor of Louisiana, revealing that it was the intention of the company to ally its territory with Spain. President Washington responded in this proclamation.

BY THE PRESIDENT OF THE UNITED STATES OF AMERICA. A PROCLAMATION.

Whereas it hath been represented to me that James O'Fallon is levying an armed force in that part of the State of Virginia which is called Kentucky, disturbs the public peace, and sets at defiance the treaties of the United States with the Indian tribes, the act of Congress intituled "An act to regulate trade and intercourse with the Indian tribes," and my proclamations of the 14th and 26th days of August last founded thereon; and it is my earnest desire that those who have incautiously associated themselves with the said James O'Fallon may be warned of their danger, I have therefore thought fit to publish this proclamation, hereby declaring that all persons violating the treaties and act aforesaid shall be prosecuted with the utmost rigor of the law.

And I do, moreover, require all officers of the United States whom it may concern to use their best exertions to bring to justice any persons offending in the premises.

In testimony whereof I have caused the seal of the United States to be affixed to these presents and signed the same with my hand.

Done at the city of Philadelphia, the 19th day of March, A.D. 1791, and of the Independence of the United States the fifteenth.

Go. Washington
By the President:
TH: Jefferson

Source: James D. Richardson, comp., *Messages and Papers of the Presidents,* 20 vols. (New York: Bureau of National Literature, 1897), 1:94.

John Jay

CHAPTER FOUR

Crises and Flashpoints

T he nation's fragile unity was threatened during Washington's presidency by a rebellion against domestic taxation. Washington met that trouble with decisive force in 1794, when he personally took command of an army of militiamen who marched to the northwestern frontier to quell the Whiskey Rebellion (see Chapter 3). In most presidential administrations, an internal rebellion would surely qualify as the gravest of crises encountered. Washington, however, faced an even greater threat to the nation in the lengthy contest over America's position in the war between Britain and France—a crisis that inflamed the passions of American citizens. President Washington knew that if he did not temper and channel those passions, the consequence might be the second war with a European power in a generation. He, more than most Americans, realized how tenuous America's victory in its War of Independence had been. If the United States went to war again with either France or Britain, it might well be at the cost of its financial credit, its unity, its western territories, or even its existence as an independent nation.

REVOLUTIONARY FRANCE IN NEED OF AMERICAN ASSISTANCE

In 1789, the year Washington took office as president, King Louis XVI of France attempted to impose new taxes on two groups previously exempt

173

from taxation, the clergy and nobility. The money was needed in part to pay debts France had incurred in helping the American colonies to win their independence. Through a complicated series of events, the king's attempt at fiscal reform led to political and social revolution. In response, the French National Assembly created a limited monarchy in 1791. The next year, the representatives of the French people declared war against Austria and abolished the monarchy. In January 1793 the French Republic executed Louis XVI and his queen, Marie Antoinette, by guillotine.

Because of France's location on the European continent, the French Revolution had dramatic consequences for the rest of Europe. It led to a Europe-wide war, the overthrow of old governments, and the formation of new states. This prolonged state of war and revolution, which lasted until 1815, formed the backdrop for the most important conflicts affecting the U.S. government from the Washington through the Madison administrations.

The United States was hardly a power to be reckoned with in 1793, the year Washington began his second term. Not only could the United States project no power in Europe, in North America it probably appeared to be the least among the participants vying for control of the continent (Meinig 1986, 422). The nation was encircled by the imperial domains of Britain and Spain, domains far larger than the landmass claimed at the time by the Americans. In the Caribbean, the United States held no territory; Britain, Spain, and France claimed for themselves all the "sugar islands" of the West Indies. The United States lacked even a navy with which to defend its interests. The Continental navy had been disbanded in 1784, and the Department of the Navy was not established until 1798. The U.S. Army was two years away from proving itself capable of defending American interests in the Ohio River Valley, and the American militia was ill equipped and poorly trained.

Despite all this, the United States had resources that were valued by the parties at war in Europe. Timber for ships came from American forests; grain for bread came from American farms. The United States also exported large quantities of tobacco, flour, indigo, rice, and even iron. Moreover, American merchant sailors were themselves a valued "commodity." Sometimes they were impressed, commandeered, by the British to serve in the Royal Navy. The French, for their part, hoped to use American merchant vessels as their own for the purpose of raiding British merchant ships.

Because the U.S. economy depended heavily on seafaring trade but had meager means of defense, American citizens were at constant risk of capture or losing property on the seas. Throughout the Washington administration, Algerian pirates preyed with relative impunity on American vessels in the Mediterranean. Indeed, President Washington, with the consent of Congress, oversaw treaty negotiations with the dey of Algiers that secured the release of American hostages through the payment of a ransom. Even greater danger awaited American ships in the Caribbean once Britain decided to use its superior naval power to its advantage by authorizing its ships to seize American vessels trading with the French.

The first threat to America from the European war came, though, not from the British capture of American ships and sailors, but from the French capture of British ships. The French wanted, and needed, the United States as a naval base from which to wage its war on British shipping; it had lost its North American presence in the French and Indian War. Because the French lacked sufficient warships to battle the British directly in the western Atlantic, they intended instead to cripple Britain, and improve their own condition, by authorizing "privateers" to attack British shipping.

French Privateers and American Ports

A privateer was a privately owned and operated ship, sailing at its own risk but by authority of the government on whose behalf it raided enemy commerce. After capturing a ship, the privateer would forcibly remove it and its crew to a friendly port. While the ship sat in harbor and its crew sat in prison, the captain and perhaps other agents of the shipowners would appear before a "prize court." If the court upheld the legality of the capture, the captured goods (including the clothes off the backs of the unfortunate sailors) would be auctioned and the proceeds distributed among the captain, crew, and ship owners. The capture of a prize was, then, only part of the struggle for a privateer. Secreting the loot to safe harbor was equally important. British privateers could repair easily enough to Canada, but the French possessed no extensive shoreline in North America. To take a captured British vessel to a French port in the Caribbean was risky, given the density of British ships in those waters. How much simpler it would be if France could operate satellite courts in the United States.

The United States acted quickly to recognize the revolutionary French government in late 1792. As Secretary of State Thomas Jefferson wrote to the American minister to France, Gouverneur Morris, "It accords with our principles to acknowledge any Government to be rightful which is formed by the will of the nation, substantially declared" (Tucker and Hendrickson 1990, 49). The French, however, wanted more than mere recognition. In 1778 the United States had made two treaties with Louis XVI. In the first, the Treaty of Amity and Commerce, the United States granted special trading privileges to France, including the right to bring into American ports British ships claimed as prizes on the seas. Under the terms of the treaty, Americans had no right to judge the legality of prizes: "It shall be lawful for the Ships of War of either Party & Privateers freely to carry whithersoever they please the Ships and Goods taken from their Enemies . . . nor shall such Prizes be arrested or seized, when they come to and enter the Ports of either Party; nor shall the Searchers or other Officers of those Places search the same or make examination concerning the lawfulness of such Prizes" (February 6, 1778, Avalon Project). In the second, the Treaty of Alliance, France and the United States promised to "guarantee mutually from the present time and forever" France's possessions in America and the "liberty, Sovereignty, and Independence" of the United States (February 6, 1778, Avalon Project). The signatories agreed that "in case of rupture between France and England," this reciprocal guarantee "shall have its full force and effect the moment such War shall break out" (February 6, 1778, Avalon Project).

Revolutionary France did not formally request that the United States go to war against Britain, because the United States had no military power to contribute to the conflict. The French did, however, assert that the commercial treaty and the treaty of alliance (not to mention the critical help that France had given to America in winning its independence) gave France the right to establish French prize courts on American soil and to equip American ships as French privateers.

Some, perhaps most, American citizens were willing to give the French all they asked for. Jefferson and his many allies within the government enthusiastically followed events in France. The European coalition that had assembled against France, the Jeffersonians believed, evinced "a desire to snuff out liberty in the Old World as a prelude to extinguishing it in the new" (Tucker and Hendrickson 1990, 45). The revolutionary government's minister to the United States, Edmund Charles Edouard Genêt ("Citizen Genêt"), naturally agreed, and did all he could to mobilize American citizens to lobby their government to come to France's aid.

The Neutrality Proclamation and the Recall of Citizen Genêt

On April 19, 1793, Washington assembled his cabinet for perhaps its most important session. For several weeks, rumors that Britain had joined in the war against France had circulated in American newspapers, which routinely published the hearsay of arriving passengers from Europe. When the rumors became too numerous and consistent to be doubted, Washington returned to Philadelphia from a short vacation at Mount Vernon, writing ahead to his cabinet members that they should be prepared for an important meeting.

If the cabinet meeting went badly and ended in angry quarrels, that might presage the failure of his hold on the government. The result could be entry by congressional fiat into a war for which the nation was not prepared. If Washington succeeded in holding together the cabinet, he might with reason anticipate holding together the government and the nation in this crisis. The first task was to shape a compromise among his cabinet members. The secretary of the Treasury, Alexander Hamilton, wanted the United States to renounce the U.S. treaties with a French government that no longer existed. In fact, Hamilton had been meeting clandestinely with the British minister to the United States, George Hammond. He had assured Hammond that he would use his influence with the president to prevent the United States from entering the war on the side of France and to throw American influence, such as it was, in Britain's favor. Secretary of State Thomas Jefferson agreed with Washington that going to war with Britain would be disastrous, but he wanted the United States to do everything short of war to assist the spread of revolution in Europe. Such an approach meant honoring America's treaties with France by allowing France to use American ports and vessels.

The cabinet debated at length the government's treaty obligations, the imminent arrival of the new French minister to the United States, and the boundaries of the president's authority to decide issues of foreign policy on behalf of the government. Jefferson's notes from the meeting recount impassioned exchanges. Hamilton, Jefferson wrote, appeared "panic-struck if we refuse our breach to every kick which Great Britain may choose to give it." Secretary of War Henry Knox, Jefferson recorded, "like a fool that he is," also took a pro-British position, while Jefferson and Attorney General Edmund Randolph argued the other side of most issues (Flexner 1972, 31). In the end, Washington, who managed to keep the exchange of views from degenerating into a free-for-all, secured unanimous approval for a policy of neutrality. Because neither Jefferson nor Hamilton wanted the term *neutrality* used, it was left out of the president's statement of the government's policy, though the intent to remain neutral was clear.

The cabinet agreed that the president should issue a proclamation of his policy, in which he would warn American citizens against doing anything that might drag the nation into war. They also agreed that the president would not call Congress into special session. At a follow-up meeting, the cabinet decided—against Hamilton's dark foreboding that war with Britain would ensue—that the United States would receive Citizen Genêt without formal reservations about the status of America's treaty obligations toward France.

The Neutrality Proclamation was issued on April 22, 1793 (Document 4.1). In it, the president asserted that war appeared to have broken out between Britain, France, and other European states and that the "duty and interest of the United States" required it to "pursue a conduct friendly and impartial toward the belligerent Powers." Any American citizen caught aiding or abetting or carrying contraband to a belligerent would "not receive the protection of the United States."

The Democratic-Republican newspapers that printed the proclamation were soon filled with angry attacks on the policy and praise for the revolution in France. "All the old Spirit of '76 is rekindling!" exulted Jefferson (Flexner 1972, 34). The leading Jeffersonian editor, Philip Freneau, published a "report" in May that Washington had issued the proclamation to save his head, which the "monocrats" (the pejorative term Jeffersonians used for "monarchists") in government had promised to separate from his body otherwise. Washington was furious and intimated to Jefferson that he withdraw Freneau's sinecure at the State Department, where Jefferson employed the editor as a translator. Because Jefferson sincerely believed that Freneau's paper, the *National Gazette,* had "saved our Constitution" (even though Freneau might at times get carried away), he declined to do as the president wished (Flexner 1972, 36).

On the day that Washington issued his proclamation, a French privateer escorted into Philadelphia harbor a captured British ship, *Little*

Sarah, renamed by the French *Little Democrat.* Thousands of Americans celebrated the capture at the wharfs. Farther south, in Charleston, where Citizen Genêt had disembarked from France in April, the new ambassador had immediately begun operating as a one-man prize court to condemn and dispose of captured property brought into that port. He also began issuing commissions to American shipowners to go raiding on behalf of France. Washington called on his cabinet to decide on a course of action. They agreed that property taken before publication of the proclamation could be kept as legitimate prizes, but privateering after the date of publication was forbidden and any prizes taken must be returned. Washington was again taking a middle course in the hope of avoiding war.

When Citizen Genêt learned of Washington's policy, he went to Philadelphia to protest. He was met first not by a representative of the government but by a mass gathering of cheering citizens. Genêt exchanged kind words with the masses, whose self-appointed leaders presented him with a paper expressing their solidarity with the French. Genêt was so moved by the people's spontaneous demonstration of affection that he decided to reveal to them something he had not yet told anyone in the American government: he had been instructed by his government not only to see that the United States honored its old treaties with France, but also to negotiate a new treaty that would bind the United States even more closely to its "sister republic" (Flexner 1972, 43).

Washington received Genêt with cold diplomatic formality. Genêt was disappointed, but concluded that the president was suffering from wounded pride because of Genêt's immense popularity and the obvious unpopularity of Washington's policy. Through the summer of 1793, Genêt continued to commission privateers and operate prize courts on American soil.

At the same time, Genêt compounded Washington's difficulty on the American frontier. Northwest of the Ohio River, the British continued to hold forts in contravention of the Peace of Paris, which concluded the Revolutionary War in 1783. Gen. Anthony Wayne's army was a year away from its famous victory at Fallen Timbers (see Chapter 3). In the Southwest, the Mississippi River was blocked to American commerce by Spain. These were familiar troubles for Washington at the outset of his second term. The French Revolution, however, brought two new challenges on the frontier. First, the revolution had driven Spain and Britain into alliance, opening for the first time the possibility of a concerted military operation against American claims to its vast western lands. Second,

Genêt confided to Secretary of State Thomas Jefferson that the French had set in motion a plan to encourage revolution in Louisiana, which would lead, Genêt hoped, to the establishment of a new sister republic in North America.

At last, Genêt had gone too far. In June Jefferson presented him with a communication from Washington notifying him that his plan to commission officers for his rebellion was an infringement of U.S. sovereignty and that his privateers would have to leave U.S. waters. In July Genêt defied the administration in sending to sea the *Little Democrat*, which had been outfitted with heavy arms in Philadelphia's harbor. Alexander Dallas, secretary of the Commonwealth of Pennsylvania, warned Genêt that the president would never approve the commissioning of the ship as a privateer. Genêt replied that in that case "he would appeal from the President to the people" (Flexner 1972, 58). Especially in the country's earliest days, this was a grave insult to the American conception of government. The president was the indirect representative of the political nation as a whole. Only he might speak on behalf of or appeal to "the people."

Before the president could decide whether to take military action to prevent the ship from sailing, it was at sea. Genêt rashly decided that he should visit the president to explain his actions, and the statement he had made to Alexander Dallas. Calling unannounced on Washington, he told the president that he was merely acting as justice dictated. After all, the Neutrality Proclamation was in contravention of sacred treaty obligations, and Genêt should not be faulted for being so much more popular than the American government. Washington merely replied that he did not read the gazettes and did not care whether his policies were popular. Genêt thought he had "won" the encounter and went to Jefferson's office the next day to boast about his triumph. "He had hardly begun his exposition when a door opened and in walked a stony-faced Washington. Genêt made one of his best bows and then noticed that Jefferson was now as stony-faced as the President. Genêt looked from one to the other for 'an invitation to remain for which I would willingly have given part of my life' " (Flexner 1972, 61). None came, and Genêt departed.

At an all-day cabinet meeting on August 1, it was agreed that the French would be asked to recall their ambassador. The cabinet could not agree, however, on whether to publish the reasons for the request, which included the insult that Genêt had leveled at the president. Hamilton wanted all the facts made known, because he saw Genêt's actions as part of a French plot to subvert the American government. Jefferson argued that Genêt was merely a most unfortunate appointment and that the United States should limit its official objections to Genêt personally, not to French policy. Washington decided that the record need not be published at that time. But "perhaps events would show whether the appeal [to the public] would be necessary or not" (Flexner 1972, 67).

Events then became even more agitated. Mobs of Americans, addressing each other as "citizen" or "citess," assembled in the streets of Philadelphia, New York, and other cities, jostling American "aristocrats" in the streets and threatening to import to America the violence of the European revolution. Newspaper stories ridiculed the president; one cartoonist even depicted his execution. Cabinet members too became more agitated in their disagreements, though they expressed themselves with more decorum than newspaper editors and cartoonists typically showed.

Secretary of the Treasury Alexander Hamilton, writing as Pacificus and Americanus, defended the president and his policy of neutrality in a series of newspaper articles (Document 4.2). At the urging of Jefferson, James Madison took up the argument on the other side, writing as Helvidius (Document 4.3). With Genêt on his way to New York, where he intended to outfit additional privateers, Sen. Rufus King of New York and Chief Justice John Jay revealed in the newspapers what everyone high in the government but nobody else knew: that Genêt had insulted the president by threatening him with an appeal to the public. Genêt responded with a public letter acknowledging the claim and suggesting that any chief executive in a free country who took umbrage at such a comment did not deserve his position. This stance, ironically, brought the public around to the side of the president. In mass meetings, where recently Washington had been condemned, the president was now defended and his policy endorsed. Because it was the recognized right of a nation to demand the recall of the ambassador of another state, the French acceded to the U.S. demand in August 1793 that Genêt be recalled. And because Washington had waited until after Genêt had publicly insulted him and turned the people to his side to demand Genêt's recall, Genêt knew he would be returning home in disgrace. In revolutionary France, the penalty for embarrassing the nation would likely be death. Washington magnanimously consented to Genêt's request for political asylum.

In his fifth annual address to Congress in 1793, President Washington spoke of the "posture of affairs, both new and delicate," on account of the war in Europe. That war, he stated in the most diplomatic of terms, had made the "connection of the United States with Europe . . . extremely interesting." He repeated the admonition of his proclamation against persons within the United States who might "array themselves in hostility against any of the powers at war, or enter upon military expeditions or enterprises within the jurisdiction of the United States" (December 3, 1793, as reprinted in Richardson 1897, 131–132). And the president's routine plea to Congress to enhance the military capacity of the nation carried new urgency on this occasion:

> The United States ought not to indulge a persuasion that, contrary to the order of human events, they will forever keep at a distance those painful appeals to arms with which the history of every other nation abounds. There is a rank due to the United States among nations which will be withheld, if not absolutely lost, by the reputation of weakness. If we desire to avoid insult, we must be able to repel it; if we desire to secure peace, one of the most powerful instruments of our rising prosperity, it must be known that we are at all times ready for war. (Richardson 1897, 132)

The Jay Treaty

The recall of Genêt coincided with changes in the European war and in the course of the revolution in France. The French government did not, on account of the collapse in 1794 of the Reign of Terror, become a model of moderation. It did, however, enter a phase of nonlethal but fractious politics at home. Hyperinflation and food shortages affected the population of France, but the French army, which lived off of the land, won important victories. The relative calm that descended on French domestic politics shortly after the recall of Genêt made France less interested in and capable of inciting discord in the United States. France's growing strength in its war against the European powers in the First Coalition made France less desperate for American assistance. What this meant for the United States was that for the rest of Washington's presidency, the gravest threat to American interests would come not from France but from Britain.

Even after France lost the "right" to operate its raiding enterprise from American soil, it continued to rely to some degree on American commercial shipping. Citing the principle that "free ships make free goods," French and American diplomats insisted that American ships be allowed to come and go freely to France and to the French West Indies. But the British saw things differently. They "declared early in the war that they would ignore this principle" in favor of the older principle of *consolato del mare,* which would authorize the British capture of French property carried on American ships and American "contraband" property headed to France. The British did not specify formally what was to be regarded as contraband, leaving the decision in the hands of British prize courts.

On November 6, 1793, just three months after Washington's cabinet had agreed to demand the recall of Citizen Genêt, the British issued an order directing British vessels to bring into prize courts all neutral ships bound to or from French territory. This directive was especially troublesome because the British government gave the order to its own merchant and naval fleet two months before bothering to release it to the world. In the interim, British warships and privateers captured roughly three hundred American ships trading in the French West Indies. After the ships were impounded, crew members who could not prove their American citizenship were impressed into service in the British navy; the rest were imprisoned.

Democratic-Republicans and Federalists in Congress agreed on a thirty-day suspension of trade with all foreign nations, beginning March 26, 1794, as the appropriate emergency response. Such a suspension would hurt Britain more than France because U.S. trade with Britain was much greater than that with France. In addition, the president took under consideration the proposal of Federalist leaders in Congress that he send to Britain a special envoy, preferably Secretary of the Treasury Alexander Hamilton. Not wanting to make such a divisive appointment, Washington simply declined to act until Hamilton himself wrote the president to inform him that he was no longer a candidate for the position of special envoy. The proper person for the job, Hamilton believed, was Chief Justice John Jay. Washington informed Congress on April 16, 1794, that "as peace ought to be pursued with unremitted zeal before the last recourse, which has so often been the scourge of nations, and can not fail to check the advanced prosperity of the United States, is contemplated, I have thought proper to nominate, and do hereby nominate,

John Jay as envoy extraordinary of the United States to His Britannic Majesty" (Washington to "Gentlemen of the Senate," in Richardson 1897, 145–146). The pro-French, pro–Democratic-Republican societies raged against the appointment. Jay, an ally of the much-hated Hamilton, was suspected of being excessively pro-British. It was even "reported" in one Philadelphia newspaper that the real reason for Washington's appointment of Jay was to remove the chief justice from the nation and thereby avoid a much-deserved post-impeachment trial (under the Constitution, the chief justice presides at the Senate trial of an impeached chief executive). The president, in the eyes of leading Democratic-Republicans such as Sen. Henry Tazewell of Virginia, did not deserve to remain in office, because in failing to come to the aid of the heroic French revolutionaries, he had lost the confidence of the American people. Yet, despite the venomous atmosphere existing at the time, Jay was confirmed by the Senate 20–8.

While Jay was in London negotiating American differences with Britain, Congress debated the continuance of the embargo on American shipping. Washington, believing he had no constitutional right to intervene in congressional deliberations, refused Hamilton's urging that he lobby Congress to prevent passage of legislation that might further antagonize Britain. Despite strong minority sentiment in the opposite direction, the embargo was halted after a second month and other anti-British legislation (such as sequestration of all debts due British subjects from American citizens) was voted down. For the remainder of 1794, Jay continued his negotiations and Congress waited.

In early winter of 1795, a rumor circulated that Jay had negotiated a treaty, but no one seemed to know what was in the document. As a result of a series of unfortunate incidents, Congress held its winter session without receiving firm news from Europe. First, a French privateer captured a ship carrying two copies of the treaty, which were thrown overboard to avoid their capture. Then, another vessel carrying another copy of the treaty encountered unfavorable winds and other misfortunes, including being stopped and searched by a French cruiser trying to intercept the rumored treaty. Finally, four months after the treaty had started its journey, "and four days after Congress had given up and adjourned in disgust," the treaty at last arrived in Philadelphia in March 1795 (Combs 1970, 160). Washington and Secretary of State Edmund Randolph (Jefferson had resigned at the end of 1793) were relieved to have it at hand, but hardly anxious to send it to Congress, where debate over its terms was bound to descend into intense partisan warfare. After a decent interval of three months, Washington called Congress back into special session. The Senate at last considered the treaty in the summer of 1795 (see Document 4.4).

In the treaty, Britain promised at last to vacate its forts in American territory and agreed that boundary disputes would be settled through arbitration. Moreover, procedures were established for the settlement of British claims against American debtors and for indemnification of Americans who claimed their ships had been illegally seized by British privateers. American ships also were granted limited freedom to trade in the British West Indies, though not to compete with British merchant ships in carrying goods directly from the sugar islands to Europe.

Although the treaty clearly contained some items of benefit to the United States, many aspects caused Americans alarm. Federalists criticized the limited nature of British concessions on American trade in the West Indies. In Article 12, the British promised only to permit small American ships (those under seventy tons) to trade there for two years, and only if they sailed their cargo to the United States. Federalists and Democratic-Republicans alike were displeased, but generally resolved to the fact that the British reserved the right under the treaty to seize as contraband any war goods intended for France, or any other enemy of Britain. The listing of contraband goods also was drafted with more - pro-British vagueness than even Hamilton approve of. Democratic-Republicans denounced the treaty for, in effect, confirming that Washington had overturned America's treaties with France. Under Jay's Treaty, the signatories agreed in Article 25 that "[n]o Shelter or Refuge shall be given in their Ports to such as have made a Prize upon the Subjects or Citizens of either of the said Parties."

Washington, troubled by the treaty, had not agreed to sign it when it was approved, 20–10, in the Senate on June 24, 1795. The Senate's approval came with condition that Article 12 be held in abeyance, pending further negotiations. While Washington consulted with his cabinet members and other advisers, Britain issued a Provisional Order authorizing seizure of American grain bound for France. France was suffering from famine, and the British winter grain crop had been poor. The matter of who would get bread from America was a potentially grave one. This situation took the notion of contraband to an extreme and complicated Washington's decision even more.

While Washington hesitated, mass meetings denounced the treaty, even in pro-British Boston. James Monroe, the American envoy to France, warned the president that the cost of avoiding war with Britain would likely be war with France. (War with France, or at least quasi-war, did in fact result in Washington's retirement—see Chapter 6.) In New York, a group of citizens, joined by a party of French sailors, burned a copy of the treaty on the steps of Jay's house. When he could temporize no more, Washington announced to his cabinet on August 12, 1795, that he would sign the treaty. A memorial attached to the treaty rejected part of Article 12 and stated that the president objected to the principle on contraband under which the Provisional Order had been issued.

The opposition, including Washington's own envoy to France, James Monroe, speculated whether the president would resign his office rather than face what they were certain would be the outrage of the American citizenry. But in Washington's seventh annual address in December 1795 (see Document 4.5), he masterfully drew the public's attention to the prosperity of the nation, a prosperity that had stemmed from peace and moderation. There would be no resignation and no widespread clamor for one. The Democratic-Republican opposition to the president did launch an attack on the treaty in the House of Representatives, demanding that the president present the chamber with documents pertaining to the treaty. But the president declined and demonstrated, in the process, the inability of the House to force the president to act contrary to his understanding of the Constitution (see Chapter 5). In fact, as the House debate went on, it began to seem that a large portion of the electorate favored the treaty, or at least continued to support the president who had signed it. The impassioned oratory of Rep. Fisher Ames of Massachusetts (Document 4.6) and the receipt of petitions from throughout the nation persuaded a majority in the House to cease its open antagonism against the chief executive.

THE PINCKNEY TREATY

In the United States, the Mississippi River was the major path for the movement of goods from the interior of the country to the wider world. On October 27, 1795, Thomas Pinckney, Washington's special envoy to Spain, successfully concluded a treaty that guaranteed American access to the Mississippi (see Document 4.7). The treaty was of great commercial importance to the growing nation and significant because it put an end to the threat of a Spanish-inspired rebellion on the country's western frontiers. Through secret agents, including Gen. James Wilkinson of the U.S. Army, and Creek leader Alexander McGillivray, the Spanish had long sought to increase the resentment of western settlers against the U.S. government. Moreover, when Spain joined England in the First Coalition against France, the specter emerged of a joint English-Spanish land grab on the American frontier.

Fortunately for the United States, Spain was never comfortable in alliance with its historic enemy, Britain, and in fact feared that the British might ally with its former colonies in North America to force Spain off the continent. After suffering defeat from invading French armies in July 1795, the Spanish concluded a peace with France. In North America, the most prudent course of action for the humbled Spanish monarchy now appeared to be cohabitation of the Mississippi with the Americans.

Under Pinckney's Treaty, Spain recognized the thirty-first parallel as the boundary between Spanish Florida and the United States, the Mississippi was opened to American navigation, and the right of American vessels to store goods temporarily at the port of New Orleans before transfer to other ships (known as the right of deposit) was assured. By Article 5 of the treaty, "the two High contracting Parties shall by all the means in their power maintain peace and harmony among the several Indian Nations who inhabit" their territories (Treaty of Friendship, Limits, and Navigation Between Spain and The United States, October 27, 1795, Avalon Project). As Hamilton observed at the time, it was "a point of the greatest moment in our system of national policy" to dissolve the combination of Britain and Spain, which the French Revolution had brought together (Tucker and Hendrickson 1990, 65).

CONCLUSION

In its earliest days, the United States was a prosperous but weak country. It was populous and expansive, but divided among states, regions, and factions. President Washington's greatest concern was to preserve what he had been entrusted to preside over: a government for the entire nation. In the early 1790s, the French Revolution set in motion a series of events that presented Washington with the greatest crisis of his presidency: war with either France or Britain. He knew that war with one of the major powers of Europe could be disastrous for America. Even if the United States somehow emerged victorious, participation in a foreign war might create the conditions for a civil war at home, where there were strong regional differences in interest and sympathy. New England could be expected to protest greatly against a war with Britain, while the South could be expected to protest just as much against war with France. Indeed, when the nation did at last succumb to full scale war, in the War of 1812 against Britain, New England Federalists flirted with succession at the infamous Hartford Convention of 1815. At the very least, war would hurt the American economy, divide the people, and set back the movement toward national integration.

The greater threat was always war with Britain, which was both a much more considerable naval power and with which America had by far the greater commercial relations. To avoid this war, Washington pursued a policy of neutrality, even though strict neutrality violated the spirit of America's wartime treaties with France. In doing so, he had to defend his policy against numerous "foes," including impassioned support for the French at home and the initial desperation of the French government. In the final years of his second term, he struggled against British policy.

Before the revolutionary and Napoleonic wars of France and England were finally concluded, Washington's fears of war with both powers would be confirmed. Under the presidency of John Adams (1797–1801), the United States engaged in an undeclared quasi-war with France, and Washington came out of retirement to lead an American ground defense against a French invasion that, thankfully, never came (see Chapter 6). During President James Madison's administration (1809–1817), the United States went to war for a second time with Britain, in 1812. During President Washington's time in office, however, it mattered most that the United States remained at peace, because the country was at its weakest. Washington saw that it did so.

BIBLIOGRAPHIC ESSAY

The Avalon Project at Yale Law School (*www.yale.edu/lawweb/avalon*) is an outstanding online depository of diplomatic materials, including the French-American Treaty of Amity and Commerce, the Treaty of Alliance, and Pinckney's Treaty. Another standard source for documents related to President Washington's administration is Volume 1 of *Messages and Papers of the Presidents*, 20 vols. (New York: Bureau of National Literature, 1897), compiled by James D. Richardson.

Washington's second term is covered in reliable detail by James Thomas Flexner in the last volume of his biography of Washington, *George Washington, Anguish and Farewell, 1793–1799* (Boston: Little, Brown, 1972). On the foreign policy of the Washington administration, see: Paul A. Varg, *Foreign Policies of the Founding Fathers* (Baltimore: Penguin, 1970); Daniel G. Lang, *Foreign Policy in the Early Republic: The Law of Nations and the Balance of Power* (Baton Rouge: Louisiana State University Press, 1985); Alexander DeConde, *Entangling Alliance: Politics and Diplomacy under George Washington* (Durham: Duke University Press, 1958); Jerald A. Combs, *The Jay Treaty: Political Battleground of the Founding Fathers* (Berkeley: University of California Press, 1970); and Robert W. Tucker and David C. Hendrickson, *Empire of Liberty: The Statecraft of Thomas Jefferson* (New York: Oxford University Press, 1990). On Federalist efforts to rally support for the Jay Treaty, which defies the stereotype of the early Federalists as uninterested in public opinion, see Todd Estes, "Shaping the Politics of Public Opinion: Federalists and the Jay Treaty Debate," *Journal of the Early Republic* 20 (fall 2000): 393–422.

Finally, the geographic context of early American statecraft can be followed in D. W. Meinig, *The Shaping of America, A Geographical Perspective on 500 Years of History*, Vol. 1, *Atlantic America, 1492–1800* (New Haven: Yale University Press, 1986).

Document 4.1   The Neutrality Proclamation, April 22, 1793

On February 1, 1793, France declared war on Britain. America was divided on what response to make. Many Americans, including Secretary of State Thomas Jefferson, felt the United States owed its support to France in return for France's support during the Revolutionary War, but they feared war with Britain. They favored permitting French ships to use American ports and otherwise giving the French any and all assistance short of actually going to war in behalf of the revolutionary republic. Others agreed with Secretary of the Treasury Alexander Hamilton that the United States should maintain strict neutrality, which would favor the British as the superior naval power. Washington convened a cabinet meeting to formulate an official policy. The result was the Neutrality Proclamation.

Whereas it appears that a state of war exists between Austria, Prussia, Sardinia, Great Britain, and the United Netherlands, of the one part, and France on the other; and the duty and interest of the United States require, that they should with sincerity and good faith adopt and pursue a conduct friendly and impartial toward the belligerent Powers;

I have therefore thought fit by these presents to declare the disposition of the United States to observe the conduct aforesaid towards those Powers respectfully; and to exhort and warn the citizens of the United States carefully to avoid all acts and proceedings whatsoever, which may in any manner tend to contravene such disposition.

And I do hereby also make known, that whatsoever of the citizens of the United States shall render himself liable to punishment or forfeiture under the law of nations, by committing, aiding, or abetting hostilities against any of the said Powers, or by carrying to any of them those articles which are deemed contraband by the modern usage of nations, will not receive the protection of the United States, against such punishment or forfeiture; and further, that I have given instructions to those officers, to whom it belongs, to cause prosecutions to be instituted against all persons, who shall, within the cognizance of the courts of the United States, violate the law of nations, with respect to the Powers at war, or any of them.

In testimony whereof, I have caused the seal of the United States of America to be affixed to these presents, and signed the same with my hand. Done at the city of Philadelphia, the twenty-second day of April, one thousand seven hundred and ninety-three, and of the Independence of the United States of America the seventeenth.

George Washington

Source: James D. Richardson, comp., *Messages and Papers of the Presidents,* 20 vols. (New York: Bureau of National Literature, 1897), 1:148–149.

Document 4.2   Pacificus, Number 1, by Alexander Hamilton, June 29, 1793

Writing under the pseudonyms "Pacificus" and "Americanus," Secretary of the Treasury Alexander Hamilton supported President Washington's Neutrality Proclamation in a series of newspaper articles. As Pacificus, Hamilton

*famously argued the executive's right to declare the position of the United States
with respect to foreign belligerents.*

As attempts are making very dangerous to the peace, and it is to be feared
not very friendly to the constitution of the UStates—it becomes the duty
of those who wish well to both to endeavour to prevent their success.

The objections which have been raised against the Proclamation of Neutrality lately issued by the President have been urged in a spirit of acrimony
and invective, which demonstrates, that more was in view than merely a
free discussion of an important public measure; that the discussion covers
a design of weakening the confidence of the People in the author of the
measure; in order to remove or lessen a powerful obstacle to the success
of an opposition to the Government, which however it may change its
form, according to circumstances, seems still to be adhered to and pursued
with persevering Industry.

This Reflection adds to the motives connected with the measure itself
to recommend endeavours by proper explanations to place it in a just light.
Such explanations at least cannot but be satisfactory to those who may not
have leisure or opportunity for pursuing themselves an investigation of the
subject, and who may wish to perceive that the policy of the Government
is not inconsistent with its obligations or its honor. . . .

[I]t is necessary to examine what is the nature and design of a proclamation of neutrality.

The true nature & design of such an act is—to make known to the
powers at War and to the Citizens of the Country, whose Government
does the Act that such country is in the condition of a Nation at Peace
with the belligerent parties, and under no obligations of Treaty, to
become an associate in the war with either of them; that this being its
situation its intention is to observe a conduct conformable with it and to
perform towards each the duties of neutrality; and as a consequence of
this state of things, to give warning to all within its jurisdiction to abstain
from acts that shall contravene those duties, under the penalties which the
laws of the land (of which the law of Nations is a part) annexes to acts of
contravention.

This, and no more, is conceived to be the true import of a Proclamation of Neutrality. . . .

It will not be disputed that the management of the affairs of this country with foreign nations is confided to the Government of the UStates.

It can as little be disputed, that a Proclamation of Neutrality, where a Nation is at liberty to keep out of a War in which other Nations are engaged and means so to do, is a usual and a proper measure. Its main object and effect are to prevent the Nation being immediately responsible for acts done by its citizens, without the privity or connivance of the Government, in contravention of the principles of neutrality.

An object this of the greatest importance to a Country whose true interest lies in the preservation of peace.

The inquiry then is—what department of the Government of the UStates is the proper one to make a declaration of Neutrality in the cases in which the engagements of the Nation permit and its interests require such a declaration.

A correct and well informed mind will discern at once that it can belong neither to the Legislative nor Judicial Department and of course must belong to the Executive.

The Legislative Department is not the organ of intercourse between the UStates and foreign Nations. It is charged neither with making nor interpreting Treaties. It is therefore not naturally that Organ of the Government which is to pronounce the existing condition of the Nation, with regard to foreign Powers, or to admonish the Citizens of their obligations and duties as founded upon that condition of things. Still less is it charged with enforcing the execution and observance of these obligations and those duties.

It is equally obvious that the act in question is foreign to the Judiciary Department of the Government. The province of that Department is to decide litigations in particular cases. It is indeed charged with the interpretation of treaties; but it exercises this function only in the litigated cases; that is where contending parties bring before it a specific controversy. It has no concern with pronouncing upon the external political relations of Treaties between Government and Government. This position is too plain to need being insisted upon.

It must then of necessity belong to the Executive Department to exercise the function in Question—when a proper case for the exercise of it occurs.

It appears to be connected with that department in various capacities, as the organ of intercourse between the Nation and foreign Nations—as the interpreter of the National Treaties in those cases in which the Judiciary is not competent, that is in the cases between Government and

Government—as that Power, which is charged with the Execution of the Laws, of which Treaties form a part—as that Power which is charged with the command and application of the Public Force.

This view of the subject is so natural and obvious—so analogous to general theory and practice—that no doubt can be entertained of its justness, unless such doubt can be deduced from particular provisions of the Constitution of the UStates.

Let us see then if cause for such doubt is to be found in that constitution.

The second Article of the Constitution of the UStates, section 1st, establishes this general Proposition, That "The Executive Power shall be vested in a President of the United States of America."

The same article in a succeeding Section proceeds to designate particular cases of Executive Power. It declares among other things that the President shall be Commander in Chief of the army and navy of the UStates and of the Militia of the several states when called into the actual service of the UStates, that he shall have power by and with the advice of the senate to make treaties; that it shall be his duty to receive ambassadors and other public Ministers and to take care that the laws be faithfully executed. . . .

The general doctrine then of our constitution is, that the Executive Power of the Nation is vested in the President; subject only to the exceptions and qu[a]lifications which are expressed in the instrument.

Two of these have been already noticed—the participation of the Senate in the appointment of Officers and the making of Treaties. A third remains to be mentioned the right of the Legislature "to declare war and grant letters of marque and reprisal."

With these exceptions the Executive Power of the Union is completely lodged in the President. This mode of construing the Constitution has indeed been recognized by Congress in formal acts, upon full consideration and debate. The power of removal from office is an important instance.

And since upon general principles for reasons already given, the issuing of a proclamation of neutrality is merely an Executive Act; since also the general Executive Power of the Union is vested in the President, the conclusion is, that the step, which has been taken by him, is liable to no just exception on the score of authority.

It may be observed that this Inference would be just if the power of declaring war had not been vested in the Legislature, but that this power naturally includes the right of judging whether the Nation is under obligations to make war or not.

The answer to this is, that however true it may be, that the right of the Legislature to declare war includes the right of judging whether the Nation be under obligations to make War or not—it will not follow that the Executive is in any case excluded from a similar right of Judgment, in the execution of its own functions.

If the Legislature have a right to make war on the one hand—it is on the other the duty of the Executive to preserve Peace till war is declared; and in fulfilling that duty, it must necessarily possess a right of judging what is the nature of the obligations which the treaties of the Country impose on the Government; and when in pursuance of this right it has concluded that there is nothing in them inconsistent with a state of neutrality, it becomes both its province and its duty to enforce the laws incident to that state of the Nation. The Executive is charged with the execution of all laws, the laws of Nations as well as the Municipal law, which recognises and adopts those laws. It is consequently bound, by faithfully executing the laws of neutrality, when that is the state of the Nation, to avoid giving a cause of war to foreign Powers. . . .

It deserves to be remarked, that as the participation of the senate in the making of Treaties and the power of the Legislature to declare war are exceptions out of the general "Executive Power" vested in the President, they are to be construed strictly—and ought to be extended no further than is essential to their execution.

While therefore the Legislature can alone declare war, can alone actually transfer the nation from a state of Peace to a state of War—it belongs to the "Executive Power," to do whatever else the laws of Nations cooperating with the Treaties of the Country enjoin, in the intercourse of the UStates with foreign Powers.

In this distribution of powers the wisdom of our constitution is manifested. It is the province and duty of the Executive to preserve to the Nation the blessings of peace. The Legislature alone can interrupt those blessings, by placing the Nation in a state of War. . . .

The President is the constitutional Executor of the laws. Our Treaties and the laws of Nations form a part of the law of the land. He who is to execute the laws must first judge for himself of their meaning. In order to the observance of that conduct, which the laws of nations combined with our treaties prescribed to this country, in reference to the present War in

Europe, it was necessary for the President to judge for himself whether there was any thing in our treaties incompatible with an adherence to neutrality. Having judged that there was not, he had a right, and if in his opinion the interests of the Nation required it, it was his duty, as Executor of the laws, to proclaim the neutrality of the Nation, to exhort all persons to observe it, and to warn them of the penalties which would attend its non observance.

The Proclamation has been represented as enacting some new law. This is a view of it entirely erroneous. It only proclaims a fact with regard to the existing state of the Nation, informs the citizens of what the laws previously established require of them in that state, & warns them that these laws will be put in execution against the Infractors of them.

Source: Harold C. Syrett et al., eds. *The Papers of Alexander Hamilton,* 26 vols. (New York and London: Columbia University Press, 1961–1979), 15:33–43.

Document 4.3   Helvidius, Number 1, by James Madison, August 24, 1793

One week after Pacificus, Number 1 was published, Secretary of State Thomas Jefferson pleaded with Rep. James Madison: "For God's sake, my dear Sir, take up your pen, select the most striking heresies and cut him to pieces in the face of the public. There is nobody else who can and will enter the lists against him" (Thomas Jefferson to James Madison, July 7, 1793, in Hutchison and Rachal 1960, 15:43). Madison then released a series of newspaper articles written under the pseudonym "Helvidius." He argued that the issuance of the proclamation encroached on Congress's powers.

No. I.

Several pieces with the signature of Pacificus were lately published, which have been read with singular pleasure and applause, by the foreigners and degenerate citizens among us, who hate our republican government, and the French revolution; whilst the publication seems to have been too little regarded, or too much despised by the steady friends to both.

Had the doctrines inculcated by the writer, with the natural consequences from them, been nakedly presented to the public, this treatment might have been proper. Their true character would then have struck every

eye, and been rejected by the feelings of every heart. But they offer themselves to the reader in the dress of an elaborate dissertation; they are mingled with a few truths that may serve them as a passport to credulity; and
they are introduced with professions of anxiety for the preservation of
peace, for the welfare of the government, and for the respect due to the
present head of the executive, that may prove a snare to patriotism.

In these disguises they have appeared to claim the attention I propose
to bestow on them: with a view to show, from the publication itself, that
under colour of vindicating an important public act, of a chief magistrate
who enjoys the confidence and love of his country, principles are advanced
which strike at the vitals of its constitution, as well as at its honour and true
interest. . . .

The basis of the reasoning [of Alexander Hamilton in Pacificus, Number 1] is, we perceive, the extraordinary doctrine, that the powers of making war, and treaties, are in their nature executive; and therefore comprehended in the general grant of executive power, where not especially and
strictly excepted out of the grant.

Let us examine this doctrine: . . .

If we consult, for a moment, the nature and operation of the two powers to declare war and to make treaties, it will be impossible not to see, that
they can never fall within a proper definition of executive powers. The natural province of the executive magistrate is to execute laws, as that of the
legislature is to make laws. All his acts, therefore, properly executive, must
presuppose the existence of the laws to be executed. A treaty is not an execution of laws: it does not presuppose the existence of laws. It is, on the
contrary, to have itself the force of a law, and to be carried into execution,
like all other laws, by the executive magistrate. To say then that the power
of making treaties, which are confessedly laws, belongs naturally to the
department which is to execute laws, is to say, that the executive department naturally includes a legislative power. In theory this is an absurdity—
in practice a tyranny.

The power to declare war is subject to similar reasoning. A declaration
that there shall be war, is not an execution of laws: it does not suppose preexisting laws to be executed: it is not, in any respect, an act merely executive. It is, on the contrary, one of the most deliberate acts that can be performed; and when performed, has the effect of repealing all the laws
operating in a state of peace, so far as they are inconsistent with a state of
war; and of enacting, as a rule for the executive, a new code adapted to the

relation between the society and its foreign enemy. In like manner, a conclusion of peace annuls all the laws peculiar to a state of war, and revives
the general laws incident to a state of peace.

These remarks will be strengthened by adding, that treaties, particularly
treaties of peace, have sometimes the effect of changing not only the external laws of the society, but operate also on the internal code, which is
purely municipal, and to which the legislative authority of the country is
of itself competent and complete.

From this view of the subject it must be evident, that although the executive may be a convenient organ of preliminary communications with foreign governments, on the subjects of treaty or war; and the proper agent
for carrying into execution the final determinations of the competent
authority; yet it can have no pretensions, from the nature of the powers
in question compared with the nature of the executive trust, to that essential agency which gives validity to such determinations.

It must be further evident, that if these powers be not in their nature
purely legislative, they partake so much more of that, than of any other
quality, that under a constitution leaving them to result to their most natural department, the legislature would be without a rival in its claim.

Another important inference to be noted is, that the powers of making
war and treaty being substantially of a legislative, not an executive nature,
the rule of interpreting exceptions strictly must narrow, instead of enlarg-
ing, executive pretensions on those subjects.

It remains to be inquired, whether there be any thing in the constitution itself, which shows, that the powers of making war and peace are considered as of an executive nature, and as comprehended within a general
grant of executive power.

It will not be pretended, that this appears from any direct position to
be found in the instrument.

If it were deducible from any particular expressions, it may be presumed,
that the publication would have saved us the trouble of the research.

Does the doctrine, then, result from the actual distribution of powers
among the several branches of the government? or from any fair analogy
between the powers of war and treaty, and the enumerated powers vested
in the executive alone?

Let us examine:

In the general distribution of powers, we find that of declaring war
expressly vested in the congress, where every other legislative power is

declared to be vested; and without any other qualification than what is common to every other legislative act. The constitutional idea of this power would seem then clearly to be, that it is of a legislative and not an executive nature.

This conclusion becomes irresistible, when it is recollected, that the constitution cannot be supposed to have placed either any power legislative in its nature, entirely among executive powers, or any power executive in its nature, entirely among legislative powers, without changing the constitution, with that kind of intermixture and consolidation of different powers, which would violate a fundamental principle in the organization of free governments. If it were not unnecessary to enlarge on this topic here, it could be shown, that the constitution was originally vindicated, and has been constantly expounded, with a disavowal of any such intermixture.

The power of treaties is vested jointly in the president and in the senate, which is a branch of the legislature. From this arrangement merely, there can be no inference that would necessarily exclude the power from the executive class: since the senate is joined with the president in another power, that of appointing to offices, which, as far as relate to executive offices at least, is considered as of an executive nature. Yet on the other hand, there are sufficient indications that the power of treaties is regarded by the constitution as materially different from mere executive power, and as having more affinity to the legislative than to the executive character.

One circumstance indicating this, is the constitutional regulation under which the senate give their consent in the case of treaties. In all other cases, the consent of the body is expressed by a majority of voices. In this particular case, a concurrence of two-thirds at least is made necessary, as a substitute or compensation for the other branch of the legislature, which, on certain occasions, could not be conveniently a party to the transaction.

But the conclusive circumstance is, that treaties, when formed according to the constitutional mode, are confessedly to have force and operation of laws, and are to be a rule for the courts in controversies between man and man, as much as any other laws. They are even emphatically declared by the constitution to be "the supreme law of the land."

So far the argument from the constitution is precisely in opposition to the doctrine. . . .

Thus it appears that by whatever standard we try this doctrine, it must be condemned as no less vicious in theory than it would be dangerous in practice. It is countenanced neither by the writers on law; nor by the nature of the powers themselves; nor by any general arrangements, or particular expressions, or plausible analogies, to be found in the constitution.

Whence can the writer have borrowed it?

There is but one answer to this question.

The power of making treaties and the power of declaring war, are *royal prerogatives in the British government*. . . .

Source: Gaillard Hunt, *The Writings of James Madison*, 9 vols. (New York: Putnam's, 1900–1910), 6:138–151.

Document 4.4   The Jay Treaty

The Jay Treaty was negotiated, debated, and ratified over a lengthy period. After his appointment as special envoy to Britain, Chief Justice John Jay traveled to London in April 1794 and negotiated the treaty throughout the summer and fall. The agreement was signed in London the following November, but because of a series of incidents, the treaty itself only reached the United States in March 1795. Despite intense popular protest, the Senate ratified it in June. Although President Washington's first impression of the Jay Treaty was negative, he thought it imperative to avoid war with Britain and signed the treaty.

ARTICLE 1.

There shall be a firm inviolable and universal Peace, and a true and sincere Friendship between His Britannick Majesty, His Heirs and Successors, and the United States of America; and between their respective Countries, Territories, Cities, Towns and People of every Degree, without Exception of Persons or Places.

ARTICLE 2.

His Majesty will withdraw all His Troops and Garrisons from all Posts and Places within the Boundary Lines assigned by the Treaty of Peace to the United States. This Evacuation shall take place on or before the first Day of June One thousand seven hundred and ninety six. . . .

ARTICLE 5.

Whereas doubts have arisen what River was truly intended under the name of the River st Croix mentioned in the said Treaty of Peace and forming a part of the boundary therein described, that question shall be referred to the final Decision of Commissioners to be appointed in the following Manner-Viz-

One Commissioner shall be named by His Majesty, and one by the President of the United States, by and with the advice and Consent of the Senate thereof, and the said two Commissioners shall agree on the choice of a third, or, if they cannot so agree, They shall each propose one Person, and of the two names so proposed one shall be drawn by Lot, in the presence of the two original Commissioners. And the three Commissioners so appointed shall be Sworn impartially to examine and decide the said question according to such Evidence as shall respectively be laid before Them on the part of the British Government and of the United States. . . .

ARTICLE 6.

Whereas it is alledged by divers British Merchants and others, His Majesty's Subjects, that Debts to a considerable amount which were bona fide contracted before the Peace, still remain owing to them by Citizens or Inhabitants of the United States, and that by the operation of various lawful Impediments since the Peace, not only the full recovery of the said Debts has been delayed, but also the Value and Security thereof, have been in several instances impaired and lessened, so that by the ordinary course of Judicial proceedings the British Creditors, cannot now obtain and actually have and receive full and adequate Compensation for the losses and damages which they have thereby sustained: It is agreed that in all such Cases where full Compensation for such losses and damages cannot, for whatever reason, be actually obtained had and received by the said Creditors in the ordinary course of Justice, The United States will make full and complete Compensation for the same to the said Creditors. . . .

For the purpose of ascertaining the amount of any such losses and damages, Five Commissioners shall be appointed and authorized to meet and act. . . .

ARTICLE 7.

Whereas Complaints have been made by divers Merchants and others, Citizens of the United States, that during the course of the War in which His Majesty is now engaged they have sustained considerable losses and damage by reason of irregular or illegal Captures or Condemnations of their vessels and other property under Colour of authority or Commissions from His Majesty, and that from various Circumstances belonging to the said Cases adequate Compensation for the losses and damages so sustained cannot now be actually obtained, had and received by the ordinary Course of Judicial proceedings; It is agreed that in all such Cases where adequate

Compensation cannot for whatever reason be now actually obtained, had and received by the said Merchants and others in the ordinary course of Justice, full and Complete Compensation for the same will be made by the British Government to the said Complainants. . . .
ARTICLE 10.

Neither the Debts due from Individuals of the one Nation, to Individuals of the other, nor shares nor monies, which they may have in the public Funds, or in the public or private Banks shall ever, in any Event of war, or national differences, be sequestered, or confiscated, it being unjust and impolitick that Debts and Engagements contracted and made by Individuals having confidence in each other, and in their respective Governments, should ever be destroyed or impaired by national authority, on account of national Differences and Discontents.
ARTICLE 11.

It is agreed between His Majesty and the United States of America, that there shall be a reciprocal and entirely perfect Liberty of Navigation and Commerce, between their respective People, in the manner, under the Limitations, and on the Conditions specified in the following Articles.
ARTICLE 12.

His Majesty Consents that it shall and may be lawful, during the time hereinafter Limited, for the Citizens of the United States, to carry to any of His Majesty's Islands and Ports in the West Indies from the United States in their own Vessels, not being above the burthen of Seventy Tons, any Goods or Merchandizes, being of the Growth, Manufacture, or Produce of the said States, which it is, or may be lawful to carry to the said Islands or Ports from the said States in British Vessels, and that the said American Vessels shall be subject there to no other or higher Tonnage Duties or Charges, than shall be payable by British Vessels, in the Ports of the United States; and that the Cargoes of the said American Vessels, shall be subject there to no other or higher Duties or Charges, than shall be payable on the like Articles, if imported there from the said States in British vessels. And His Majesty also consents that it shall be lawful for the said American Citizens to purchase, load and carry away, in their said vessels to the United States from the said Islands and Ports, all such articles being of the Growth, Manufacture or Produce of the said Islands, as may now by Law be carried from thence to the said States in British Vessels, and subject only to the same Duties and Charges on Exportation to which British Vessels and their Cargoes are or shall be subject in similar circumstances.

Provided always that the said American vessels do carry and land their Cargoes in the United States only, it being expressly agreed and declared that during the Continuance of this article, the United States will prohibit and restrain the carrying any Melasses, Sugar, Coffee, Cocoa or Cotton in American vessels, either from His Majesty's Islands or from the United States, to any part of the World, except the United States, reasonable Sea Stores excepted. Provided also, that it shall and may be lawful during the same period for British vessels to import from the said Islands into the United States, and to export from the United States to the said Islands, all Articles whatever being of the Growth, Produce or Manufacture of the said Islands, or of the United States respectively, which now may, by the Laws of the said States, be so imported and exported. And that the Cargoes of the said British vessels, shall be subject to no other or higher Duties or Charges, than shall be payable on the same articles if so imported or exported in American Vessels.

It is agreed that this Article, and every Matter and Thing therein contained, shall continue to be in Force, during the Continuance of the war in which His Majesty is now engaged; and also for Two years from and after the Day of the signature of the Preliminary or other Articles of Peace by which the same may be terminated

And it is further agreed that at the expiration of the said Term, the Two Contracting Parties will endeavour further to regulate their Commerce in this respect, according to the situation in which His Majesty may then find Himself with respect to the West Indies, and with a view to such Arrangements, as may best conduce to the mutual advantage and extension of Commerce. And the said Parties will then also renew their discussions, and endeavour to agree, whether in any and what cases Neutral Vessels shall protect Enemy's property; and in what cases provisions and other articles not generally Contraband may become such. But in the mean time their Conduct towards each other in these respects, shall be regulated by the articles hereinafter inserted on those subjects. . . .

ARTICLE 14.

There shall be between all the Dominions of His Majesty in Europe, and the Territories of the United States, a reciprocal and perfect liberty of Commerce and Navigation. . . .

ARTICLE 17.

It is agreed that, in all Cases where Vessels shall be captured or detained on just suspicion of having on board Enemy's property or of carrying to the Enemy, any of the articles which are Contraband of war; The said Ves-

sel shall be brought to the nearest or most convenient Port, and if any property of an Enemy, should be found on board such Vessel, that part only which belongs to the Enemy shall be made prize, and the Vessel shall be at liberty to proceed with the remainder without any Impediment. And it is agreed that all proper measures shall be taken to prevent delay, in deciding the Cases of Ships or Cargoes so brought in for adjudication, and in the payment or recovery of any Indemnification adjudged or agreed to be paid to the masters or owners of such Ships.
ARTICLE 18.

In order to regulate what is in future to be esteemed Contraband of war, it is agreed that under the said Denomination shall be comprized all Arms and Implements serving for the purposes of war by Land or Sea; such as Cannon, Muskets, Mortars, Petards, Bombs, Grenades Carcasses, Saucisses, Carriages for Cannon, Musket rests, Bandoliers, Gunpowder, Match, Saltpetre, Ball, Pikes, Swords, Headpieces Cuirasses Halberts Lances Javelins, Horsefurniture, Holsters, Belts and, generally all other Implements of war, as also Timber for Ship building, Tar or Rosin, Copper in Sheets, Sails, Hemp, and Cordage, and generally whatever may serve directly to the equipment of Vessels, unwrought Iron and Fir planks only excepted, and all the above articles are hereby declared to be just objects of Confiscation, whenever they are attempted to be carried to an Enemy. . . .
ARTICLE 21.

It is likewise agreed that the Subjects and Citizens of the Two Nations, shall not do any acts of Hostility or Violence against each other, nor accept Commissions or Instructions so to act from any Foreign Prince or State, Enemies to the other party, nor shall the Enemies of one of the parties be permitted to invite or endeavour to enlist in their military service any of the Subjects or Citizens of the other party; and the Laws against all such Offences and Aggressions shall be punctually executed. And if any Subject or Citizen of the said Parties respectively shall accept any Foreign Commission or Letters of Marque for Arming any Vessel to act as a Privateer against the other party, and be taken by the other party, it is hereby declared to be lawful for the said party to treat and punish the said Subject or Citizen, having such Commission or Letters of Marque as a Pirate. . . .
ARTICLE 23.

The Ships of war of each of the Contracting Parties, shall at all times be hospitably received in the Ports of the other, their Officers and Crews paying due respect to the Laws and Government of the Country. The offi-

cers shall be treated with that respect, which is due to the Commissions which they bear. And if any Insult should be offered to them by any of the Inhabitants, all offenders in this respect shall be punished as Disturbers of the Peace and Amity between the Two Countries. . . .
ARTICLE 24.

It shall not be lawful for any Foreign Privateers (not being Subjects or Citizens of either of the said Parties) who have Commissions from any other Prince or State in Enmity with either Nation, to arm their Ships in the Ports of either of the said Parties, nor to sell what they have taken, nor in any other manner to exchange the same, nor shall they be allowed to purchase more provisions than shall be necessary for their going to the nearest Port of that Prince or State from whom they obtained their Commissions.
ARTICLE 25.

It shall be lawful for the Ships of war and Privateers belonging to the said Parties respectively to carry whithersoever they please the Ships and Goods taken from their Enemies without being obliged to pay any Fee to the Officers of the Admiralty, or to any Judges what ever; nor shall the said Prizes when they arrive at, and enter the Ports of the said Parties be detained or seized, neither shall the Searchers or other Officers of those Places visit such Prizes (except for the purpose of preventing the Carrying of any part of the Cargo thereof on Shore in any manner contrary to the established Laws of Revenue, Navigation or Commerce) nor shall such Officers take Cognizance of the Validity of such Prizes; but they shall be at liberty to hoist Sail, and depart as speedily as may be, and carry their said Prizes to the place mentioned in their Commissions or Patents, which the Commanders of the said Ships of war or Privateers shall be obliged to shew. No Shelter or Refuge shall be given in their Ports to such as have made a Prize upon the Subjects or Citizens of either of the said Parties; . . .

Neither of the said parties shall permit the Ships or Goods belonging to the Subjects or Citizens of the other to be taken within Cannon Shot of the Coast, nor in any of the Bays, Ports or Rivers of their Territories by Ships of war, or others having Commission from any Prince, Republic or State whatever. . . .
ARTICLE 28.

It is agreed that the first Ten Articles of this Treaty shall be permanent and that the subsequent Articles except the Twelfth shall be limited in their duration to Twelve years to be computed from the Day on which the Ratifications of this Treaty shall be exchanged, but subject to this Condition that whereas the said Twelfth Article will expire by the Limitation therein contained at the End of two years from the signing of the Preliminary or other Articles of Peace, which shall terminate the present War, in which His Majesty is engaged; . . .

In Faith whereof We the Undersigned, Ministers Plenipotentiary of His Majesty The King of Great Britain; and the United States of America, have signed this present Treaty, and have caused to be affixed thereto, the Seal of Our Arms.

Done at London, this Nineteenth Day of November, One thousand seven hundred and ninety Four.

GRENVILLE [Seal) JOHN JAY [Seal]

Source: Avalon Project, Yale Law School (*www.yale.edu/lawweb/avalon/diplomacy/britian/jay.htm*).

Document 4.5   Seventh Annual Address, December 8, 1795

President Washington surprised his critics by declining in his seventh annual address to defend the unpopular Jay Treaty in any detail. Rather, he drew Congress's and the public's attention to the blessings of prosperity that he argued came from the nation's steady pursuit of moderation and neutrality.

Fellow Citizens of the Senate and of the House of Representatives:

I trust I do not deceive myself when I indulge the persuasion that I have never met you at any period when more than at the present the situation of our public affairs has afforded just cause for mutual congratulation, and for inviting you to join with me in profound gratitude to the Author of all Good for the numerous and extraordinary blessings we enjoy.

The termination of the long, expensive, and distressing war in which we have been engaged with certain Indians northwest of the Ohio is placed in the option of the United States by a treaty which the commander of our army has concluded provisionally with the hostile tribes in that region. . . .

The Creek and Cherokee Indians, who alone of the Southern tribes had annoyed our frontiers, have lately confirmed their preexisting treaties with us, and were giving evidence of a sincere disposition to carry them into effect by the surrender of the prisoners and property they had taken. . . .

The latest advices from our envoy at the Court of Madrid give, moreover, the pleasing information that he had assurances of a speedy and satisfactory conclusion of his negotiation. While the event depending upon unadjusted particulars can not be regarded as ascertained, it is agreeable to cherish the expectation of an issue which, securing amicably very essential interests of the United States, will at the same time lay the foundation of lasting harmony with a power whose friendship we have uniformly and sincerely desired to cultivate.

Though not before officially disclosed to the House of Representatives, you, gentlemen, are all apprised that a treaty of amity, commerce, and navigation has been negotiated with Great Britain, and that the Senate have advised and consented to its ratification upon a condition which excepts part of one article. Agreeably thereto, and to the best judgment I was able to form of the public interest after full and mature deliberation, I have added my sanction. The result on the part of His Britannic Majesty is unknown. When received, the subject will without delay be placed before Congress.

This interesting summary of our affairs with regard to the foreign powers between whom and the United States controversies have subsisted, and with regard also to those of our Indian neighbors with whom we have been in a state of enmity or misunderstanding, opens a wide field for consoling and gratifying reflections. If by prudence and moderation on every side the extinguishment of all the causes of external discord which have heretofore menaced our tranquility, on terms compatible with our national rights and honor, shall be the happy result, how firm and how precious a foundation will have been laid for accelerating, maturing, and establishing the prosperity of our country.

Contemplating the internal situation as well as the external relations of the United States, we discover equal cause for contentment and satisfaction. While many of the nations of Europe, with their American dependencies, have been involved in a contest unusually bloody, exhausting, and calamitous, in which the evils of foreign war have been aggravated by domestic convulsion and insurrection; in which many of the arts most useful to society have been exposed to discouragement and decay; in which scarcity of subsistence has imbittered other sufferings; while even the anticipations of a return of the blessings of peace and repose are alloyed by the sense of heavy and accumulating burthens, which press upon all the departments of industry and threaten to clog the future springs of government, our favored country, happy in a striking contrast, has enjoyed tranquility—a tranquility the more satisfactory because maintained at the expense of no duty. Faithful to ourselves, we have violated no obligation to others.

Our agriculture, commerce, and manufactures prosper beyond former example, the molestations of our trade (to prevent a continuance of which, however, very pointed remonstrances have been made) being overbalanced by the aggregate benefits which it derives from a neutral position. Our population advances with a celerity which, exceeding the most sanguine calculations, proportionally augments our strength and resources, and guarantees our future security.

Every part of the Union displays indications of rapid and various improvement; and with burthens so light as scarcely to be perceived, with resources fully adequate to our present exigencies, with governments founded on the genuine principles of rational liberty, and with mild and wholesome laws, is it too much to say that our country exhibits a spectacle of national happiness never surpassed, if ever before equaled?

Placed in a situation every way so auspicious, motives of commanding force impel us, with sincere acknowledgment to Heaven and pure love to our country, to unite our efforts to preserve, prolong, and improve our immense advantages. To cooperate with you in this desirable work is a fervent and favorite wish of my heart.

It is a valuable ingredient in the general estimate of our welfare that the part of our country which was lately the scene of disorder and insurrection now enjoys the blessings of quiet and order. The misled have abandoned their errors, and pay the respect to our Constitution and laws which is due from good citizens to the public authorities of the society. These circumstances have induced me to pardon generally the offenders here referred to, and to extend forgiveness to those who had been adjudged to capital punishment. For though I shall always think it a sacred duty to exercise with firmness and energy the constitutional powers with which I am vested, yet it appears to me no less consistent with the public good than it is with my personal feelings to mingle in the operations of Government every degree of moderation and tenderness which the national justice, dignity, and safety may permit.

Gentlemen: Among the objects which will claim your attention in the course of the session, a review of our military establishment is not the least important. . . .

With the review of our Army establishment is naturally connected that of the militia. . . .

While we indulge the satisfaction which the actual condition of our Western borders so well authorizes, it is necessary that we should not lose sight of an important truth which continually receives new confirmations, namely, that the provisions heretofore made with a view to the protection of the Indians from the violences of the lawless part of our frontier inhabitants are insufficient. . . .

The accomplishment of this work, if practicable, will reflect undecaying luster on our national character and administer the most grateful consolations that virtuous minds can know.

Source: James D. Richardson, comp., *Messages and Papers of the Presidents,* 20 vols. (New York: Bureau of National Literature, 1897), 1:174–177.

Document 4.6   Rep. Fisher Ames on the Jay Treaty, April 28, 1796

In 1796, after the Senate had consented to the Jay Treaty, President Washington had signed it, and Britain and the United States had proclaimed it, a congressional appropriation was needed to execute the treaty. As the nation followed the debate in the partisan presses of the day, Rep. Fisher Ames of Massachusetts was asked by the Federalists to deliver an oration on the subject before the House of Representatives. In ailing health, the thirty-eight-year-old Ames, who was absent for the early part of the debate, made the trip from Massachusetts to Philadelphia. In his speech, he stressed that any action to impair the constitutional authority of the president and Senate to make treaties would cripple the country and remove public faith in government. After uttering his final words, Ames collapsed; his speech, which served as the climax of the debate, brought tears to his colleagues' eyes. Two days later, the House appropriated $80,800 to execute the Jay Treaty.

Mr. Chairman: I entertain the hope, perhaps the rash one, that my strength will hold me out to speak a few minutes. . . .

[A]n attempt has been made to produce an influence of a nature more stubborn and more unfriendly to truth. It is very unfairly pretended that the constitutional right of this House is at stake, and to be asserted and preserved only by a vote in the negative. We hear it said that this is a struggle for liberty, a manly resistance against the design to nullify this assembly, and to make it a cypher in the government. That the PRESIDENT and Senate, the numerous meetings in the cities, and the influence of the general alarm of the country, are the agents and instruments of a scheme of coercion and terror, to force the Treaty down our throats, though we loathe it, and in spite of the clearest convictions of duty and conscience.

It is necessary to pause here and inquire, whether suggestions of this kind be not unfair in their very texture and fabric, and pernicious in all their influences? . . .

The doctrine has been avowed, that the Treaty, though formally ratified by the Executive power of both nations, though published as a law for our own, by the PRESIDENT's Proclamation, is still a mere proposition submitted to this assembly, no way distinguishable in point of authority, or obligation from a motion for leave to bring in a bill, or any other original act of ordinary legislation. This doctrine, so novel in our country, yet, so dear to many, precisely for the reason that, in the contention of power, victory is always dear, is obviously repugnant, to the very terms, as well as the fair interpretation of our own resolutions. . . . We declare that the treaty-making power is exclusively vested in the PRESIDENT and the Senate, and not in this House. Need I say that we fly in the face of that resolution when we pretend that the acts of that power are not valid until we have concurred in them? It would be nonsense, or worse, to use the language of the most glaring contradiction, and to claim a share in a power which we, at the same time, disclaim as exclusively vested in other departments. . . .

The Treaty is bad, fatally bad, is the cry. It sacrifices the interest, the honor, the independence of the United States, and the faith of our engagements to France. If we listen to the clamor of party intemperance, the evils are of a number not to be counted, and of a nature not to be borne, even in idea. The language of passion and exaggeration may silence that of sober reason in other places, it has not done it here. The question here is, whether the Treaty be really so very fatal as to oblige the nation to break its faith? I admit that such a treaty ought not to be executed. I admit that self-preservation is the first law of society, as well as of individuals. It would, perhaps, be deemed an abuse of terms to call that a treaty which violates such a principle. I waive, also, for the present, any inquiry what departments shall represent that nation, and annul the stipulations of a treaty. I content myself with pursuing the inquiry, whether the nature of this compact be such as to justify our refusal to carry it into effect? . . .

It is in vain to allege that our faith plighted to France is violated by this new Treaty. Our prior Treaties are expressly saved from the operation of the British Treaty. And what do those mean, who say, that our honor was forfeited by treating at all, and especially by such a Treaty? Justice, the laws and practice of nations, a just regard for peace as a duty to mankind, and the known wish of our citizens, as well as that self-respect which required it of the nation to act with dignity and moderation—all these forbid an appeal to arms before we had tried the effect of negotiation. The honor of the United States was saved, not forfeited, by treating. The Treaty itself, by its stipulations for the posts, for indemnity, and for a due observance of our neutral rights, has justly raised the character of the nation. Never did the name of America appear in Europe with more lustre than upon the event of ratifying this instrument. The fact is of a nature to overcome all contradiction.

But *the independence of the country—we are colonists again.* This is the cry of the very men who tell us that France will resent our exercise of the rights of an independent nation to adjust our wrongs with an aggressor, without giving her the opportunity to say those wrongs shall subsist and shall not be adjusted. This is an admirable specimen of independence. The Treaty with Great Britain, it cannot be denied is unfavorable to this strange sort of independence.

Few men, of any reputation for sense, among those who say the Treaty is bad, will put that reputation so much at hazard as to pretend that it is so extremely bad as to warrant and require a violation of public faith. The proper ground of the controversy, therefore, is really unoccupied by the opposers of the Treaty; as the very hinge of the debate is on the point, not of its being good, or otherwise, but whether it is intolerably and fatally pernicious? . . .

This Treaty, like a rainbow on the edge of the cloud, marked to our eyes the space where it was raging, and afforded at the same time the sure prognostic of fair weather. If we reject it, the vivid colors will grow pale; it will be a baleful meteor, portending tempest and war. . . .

I have thus been led by my feelings to speak more at length than I had intended; yet I have, perhaps, as little personal interest in the event as any one here. There is, I believe, no member who will not think his chance to be a witness of the consequences greater than mine. If, however, the vote should pass to reject, and a spirit should rise, as it will with the public disorders to make confusion worse confounded, even I, slender and almost broken as my hold upon life is, may outlive the government and Constitution of my country.

Source: W. B. Allen, ed., *Works of Fisher Ames* (as published by his son Seth Ames) (Indianapolis: Liberty Classics, 1983), 1143–1182.

Document 4.7   Pinckney's Treaty, formally known as Treaty of Friendship, Limits, and Navigation, signed at San Lorenzo el Real, October 27, 1795

From 1792 on, President Washington had sought to negotiate a treaty with "His Catholic Majesty," as the Spanish government was known in diplomatic circles. This treaty, ratified by the United States on March 7, 1796, and by Spain on April 25, 1796, guaranteed U.S. citizens the right of access to the Mississippi River, and represented Spain's acknowledgment that the United States had successfully colonized its interior up to the borders of Spanish North America. By this treaty, the United States freed itself from anxiety that it might at some point have to make war against Spain to assert its territorial claims east of the Mississippi. The preamble's recitation of the qualifications of the signatories to the treaty gives testimony to the vast distance that separated the nobility-encrusted political culture of Spain from that of the more democratic United States.

His Catholic Majesty and the United States of America desiring to consolidate on a permanent basis the Friendship and good correspondence which happily prevails between the two Parties, have determined to establish by a convention several points, the settlement whereof will be productive of general advantage and reciprocal utility to both Nations. With this intention his Catholic Majesty has appointed the most Excellent Lord Don Manuel de Godoy and Alvarez de Faria, Rios, Sanchez Zarzosa, Prince de la Paz Duke de la Alcudia Lord of the Soto de Roma and of the State of Albala: Grandee of Spain of the first class: perpetual Regidor of the Citty of Santiago: Knight of the illustrious Order of the Golden Fleece, and Great Cross of the Royal and distinguished Spanish order of Charles the III. Commander of Valencia del Ventoso, Rivera, and Aceuchal in that of Santiago: Knight and Great Cross of the religious order of St John: Counsellor of State: First Secretary of State and Despacho: Secretary to the Queen: Superintendent General of the Posts and High Ways: Protector of the Royal Academy of the Noble Arts, and of the Royal Societies of natural history, Botany, Chemistry, and Astronomy: Gentleman of the King's Chamber in employement: Captain General of his Armies: Inspector and Major of the Royal Corps of Body Guards &a &a &a and the President of the United States with the advice and consent of their Senate, has appointed Thomas Pinckney a Citizen of the United States, and their

Envoy Extraordinary to his Catholic Majesty. And the said Plenipotentiaries have agreed upon and concluded the following Articles.
ART. I.

There shall be a firm and inviolable Peace and sincere Friendship
between His Catholic Majesty his successors and subjects, and the United
Estates and their Citizens without exception of persons or places.
ART. II.

To prevent all disputes on the subject of the boundaries which separate
the territories of the two High contracting Parties, it is hereby declared and
agreed as follows: to wit: The Southern boundary of the United States which
divides their territory from the Spanish Colonies of East and West Florida,
shall be designated by a line beginning on the River Mississipi at the
Northermost part of the thirty first degree of latitude North of the Equator,
which from thence shall be drawn due East to the middle of the River
Apalachicola or Catahouche, thence along the middle thereof to its junction
with the Flint, thence straight to the head of St Mary's River, and thence
down the middle there of to the Atlantic Ocean. And it is agreed that if
there should be any troops, Garrisons or settlements of either Party in the
territory of the other according to the above mentioned boundaries, they
shall be withdrawn from the said territory within the term of six months after
the ratification of this treaty or sooner if it be possible and that they shall be
permitted to take with them all the goods and effects which they possess.
ART. III.

In order to carry the preceding Article into effect one Commissioner
and one Surveyor shall be appointed by each of the contracting Parties who
shall meet at the Natchez on the left side of The River Mississipi before the
expiration of six months from the ratification of this convention, and they
shall proceed to run and mark this boundary according to the stipulations
of the said Article. They shall make Plats and keep journals of their proceedings which shall be considered as part of this convention, and shall
have the same force as if they were inserted therein. . . .
ART. IV.

It is likewise agreed that the Western boundary of the United States
which separates them from the Spanish Colony of Louissiana, is in the middle of the channel or bed of the River Mississipi from the Northern boundary of the said States to the completion of the thirty first degree of latitude
North of the Equator; and his Catholic Majesty has likewise agreed that
the navigation of the said River in its whole breadth from its source to the
Occean shall be free only to his Subjects, and the Citizens of the United

States, unless he should extend this privilege to the Subjects of other Powers by special convention.

ART. V.

The two High contracting Parties shall by all the means in their power maintain peace and harmony among the several Indian Nations who inhabit the country adjacent to the lines and Rivers which by the proceeding Articles form the boundaries of the two Floridas; and the teeter to obtain this effect both Parties oblige themselves expressly to restrain by force all hostilities on the part of the Indian Nations living within their boundaries: so that Spain will notsuder her Indians to attack the Citizens of the United States, nor the Indians inhabiting their territory; nor will the United States permit these last mentioned Indians to commence hostilities against the Subjects of his Catholic Majesty, or his Indians in any manner whatever. . . .

ART. XXI.

In order to terminate all differences on account of the losses sustained by the Citizens of the United States in consequence of their vessels and cargoes having been taken by the Subjects of his Catholic Majesty during the late war between Spain and France, it is agreed that all such cases shall be referred to the final decision of Commissioners. . . .

ART. XXII.

The two high contracting Parties hopping that the good correspondence and friendship which happily reigns between them will be further increased by this Treaty, and that it will contribute to augment their prosperity and opulence, will in future give to their mutual commerce all the extension and favor which the advantage of both Countries may require; and in consequence of the stipulations contained in the IV. article his Catholic Majesty will permit the Citizens of the United States for the space of three years from this time to deposit their merchandise and effects in the Port of New Orleans, and to export them from thence without paying any other duty than a fair price for the hire of the stores, and his Majesty promises either to continue this permission if he finds during that time that it is not prejudicial to the interests of Spain, or if he should not agree to continue it there, he will assign to them on another part of the banks of the Mississipi an equivalent establishment.

ART. XXIII.

The present Treaty shall not be in force untill ratified by the Contracting Parties, and the ratifications shall be exchanged in six months from this time, or sooner if possible.

In Witness whereof We the underwritten Plenipotentiaries of His Catholic Majesty and of the United States of America have signed this present Treaty of Friendship, Limits and Navigation and have "hereunto affixed our seals respectively.

Done at San Lorenzo el Real this seven and twenty day of October one thousand seven hundred and ninety five.

THOMAS PINCKNEY
[Seal]
EL PRINCIPE DE LA PAZ
[Seal]

Source: Avalon Project, Yale Law School (*www.yale.edu/lawweb/avalon/diplomacy/ spain/sp1795.htm*).

Copyright 1876 by Currier & Ives N.Y.

GEORGE WASHINGTON.   GENL HENRY KNOX, Secy of War.   ALEXANDER HAMILTON, Secy of the Treasury   THOMAS JEFFERSON, Secy of State   EDMUND RANDOLPH, Attorney General

WASHINGTON AND HIS CABINET.

Political parties emerged in part from differences over policy in President George Washington's cabinet. Left to right: President Washington, Secretary of War Henry Knox, Secretary of the Treasury Alexander Hamilton, Secretary of State Thomas Jefferson, and Attorney General Edmund Randolph.

CHAPTER FIVE

Institutional Relations

Two stories arise from President Washington's relationship with major institutions. One story depicts a drama in which Washington, working with and sometimes against other constitutionally sanctioned institutions, established the boundaries of presidential power. The result would have pleased those who established the Constitution and recruited Washington to preside over the new government. Washington forcefully demonstrated the presidency's importance in the administration and enforcement of laws. Meanwhile, the chief executive's supremacy in foreign affairs was upheld, but was balanced by Congress's dominance in legislation.

The other story, that of Washington's relations with extraconstitutional institutions, is equally important. As modern political scientists routinely argue, the formal institutions of democracy are not sufficient for real democracy to flourish. Without a free press, political parties, and a multiplicity of other organizations that give average citizens a voice in public affairs, a formal democracy can mask what is in fact an authoritarian regime.

CONGRESS

President Washington did not believe he had any right to lead Congress to enact the laws that he was certain were in the public's interest.

In discussing legislation to promote better agricultural practices, he wrote, "However convinced I am of the great advantages to be derived to the Community, I know not whether I can with propriety do any thing more at present than what I have already done" (Phelps 1993, 141). He had, he went on to observe, already recommended the subject in question to the attention of Congress in one of his annual addresses. The rest was up to the members of the legislature.

Washington felt comfortable recommending legislation to Congress's attention only because the Constitution stipulates in Article II, Section 3, that the president "shall from time to time give to the Congress Information of the State of the Union, and recommend to their Consideration such Measures as he shall judge necessary and expedient." In accordance with this obligation, Washington appeared personally before Congress to deliver his annual message, or State of the Union address. (After President Thomas Jefferson [1801–1809] discontinued the practice, finding a written message more in keeping with the republican simplicity he sought to impose on the office, presidents did not deliver their annual messages to Congress in person until President Woodrow Wilson restored the tradition in 1913.) In those speeches, the president would recommend, typically in broad terms, topics for legislative action. In only one instance, the creation of a more uniform militia, did Washington personally draft legislation that he then gave to his secretary of war, Henry Knox, to present to Congress.

Washington's cautious perspective on executive-congressional relations was evident, for example, in the role he assigned himself in passage of the Bill of Rights. Some states had ratified the Constitution with the understanding that a set of amendments, a "bill of rights," guaranteeing the people and the states their traditional liberties would be considered at the earliest opportunity. Washington explained the situation to his friend the Marquis de Lafayette before he took office as president. "[T]here are many things in the Constitution," he wrote on April 28, 1788, from Mount Vernon, "which only need to be explained, in order to prove equally satisfactory to all parties. For example: there was not a member of the convention, I believe, who had the least objection to what is contended for by the Advocates for a *Bill of Rights and Tryal by Jury*" (Fitzpatrick 1931–1944, 29:478). Believing, then, that there was a consensus on the advisability of such amendments, Washington went so far in his inaugural address as to delicately remind Congress of the matter before it. "[I]t will remain with your judgment," the new president announced, "to decide how far an exercise of the occasional power delegated by the fifth article of the Constitution [pertaining to amendments] is rendered expedient at the present juncture" (Richardson 1897, 45). Washington then left it entirely to Congress to act on his "recommendation."

George Washington was not, then, in any sense a legislative leader (see Chapter 3). His rejection of this role was in keeping with the plan of the framers, who believed that the legislative branch had full responsibility for deliberating on legislation. After Washington recommended legislation to Congress, he declined to lobby in its behalf. In his consultations with members of Congress, the president was careful not to give his critics any occasion for suspicion that he was attempting to influence congressional deliberations. When he invited members of the House and Senate to dine with him, he extended invitations by rotation to maintain the appearance of strict noninterference (see Chapter 1). The president did consult with James Madison, his longtime friend who emerged in the Washington presidency as a leader of the House. When he did so, however, it was typically to request Madison's perspective as a constitutional framer, not for Madison's contemporary partisan views (Wills 2002, 40–42).

The clearest instance of Washington's constitutional reticence occurred in the context of the Jay Treaty. In 1794, after the president sent Supreme Court Chief Justice John Jay to Britain to negotiate a treaty that he hoped would avoid war between France and Britain, Secretary of the Treasury Alexander Hamilton urged the president to lobby Congress to prevent passage of the provocative measures, such as confiscation of British property in American hands, it was debating. Washington, however, refused to speak out publicly on the pending legislation. In the Senate, only Vice President John Adams's use of his power to break a tie vote prevented that body from passing anti-British legislation at a moment of critical importance to Washington's policy of neutrality.

Such was Washington's reputation, however, that even in silence the president exercised what some members of Congress saw as an overbearing influence on events. Everyone knew Washington was opposed to legislation that might undermine his own choice of a foreign policy, and apparently that was enough to give many middle-of-the road members of Congress pause. "The influence of the ex[ecutive] on events . . . ," wrote James Madison to retired Secretary of State Jefferson, "and the public confidence in the P[resident] are an overmatch for all the efforts Republicanism can make" (Flexner 1972, 153).

The Veto

At the Constitutional Convention in Philadelphia, Washington had expressed to his fellow Virginia delegates his wish that the executive have exclusive use of the veto—that is, the president would not to have to share that power with a council. On this point, Washington was with the majority. He also had hoped that the Constitution would make it extremely difficult for Congress to override an executive veto, desiring a three-fourths vote threshold rather than the two-thirds vote that was adopted. As the first president, Washington was more willing to veto, and to entertain use of the veto, than either John Adams or Thomas Jefferson, his immediate successors. During his eight years in office, Washington issued two vetoes, both of which were upheld. Presidents Adams and Jefferson did not exercise the veto at all. In fact, of the six presidents who held office from Washington to the revolutionary administration of Andrew Jackson, only three vetoed any legislation (Nelson 1999, 476).

Washington first considered issuing a veto after Congress passed its first revenue bill, which placed tariffs on certain imported items and rejected the principle of "discrimination" against British goods. Washington believed that the United States should place higher tariffs on British imports in retaliation for Britain's refusal to enter into a commercial treaty with its former adversary. Yet despite his reservations about its merits, Washington signed the bill into law. But before doing so, he discussed the legislation with influential members of Congress, who assured him that it was not their intent with this bill to close the debate on discrimination, and that they, in fact, already planned further deliberations on the issue. On another occasion, in 1791, after Congress passed legislation to redeem the public debt and to establish a Bank of the United States (see Chapter 3), Washington waited until Congress sent him its bill to decide whether he would support the legislation initiated by his own secretary of the Treasury. He finally signed the bill, but only after soliciting lengthy arguments pro and con from his Treasury secretary and James Madison, leader of the anti-Hamilton faction in the House.

Washington's first veto was of a bill passed by Congress to reapportion House seats after the nation's first census. The bill would have violated the constitutional dictate that "[t]he Number of Representatives shall not exceed one for every thirty Thousand" (Article I, Section 2). In issuing this veto (Document 5.1), Washington upheld the role of the president as guardian of the Constitution. This role was especially important at the time, because the Supreme Court had not yet utilized the right of judicial review by which federal courts set aside laws and executive actions that violate the Constitution.

Washington's second veto (Document 5.2), of a law that would have made dangerous and unfair cuts in military personnel, more resembled the kind of veto exercised by modern presidents—that is, used to strike down bills viewed as constitutional but bad policy. Because in his second veto Washington sought to give voice to the people's will (something not commonly thought to be a presidential priority), that veto established no precedent and even today is often overlooked (Phelps 1989, 268). Washington never sought to explain this potentially radical use of the veto power. One can only surmise that his special feeling of responsibility for the lives of American citizens, and his historically grounded concern for the welfare of the nation's soldiers, compelled him to issue this unusual veto.

Treaty Making

The Constitution stipulates in Article II, Section 2, that the president "shall have Power, by and with the Advice and Consent of the Senate, to make Treaties, provided two thirds of the Senators present concur." Thinking to solicit in person the advice and consent of the Senate, the president traveled to the Senate chambers early in his first term to seek that body's opinion of draft instructions to be given to commissioners who soon would be negotiating a treaty with the Cherokees. The senators, reluctant to debate the matter while the president sat watching, told Washington to come back the next day. Washington did so, but vowed never to repeat the experiment (see Document 5.3). From that time on, treaties would be negotiated by presidents and their agents and then presented to the Senate for its retrospective advice. And presidents would routinely take into their confidence in the early stages of treaty formation members of the Senate whose views they thought to be personally and politically valuable. Washington himself followed this informal ad hoc practice while choosing an envoy to send to Britain in 1794.

War Powers

President Washington never claimed that as president he possessed "war powers." Congress was responsible, in Washington's interpretation of the Constitution, for deciding whether and when to go to war. In declaring his policy of neutrality between the warring powers of Europe (see Chapter 4 and Document 4.1), Washington asserted that he was not usurping a congressional prerogative, but merely declaring what the government's policy was. Until such time as Congress might change the policy, the United States was at peace with all the parties in the European war. However, because neutrality meant in practice partiality toward Britain, Washington's decision unleashed vicious attacks on his administration and a famous exchange of opinions by Hamilton and Madison (see Documents 4.2 and 4.3).

Hamilton claimed that the difference between the vesting clauses of Articles I and II of the Constitution was intended to suggest that the president had a residuum of discretionary power to use as he saw fit. Article I, in vesting power in Congress, stipulates carefully that Congress is to have "[a]ll legislative Powers herein granted." The complementary clause in Article II states that the "executive Power shall be vested in a President of the United States of America." According to Hamilton, the "executive Power" included all powers normally exercised by an executive, such as a king, even if those powers were not expressly mentioned as belonging to the American executive. Hamilton's argument struck Madison and his patron, Jefferson, as the most extreme of "heresies" (Nelson 1999, 39).

Hamilton's argument as Pacificus (see Chapter 4) contained seeds of presidential prerogative that would germinate in future presidencies, and would be used by presidents to justify bypassing Congress when going to war. Washington himself was content to use Hamilton's argument simply as a defense for his Neutrality Proclamation of 1793. In ordering military personnel into harm's way, Washington acted only after securing congressional authorization.

In the Indian war in the Northwest Territory, Washington acted under authority given by Congress on September 29, 1789, in an act "for the purpose of protecting the inhabitants of the frontiers of the United States from the hostile incursions of the Indians" (Fisher 1995, 13). That act provided that the president might "call into service from time to time, such part of the militia of the states respectively, as he may judge necessary for the purpose aforesaid." In the years that followed, Congress passed additional authorizations extending the time during which the president might call on the militia in the Northwest Territory.

In the Whiskey Rebellion of 1794, the president acted with force after Associate Justice James Wilson informed him that the laws of the nation could not be upheld by normal means in western Pennsylvania. Wilson made this communication pursuant to a 1792 act of Congress that had spelled out the procedure to be followed if the president were ever to call on the militia to quell a domestic disturbance. According to the act, whenever the laws of the nation were obstructed "by combinations too powerful to be suppressed by the ordinary course of judicial proceedings, or by the powers vested in the marshals by this act," the president should be notified by a member of the federal court. Only then could the president call on the militia to suppress the "combinations" (Phelps 1993, 16).

Even after receiving the requisite notification from Wilson, Washington attempted to avoid calling the militia into federal service. Because the dissension was located in western Pennsylvania, the president attempted to persuade the governor of that state, Thomas Mifflin, to call into service his own state's militia. Mifflin, however, was as reluctant as Washington to resort to arms and declined to do so. Washington therefore called into service a militia from several states, which he personally led across the mountains.

Appointments

In making appointments, Washington's criteria included political items such as geographic balance and support for the Constitution. His principal concern, however, was for reputation. Did the candidate have the confidence of those on whose behalf he had previously exercised some public authority as a state official, judge, assemblyman, or military officer? Confident in himself as a judge of character, Washington was offended whenever the Senate declined to ratify his selections. Nevertheless, he accepted the practice of "senatorial courtesy," whereby the Senate agrees not to endorse the president's nomination of any candidate for high office who is personally or politically repugnant to the senatorial delegation from the candidate's home state (see Document 5.4).

As for the president's right to replace Senate-confirmed appointees, on July 14, 1789, Vice President John Adams cast the tie-breaking vote in the Senate in favor of executive independence. His vote was on a motion to strike, from a bill creating the State Department, language indicating that the secretary of that department "shall be removed from office by the President of the United States." After four days, the bill passed with the controversial clause intact, and was signed into law nine days later (Nelson, 1999, 35–36). The issue was thus settled for the duration of Washington's time in office, although it would be revived in future administrations. The president's right to replace Senate-confirmed appointees was more important than it might seem, because without the power to fire an official without Senate approval, a president might lose control of the executive branch of government. Department heads incurring the displeasure of the president might even seek an alliance with the Senate against the president on matters of controversial policy. Because the Constitution was silent about the president's relationship with the heads of the major departments, the Senate's vote to make department heads responsible to the executive alone once confirmed was of historic importance.

Congressional Investigations

When Maj. Gen. Arthur St. Clair's army met disaster in the Northwest on November 4, 1791, Secretary of War Henry Knox urged the chastened general to seek a presidential inquiry into his leadership. Congress deliberated and decided that the House, not the president, should conduct the investigation. The special committee impaneled for the task was authorized to ask the executive for relevant documents. Washington convened his cabinet to consider the executive's reply. The secretaries of the departments then asked for time to study the matter and, when reconvened two days later, agreed that such requests should be directed to the president himself and not to the head of one of the departments, and that the president should decide on a case-by-case basis. In this case, none of the papers requested would injure the public, so all were released. The president therefore complied with Congress, but in the process he made the first official argument in behalf of executive privilege.

The president gave Congress a different response when the House of Representatives demanded on March 2, 1796, that he present to them the same documents that he had presented to the Senate in the latter's consideration of the Jay Treaty. The House reasoned that its responsibility to appropriate funds to implement a treaty gave it the right to review such documents and to debate the merits of a treaty it would have to fund. The executive refused this demand on the grounds that, within

Congress, the Constitution grants the Senate sole power to advise and consent to treaties.

The president, however, was not always hesitant to give Congress what it wanted to conduct an investigation. In 1793, when Democratic-Republicans in the House began an inquiry into the financial conduct of Secretary of the Treasury Alexander Hamilton, the president saw no reason to withhold from Congress what it requested for its investigation. Congress actually wanted Hamilton to appear before it to report on the use of appropriated funds. Although he did not compel Hamilton to appear, Washington indicated clearly that he thought it would be proper for him to do so. On his part, Hamilton resented Washington's failure to shield him from his critics, but he knew that in one way he was getting off easy with his Democratic-Republican opponents. After all, a man had approached some Democratic-Republican members of Congress, claiming to possess evidence against the secretary that would ruin him. The evidence turned out to be of a personal nature, however, and the members of Congress, after consulting Jefferson himself, declined to use it. (Hamilton had had an affair with the man's wife. Although he paid money to keep the affair quiet, Hamilton did refuse the husband's demands that Hamilton use his influence to place the husband on the government's payroll.)

The Jeffersonians had hoped for evidence of public, not private, corruption. All they found was that Hamilton had at times applied funds appropriated for one thing toward some other thing also authorized by the legislature. In 1789 Washington himself had spent money appropriated for treaty negotiations in the South for a survey to fix the nation's border in the North. Democratic-Republicans trusted President Washington with discretion, however, but not Secretary Hamilton. In fact, Hamilton's fellow cabinet member, Jefferson, drafted a list of charges condemning Hamilton's conduct. Most of the charges asserted as fact the alleged misdeeds that Hamilton had been forced to defend himself against—for example, that he had used funds appropriated for one purpose for another, and had done so "without the instruction of the President of the United States" (Cunningham 2000, 104). The last two resolutions made plain Jefferson's desires for his nemesis and his office:

9. *Resolved,* That at the next meeting of Congress, the act of Sep 2d, 1789, establishing a Department of the Treasury should be so amended

as to constitute the office of the Treasurer of the United States a separate department, independent of the Secretary of the Treasury.

10. *Resolved,* That the Secretary of the Treasury has been guilty of maladministration in the duties of his office, and should, in the opinion of Congress, be removed from his office by the President of the United States.

The list, edited to remove these last two most radical charges and entered into debate as resolutions of the House, was voted down. Only five members, including James Madison, voted for all charges. Disappointed at the result in the House, Sen. James Monroe published a lengthy tirade, "An Examination of the Late Proceedings in Congress Respecting the Official Conduct of the Secretary of the Treasury," in which he leveled against Hamilton the charges that had been aired in the House. Hamilton responded by distributing the House proceedings themselves. The partisan presses urged members on both sides of the conflict to continue the battle.

During Washington's second term, the House again investigated Hamilton, with the same result. This time, though, the Republicans goaded Hamilton into a defense that dragged the president into the inquiry. Hamilton declared that when in the past he had diverted funds appropriated for one purpose to another, he had in fact done so *with Washington's approval.* The president did not recall giving Hamilton any such authorization, however, and made this plain in a letter to Hamilton. Hamilton asked Washington to revise his statement, or at least to meet personally with Hamilton on the matter. To the outrage of Federalists in Congress and the delight of Democratic-Republicans, Washington declined to do both. A precedent was established that a president's department heads should be prepared to defend themselves before Congress and not to bring the president into the conflict.

THE CABINET

When George Washington began his first term, he and the vice president, and Washington's longtime personal secretary, Tobias Lear, were the executive branch of the new government. Holdovers from the Articles of Confederation government continued to be available to the president for advice and assistance, but clearly the president needed help. Exactly what help would the new president have?

After three months of debate in 1789, Congress passed bills creating departments to oversee war, foreign affairs, and the Treasury. The heads of the three departments, and eventually the attorney general, a position created in the Judiciary Act passed the same year, made up what became known as the president's cabinet. Washington first began to refer to this group as his "Cabinet" in April 1793 (Flexner 1970, 214).

The old Department of Foreign Affairs was renamed the Department of State, because Congress made the same department responsible for some domestic matters such as weights and measures. The department for war and war preparations was called, in the straightforward style of the time, the Department of War. Both departments were understood to be uniquely executive; their heads were to report to the president. The bill establishing the Department of the Treasury was worded differently, so that the head of that department would be responsible, in theory, to Congress as well as to the president. In Section 2 of the act creating the Treasury Department, Congress specified that it was the duty of the head of that department "to make report, and give information to either branch of the legislature, in person or in writing (as he may be required), respecting all matters referred to him by the Senate or House of Representatives, or which shall appertain to his office" (*www.ustreas.gov/education/fact-sheets/history/act-congress.html*). This designation was intended to balance the president's right to request such information, as provided in the Constitution (Article II, Section 2). Given the vigor of the first secretary, Alexander Hamilton, Congress was not able to use this meager paper job description to keep the Treasury from entering into the executive orbit. The head of the Treasury, like the heads of war and state, would take his place in the president's cabinet at the pleasure of the chief executive, and would therefore be responsible first and foremost to the president.

The attorney general held a special place at the margins of the cabinet. The position was not at first that of the head of an executive department. In fact, the first attorney general, the nation's chief legal officer, had no staff and a salary that was half that of the heads of departments. The position was understood to be part time, and early attorneys general maintained private law practices in their home states. The attorney general's responsibilities, as established by Congress, were to serve as the government's advocate in the Supreme Court and to advise the president and the department heads on legal matters.

Washington was determined to use his cabinet officers, at first singly and then as a group, in an orderly manner, so that he could avoid spending his time on details best left to subordinate officials. For this reason, he declined to discuss foreign relations directly with the French minister to the United States, insisting instead that the minister speak with the secretary of state. Washington wanted the ordinary business of the government to come to him after being "digested and prepared" by the head of the relevant department (Flexner 1970, 213). Similarly, Washington made it clear that he expected his department heads to be available to him, daily if necessary, to answer questions and to prepare reports. In his first several years in office, Washington typically met privately with the heads of the executive department, or exchanged correspondence with them, as suited his needs at the moment.

By 1792, the final year of his first term, Washington was calling regular meetings of his department heads, plus the attorney general, in an apparent attempt to "iron out in advance the disagreements to which his advisers were becoming prone" (Flexner 1970, 353). Most modern presidents have continued this practice; they use meetings of this ostensibly advisory body primarily to remind its members of the loyalty they owe to its head and to impress on all members the importance of presenting a united front to Congress and the wider world beyond. Washington looked to his trusted adviser, Attorney General Edmund Randolph, in particular, for help in finding common ground between Hamilton and Jefferson. But as in many modern administrations, the attempt to forge consensus proved futile. Jefferson and Hamilton were not to be restrained. Each looked jealously at the president's relationship with the other for any signs of favoritism. Contemporary myth to the contrary notwithstanding, Washington sided more often on controversial points with Jefferson than with Hamilton (Malone 1948–1981, 3:11, 448–449). Yet because Washington had sided early on with Hamilton on the critically important issues of the bank and debt redemption (see Chapter 3), Jefferson and his allies, with reason, viewed themselves as the "underdogs" in the contest for the president's support.

The difficulties Washington had with his two most famous cabinet members were rivaled by the trouble he encountered when he made Randolph secretary of state, replacing Jefferson, who had resigned at the end of 1793. As noted, in the cabinet Randolph often had sought the middle ground in the disputes between Hamilton and Jefferson, who was his cousin. But despite the family connection, Jefferson disapproved of the appointment, thinking that Randolph had gone too far in support of Hamilton's schemes. In a letter to Washington, Jefferson reminded the president that Randolph's reputation with Virginia merchants and shop-keepers was poor and that his "character of independence" had been compromised by the fact that he was perpetually short of funds (Flexner 1972, 107).

The Federalists did not fully appreciate the animosity between the out-going and incoming secretaries, however, and expected Randolph to be a tool of Jeffersonian republicanism. For this reason, when the British minister to the United States revealed to the Federalist-aligned Ameri-can secretaries of war and Treasury a captured French document that seemed to implicate Randolph in a scheme to use French funds to incite violence against the government in the Whiskey Rebellion, they hurried to show the incriminating evidence to the president.

The captured document, which was not wholly intact, reported that Randolph was the secret head of the pro-French Philadelphia Democratic Society, and suggested that he had asked the French agent for money: "A few thousand dollars would have decided between war and peace! So the consciences of the so-called American patriots already have their price!" (Schultz 2000, 10). The document suggested that because the French would not pay the demanded bribe, the pro-French Democratic Society came out in support of Washington's use of force against a pro-French, pro-revolution rebellion beyond the mountains.

Washington confronted Randolph with the "evidence" in the presence of Secretary of War Timothy Pickering and Secretary of the Treasury Oliver Wolcott. Randolph insisted that he was innocent, and expressed anger at Washington's ill treatment and lack of confidence. He fled from the room without defending himself in any detail, revealing to Washing-ton's satisfaction his guilt. Randolph then resigned, and after four months published a 108-page *Vindication*, in which he argued he had sought money from the French, but not for himself. He had wanted to uncover British complicity in the Whiskey Rebellion. Pennsylvania merchants had evidence that the British had instigated the rebellion to spur moderate Americans to look with horror on pro-French, pro-revolutionary senti-ment in their midst. These merchants would not reveal their secrets, how-ever, so long as they were in debt to British factors. If the French would pay off their debts, these merchants would be free to tell all they knew of

British perfidy. It was, Randolph insisted, perfectly innocent, and merely a passing thought. The *Vindication* went on to charge Washington with hypocrisy, disloyalty, and something close to senility. Indeed, Randolph hinted in this open letter to the president that Washington had lost his faculties (Randolph 1855, 75).

SUPREME COURT

President Washington's relationship with the Supreme Court was shaped by his personal regard for the first chief justice, John Jay. The early Court was composed of five associate justices and one chief justice. Based on his lengthy experience in national affairs, Washington made his own selections of the men to fill these positions. Sometimes, however, he consulted with an adviser. In seeking a chief justice, he solicited informally the advice of his friend and ally James Madison. Indeed, at the beginning of his presidency Washington often sought Madison's advice—but because of the men's personal relationship, not because of any congruence of constitutional responsibilities (the House, of which Madison was a member, had no role in the confirmation of a justice).

While the new government was being created, Jay was serving abroad as minister of foreign affairs under the Articles of Confederation. Jay, who already had turned down the offer to be secretary of state, was chosen for the Court because he had been a leading advocate of the Constitution and coauthor with Hamilton and Madison of *The Federalist Papers*. He was confirmed by the Senate in a voice vote.

Because of Washington's respect for Jay, and because the early Supreme Court had at first virtually no work to do, Washington felt free to consult with Jay on a wide range of matters. In preparation for his annual message to Congress of 1790, the president wrote to Jay: "If any thing in the judiciary line, if any thing of a more general nature, proper for me to communicate to that body at the opening of the session, has occurred to you, you would oblige me by submitting them with the freedom and frankness of friendship" (Johnston 1891, 3:409). Jay obliged the president with a lengthy letter covering diverse issues such as the coinage of silver, the repair of post roads, the military utility of the fortification at West Point, and conservation of timber from which to make ships' masts (Jay to Washington, November 13, 1790, in Johnston 1891, 3:405–408). In addition, Jay and Hamilton exchanged confidences on the government and administration policy. It was then not surprising that when Hamilton at last withdrew from consideration as special envoy to Britain during the crisis of Washington's second term, he put forward Jay as the only suitable alternative (see Chapter 4).

The relationship between the president and the Supreme Court was not always as open as Washington would have liked. In the crisis with France that accompanied Citizen Genêt across the Atlantic (see Chapter 4), the president attempted at one point to pass on to his cabinet responsibility for deciding precisely what the president's own policy of neutrality would allow with regard to French seizure of British shipping. Unable to lead his cabinet to a consensus, he instructed its members to meet without him and come to some sort of decision. The cabinet, following Jefferson's lead, told the president he should ask the Supreme Court to decide. Writing for the Court, Chief Justice Jay declined, stating that the doctrine of separation of powers made it inappropriate for the Court to issue advisory opinions (see Document 5.5). The members of the Court might advise the president informally, but they would not put the authority of the Court behind such advice. One analyst of the opinion holds that the 1793 "incident provides the source for not only the prohibition against advisory opinions but an entire constellation of doctrines falling under the label of justiciability: mootness, standing, ripeness, political questions, the doctrine of independent state grounds, the principle that constitutional questions are reached only as a last resort, and its related doctrine favoring a narrow basis for decision" (Stewart 1997, 171).

EXTRACONSTITUTIONAL INSTITUTIONS

President Washington recognized the importance and legitimacy of extraconstitutional institutions. He acknowledged at various times the importance of family, the militia company, school and college, church and temple (see Document 5.6), and even, within limits, the press. The president was not at all pleased, however, by the growth of party spirit within his administration and in Congress. He was particularly distressed at the part that his most illustrious cabinet members were playing in the establishment of party conflict.

The conflict between the supporters of a strong national government and those who feared such a government was keenly felt in the

Washington administration because of the presence there of Alexander Hamilton and Thomas Jefferson. Neither man trusted the motives or the loyalties of the other, to the extent that both felt justified in using extraordinary, and extraconstitutional, means to diminish the influence in government of the other.

The Press

In the prelude to the American Revolution, George Washington, like all rebels, relied on the free circulation of pamphlets and newspapers for information and points of view about events in the colonies. Freedom of the press had been indispensable to the freedom of the republic and was guaranteed in the Bill of Rights, whose adoption Washington favored. Like many a president, however, Washington's support for a free press was sorely tested when columnists turned their ire against the chief executive.

During the Washington administration, a number of newspapers, some lasting only months, offered readers information and commentary on political events. The two most important papers were the *Gazette of the United States* and the *National Gazette,* under the influence, respectively, of Alexander Hamilton and Thomas Jefferson.

In 1789 John Fenno, a businessman from Boston, launched the pro-administration *Gazette of the United States,* and set up operations in the nation's temporary capital, New York. Alexander Hamilton became the unofficial sponsor of the paper, writing for it under pseudonyms and "lending" Fenno money without asking for repayment (Pasley 2001, 58). In Fenno's newspaper, the pomp and ceremony of the early Washington presidency were covered in detail and praised as befitting the majesty of the new government. This kind of coverage alarmed Thomas Jefferson and James Madison, who then set in motion a plan for a rival paper, the *National Gazette.* Jefferson employed the paper's editor, Philip Freneau, as his department's official French-English translator, but made it clear that Freneau would have "so little to do" that he could pursue another calling. The *National Gazette* portrayed Washington as a tragic figure: a great man who was increasingly under the influence of "the aristocratic few and their contemptible minions of speculators, torries and British emissaries" (Humphrey 1996, 48).

By the last year of his first term, personal criticism of Washington began to surface in the opposition press. Freneau, in his paper, went so far as to denounce "reverence [for] the supporter of a principle, instead of the principle itself," suggesting that if only citizens would stop idolizing Washington they might rally to the opposition against his policies supporting a strong central government (Sharp 1993, 54). In an exchange of letters in the summer of 1792, Washington, Jefferson, and Hamilton debated who was at fault for the newspaper war and the divide within the government that it reflected. Jefferson initiated the correspondence when he sent the president a lengthy letter detailing multiple charges against Hamilton and his allies. Jefferson included among his adversary's allies the editor and contributors to the *Gazette*. These persons were, said Jefferson, a "corrupt squadron" who were bent on preparing "the way for a change, from the present form of government, to that of a monarchy" (Cunningham 2000, 79). Washington recast Jefferson's charges in his own words and sent them to Hamilton, asking him for his response to "a variety of matters" which unnamed "others, less friendly perhaps to the Government, and more disposed to arraign the conduct of its officers" had brought to his attention (Document 5.7). In his reply, Hamilton answered the charges item by item, and included his own countercharges against his antagonists.

In private letters to both men later that summer, Washington scolded Hamilton and Jefferson alike, reminding them that "differences in political opinions are as unavoidable as, to a certain point, they may be necessary," but that "liberal allowances" must be made for the motives of those with different opinions. There must be, he wrote in identical language to both men, "mutual forbearances and temporizing yieldings *on all sides*" (Cunningham 2000, 94).

Hamilton and Jefferson replied on the same day. Hamilton agreed with the president that the current state of affairs in his administration was bound to "destroy the energy of Government" if it did not abate (Document 5.8). Hamilton insisted, though, that he had shown forbearance against the party of Jefferson, but that when he determined that Jefferson's intent was "subversion of measures, which in its consequences would subvert the Government," he yielded to the impulse to retaliate. "I cannot doubt, from the evidence I possess," Hamilton wrote, "that the National Gazette was instituted by him for political purposes and that one leading object of it has been to render me and all the measures connected with my department as odious as possible" (Document 5.8). He did not apologize for retaliating, though he pledged to abide by

Washington's leadership "if you shall hereafter form a plan to reunite the members of your administration."

Jefferson's reply was lengthier and less conciliatory (see Document 5.9). He claimed that Hamilton had "duped" him into supporting the creation of the Bank of the United States (see Chapter 3). He now realized, he wrote, that Hamilton's financial plan "was calculated to undermine and demolish the republic." The man himself, Jefferson wrote angrily, will be remembered by history, if he is remembered at all, as but "a tissue of machinations against the liberty of the country which has not only received and given him bread, but heaped its honors on his head."

When Jefferson shortly afterward retired from the administration, Freneau's newspaper folded for lack of funds. Ironically, this only worsened the president's relations with the opposition press. The Philadelphia *Aurora,* edited by Benjamin Franklin Bache (Benjamin Franklin's grandson), took up the torch for the Jeffersonian cause and began to attack Washington himself. "If ever a nation was debauched by a man," Bache commented on Washington after his Farewell Address, "the American nation has been debauched by Washington" (Document 5.10).

Political Parties and Other "Self-Created Societies"

Washington is sometimes criticized for hypocrisy in continuing to assert nonpartisanship, while, in reality, he became a strong Federalist partisan. Washington's relationship to parties was actually too complex to support any such generalization. He struggled throughout his presidency to bring the opposition back into the consensus he hoped to leave as a legacy of his administration. Washington's quest for consensus, even unanimity of opinion, reflected his belief, common at the time, that parties were an abomination. Even the founders of the first political parties shared this view. Hamilton sincerely believed that Jefferson intended to subvert the government and destroy its constitutional foundations. Jefferson believed the same of Hamilton. Once the wars of Europe became the subject of American political divisions, both also became convinced that the other intended not just to destroy the government, but also to make the nation subservient to a foreign master. As the war abroad and at home continued, the Democratic-Republican press unleashed a multitude of attacks upon the president (Document 5.10). The president, nonetheless, resisted identification with the anti–Democratic-Republican, or Federalist Party, and even declined to endorse John Adams, the Federalist candidate and his own vice president, as his successor in the presidential contest of 1796.

The incredible thing is not that party spirit developed, or that it developed through the exchange of sometimes scurrilous newspaper articles, but that it did not descend into the chaos or tyranny that was widely feared. The moment of supreme danger, from Washington's perspective, came in 1794 during the Whiskey Rebellion. The year before, "Democratic Societies" had formed in Philadelphia and elsewhere. At the time of the Whiskey Campaign, there were perhaps thirty-five such political clubs, all supporting the Jeffersonian opponents of the president. The president believed that the Philadelphia Democratic Society had helped to instigate the uprising in western Pennsylvania, and he assailed a certain "self created society" in his annual message to Congress delivered in November 1794 (see Document 3.12). Madison saw Washington's denunciation of the societies as part of a Federalist plot. "The game was to connect the democratic societies with the odium of the insurrection, to connect the Democratic-Republicans in Congress with these societies, to put the President ostensibly at the head of the other party in opposition to both" (Hofstadter 1969, 94). The consequence was the rapid dissolution of the societies.

Fortunately for Americans and their new government, the American people had more in common with each other than they sometimes realized. The rough agreement of the political class, the freeholders, on the legitimacy of constitutional governance, and the fact that amidst the political turmoil of these early years Americans continued to prosper in their private lives, proved to be in retrospect sufficient safeguards against true "subversion." The president acted as a balance wheel. Although his cabinet was uniformly Federalist after the debacle with Randolph as secretary of state, Washington did not openly side with the Federalists as a party until he was freed from the constitutional responsibility of the presidency.

The States

When George Washington at last agreed to reenter public life by attending the Constitutional Convention of 1787, he was motivated by a desire to strengthen the national government. As commander in the Revolutionary War, he had seen firsthand the unfortunate consequences of state supremacy (see Chapter 1). Washington's policies as president were intended to unite the nation, even as it expanded (see Chapter 3). As a result of his beliefs and his policies, President Washington sometimes had tense relations with the states and the defenders of state sovereignty.

Washington's first occasion to uphold the superior power of the national government under the new Constitution was in Congress's first session, when it passed a routine resolution calling for a day of national thanksgiving. Such days of thanksgiving had been proclaimed many times under the Articles of Confederation, and defenders of states' power expected the new president to follow the old practice by transmitting to the governors the national government's request for the special day. Washington decided instead to issue the proclamation himself, speaking directly to the citizens of the Republic (Document 5.11). And as political scientist Glenn Phelps has observed, "not only was his proclamation directed to the people of the United States, but it asked a special blessing for the national government and the Constitution, but not the states!" (Phelps 1993, 128).

On other occasions as well the president took issue with those who would deny the superior power and dignity of the national government vis-à-vis the states. In his tour of the northern states, the president engaged in and won a contest of wills with Gov. John Hancock of Massachusetts, forcing the governor to acknowledge in protocol the supremacy of the national government (see Chapter 1). These battles over symbolism made it easier for the president to assert the powers of the national government when it really mattered, such as when he commanded certain states to send to the national government sufficient militia to quell the Whiskey Rebellion (see Chapter 3). In placing state militias directly under the control of officers of the U.S. Army in three successive campaigns against Indians in the Northwest, the president had similarly demonstrated his understanding of the strength of the national government to command action and obedience from the states (see Chapter 3).

A REPUBLIC FOR THE REAL WORLD

Washington sometimes acted, wrote, and spoke as if he were president of an ideal, classical republic, where the government rests on the strict virtue of the citizenry. For example, in a state such as republican Rome only the most upright citizenry could be kept in check, because institutions devoted to efficiently working out differences of opinion were few and easily corrupted. The resort to force was unnervingly common, because there was no public police force or civil service. Without unanimity or something close to it, violent chaos could and did ensue. Washington, who pined for "unanimity," seems not to have appreciated how different the United States was (Hofstadter 1969, 100–101). Its constitutional form of government was a check against tyranny, while the predominantly individualistic political culture among its mostly middle-class, free, white population gave presidents and other public leaders ample opportunity to forge compromises that would find support among a majority of voters. The president's ability to work with and through a variety of constitutional and extraconstitutional institutions was critical to the success of the American experiment in republican government.

BIBLIOGRAPHIC ESSAY

Standard sources on Washington's presidency contain considerable information on the president's relations with major institutions. See the latter two volumes of James Thomas Flexner's biography of Washington: *George Washington and the New Nation, 1783–1793* (Boston: Little, Brown, 1970), and *George Washington: Anguish and Farewell, 1793–1799* (Boston: Little, Brown, 1972). Also see Willard Sterne Randall's *George Washington, A Life* (New York: Henry Holt, 1997), and James D. Richardson's compilation of presidential documents, *Messages and Papers of the Presidents,* 20 vols. (New York: Bureau of National Literature, 1897).

More specialized resources on this topic include: Glenn A. Phelps, "George Washington: Precedent Setter," in *Inventing the American Presidency,* ed. Thomas E. Cronin (Lawrence: University Press of Kansas, 1989), 259–281, which is cited here, and which is elaborated on in Phelps, *George Washington and American Constitutionalism* (Lawrence: University Press of Kansas, 1993). Also see Louis Fisher's *Presidential War Power* (Lawrence: University Press of Kansas, 1995), and *The Politics of Shared Power* (College Station: Texas A&M University Press, 1998).

Washington's relations with his judiciary can be followed in more detail in: William R. Casto, *The Supreme Court in the Early Republic: The Chief Justiceships of John Jay and Oliver Ellsworth* (Columbia: University of South Carolina Press, 1995), and two essays in Scott Douglas Gerber, *Seriatim: The Supreme Court before John Marshall* (New York: New York University

Press, 1998)—the first by the editor, "Introduction: The Supreme Court before John Marshall," 1–25, and the second by Sandra Frances Van-Burkle, "'Honour, Justice, and Interest': John Jay's Republican Politics and Statesmanship on the Federal Bench," 26–69. In addition, see Jay Stewart, *Most Humble Servants: The Advisory Role of Early Judges* (New Haven: Yale University Press, 1997). On the attorney general in the early republic, see Cornell W. Clayton, *The Politics of Justice: The Attorney General and the Making of Legal Policy* (Armonk, N.Y.: M. E. Sharpe, 1992), and Daniel J. Meador, *The President, The Attorney General, and the Department of Justice* (Charlottesville: White Burkett Miller Center for Public Affairs, University of Virginia, 1980).

On Washington's relations with Hamilton and other financial elites, see Philip H. Burch Jr., *Elites in American History: The Federalist Years to the Civil War* (New York: Holmes and Meier, 1981). For Edmund Randolph's *Vindication*, see the reprint edition, *A Vindication of Edmund Randolph, Written by Himself and Published in 1795* (Richmond: no publisher specified, 1855). For a documentary history of the Jefferson versus Hamilton controversy, see Noble E. Cunningham Jr., *Jefferson vs. Hamilton: Confrontations that Shaped a Nation* (Boston: Bedford/St. Martin's, 2000).

On the press in the Washington era, see: Jeffrey L. Pasley, *"The Tyranny of Printers": Newspaper Politics in the Early American Republic* (Charlottesville: University Press of Virginia, 2001); Carol Sue Humphrey, *The Press of the Young Republic, 1783–1833* (Westport, Conn.: Greenwood Press, 1996); Donovan H. Bond and W. Reynolds McLeod, eds., *Newsletters to Newspapers: Eighteenth Century Journalism* (Morgantown: School of Journalism, West Virginia University, 1977); and Donald H. Stewart, *The Opposition Press of the Federalist Period* (Albany: State University of New York Press, 1969).

On the formation of the party system, see: Richard Hofstadter, *The Idea of a Party System: The Rise of Legitimate Opposition in the United States, 1780–1840* (Berkeley: University of California, 1969); Saul Cornell, *The Other Founders: Anti-Federalism and the Dissenting Tradition in America, 1788–1828* (Chapel Hill: University of North Carolina Press, 1999); John L. Brooke, "Ancient Lodges and Self-Created Societies: Voluntary Associations and the Public Sphere in the Early Republic," in *Launching the Extended Republic: The Federalist Era*, ed. Ronald Hoffman and Peter J. Albert (Charlottesville: University Press of Virginia, 1996), 273–359; and the excellent collection of essays in Doron Ben-Atar and Barbara B. Oberg, eds., *Federalists Reconsidered* (Charlottesville: University Press of Virginia, 1998).

Document 5.1   The First Presidential Veto Message, April 5, 1792

George Washington vetoed two bills while in office—one each term. The first veto was in response to a House reapportionment bill that followed the 1790 census. Washington rejected the measure as overly favorable to northern states. The House, after failing to override the veto, revised the bill to meet the president's objections.

Gentlemen of the House of Representatives: I have maturely considered the Act passed by the two Houses, intitled, "An Act for an apportionment of Representatives among the several States according to the first enumeration," and I return it to your House, wherein it originated, with the following objections.

First: The Constitution has prescribed that Representatives shall be apportioned among the several States, according to their respective Numbers: and there is no one proportion or division which, applied to the respective numbers of the States, will yield the number and allotment of Representatives proposed by the bill.

Second. The Constitution has also provided that the number of Representatives shall not exceed one for every thirty thousand: which restriction is, by the context, and by fair and obvious construction, to be applied to the seperate and respective numbers of the States: and the bill has allotted to eight of the States more than one for thirty thousand.

Source: John C. Fitzpatrick, ed., *The Writings of Washington from the Original Manuscript Sources, 1745–1799,* 39 vols. (Washington, D.C.: Government Printing Office, 1931–1944), 32:16–17, 35:405–406.

Document 5.2   Second Presidential Veto, February 28, 1797

The president delivered the following message to the House after receiving a bill he believed would have made dangerous and unfair cuts in military personnel. In this second veto, the president made the first use of his "negative" to reject a law that he deemed constitutional but inexpedient.

Gentlemen of the House of Representatives: Having maturely considered the Bill to alter and amend an Act entitled an Act to ascertain and fix the military establishment of the United States which was presented to me on the twenty second day of this Month I now return it to the House of Representatives, in which it originated with my objections. First. If the Bill passes into a law the two Companies of light dragoons will be from that moment legally out of service, though they will afterwards continue actually in service, and for their services during this interval, namely from the time of legal to the time of actual discharge, it will be unlawful to pay them, unless some future provision be made by law. Though they may be discharged at the pleasure of Congress, in justice they ought to receive their pay not only to the time of passing the law, but at least to the time of their actual discharge. Secondly. It will be inconvenient and injurious to the public to dismiss the light Dragoons as soon as notice of the law can be conveyed to them; one of the Companies having been lately destined to a necessary and important service. Thirdly. The Companies of Light Dragoons consist of one hundred and twenty six non commissioned Officers and privates, who are bound to serve as dismounted Dragoons, when ordered so to do; they have received in bounties about two thousand dollars; one of them is completely equipped, and above half of the non commissioned Officers and privates have yet to serve more than one third the term of their inlistment; and besides there will in the course of the year be a considerable deficiency in the complement of infantry intended to be continued. Under these circumstances to discharge the Dragoons does not seem to comport with economy. Fourthly. It is generally agreed that some Cavalry either Militia or regular will be necessary and according to the best information I have been able to obtain, it is my opinion, that the latter will be less expensive and more useful than the former, in preserving peace between the frontier settlers, and the Indians and therefore a part of the Military establishment should consist of Cavalry.

Source: John C. Fitzpatrick, ed., *The Writings of Washington from the Original Manuscript Sources, 1745–1799,* 39 vols. (Washington, D.C.: Government Printing Office, 1931–1944), 35:405–406.

Document 5.3   Sen. William Maclay, August 22, 1789

To preserve the confidentiality of its deliberations, the first Senate kept no official record of its debates. Fortunately for posterity, one senator kept a comprehensive diary. Unfortunately for George Washington, that senator was William Maclay, one of the administration's harshest critics. In this excerpt from the Pennsylvania senator's diary, Maclay describes a historic meeting of the president with the Senate.

Senate met and went on the Coasting bill, The Door Keeper soon told Us of the Arrival of the President. The President was introduced and took our President's chair—he rose and told us bluntly that he had called on Us for our advice and consent to some propositions respecting the Treaties to be held with the Southern Indians—said he had brought Genl. Knox with him who was well acquainted with the business. He then turned to Genl. Knox Who was seated {at his} on the left of the Chair. Genl. Knox handed him a paper which he handed to the President of the Senate, who was seated on a Chair on the floor to his right. our President hurried over the Paper. Carriages were driving past and such a Noise I could tell it was something about Indians, but was not master of one Sentence of it. Signs were made to the door Keeper to shut down the Sashes. Seven heads (as we since learn) were stated at the End of the Paper which the Senate were to give their advice and consent to. they were so framed that this could be done by Aye or No. {Our Presid.} The President told Us a paper from an Agent of the Cherokees was given to him just as he was coming to the Hall. he motioned to General Knox for it, and handed it to the President of the Senate. it was read, it complained hard of the unjust Treatment of the People of North Carolina & ca. their Violation of Treaties & ca. Our President now read off, the first article to which our advice and consent was requested. it referred back principally to some statements in the body of the Writing which had been read. Mr. Morris rose and said the Noise of carriages had been so great that he really could not say that he had heard the body of the paper which was read and prayed it might be read again. it was so. It was no sooner read than our President. immediately read the first head over and put the Question do you advise and consent & ca. There was a dead pause. Mr. Morris wispered me, we will see who will venture to break silence first. {Our Presi}—Our President was proceeding As many As—I rose reluctantly indeed, and from the length of the pause, the hint given by Mr. Morris, and the proceeding of our President, it appeared to me, that if I did not, no other one would. and we could have these advices and consents ravish'd in a degree from us. Mr. President. The paper which you have now read to Us appears to have for it's basis Sundry Treaties and public Transactions, between the southern Indians and the United States & and the States of Georgia North and south Carolina. The business is new to the Senate, it is of importance, it is our duty to inform ourselves as well as possible on the Subject. I therefore call for the reading of the Treaties and other documents alluded to in the paper now before Us. I cast an Eye at the President of the United States, I saw he wore an aspect of Stern displeasure. General Knox turned up some of the Acts of Congress, and the protests of One Blount Agent for North Carolina. Mr. Lee rose and named a particular Treaty which he wished to read. the Business laboured with the Senate, there appeared an evident reluctance to proceed. The first Article was about the Cherokees, it was hinted that the Person just come from then, might have more information. The President of U.S. rose said he had no objection to that article being postponed and in the mean time he could see the Messenger. the 2d Article which was about the Chickasaws and Choctaws was likewise postponed. The 3d Article more immediately concerned Georgia and the Creeks. Mr. Gun from Georgia moved this to be postponed to Monday he was seconded by Few Genl. Knox was asked, when Genl. Lincoln would be here on his way to Georgia. he answered, not untill Saturday next the Whole House seemed against Gun and Few. I rose & said When I considered the Newness and the importance of the subject, that One Article had already been postponed, That Genl. Lincoln the first named of the {Trustees had} Commissioners would not be here for a week. The deep interest Georgia had in this affair, I could not think it improper that the Senators from that State should be indulged in a postponement untill monday. more especially as I had not heard any inconvenience pointed out that could possibly flow from it. the Question was put and actually carried. But Elsworth immediately began a long discourse on the Merits of the Business. he was answered by Mr. Lee Who appeald to the Consti[tu]tion with regard to the powers of making War. Butler & Izard answered & ca.Mr. Morris at last informed the disputants that they were debating on a Subject that was actually postponed. Mr. Adams denied in the face of the House that it had been postponed. this very trick has been played by him and his New England Men more than Once. the Question was however put a 2d time and carried. I had at an early stage wispered Mr. Morris that I thought the best way to conduct the business was to have all the papers committed—my reasons were that I saw no chance of a fair investigation of subjects while the President of the U.S. sat there with his Secretary at War, to support his Opinions and over awe the timid and neutral part of the Senate—Mr. Morris hastily rose and moved that the papers communicated to the Senate by the P. of the U.S. should be referred to a committee of 5, to report immediately as soon as might be, on them. he was seconded by Mr. Gun. several Members Grumbled some Objections. Mr. Butler rose made a lengthy speech against committment. said we were acting as a Council no Councils ever committed anything, Committees were an improper mode of doing business, it threw business out of the hands of the Many into the hands of the few. &ca. I rose and supported the mode of doing business by Committees, asserted that Executive Councils did make use of Councils committees, that Committees were used in all public deliberative bodies &c. &ca. I thought I did the Subject Justice, but concluded, the Committment cannot be attended with any possible inconvenience, some articles are already postponed untill Monday, Whoever the Committee are (if committed) they must make their report on Monday morning. I spoke thro' the Whole in a low tone of Voice. Peevishness itself I think could not have taken offence at anything I said. as I sat down the President of the U.S. started up in a Violent fret. This defeats every purpose of my coming here, were the first words that he said, he then went on that he had brought his Secretary at War with him to give every necessary information, that the Secretary knew all about the Business—and yet he was delayed and could not go on with the Matter—he cooled however by Degrees said he had no objection to putting off the Matter untill Monday, but declared he did not understand the Matter of Committment, he might be delayed he could not tell how long, he rose a 2d time and said he had no Objection to postponement untill Monday at 10 O'clock. by the looks of the Senate this seemed agreed to. a pause for some time ensued. We waited for him to withdraw, he did so with a discontented Air. had it been any other, than the Man who I wish to regard as the first Character in the World, I would have said with sullen dignity I cannot now be mistaken the President wishes to tread on the Necks of the Senate. Committment will bring this matter to discussion, at least in the Committee when he is not present. he wishes Us to see with he Eyes and hear with the ears of his Secretary only, the Secretary to advance the Premisses the President to draw Conclusions. and to bear down our deliberations with his personal Authority & Presence, form only will be left for Us—This will not do with Americans. but let the Matter Work it will soon cure itself.

Source: Kenneth R. Bowling and Helen E. Veit, eds., *The Diary of William Maclay and Other Notes on Senate Debates* (Baltimore: Johns Hopkins University Press, 1988), 128–131.

Document 5.4   Washington to the Senate, August 6, 1789

President Washington accepted the Senate's right to dissent from his appointments to executive office, thereby doing his part to establish the precedent of senatorial courtesy. The president was not, however, pleased by the Senate's rejection of his candidate for the position of federal tax collector in the port of Savannah, Georgia. In this letter, he details his reasons for nominating Benjamin Fishbourn. The president's concern for personal character and his indifference to partisan political considerations are clear in this communication.

Gentlemen of the Senate:

My nomination of Benjamin Fishbourn for the place of naval officer of the port of Savannah not having met with your concurrence, I now nominate Lachlan McIntosh for that office.

Whatever may have been the reasons which induced your dissent, I am persuaded they were such as you deemed sufficient. Permit me to submit to your consideration whether on occasions where the propriety of nominations appear questionable to you it would not be expedient to communicate that circumstance to me, and thereby avail yourselves of the information which led me to make them, and which I would with pleasure lay before you. Probably my reasons for nominating Mr. Fishbourn may tend to show that such a mode of proceeding in such cases might be useful. I will therefore detail them.

First. While Colonel Fishbourn was an officer in actual service and chiefly under my own eye, his conduct appeared to me irreproachable; nor did I ever hear anything injurious to his reputation as an officer or a gentleman. At the storm of Stony Point his behavior was represented to have been active and brave, and he was charged by his general to bring the account of that success to the headquarters of the Army.

Secondly. Since his residence in Georgia he has been repeatedly elected to the assembly as a representative of the county of Chatham, in which the port of Savannah is situated, and sometimes of the counties of Glynn and Camden; he has been chosen a member of the executive council of the State and has lately been president of the same; he has been elected by the officers of the militia in the county of Chatham lieutenant-colonel of the militia in that district, and on a very recent occasion, to with, in the month of May last, he has been appointed by the council (on the suspension of the late collector) to an office in the port of Savannah nearly similar to that for which I nominated him, which office he actually holds at this time. To these reasons for nominating Mr. Fishbourn I might add that I received private letters of recommendation and oral testimonials in his favor from some of the most respectable characters in that State; but as they were secondary considerations with me, I do not think it necessary to communicate them to you.

It appeared, therefore, to me that Mr. Fishbourn must have enjoyed the *confidence* of the militia officers in order to have been elected to a military rank; the *confidence* of the freemen to have been elected to the assembly; the *confidence* of the assembly to have been selected for the council, and the *confidence* of the council to have been appointed collector of the port of Savannah.

Go. Washington

Source: James D. Richardson, comp., *Messages and Papers of the Presidents,* 20 vols. (New York: Bureau of National Literature, 1897), 1:50–51.

Document 5.5   The Supreme Court Rejects Advisory Opinion Role

At the request of President Washington, Secretary of State Thomas Jefferson wrote the Supreme Court in the midst of a crisis created by France's commissioning of privateers in American ports and France's operation of prize courts on American soil. The president had proclaimed American neutrality, which might seem to proscribe such activities. At the same time, the United States had not negated its treaty obligations with France, which specifically authorized at least some of the controversial actions of French agents in American ports. The president wanted the Court's advice on whether the United States could prohibit French agents in America from commissioning as a privateer a ship captured before Washington proclaimed American neutrality. The president also wondered where the line should be drawn between what was permissible and what was not.

The Court declined the president's request for an opinion. In doing so, it set a powerful precedent against issuing "advisory opinions" and drew a line between the judiciary and the executive. The Court's response, drafted by Jay, was not a unique statement. Jay had defended the separation of powers on other occasions as well, most conspicuously in a writ of mandamus issued in Hayburn's Case (1792) in a New York circuit court. This decision eased the way for the Marshall Court's famous assertion of the Court's power to overturn acts of Congress for unconstitutionality in Marbury v. Madison *(1803).*

Thomas Jefferson to Chief Justice John Jay and Associate Justices, July 18, 1793

Gentlemen:

The war which has taken place among the powers of Europe produces frequent transactions within our ports and limits, on which questions arise of considerable difficulty, and of greater importance to the peace of the United States. These questions depend for their solution on the construction of our treaties, on the laws of nature and nations, and on the laws of the land, and are often presented under circumstances *which do not give a cognizance of them to the tribunals of the country.* Yet their decision is so little analogous to the ordinary functions of the executive, as to occasion much embarrassment and difficulty to them. The President therefore would be much relieved if he found himself free to refer questions of this description to the opinions of the judges of the Supreme Court of the United States, whose knowledge of the subject would secure us against errors dangerous to the peace of the United States, and their authority insure the respect of all parties.

Chief Justice John Jay and Associate Justices to Washington, August 8, 1793

Sir:

We have considered the previous question stated in a letter written by your direction to us by the Secretary of State on the 18th of last month, [regarding] the lines of separation between the three departments of the government. There being in certain respects checks upon each other, and our being judges of a court in the last resort, are considerations which afford strong arguments against the propriety of our extra-judicially deciding the questions alluded to, especially as the power given by the Constitution to the President, of calling on the heads of departments for opinions, seems to have been *purposely* as well as expressly united to the *executive* departments.

We exceedingly regret every event that may cause embarrassment to your administration, but we derive consolation from the reflection that your judgment will discern what is right, and that your usual prudence, decision, and firmness will surmount every obstacle to the preservation of the rights, peace, and dignity of the United States.

We have the honour to be, with perfect respect, sir, your most obedient and most humble servants.

Source: Henry P. Johnston, *Correspondence and Public Papers of John Jay,* 4 vols. (New York: Putnam's Sons, 1890–1893), 3:486–489.

Document 5.6   Address to the Hebrew Congregation, August 18, 1790

Newport, Rhode Island, was home to the largest Jewish population of the American colonies. On the occasion of Washington's visit to the town, Moses Seixes, a leader of Yeshut Israel, delivered a message to the president extolling the new government as one "which to bigotry gives no sanction" (Twohig 1996, 6:284). Washington's strongest remarks on the topic of religious toleration were delivered in response.

Gentlemen.

While I receive, with much satisfaction, your Address replete with expressions of affection and esteem; I rejoice in the opportunity of assuring you, that I shall always retain a grateful remembrance of the cordial welcome I experienced in my visit to Newport, from all classes of Citizens.

The reflection on the days of difficulty and danger which are past is rendered the more sweet, from a consciousness that they are succeeded by days of uncommon prosperity and security. If we have wisdom to make the best use of the advantages with which we are now favored, we cannot fail, under the just administration of a good Government, to become a great and a happy people.

The Citizens of the United States of America have a right to applaud themselves for having given to mankind examples of an enlarged and liberal policy: a policy worthy of imitation. All possess alike liberty of conscience and immunities of citizenship. It is now no more that toleration is spoken of, as if it was by the indulgence of one class of people, that another enjoyed the exercise of their inherent natural rights. For happily the Government of the United States, which gives to bigotry no sanction, to persecution no assistance requires only that they who live under its protection should demean themselves as good citizens, in giving it on all occasions their effectual support.

It would be inconsistent with the frankness of my character not to avow that I am pleased with your favorable opinion of my Administration, and fervent wishes for my felicity. May the Children of the Stock of Abraham, who dwell in this land, continue to merit and enjoy the good will of the other Inhabitants; while every one shall sit in safety under his own vine and figtree, and there shall be none to make him afraid. May the father of all mercies scatter light and not darkness in our paths, and make us all in our several vocations useful here, and in his own due time and way everlastingly happy.

Go: Washington

Source: Dorothy Twohig, ed., *The Papers of George Washington, Presidential Series,* Vol. 6, *July–November 1790* (Charlottesville: University Press of Virginia, 1996), 285–286.

Document 5.7   Washington to Alexander Hamilton, July 29, 1792

In late May 1792 Secretary of State Thomas Jefferson wrote the president to urge him not to retire at the close of his first term because of the partisan rancor afflicting the country and its government. "Should an honest majority" result in Congress from the elections of 1792, then Washington might retire before his second term expired, Jefferson suggested. But at present, he told Washington, the "confidence of the whole union is centered in you." The rest of Jefferson's letter was taken up with charges "hackneyed in the public papers in detail," but worth repeating for the president's benefit (Cunningham 2000, 79, 81). In this indirect way Jefferson made certain that the president was aware of the perfidy of which Jefferson believed Secretary of the Treasury Alexander Hamilton and his allies were guilty. In a letter to Hamilton a month later, Washington repeated the charges almost verbatim, while being careful not to reveal their source.

My dear Sir:

. . . On my way home, and since my arrival here, I have endeavoured to learn from sensible and moderate men—known friends to the Government—the sentiments which are entertained of public measures. These all agree that the Country is prosperous and happy; but they seem to be alarmed at that system of policy, and those interpretations of the Constitution which have taken place in Congress.

Others, less friendly perhaps to the Government, and more disposed to arraign the conduct of its Officers . . . go further, & enumerate a variety of matters, wch. as well as I can recollect, may be adduced under the following heads. Viz.

First That the public debt is greater than we can possibly pay before other causes of adding new debt to it will occur; and that this has been artificially created by adding together the whole amount of the debtor and creditor sides of the accounts, instead of taking only their balances; which could have been paid off in a short time.

2d. That this accumulation of debt has taken for ever out of our power those easy sources of revenue, which, applied to the ordinary necessities and exigencies of Government, would have answered them habitually, and covered us from habitual murmurings against taxes and tax gatherers; reserving extraordinary calls, for extraordinary occasions, would animate the People to meet them.

3d. That the calls for money have been no greater than we must generally expect, for the same or equivalent exigencies; yet we are already obliged to strain the *impost* till it produces clamour, and will produce evasion, and war on our citizens to collect it, and even to resort to an *Excise* law, of odious character with the people; partial in its operation; unproductive unless enforced by arbitrary & vexatious means; and committing the authority of the Government in parts where resistance is most probable, & coercion least practicable. . . .

18th. Of all the mischiefs objected to the system of measures before-mentioned, none they add is so afflicting, & fatal to every honest hope, as the corruption of the legislature. As it was the earliest of these measures it became the instrument for producing the rest, and will be the instrument for producing in future a King, Lords & Commons; or whatever else those who direct it may chuse. . . . [T]hey will form the worst Government upon earth, if the means of their corruption be not prevented. . . .

These, as well as my memory serves me, are the sentiments which, directly and indirectly, have been disclosed to me.

Source: As reprinted in Noble E. Cunningham Jr., *Jefferson vs. Hamilton: Confrontations that Shaped a Nation* (Boston: Bedford/St. Martin's, 2000), 83–86.

Document 5.8   Alexander Hamilton to Washington, September 9, 1792

This is Alexander Hamilton's reply to the president's letter pleading with both Secretary of the Treasury Hamilton and Secretary of State Thomas Jefferson to demur from further machinations against one another.

Sir:

I have the pleasure of your private letter of the 26th of August.

The feelings and views which are manifest in that letter are such as I expected would exist. And I most sincerely regret the causes of the uneasy sensations you experience. It is my most anxious wish, as far as may depend upon me, to smooth the path of your administration, and to render it prosperous and happy. And if any prospect shall open of healing or terminating the differences which exist, I shall most cheerfully embrace it; though I consider myself as the deeply injured party. The recommendation of such a spirit is worthy of the moderation and wisdom which dictated it; and if your endeavours should prove unsuccessful, I do not hesitate to say that in my opinion the period is not remote when the public good will require *substitutes* for the *differing members* of your administration. The continuance of a division there must destroy the energy of Government, which will be little enough with the strictest Union. On my part there will be a most cheerful acquiescence in such a result.

I trust, Sir, that the greatest frankness has always marked and will always mark every step of my conduct towards you. In this disposition, I cannot conceal from you that I have had some instrumentality of late in the retaliations which have fallen upon certain public characters and that I find myself placed in a situation not to be able to recede *for the present.*

I considered myself compelled to this conduct by reasons public as well as personal of the most cogent nature. I *know* that I have been an object of uniform opposition from Mr. Jefferson, from the first moment of his coming to the city of New York to enter upon his present office. I *know,* from the most authentic sources, that I have been the frequent subject of the most unkind whispers and insinuating from the same quarter. I have long seen a formed party in the Legislature, under his auspices, bent upon my subversion. I cannot doubt, from the evidence I possess, that the National Gazette was instituted by him for political purposes and that one leading object of it has been to render me and all the measures connected with my department as odious as possible. . . .

As long as I saw no danger to the Government, from the machinations which were going on, I resolved to be a silent sufferer of the injuries which were done me. . . . But when I no longer doubted, that there was a formed party deliberately bent upon the subversion of measures, which in its consequences would subvert the Government—when I saw, that the undoing of the funding system in particular (which, whatever maybe the original merits of that system, would prostrate the credit and honor of the Nation, and bring the Government into contempt with that description of Men, who are in every society the only firm supporters of government) was an avowed object of the party; and that all possible pains were taking to produce that effect by rendering it odious to the body of the people, I considered it as a duty, to endeavour to resist the torrent, and as an essential means to this end, to draw aside the veil from the principal Actors. To this strong impulse, to this decided conviction, I have yielded. And I think events will prove that I have judged rightly.

Nevertheless I pledge my honor to you Sir, that if you shall hereafter form a plan to unite the members of your administration, upon some steady principle of cooperation, I will faithfully concur in executing it during my continuance in office. And I will not directly or indirectly say or do a thing, that shall endanger a feud.

. . . With the most faithful and affectionate attachment I have the honor to remain

Sir

Your most Obed & humble servant
A HAMILTON

Source: Noble E. Cunningham Jr., *Jefferson vs. Hamilton: Confrontations that Shaped a Nation* (Boston: Bedford/St. Martin's, 2000), 95–97.

Document 5.9   Thomas Jefferson to Washington, September 9, 1792

Secretary of State Thomas Jefferson replied to Washington's chastisement with considerable passion. It was his nemesis, Treasury Secretary Alexander Hamilton, he protested, who was responsible for the division in the government.

Dear Sir:

I received on the 2d. inst the letter of August 23. which you did me the honor to write me; but the immediate return of our post, contrary to his custom, prevented my answer by that occasion. . . .

I now take the liberty of proceeding to that part of your letter wherein you notice the internal dissentions which have taken place within our government, and their disagreeable effect on its movements. That such dissentions have taken place is certain, and even among those who are nearest to you in the administration. To no one have they given deeper concern than myself; to no one equal mortification at being myself a part of them. Tho' I take to myself no more than my share of the general observations of your letter, yet I am so desirous ever that you should know the whole truth, and believe no more than the truth, that I am glad to seize every occasion of developing to you whatever I do think relative to the government; . . .

While I embarked in the government, it was with a determination to intermeddle not at all with the legislature, and as little as possible with my co-departments. The first and only instance of variance from the former part of my resolution, I was duped into by the Secretary of the treasury, and made a tool for forwarding his schemes, not then sufficiently understood by me; and off all the errors of my political life, this has occasioned me the deepest regret. It has ever been my purpose to explain this to you, when, from being actors on the scene, we shall have become uninterested spectators only. The second part of my resolution has been religiously observed with the war department; and as to that of the Treasury, has never been farther swerved from, than by the mere enunciation of my sentiments in conversation, and chiefly among those who, expressing the same sentiments, drew mine from me. If it has been supposed that I have ever intrigued among the members of the legislature to defeat the plans of the Secretary of the Treasury, it is contrary to all truth. As I never had the desire to influence the members, so neither had I any other means than my friendships, which I valued too highly to risk by usurpations on their freedom of judgment, and the conscientious pursuit of their own sense of duty. That I have utterly, in my private conversations, disapproved of the system of the Secretary of the treasury, I acknolege and avow: and this was not merely a speculative difference. His system flowed from principles adverse to liberty, and was calculated to undermine and demolish the republic, by creating an influence of his department over the members of the legislature. I saw this influence actually produced, and it's first fruits to be the establishment of the great outlines of his project by the votes of the very persons who, having swallowed his bait were laying themselves out to profit by his plans: and that had these persons withdrawn, as those interested in a question ever should, the vote of the disinterested majority was clearly the reverse of what they made it. These were no longer the votes then of the representatives of the people, but of deserters from the rights and interests of the people. . . . If what was actually doing begat uneasiness in those who wished virtuous government, what was further proposed was not less threatening to the friends of the constitution. For, in a Report on the subject of manufactures, (still to be acted on) it was expressly assumed that the general government has a right to exercise all powers which may be for the *general welfare,* that is to say, all the legitimate powers of government . . . [with regard to America's relations with France and Britain] my system was to give some satisfactory distinctions to the former, of little cost to us, I return for the solid advantages yielded us by them; and to have met the English with some restrictions which might induce them to abate their severities against our commerce. I have always supposed this coincided with your sentiments. Yet the Secretary of the treasury, by his cabals with members of the legislature, and by high toned declamation on other occasions, has forced down his own system. . . . So that if the question be By whose fault is it that Colo. Hamilton and myself have not drawn together? The answer will depend on that to two other questions; Whose principles of administration, by their purity, best justify conscientious adherence? And Which of us has, notwithstanding, stepped farthest into the control of the department of the other? . . .

If my own justification, or the interests of the republic shall require it, I reserve to myself the right of then [after retirement] appealing to my country, subscribing my name to whatever I write, and using with freedom and truth the facts and names necessary to place the cause in it's just form before that tribunal. To a thorough disregard of the honors and emoluments of office, I join as great a value for the esteem of my countrymen; and conscious of having merited it by an integrity which cannot be reproached, and by an enthusiastic devotion to their rights and liberty, I will not suffer my retirement to be clouded by the slanders of a man whose history, from the moment at which history can stoop to notice him, is a tissue of machinations against the liberty of the country which has not only received and given him bread, but heaped it's honors on his head. Still . . . I hope I may promise, both to you and to myself, that none will receive ailment from me during the short space I have to remain in office, which will find ample employment in closing the present business of the department. . . .

In the mean time and ever I am with great and sincere affection & respect, dear Sir, your most obedient and humble servant

TH: JEFFERSON

Source: Noble E. Cunningham Jr., *Jefferson vs. Hamilton: Confrontations that Shaped a Nation* (Boston: Bedford/St. Martin's, 2000), 97–102.

Document 5.10   The Partisan Press

When the American press was the agent of an American revolution, Washington argued that "in a free and republican government, you cannot restrain the voice of the multitude; every man will speak as he thinks" (letter, Washington to Marquis de Lafayette, September 1, 1778, in George Wash-

ington Papers at the Library of Congress, 1741–1799: Series 3h Varick Transcripts). After struggling as president to maintain harmony within his divided cabinet, Washington had come to appreciate the costs as well as the benefits of a free press. "If the government and the officers of it are to be the constant theme for newspaper abuse . . . it will be impossible, I conceive, for any man living to manage the helm or to keep the machine together" (letter, Washington to Edmund Randolph, August 26, 1792, in George Washington Papers at the Library of Congress, 1741–1799: Series 2 Letterbooks).

The excerpts here highlight the fierce tone of public attacks against the president.

If ever a nation was debauched by a man, the American nation has been debauched by Washington. If ever a nation has suffered from the improper influence of a man, the American nation has suffered from the influence of Washington. If ever a nation was deceived by a man, the American nation has been deceived by Washington. Let his conduct then be an example to future ages. Let it serve to be a warning that no man may be an idol, and that a people may confide in themselves rather than in an individual. Let the history of the federal government instruct mankind, that the masque of patriotism may be worn to conceal the foulest designs against the liberties of the people.
Source: *Philadelphia Aurora*, December 23, 1796.

Retire immediately; let no flatterer persuade you to rest one hour longer at the helm of state. You are utterly incapable to steer the political ship into the harbour of safety. If you have any love for your country, leave its affairs to the wisdom of your fellow citizens; do not flatter yourself with the idea that you know their interests better than other men; there are thousands amongst them who equal you in capacity, and who excel you in knowledge.
Source: *Philadelphia Aurora*, November 20, 1795.

The man who is the source of all the misfortunes of our country, is this day reduced to a level with his fellow citizens, and is no longer possessed of power to multiply evils upon the United States. If there was ever a period for rejoicing, this is the moment—every heart in unison with the freedom and happiness of the people ought to beat high, with the exultation that the name of Washington from this day ceases to give a currency to political iniquity, and to legalized corruption.
Source: *Philadelphia Aurora*, March 6, 1797.

256   CHAPTER FIVE

Contrast the boasted prosperity, blasphemy in contempt of truth! so loudly and daringly vociferated by the executive of the United States, and reverberated by Congress; by the Executives of the states and re-echoed by their legislatures, with existing truths glaring as a summer's sun, with the loudly crying facts. Our apparent prosperity alas has been the result of our fictitious credit of funding and banking systems, and withal rifling out of the miseries, the imperious necessities and wants of a sister republic, who raised America into existence among the nations of the earth struggling for freedom with the combined despots of Europe. Is this the prosperity of which Americans should exceedingly boast? God forbid. And this apparent prosperity is impudently ascribed, too, to the six years glorious Washington administration.
Source: *Bache's General Advertiser*, December 17, 1796.

Mr. Washington, the Cincinnatus of America, did not feed on roasted turnips, nor fellow the plow like the Venerable Roman of that name; he rode in a coach and fix, $25000, a sum much larger than the yearly income of many of our younger princes, was thought insufficient to supply his table and it is said, the austere republican chief of the Western world was obliged to add many thousands of his own money, before he could eat and drink, and sleep in a manner worthy of his high station.
Source: *Philadelphia Aurora*, October 20, 1797.

It has been a serious misfortune to our country, that the President of the United States has been substituted for a Providence, and that the Gifts of Heaven have been ascribed for his agency. The Flattery, nay, the adoration that has been heaped upon him, has made him forget that he is mortal, and he may have been persuaded to believe, and indeed his actions squint that way, that like Alexander he is an immediate offspring of the gods. During the revolution it was necessary to give a consequence to the commander-in-chief by ascribing to him extraordinary qualifications. The delusion was useful, as it inspired confidence . . . but what was then was policy in the end became habit, and as the people were instructed to believe in the pre-eminent talents and virtues of the General, the belief continued when it was no longer necessary or useful. George III, it seems, became his example, and like George, he was only to be approached at a levee dragged in a coach and fix. The pomp, ostentation and parade of a British monarch was to be appended to the first magistrate of a free people, and hosannas were to be sung to him as the province of our country. This is an epitome

of the conduct of George Washington.
Source: *Bache's General Advertiser*, December 23, 1796.

I maintain that it was lawful and laudable to hang Jay in effigy, and that Washington ought to have been treated in the same manner if he had not been so popular.
Source: "The Creed of a Full-Blooded Jacobin," *Columbian Centinel,* August 27, 1800.

Source: A compilation of anti-Washington newspaper clippings compiled by Sushila Nayak for Marcus Raskin, "Presidential Disrespect: A History of Presidential Denigration from Washington to Clinton," Institute for Policy Studies, Washington, D.C.

Document 5.11   Proclamation: A National Thanksgiving, October 3, 1789

Since 1623, governments in America have traditionally issued a formal proclamation of thanks to God for particular blessings or events. In this first year of his presidency, Congress requested that the president follow this tradition, communicating to the states the government's desire for such a day to be recognized in November, the time for the even more ancient celebration of the fall harvest. Rather than merely pass on the call for thanks to the states, Washington asserted the prerogative of the president to speak to, and on behalf of, the American people directly.

Whereas it is the duty of all nations to acknowledge the providence of Almighty God, to obey His will, to be grateful for His benefits, and humbly to implore His protection and favor; and

Whereas both Houses of Congress have, by their joint committee, requested me "to recommend to the people of the United States a day of public thanksgiving and prayer, to be observed by acknowledging with grateful hearts the many and signal favors of Almighty God, especially by affording them an opportunity peaceably to establish a form of government for their safety and happiness:"

Now, therefore, I do recommend and assign Thursday, the 26th day of November next, to be devoted by the people of these States to the service of that great and glorious Being who is the beneficent author of all the good that was, that is, or that will be; that we may then all unite in rendering unto Him our sincere and humble thanks for His kind care and protection of the people of this country previous to their becoming a nation; for the signal and manifold mercies and the favorable interpositions of His providence in the course and conclusion of the late war; for the great degree of tranquility, union, and plenty which we have since enjoyed; for the peaceable and rational manner in which we have been enabled to establish constitutions of government for our safety and happiness, and particularly the national one now lately instituted; for the civil and religious liberty with which we are blessed, and the means we have of acquiring and diffusing useful knowledge; and, in general, for all the great and various favors which He has been pleased to confer upon us.

And also that we may then unite in most humbly offering our prayers and supplications to the great Lord and Ruler of Nations, and beseech Him to pardon our national and other transgressions; to enable us all, whether in public or private stations, to perform our several and relative duties properly and punctually; to render our National Government a blessing to all the people by constantly being a Government of wise, just, and constitutional laws, discreetly and faithfully executed and obeyed; to protect and guide all sovereigns and nations (especially such as have shown kindness to us), and to bless them with good governments, peace, and concord; to promote the knowledge and practice of true religion and virtue, and the increase of science among them and us; and, generally, to grant unto all mankind such a degree of temporal prosperity as He alone knows to be best.

Given under my hand, at the city of New York, the 3d day of October, A.D. 1789, Go. Washington

Source: James D. Richardson, comp., *Messages and Papers of the Presidents,* 20 vols. (New York: Bureau of National Literature, 1897), 1:56.

Life of George Washington – The Farmer. Lithograph, 1853. Claude Regnier after Junius Brutus Stearns.

CHAPTER SIX

After the White House: Washington in Retirement

P resident Washington took no part in the election of his successor. In fact, apparently he never even mentioned the election in his private correspondence. He clearly preferred John Adams to Thomas Jefferson, but gave his vice president no assistance in the election and offered him no public endorsement. Just as it was considered not proper at the time for a presidential candidate to politick for the office, it was considered not appropriate for a sitting president to influence the choice of his successor. As for Adams, he did not resent Washington's failure to help him win election, but he did resent the fact that Washington stole the show from him at his own inauguration.

As Adams confided to his wife in successive letters, on the day of his accession to office all eyes were turned to Washington. Afterward, Adams complained that "everybody talks of the tears, of the full eyes, the streaming eyes, the trickling eyes, etc., etc., but all is enigma beyond. No one descends to particulars to say why or wherefore. I am, therefore, left to suppose that it was all grief for the loss of their beloved" (Flexner 1972, 333). Washington seems, then, to have triumphed over Adams on what was supposed to have been Adams's finest day. "Methought I heard him say," Adams wrote, " 'Ay! I'm fairly out and you fairly in. See which of us will be happiest!'"

AT MOUNT VERNON

George Washington had always found happiness at Mount Vernon. Moreover, his passion for a *private* life at his homestead was an integral part of his *public* image. Like the Roman hero with whom he was associated, Lucius Quintus Cincinnatus, Washington continually demonstrated his reluctance to hold power and his eagerness to retreat to the countryside. Twice before, he had relinquished military commissions and returned to Mount Vernon—after the French and Indian War and after the Revolutionary War. In 1797 Washington bade farewell to another type of war, the partisan squabbling that suffused his presidency, and he retired a final time to his plantation on the shores of the Potomac. He intended, he told a friend, never to travel more than twenty miles from his home again (see Document 6.1).

Mount Vernon had suffered, as it always did, from Washington's absence. Although the plantation, its five separate farms, numerous gardens, workshops, mills, fisheries, granaries, storerooms, kitchens, quarters, and barns were staffed with several hundred slaves and under the supervision of slave foremen, white overseers, and a general manager, Washington was personally absorbed in the business of his plantation and was constantly busy with plans for the improvement of his properties.

At Mount Vernon, Washington settled into the routines of a gentleman farmer. In addition to worrying over his property, Washington maintained his heavy correspondence, sat for portraits and family paintings, and entertained an unceasing procession of guests. Guests, both invited and uninvited, were an essential part of plantation life. Washington learned as much from his many visitors as he could, putting to them numerous questions about their travels or their fields of expertise (see Document 6.2).

Months after retiring to Mount Vernon, Washington arranged for his nephew Lawrence Lewis to come live at the plantation to help entertain company. "As both your Aunt and I," Washington wrote, "are in the decline of life, and regular in our habits, especially in our hours of rising & going to bed; I require some person (fit & Proper) to ease me of the trouble of entertaining company; particularly of Nights, as it is my inclination to retire (and unless prevented by very particular company, always do retire) either to bed, or to my study, soon after candle light" (Rasmussen and Tilton 1999, 250).

While at Mount Vernon, Lewis became engaged to Eleanor Parke Custis, George Washington's stepgrandchild. "Nelly" was universally described as a beautiful and accomplished young lady, and Washington legally adopted her so he could give her away in marriage to his nephew. Soon afterward, Lewis and Nelly took up residence at Dogue Run Farm, one of Washington's Mount Vernon properties.

Also in residence at Mount Vernon during Washington's retirement was a second grandchild who was raised there, George Washington Parke Custis, the seventh and youngest child of Martha Washington's son John. After Washington's death, Custis came into his own as a writer and playwright. His book of recollections of Washington, published in 1859, interpreted the Washington legend for a new generation (Custis, 1859).

COMMANDER IN CHIEF OF A PROVISIONAL ARMY

Guests to Mount Vernon sometimes recounted that Washington would grow silent and even resentful if one of their number endeavored to steer the conversation to politics. But the former president could not avoid the subject altogether, because during his retirement events raised the stakes, once again, to the very survival of the American nation.

The conflict over American foreign policy that had so troubled Washington's second term had worsened under President John Adams. French privateers were raiding American vessels, and there was talk of war unless a new treaty could be negotiated between the French and the Americans. On May 17, 1797, Adams lectured a special session of Congress on the need for a studied neutrality, but at the same time he called on Congress to build up America's defenses. Adams also appointed John Marshall, Elbridge Gerry, and Charles Pinckney to engage in talks between the two countries. On their arrival in Paris, the American agents of the president were visited by three representatives of French foreign minister, Charles Maurice Talleyrand. These men, referred to in American dispatches as X, Y, and Z, demanded a bribe for Talleyrand and a large loan for France merely to open negotiations.

The American agents refused to agree to these demands, and their description of the attempted extortion was published in the American press. Public reaction against the French as a result of the so-called XYZ affair produced a war fever in parts of the United States, including Virginia. Washington continued to believe in the practical necessity of neutrality for the new and still weak nation, but "if my services should be required by my Country," he wrote to Adams, he could not decline to do his duty (Rasmussen and Tilton 1999, 248).

The pro-French Democratic-Republicans rushed to defend the French government, placing the blame for the XYZ affair on the alleged pro-British policy pursued by the Washington administration. A letter from Thomas Jefferson was reprinted throughout the nation implying that Washington was an "apostate" guilty of monarchical "heresies" (Flexner 1972, 382). The former American minister to France, James Monroe, issued a five-hundred-page annotated compendium of documents intended to demonstrate that current troubles with France stemmed from Washington's errors in foreign policy. The former president was incredulous. "Cowardly, illiberal, and assassin-like" means were being used against the American executive. Washington had supposed "until lately," he wrote on March 1, 1798, that all Americans would rally behind President Adams in response to the French insult, but instead partisan rancor had only worsened. Whether the nation could resolve its difficulties "at any point short of confusion and anarchy," Washington wrote, "is *now* in my opinion more problematical than ever" (Flexner 1972, 384).

To meet the apparent threat of French invasion, the government passed legislation in 1798 that established a Department of the Navy and a marine corps, improved coastal defenses, and authorized a "Provisional Army" of ten thousand federal volunteers to be raised "in the event of a declaration of war against the United States, . . . actual invasion . . . or of imminent danger of such invasion" (Palmer and Stryker 1986, 50). Adams desired that Washington, or at least his name, appear at the head of the new military enterprise. Adams wrote his predecessor: "We must have your name if you will, in any case, permit us to use it. There will be more efficacy in it than in many an army" (Flexner 1972, 394).

Washington replied, "In the case of an *actual* invasion by a formidable force, I certainly should not entrench myself under the cover of age and retirement" (Flexner 1972, 395). Though he thought the French "intoxicated and lawless," Washington did not believe that they actually would invade the United States. Nevertheless, he was a cautious man, and dutifully turned his attention to the details of his provisional command.

Washington wanted his command announced by Adams only should the emergency of an impending French invasion "become evident" (Washington to James McHenry, 5 July 1798, in Fitzpatrick 1931–1944,

36:318–320). Adams, however, was contending with another kind of emergency: a concerted effort to persuade him to give the command instead to Alexander Hamilton—someone Adams distrusted for his ambition and fondness for monarchy. In haste, Adams named Washington lieutenant general and commander of all the military forces of the nation and sent Secretary of War Henry Knox to Mount Vernon to inform the commander of his new appointment. The newspapers, however, were faster than Knox, and Washington learned of the appointment in the press.

Washington spent several months attempting to organize his command. Of particular importance to the aging general, as well as to Adams, was the selection of his three principal aides, all of whom were to have rank of major general, but who were to stand in relation to one another in a clear chain of command. The order of the three became the subject of bitter controversy. Henry Knox, one of Washington's dearest and oldest friends, could not accept that he was unfit by advanced age to serve in the number two position, directly under Washington. Knox lobbied Adams, his fellow Bay State colleague, to place him first. Adams agreed and so informed Washington, complaining to Secretary of War James McHenry that "there has been too much intrigue in this business with General Washington and me" (Flexner 1972, 407). Washington responded in barely controlled fury, intimating to the president in writing that he would resign his commission if he were not allowed to name the order of his own major generals. Adams capitulated, and Hamilton, Washington's choice, was named second in command.

On November 5, 1798, Washington set out for Philadelphia, where he spent five weeks assembling, on paper at least, the new army. Washington's principal task was to select the officers for the envisioned regiments and assign them to their commands. Because of the nature of the enemy, Washington was unwilling to contemplate the appointment of men who had previously sided with the pro-French party in America, or who were recommended by Democratic-Republican congressmen. Though complaining of his exhausting workload, Washington took pleasure in being again at the center of events in the nation's most populous city. He dined with old friends and consulted with Philadelphia's finest tailor on the manufacture of the uniform that he had designed for himself. Before departing once more for Mount Vernon, Washington lectured President Adams on the need to continue with plans for the provisional army lest the French gain courage from any interruption of the American preparedness campaign.

As Adams feared, Hamilton briefly took command of the army, from December 1799, upon Washington's death, to June 1800. By that time, however, Adams had hit on a plan to avoid war and frustrate the growing power of Hamilton within the Federalist Party. The president surprised his cabinet by reopening negotiations with the French in the winter of 1798. Pro-war Federalists attempted to rally Washington to their cause, flooding him with pleas to use his immense prestige against Adams's new policy of peace, and even to accept another draft for the presidency. Washington replied cautiously, "I have for some time past viewed the political concerns of the United States with an anxious and painful eye. They appear to me to be moving by hasty strides to some awful crisis, but in what they will result, that Being who sees, foresees, and directs all things alone can tell. The vessel is afloat or very nearly so, and considering myself as a passenger only, I shall trust to the mariners whose duty it is to watch, to steer it into a safe port" (Flexner 1972, 431). As James Thomas Flexner observed, "This statement was George Washington's last important political act."

WASHINGTON'S DEATH

In the month before the close of the century, Washington looked forward to the year 1800 at Mount Vernon. He drew up for James Anderson, his elderly plantation manager, lengthy instructions on the operation of the farms, urging that the crops be rotated as per his previous instructions and attempting once again to impress upon his manager the importance of system and regularity. He also wrote of the importance of personally inspecting operations, particularly "in severe weather, when attention and care is most needed" (Rasmussen and Tilton 1999, 258).

Heeding his own admonitions, Washington set out on horseback to inspect his farms on December 12, 1799, despite rain, snow, and hail. The next day, having contracted a cold and a sore throat, Washington ignored the apparently minor malady and marked trees on the front lawn for removal to improve the view of the residence from the approaching road. That evening, he declined Martha's offer to summon help for his worsening condition. Very late in the next day, attended by several physicians, his wife, his secretary, and his body servant, Washington died.

Washington did not brood on his age in retirement, but neither did he fail to acknowledge the obvious. He was an old man for his time, and his family was short-lived. He had had occasion to form his own opinions about death, and viewed it with the stoicism that he had developed as a young man. "When the summons comes," he had written in 1799 upon the death of his sole surviving brother, "I shall endeavour to obey it with a good grace" (Henriques 2001, 252).

Unfortunately for Washington, his fatal condition was exceedingly painful, and was made more so by the care he received from his doctors (see Document 6.3). According to the latest medical theory, Washington died from acute epiglottitis caused by virulent bacteria. The disease inflames the throat and blocks the airway. During the course of Washington's final day, his doctors applied the all-purpose treatment of the day: bleeding—four times. An emergency tracheotomy might have saved the patient's life, but it was a new and controversial procedure (Wallenborn 1997).

"Let me go off quietly," Washington begged of his earnest but mistaken physicians (Document 6.3). Throughout the ordeal, Washington expressed his concern for those attending him, and at last passed quietly. Washington was buried in the family vault at Mount Vernon.

LAST WILL AND TESTAMENT

Washington spent considerable time in the summer of 1799 writing out a new will (Document 6.4). For the final draft, Washington ordered special paper, bearing a watermark fusing agricultural and ideological themes. A goddess of agriculture repined on a plough in the middle of the seal, holding a liberty pole in one hand. The will made clear that Washington died a wealthy man, with an estate valued at roughly $500,000. Martha received upon his death a life interest in the majority of his estate. Otherwise, Washington scattered his wealth among his heirs. He instructed that his land holdings out west be sold and the proceeds divided into twenty-three parts—the number of relations he wished to remember in his will. Even Mount Vernon itself was to be broken up into three farms. The mansion, nearby acreage, and Washington's public papers were deeded to Bushrod Washington, his nephew, in honor of a promise Washington made to Bushrod's father when they served together in the French and Indian War.

During his lifetime, Washington "moved into the category of 'good' slave master. He stopped selling slaves because he thought the practice was cruel, even though this new policy made his farms unprofitable and caused him to pile up debt" (Wilkins 2001, 81–83). Privately, he voiced his support for legal efforts to put an end to slavery. "I never mean (unless some particular circumstance should compel me to it) to possess another slave by purchase;" Washington wrote to a friend in 1786, "it being among my first wishes to see some plan adopted by the legislature, by which slavery in this Country may be abolished by slow, sure & imperceptible degrees" (Twohig 2001, 121).

Washington's objections were practical as well as moral—that is, he recognized that slave laborers lacked the requisite incentive to work with efficiency. He was distressed on one occasion to calculate that a group of his slaves at Mount Vernon could hew a particular quantity of lumber from logs four times faster when he personally timed the activity than when working on their own. He also routinely calculated the expense he incurred caring for the several hundred slaves on his properties, and, with regret, compared that expense with the lesser amount of money earned from their labor. All told, at the time of his death Washington had 317 slaves under his control at Mount Vernon (see Document 6.5).

Washington did not speak out publicly against slavery during his lifetime. In his will, however, he took the unusual step of providing for the manumission of his slaves upon the death of his widow. "To emancipate them during her life," he wrote, "would, tho' earnestly wished by me, be attended with such insuperable difficulties on account of their intermixture by Marriages with the dower Negroes [those Mrs. Washington owned during her lifetime, as an inheritance from her first husband], as to excite the most painful sensations, if not disagreeable consequences from the latter, while both descriptions are in the occupancy of the same Proprietor."

In addition, Washington specified in his will that the old and infirm should be provided for by Washington's heirs while they lived, and that, once free, the young were to be taught to read and write and "brought up to some useful occupation" (Flexner 1972, 446). But Washington's plans for the education of his freed slaves could not be implemented because of laws passed after Washington's death prohibiting the education of blacks.

SYMBOL OF THE NATION

In death, Washington almost immediately regained the stature he had enjoyed at the close of the Revolutionary War. Congress declared a day of national mourning, and some eighteen hundred memorial services were held in the roughly two hundred cities and towns in the United States. In the words of a somewhat cynical British traveler, orators all over the country "called all their tropes and metaphors together; collected all the soldiers and statesmen of history, and made them cast garlands at the feet of his statue" (Bryan 1952, 55). Indeed, eulogists struggled to find fit subjects to compare to Washington. In Worcester, Massachusetts, Aaron Bancroft compared Washington to the biblical prophet Joshua, but found even that comparison wanting, because the American president "was free from the vices and weaknesses" which were "the shade" of the Old Testament king's greatness (Bryan 1952, 63). Jedidiah Morse, at Charlestown, Massachusetts, used his eulogy to liken Washington to Moses, to demonstrate that Washington's leadership was as surely heaven-sent as that of Moses (Bryan 1952, 63). Maj. Gen. Henry Lee of Virginia famously summarized the late president's place in American memory in a eulogy delivered before his congressional colleagues. Washington, he proclaimed, had been "first in war, first in peace and first in the hearts of his countrymen" (Document 6.6). Open opponents of the Washington administration, which by this time included Vice President Thomas Jefferson, maintained a respectful silence. Jefferson was not asked to speak at the congressional ceremonies. Rather than listen to Lee, Jefferson's avowed enemy in Virginia politics, Jefferson busied himself with business outside the capital.

In the years after Washington's death, long after the Jeffersonian opposition had become the dominant party in American politics and the Federalist Party had ceased to exist, Washington's centrality to the nation's sense of itself remained unshaken. A steady stream of books and poems recounted and embellished the stories of his life (see Document 6.7). Incredibly, two historians have found that "of the approximately twenty-two hundred books printed by American presses in the early years of the nineteenth century, some four hundred addressed either Washington's life as a whole or some aspect of it" (Rasmussen and Tilton 1999, 261). Washington's image was circulated in prints and engravings. One popular print by John James Barralet, made in 1802, depicted

Washington ascending to heaven borne by Father Time and an angel. In the background, the nation's mothers weep, while in the foreground Liberty hangs her head, as does a Native American warrior. Commenting on the popularity of images of Washington, a Russian traveler to America observed in 1815 that "every American considers it his sacred duty to have a likeness of Washington in his house, just as we have images of God's Saints" (Rasmussen and Tilton 1999, 261).

LEGACY

Upon his death, then, Washington was "almost immediately elevated to mythic status" (Rasmussen and Tilton 1999, 261). The mythic Washington is still present in America, at Mount Vernon, which is visited by over one million persons a year, and in other physical embodiments such as the Washington Monument. But in the many years since his passing, his image has naturally been partly obscured and his reputation subject to revisionist critiques. Washington was, after all, a man of his time, and times have changed considerably since the eighteenth century.

To begin with, George Washington was a very wealthy man. In the early 1900s, American historians and political scientists began to investigate the thesis that the independence movement and, especially, the movement to put the new nation under a strong central government were fueled by self-interest. The rich were not satisfied with the status quo; they created a new nation so they might be free to grow as rich as they liked. Their new government would keep power out of the hands of hapless debtors such as Daniel Shays, who in 1786 led an armed rebellion against the Massachusetts courts that were foreclosing on the farms of penniless veterans. Washington and other elites viewed Shays as a dangerous lawbreaker, and strengthened the government through the Constitution to prevent the likes of Shays from spreading civil unrest through the states. Contemporaries, viewing history from the perspective of ordinary people, sometimes portray Shays as a hero (Calliope Film Resources 2000). From such a perspective, what is so glorious about independence and the Constitution?

Not only was Washington rich; he was also proud. As a consequence, "[i]n modern times Washington is commonly criticized because he was not, in his years of fame, a simply friendly soul like your neighbor who will, in a pinch, come over and sit with the baby" (Flexner 1974, 494). Washington was, in fact, never truly at home with the average American of his day. For example, he regarded the West as a land of opportunity, and once urged a neighbor to move to the frontier, where an enterprising man with limited means might become wealthy or at least independent through the purchase and improvement of unsettled land. Yet when he first encountered colonists living on the frontier, he remarked in his diary that they were "as ignorant a set of people as the Indians" (Jackson and Twohig 1976–1979, 1:22). He loved the land of America, and loved the promise of independence it offered to enterprising men such as himself and his neighbor, but he was not, at least as a young man, personally fond of the mass of people who would come to revere him. Such elitism does not win favor among socially democratic commentators.

Finally, and most seriously, there is the issue of Washington's relationship with Native Americans and African Americans. He had greater respect for Indians than did many other leading men of his day and later, such as Andrew Jackson. And he felt more personally the immorality of slavery than did most other elites of his time, including the presumably more egalitarian Thomas Jefferson. Washington, unlike Jefferson, quietly favored legislation in Virginia that would have banned slavery, and in his will he freed his slaves, effective upon his wife's death. But Washington nevertheless devoted his life to the service of a slave-owning, Indian-banishing people and their government. Is such a man a fit symbol for the nation now that it has been refashioned as a land of opportunity for persons of all races, and now that the conquest of the continent by Europeans is no longer discussed without recognition of the human costs to its original inhabitants?

For these reasons, Washington has been subjected to both popular and intellectual criticism. Modern artists have depicted him in paintings whose satiric titles say as much as their images. "George Washington *Carver* Crossing the Delaware" was painted by Robert Colescott in 1975 (emphasis added). In 1994 Alfred Quiroz contributed "George Washington inspects the hemp crop" (Mitnick 1999, 147–148). In historians' ratings of presidents, Washington still manages to finish second or third, but the top position has been reserved since 1948 for Abraham Lincoln (Stanley and Niemi 2001, 244–245). In popular estimations, Washington has fallen behind not only Lincoln (and Franklin D. Roosevelt), but more recent presidents such as John F. Kennedy and Ronald Reagan (Simmons 2001).

In the end, no matter what one decides about Washington's place in the pantheon of American leaders, his positive legacies must be confronted. He has been a central symbol of the American national identity to generations. His exaltation at the founding, according to a careful chronicler of nationalism's different paths in a number of countries, was in fact the dominant factor in making American nationalism viable (Greenfeld 1992, 423). And he was the preeminent symbol of national unity as the country approached disunion in the Civil War. As the poet Walt Whitman recounted two years before Lincoln was first elected president, Washington's name was "constantly on our lips" (Schwartz 1987, 195).

In addition to his symbolic legacy, Washington left a legacy in the institutions of the government and in how they operate. His presence at the Constitutional Convention gave the framers the courage to create an executive office strong enough to exert energy in times of crisis. Washington's exercise of the presidency set a model for other presidents to follow and gave meaning to constitutional provisions such as the president's role as commander in chief and the president's duty to "from time to time give to the Congress Information of the State of the Union" (Article II, Section 3).

Washington's assertion of executive privilege in a treaty dispute with Congress also helped to establish the limits to Congress's role in diplomacy. His reticence on most legislative matters established another precedent, one that held for over a hundred years: the president should not abridge the legislature's deliberative role. When Washington took office and throughout the next century, presidents did not routinely claim a "mandate" from the people to lead Congress in passing legislation. Similarly, Washington's reticence in his campaigns for office set a precedent that was followed by most candidates for the position until the twentieth century. The office that Washington first held was political, but it also was clearly not like any other elective position in government.

Finally, though the consequence was unintended (see Chapter 2), Washington's decision to retire after two terms set a precedent, limiting the power of any one president. The two-term tradition held until Franklin D. Roosevelt was elected to four terms. Since 1951, presidents have been limited to two elective terms by the Twenty-first Amendment.

BIBLIOGRAPHIC ESSAY

James Thomas Flexner's fourth volume, *George Washington, Anguish and Farewell, 1793–1799* (Boston: Little, Brown, 1972), covers in detail

Washington's final retirement to Mount Vernon. William M. S. Rasmussen and Robert S. Tilton's *George Washington: The Man Behind the Myths* (Charlottesville: University Press of Virginia, 1999), a book written to accompany a museum display, is an excellent source of visual imagery and commentary on Washington's life, including his retirement. The final volume of *The Writings of George Washington from the Original Manuscript Sources, 1745–1799*, 39 vols. (Washington, D.C.: Government Printing Office, 1931–1944), edited by John C. Fitzpatrick, is the standard source on Washington's papers from this period.

On Washington's perspective on slavery, see Fritz Hirschfeld, *George Washington and Slavery: A Documentary Portrayal* (Columbia: University of Missouri Press, 1997), and Dorothy Twohig, " 'That Species of Property': Washington's Role in the Controversy over Slavery," in *George Washington Reconsidered*, ed. Don Higginbotham (Charlottesville: University Press of Virginia, 2001), 114–140. Also in *George Washington Reconsidered*, see Peter R. Henriques, "The Final Struggle between George Washington and the Grim King: Washington's Attitude toward Death and an Afterlife," 250–274, and Robert F. Dalzell Jr. and Lee Baldwin Dalzell, "Interpreting George Washington's Mount Vernon," 94–113. See as well Roger Wilkins, *Jefferson's Pillow: The Founding Fathers and the Dilemma of Black Patriotism* (Boston: Beacon Press, 2001), 81–83.

Washington's fatal illness is considered in "George Washington's Terminal Illness: A Modern Medical Analysis of the Last Illness and Death of George Washington" by White McKenzie Wallenborn, M.D. This essay is based on a speech delivered on November 5, 1997, and is archived on the Web site of Washington Papers project at the University of Virginia (*www.virginia.edu/gwpapers/articles/wallenborn/index.html*).

For background on the military affairs in which Washington was involved during his retirement, see Dave Richard Palmer and James W. Stryker, *Early American Wars and Military Institutions,* a volume of *The West Point Military History Series,* ed. Thomas E. Griess, Department of Military History, U.S. Military Academy, West Point, New York (Wayne, N.J.: Avery Publishing, 1986). For a modern perspective on Shays's Rebellion, which evinces great sympathy for the rebellious farmers, see this curricular resource: Calliope Film Resources, "Shays' Rebellion" (*www.calliope.org/shays/shays2.html*).

Document 6.1   Washington to John Sinclair, December 10, 1796

John Sinclair, a well-known British agricultural economist and member of Parliament, invited Washington to spend time with him in England during his retirement. Sinclair was working on A Statistical Account of Scotland, *a book on Scotland's farm industry, population, and history while serving as president of Parliament's newly founded Board of Agriculture. In this response, Washington outlines his plans for retirement.*

Sir: Since I had the honor of writing to you in June last, I have been favoured with your letters of the 14th and the 30th of May and 10th of September; accompanying the additional appendix to the chapter on manures; your address to the Board of Agriculture; and other valuable productions relative to that important subject.

For your goodness in sending them to me, I pray you to accept my best thanks. . . .

A few months more, say the third of March next, and the scenes of my political life will close, and leave me in the shades of retirement; when, if a few years are allowed me to enjoy it (many I cannot expect, being upon the verge of Sixty five), and health is continued in me, I shall peruse with pleasure and edification, the fruits of your meritorious labors, for the improvement of Agriculture; and shall have leisure, I trust, to realize some of the useful discoveries which have been made in the science of Husbandry, Patronized by you, so much for the interest of mankind, and your own honor.

Until the above period shall have arrived, and particularly during the present Session of Congress, which commenced the 5th instant; I can give but little attention to matters out of the line of my immediate avocations; I did not, however, omit the occasion at the opening of the Session, to call the attention of that body to the importance of Agriculture. What will be the result I know not at present, but if it should be favourable, the hints which you will have it in your power to give, cannot fail of being gratefully received by the members who may constitute the Board.

The articles entrusted to the care of Doctor Edwards came safe, and while all of them are curious; and entitled to my particular acknowledgements, none deserve to be held in higher estimation than the heads of the Egyptian Wheat. They came much too late however for our usual seed time, but I delayed not a moment in sending them to my Manager at

Mount Vernon, with particular directions how to dispose of them to the best advantage; reserving one head a resource, in case of failure from late Sowing. . . .

The Gentlemen whose names you have mentioned in your letter of the 10th of September, will, I am persuaded, be gratified for your civilities. The true policy of this country is to live in peace and amity with all the World; and I am sure it is the wish of the government that it should do so, as long as is consistent with the respect that is due to itself.

I cannot conclude without requesting your acceptance of my grateful acknowledgements, for the expression of your wish to see me in Great Britain, and under your hospitable roof; But I believe there are few things more certain than that after I have retired to Mount Vernon, I shall never go twenty miles beyond the limits of it; unless perchance, I should visit some landed property (under lease) at the distance of about Seventy miles from it. With very great esteem etc.

Source: John C. Fitzpatrick, ed., *The Writings of Washington from the Original Manuscript Sources, 1745–1799,* 39 vols. (Washington, D.C.: Government Printing Office, 1931–1944), 35:321–323.

Document 6.2   Recollections about Washington

Benjamin Latrobe, an English-born, German-educated architect, came to America on March 20, 1796. He found himself face to face with George Washington while delivering a letter to Mount Vernon from the former president's nephew. The "Bath" referred to in this document was not the ancient spa city in southwestern England, but an eponymous warm springs "resort" in the Shenandoah Mountains.

On Sunday, the 16th of July, I set off on horseback for Mount Vernon, having a letter to the President from his nephew, my particular friend, Bushrod Washington, Esq. . . .

Having alighted at Mount Vernon, I sent in my letter of introduction, and walked into the portico next to the river. In about ten minutes the President came to me. He was attired in a plain blue coat, his hair dressed and powdered. There was a reserve but no hauteur in his manner. He shook me by the hand, said he was glad to see a friend of his nephew's, drew a chair, and desired me to sit down. Having inquired after the family

I had left, the conversation turned to Bath, to which they were going. He said he had known the place when there was scarce a house upon it fit to step in, that the accommodations were, he believed, very good at present. He thought the best thing a family, regularly and constantly visiting Bath, could do would be to build a house for their separate accommodation, the expense of which might be two hundred pounds. He has himself a house there which he supposes must be going to ruin. Independent of his public situation, the increased dissipation and frequency of visitors would be an objection to his visiting it again, unless the health of himself or a family should render it necessary. At first that was the motive, he said, that induced people to encounter the badness of the roads and the inconvenience of the lodgings, but at present few, he believed, in comparison of the whole number, had health in view. Even those whose object it was, were interrupted in their quiet by the dissipation of the rest. This, he observed, must naturally be the case in every large collection of men whose minds were not occupied by pressing business or personal interest. In these and many more observations of the same kind there was no moroseness nor anything that appeared as if the rapidly increasing immorality of the citizens particularly impressed him at the time he made them. They seemed the well-expressed remarks of a man who has seen and knows the world.

The conversation then turned upon the rivers of Virginia. He gave me a very minute account of all their directions, their natural advantages, and what he conceived might be done for their improvement by art. He then inquired whether I had seen the Dismal Swamp, and seemed particularly desirous of being informed upon the subject of the canal going forward there. . . .

After conversing with me for more than two hours he got up and said that "we should meet again at dinner." I then prowled about the lawn and took some views. Upon my return to the house, I found Mrs. Washington and her granddaughter, Miss Custis, in the hall. I introduced myself to Mrs. Washington, as a friend of her nephew, and she immediately entered into a conversation upon the prospect from the lawn, and presently gave me an account of her family in a good-humored free manner that was extremely pleasant and flattering. She retains strong remains of considerable beauty, seems to enjoy very good health, and to have a good humor. She has no affectation of superiority in the slightest degree, but acts completely in the character of the mistress of the house of a respectable and opulent country gentleman. . . .

As much as I wished to stay, I thought it a point of delicacy to take up as little of the time of the President as possible, and I therefore requested Mrs. Washington's permission to order my horses. She expressed a slight wish that I would stay, but I did not think it sufficiently strong in etiquette to detain me, and ordered my horses to the door. I waited a few minutes till the President returned. He asked me whether I had any very pressing business to prevent my lengthening my visit. I told him I had not, but that I considered it an intrusion upon his more important engagements, I thought I could reach Colchester that evening by daylight. "Sir," said he, "you see I take my own way. If you can be content to take yours at my house, I shall be glad to see you here longer."

Coffee was brought about six o'clock. When it was removed the President, addressing himself to me, inquired after the state of the crops about Richmond. I told him all I had heard. A long conversation upon farming ensued, during which it grew dark, and he then proposed going into the hall. He made me sit down by him and continued the conversation for above an hour. . . .

Washington has something uncommonly majestic and commanding in his walk, his address, his figure, and his countenance. His face is characterized, however, more by intense and powerful thought than by quick and fiery conception. There is a mildness about its expression, and an air of reserve in his manner lowers its tone still more. He is sixty-four, but appears some years younger, and has sufficient apparent vigor to last many years yet. He was frequently entirely silent for many minutes, during which time an awkwardness seemed to prevail in everyone present. His answers were often short and sometimes approached moroseness. He did not at any time speak with very remarkable fluency; perhaps the extreme correctness of his language, which almost seemed studied, prevented that effect. He appeared to enjoy a humorous observation, and made several himself. He laughed heartily several times in a very good-humored manner. On the morning of my departure he treated me as if I had lived for years in his house, with ease and attention, but in general I thought there was a slight air of moroseness about him as if something had vexed him.

Source: Benjamin Henry Latrobe, *Journal* (New York: 1905), 50–63.

Document 6.3   Washington's Final Days

Tobias Lear worked as George Washington's private secretary from the end of the Revolutionary War through Washington's first term as president. During the president's second term, Lear left to pursue a career brokering land deals in the District of Columbia. After his business failed, Lear journeyed the short distance to Mount Vernon in 1798 to resume the position of secretary to his now elderly boss. At Washington's request, Lear took on one final task—that of organizing the former president's papers. This is Tobias Lear's description of Washington's final days.

Saturday, Decr. 14th. 1799.

This day being marked by an event which will be memorable in the History of America, and perhaps of the World, I shall give a particular statement of it, to which I was an eye witness—

The last illness and death of General Washington

On Thursday Decr. 12th. the General rode out to his farms about ten o'clock, and did not return home till past three. Soon after he went out the weather became very bad, rain, hail, and snow falling alternately with a cold wind: When he came in, I carried some letters to him to frank, intending to send them to the Post-Office in the evening. He franked the letters; but said the Weather was too bad to send a servant to the Office that evening. I observed to him that I was afraid he had got wet; he said no, his great Coat had kept him dry; but his neck appeared to be wet, and the snow was hanging upon his hair. He came to dinner (which had been Waiting for him) without changing his dress. In the evening he appeared as well as usual.

A heavy fall of snow took place on Friday (which prevented the General from riding out as usual). He had taken cold (undoubtedly from being so much exposed the day before) and complained of a sore throat: he however went out in the afternoon into the ground between the House and the River to mark some trees which were to be cut down in the improvement of that spot. He had a Hoarseness which increased in the evening; but he made light of it. In the evening the Papers were brought from the Post Office, and he sat in the Parlour, with Mrs. Washington & myself reading them till about nine o'clock—when Mrs. W. went up into Mrs. Lewis's room, who was confined in Child Bed, and left the General & myself reading the papers. He was very cheerful and when he met with anything interesting or entertaining, he wd. read it aloud as well as his hoarseness would permit him. He requested me to read to him the debates of the Virginia Assembly on the election of a Senator and a Governor— and on hearing Mr. Madison's observations respecting Mr. Monroe, he appeared much affected and spoke with some degree of asperity on the subject, which I endeavored to moderate, as I always did on such occasions. On his retiring I observed to him that he had better take something to remove his cold. He answered no; "you know I never take any thing for a cold. Let it go as it came."

Between two & three o'clock on Saturday morning, he awoke Mrs. Washington, and told her he was very unwell, and had had an ague. She observed that he could scarcely speak and breathed with difficulty; and would have got up to call a Servant; but he would not permit her lest she should take cold. As soon as the day appeared, the Woman (Caroline) went into the Room to make a fire, and Mrs. Washington sent her immediately to call me. I got up, put on my clothes as quickly as possible, and went to his Chamber. Mrs. Washington was then up, and related to me his being taken ill as before stated. I found the General breathing with difficulty, and hardly able to utter a word intelligibly. He desired that Mr. Rawlins (one of the overseers) might be sent for to bleed him before the Dr. could arrive. I dispatched a servant instantly for Rawlins, and another for Dr. Craik, and returned again to the General's Chamber, where I found him in the same situation as I had left him. A mixture of Molasses, Vinegar & butter was prepared to try its effects in the throat; but he could not swallow a drop. Whenever he attempted it he appeared to be distressed, convulsed and almost suffocated. Rawlins came in soon after sunrise, and prepared to bleed him. When the arm was ready the General observing that Rawlins appeared to be agitated, said, as well as he could speak "Don't be afraid." And after the incision was made, he observed, "The orifice is not large enough." However the blood ran pretty freely. Mrs. Washington not knowing whether bleeding was proper or not in the General's situation, begged that much might not be taken from him, lest it should be injurious, and desired me to stop it; but when I was about to untie the string the General put up his hand to prevent it, and as soon as he could speak, said—"More, more." Mrs. Washington being still very uneasy lest too much blood should be taken, it was stopped after taking about half a pint. Finding that no relief was obtained from bleeding, and that nothing would go down the throat, I proposed bathing it externally with salvolatila, which was done; and in the operation, which was with the hand, and in the gentlest manner, he observed "tis very sore." A piece of flannel dip'd in salvolatila was put around his neck, and his feet bathed in warm water; but without affording any relief.

In the mean time, before Dr. Craik arrived Mrs. Washington desired me to send for Dr. Brown of Post Tobacco, whom Dr. Craik had recommended to be called, if any case should ever occur that was seriously alarming. I dispatched a messenger (Cyrus) immediately for Dr. Brown (between 8 & 9 o'clock). Dr. Craik came in soon after, and upon examining the General, he put a blister of Cantharides on the throat, took some more blood from him, and had a gargle of Vinegar & sage tea, and ordered some Vinegar and hot water for him to inhale the steam which he did;—but in attempting to use the gargle he was almost suffocated. When the gargle came from his throat some phlegm followed it, and he attempted to Cough, which the Doctor encouraged him to do as much as possible; but he could only attempt it. About eleven o'clock Dr. Craik requested that Dr. Dick might be sent for, as he feared Dr. Brown would not come in time. A messenger was accordingly dispatched for him. About this time the General was bled again. No effect however was produced by it, and he remained in the same state, unable to swallow anything. A blister was administered about 12 o'clock, which produced an evacuation; but caused no alteration in his complaint.

Dr. Dick came in about 3 o'clock, and Dr. Brown arrived soon after. Upon Dr. Dick's seeing the General and consulting a few minutes with Dr. Craik he was bled again; the blood came very slow, was thick, and did not produce any symptoms of fainting. Dr. Brown came into the chamber soon after; and upon feeling the General's pulse &c. the Physicians went out together. Dr. Craik returned soon after. The General could now swallow a little. Calomel & tarter em. were administered, but without any effect.

About half past 4 o'clock he desired me to call Mrs. Washington to his bed side, when he requested her to go down into his room, and take from his desk two Wills which she would find there, and bring them to him, which she did. Upon looking at them he gave her one which he observed was useless, as being superseded by the other, and desired her to burn it, which she did, and took the other and put it into her Closet.

After this was done, I returned to his bedside, and took his hand. He said to me, "I find I am going, my breath can not last long. I believed from the first that the disorder would prove fatal. Do you arrange and record all my late military letters and papers. Arrange my accounts and settle my books, as you know more about them than any one else, and let Mr. Rawlins finish recording my other letters which he has begun." I told him this should be done. He then asked if I recollected anything which it was essential for him to do, as he had but a very short time to continue among us. I told him I could recollect nothing; but that I hoped he was not so near his end; he observed smiling, that he certainly was, and that as it was the debt that all must pay, he looked to the event with perfect resignation.

In the course of the afternoon he appeared to be in great pain and distress, from the difficulty of breathing, and frequently changed his position in the bed. On these occasions I lay upon the bed, and endeavored to raise him, and turn him with as much care as possible. He appeared penetrated with gratitude for my attentions, & often said, I am afraid I shall fatigue you too much, and upon my assuring him that I could feel nothing but a wish to give him ease, he replied, "Well it is a debt we must pay to each other, and I hope when you want aid of this kind you will find it."

He asked when Mr. Lewis & Washington Custis would return, (they were in New Kent) I told him about the 20th. of the month.

About 5 o'clock Dr. Craik came again into the room & upon going to the bed side the Genl. said to him, Doctor, I die hard; but I am not afraid to go; I believed from my first attack that I should not survive it; my breath can not last long.

The Doctor pressed his hand, but could not utter a word. He retired from the bed side, & sat by the fire absorbed in grief.

Between 5 & 6 o'clk Dr. Dick & Dr. Brown came into the room, and with Dr. Craik went to the bed; when Dr. Craik asked him if he could sit up in the bed? He held out his hand & I raised him up. He then said to the Physicians, "I feel myself going, I thank you for your attentions; but I pray you to take no more trouble about me, let me go off quietly, I can not last long." They found that all which had been done was without effect; he laid down again and all retired except Dr. Craik. He continued in the same situation, uneasy & restless, but without complaining; frequently asking what hour it was. When I helped him to move at this time he did not speak, but looked at me with strong expressions of gratitude.

About 8 o'clock the Physicians came again into the room and applied blisters and cataplasms of wheat bran to his legs and feet; after which they went out (except Dr. Craik) without a ray of hope. I went out about this time and wrote a line to Mr. Law & Mr. Peter, requesting them to come with their wives (Mrs. Washington's Granddaughters) as soon as possible to Mt Vernon.

About ten o'clk he made several attempts to speak to me before he could effect it, at length he said,—"I am just going. Have me decently buried; and do not let my body be put into the Vault in less than three days after I am dead." I bowed assent, for I could not speak. He then looked at me again and said, "Do you understand me?" I replied "Yes." "'Tis well" said he.

About ten minutes before he expired (which was between ten & eleven o 'clk) his breathing became easier; he lay quietly;—he withdrew his hand from mine, and felt his own pulse. I saw his countenance change. I spoke to Dr. Craik who sat by the fire;—he came to the bed side. The General's hand fell from his wrist—I took it in mine and put it into my bosom. Dr. Craik put his hands over his eyes and he expired without a struggle or a sigh!

While we were fixed in silent grief, Mrs. Washington (who was sitting at the foot of the bed) asked with a firm & collected voice, Is he gone? I could not speak, but held up my hand as a signal that he was no more. 'Tis well, said she in the same voice, "All is now over I shall soon follow him! I have no more trials to pass through!"

Source: "Account of George Washington's Last Illness and Death, December 14–25, 1799," *Tobias Lear's Journal* (New York: 1906), 21–24.

Document 6.4   Washington's Will, July 9, 1799

George Washington's will reveals the nature of his ideals. Not only does he guarantee freedom for his slaves, but he also outlines specific procedures for educating them. Upon his wife's death, the slaves would be taught to read and write and would generally be cared for as the laws commanded for the care of poor (white) orphans. Washington's support for education is evidenced by his bequests to universities and schools.

In the name of God amen I George Washington of Mount Vernon—a citizen of the United States, and lately President of the same, do make, ordain and declare this Instrument; which is written with my own hand and every page thereof subscribed with my name, to be my last Will & Testament, revoking all others.

Imprimus. All my debts, of which there are but few, and none of magnitude, are to be punctually and speedily paid—and the Legacies hereinafter bequeathed, are to be discharged as soon as circumstances will permit, and in the manner directed.

Item. To my dearly beloved wife Martha Washington I give and bequeath the use, profit and benefit of my whole Estate, real and personal, for the term of her natural life—except such parts thereof as are specifically disposed of hereafter: My improved lot in the Town of Alexandria, situated on Pitt & Cameron streets, I give to her and her heirs forever; as I also do my household & Kitchen furniture of every sort & kind, with the liquors and groceries which may be on hand at the time of my decease; to be used & disposed of as she may think proper.

Item. Upon the decease of my wife, it is my Will & desire that all the Slaves which I hold in my own right, shall receive their freedom. To emancipate them during her life, would, tho' earnestly wished by me, be attended with such insuperable difficulties on account of their intermixture by Marriages with the dower Negroes, as to excite the most painful sensations, if not disagreeable consequences from the latter, while both descriptions are in the occupancy of the same Proprietor; it not being in my power, under the tenure by which the Dower Negroes are held, to manumit them. And whereas among those who will receive freedom according to this devise, there may be some, who from old age or bodily infirmities, and others who on account of their infancy, that will be unable to support themselves; it is my Will and desire that all who come under the first & second description shall be comfortably clothed & fed by my heirs while they live; and that such of the latter description as have no parents living, or if living are unable, or unwilling to provide for them, shall be bound by the Court until they shall arrive at the age of twenty five years; and in cases where no record can be produced, whereby their ages can be ascertained, the judgment of the Court, upon its own view of the subject, shall be adequate and final. The Negroes thus bound, are (by their Masters or Mistresses) to be taught to read & write; and to be brought up to some useful occupation, agreeably to the Laws of the Commonwealth of Virginia, providing for the support of Orphan and other poor Children. And I do hereby expressly forbid the Sale, or transportation out of the said Commonwealth, of any Slave I may die possessed of, under any pretence whatsoever. And I do moreover most pointedly, and most solemnly enjoin it upon my Executors hereafter named, or the Survivors of them, to see that this clause respecting Slaves, and every part thereof be religiously fulfilled at the Epoch at which it is directed to take place; without evasion, neglect or delay, after the Crops which may then be on the ground are harvested, particularly as it respects the aged and infirm; seeing that a regular and permanent fund be established for their support so long as there are subjects requiring it; not trusting to the uncertain provision to be made by individuals. And to my Mulatto man William (calling himself William Lee) I give immediate freedom; or if he should prefer it (on account of the accidents which have befallen him, and which have rendered him incapable of walking or of any active employment) to remain in the situation he now is, it shall be optional in him to do so: In either case however, I allow him an annuity of thirty dollars during his natural life, which shall be independent of the victuals and clothes he has been accustomed to receive, if he chooses the last alternative; but in full, with his freedom, if he prefers the first; & this I give him as a testimony of my sense of his attachment to me, and for his faithful services during the Revolutionary War.

Item. To the Trustees (Governors, or by whatsoever other name they may be designated) of the Academy in the Town of Alexandria, I give and bequeath, in Trust, four thousand dollars, or in other words twenty of the shares which I hold in the Bank of Alexandria, towards the support of a Free school established at, and annexed to, the said Academy; for the purpose of Educating such Orphan children, or the children of such other poor and indigent persons as are unable to accomplish it with their own means; and who, in the judgment of the Trustees of the said Seminary, are best entitled to the benefit of this donation. The foresaid twenty shares I give & bequeath in perpetuity; the dividends only of which are to be drawn for, and applied by the said Trustees for the time being, for the uses above mentioned; the stock to remain entire and untouched; unless indications of a failure of the said Bank should be so apparent, or a discontinuance thereof should render a removal of this fund necessary; in either of these cases, the amount of the Stock here devised, is to be vested in some other Bank or public Institution, whereby the interest may with regularity & certainty be drawn, and applied as above. And to prevent misconception, my meaning is, and is hereby declared to be, that these twenty shares are in lieu of, and not in addition to, the thousand pounds given by a missive letter some years ago; in consequence whereof an annuity of fifty pounds has since been paid towards the support of this Institution.

Item. Whereas by a Law of the Commonwealth of Virginia, enacted in the year 1785, the Legislature thereof was pleased (as an evidence of Its approbation of the services I had rendered the Public during the Revolution—and partly, I believe, in consideration of my having suggested the vast advantages which the Community would derive from the extensions of its Inland Navigation, under Legislative patronage) to present me with one hundred shares of one hundred dollars each, in the incorporated company established for the purpose of extending the navigation of James River from tide water to the Mountains: and also with fifty shares of one hundred pounds Sterling each, in the Corporation of another company, likewise established for the similar purpose of opening the Navigation of the River Potomac from tide water to Fort Cumberland, the acceptance of which, although the offer was highly honourable, and grateful to my feelings, was refused, as inconsistent with a principle which I had adopted, and had never departed from—namely—not to receive pecuniary compensation for any services I could render my country in its arduous struggle with great Britain, for its Rights; and because I had evaded similar propositions from other States in the Union; adding to this refusal, however, an intimation that, if it should be the pleasure of the Legislature to permit me to appropriate the said shares to public uses, I would receive them on those terms with due sensibility; and this it having consented to, in flattering terms, as will appear by a subsequent Law, and sundry resolutions, in the most ample and honourable manner, I proceed after this recital, for the more correct understanding of the case, to declare that as it has always been a source of serious regret with me, to see the youth of these United States sent to foreign Countries for the purpose of Education, often before their minds were formed, or they had imbibed any adequate ideas of the happiness of their own; contracting, too frequently, not only habits of dissipation & extravagance, but principles unfriendly to Republican Government and to the true & genuine liberties of Mankind; which, thereafter are rarely overcome. For these reasons, it has been my ardent wish to see a plan devised on a liberal scale, which would have a tendency to sprd systemactic ideas through all parts of this rising Empire, thereby to do away local attachments and State prejudices, as far as the nature of things would, or indeed ought to admit, from our National Councils. Looking anxiously forward to the accomplishment of so desirable an object as this is (in my estimation) my mind has not been able to contemplate any plan more likely to effect the measure than the establishment of a UNIVERSITY in a central part of the United States, to which the youth of fortune and talents from all parts thereof might be sent for the completion of their Education in all the branches of polite literature; in arts and Sciences, in acquiring knowledge in the principles of Politics & good Government; and (as a matter of infinite Importance in my judgment) by associating with each other, and forming friendships in Juvenile years, be enabled to free themselves in a proper degree from those local prejudices & habitual jealousies which have just been mentioned; and which, when carried to excess, are never failing sources of disquietude to the Public mind, and pregnant of mischievous consequences to this Country: Under these impressions, so fully dilated.

Item. I give and bequeath in perpetuity the fifty shares which I hold in the Potomac Company (under the aforesaid Acts of the Legislature of Virginia) towards the endowment of a UNIVERSITY to be established within the limits of the District of Columbia, under the auspices of the General Government, if that government should incline to extend a fostering hand towards it; and until such Seminary is established, and the funds arising on these shares shall be required for its support, my further Will & desire is that the profit accruing therefrom shall, whenever the dividends are made, be laid out in purchasing Stock in the Bank of Columbia, or some other Bank, at the discretion of my Executors; or by the Treasurer of the United States for the time being under the direction of Congress; provided that Honourable body should Patronize the measure, and the Dividends proceeding from the purchase of such Stock is to be vested in more stock, and so on, until a sum adequate to the accomplishment of the object is obtained, of which I have not the smallest doubt, before many years passes away; even if no aid or encouraged is given by Legislative authority, or from any other source. . . .

Item. To my Nephew Bushrod Washington, I give and bequeath all the Papers in my possession, which relate to my Civil and Military Administration of the affairs of this Country; I leave to him also, such of my private Papers as are worth preserving; and at the decease of wife, and before—if she is not inclined to retain them, I give and bequeath my library of Books and Pamphlets of every kind. . . .

And by way of advice, I recommend it to my Executors not to be precipitate in disposing of the landed property (herein directed to be sold) if from temporary causes the Sale thereof should be dull; experience having fully evinced, that the price of land (especially above the Falls of the Rivers, & on the Western Waters) have been progressively rising, and cannot be long checked in its increasing value. And I particularly recommend it to such of the Legatees (under this clause of my Will) as can make it convenient, to take each a share of my Stock in the Potomac Company in preference to the amount of what it might sell for; being thoroughly convinced myself, that no uses to which the money can be applied will be so productive as the Tolls arising from this navigation when in full operation (and this from the nature of things it must be 'ere long) and more especially if that of the Shenandoah is added thereto.

The family Vault at Mount Vernon requiring repairs, and being improperly situated besides, I desire that a new one of Brick, and upon a larger Scale, may be built at the foot of what is commonly called the Vineyard Enclosure, on the ground which is marked out. In which my remains, with those of my deceased relatives (now in the old Vault) and such others of my family as may choose to be entombed there, may be deposited. And it is my express desire that my Corpse may be Interred in a private manner, without parade, or funeral Oration.

Lastly I constitute and appoint my dearly beloved wife Martha Washington, My Nephews William Augustine Washington, Bushrod Washington, George Steptoe Washington, Samuel Washington, & Lawrence Lewis, & my ward George Washington Parke Custis (when he shall have arrived at the age of twenty years) Executrix & Executors of this Will & testament, In the construction of which it will readily be perceived that no professional character has been consulted, or has had any Agency in the draught—and that, although it has occupied many of my leisure hours to digest, & to through it into its present form, it may, notwithstanding, appear crude and incorrect. But having endeavored to be plain, and explicit in all Devises—even at the expense of prolixity, perhaps of tautology, I hope, and trust, that no disputes will arise concerning them; but if, contrary to expectation, the case should be otherwise from the want of legal expression, or the usual technical terms, or because too much or too little has been said on any of the Devises to be consonant with law, My Will and direction expressly is, that all disputes (if unhappily any should arise) shall be decided by three impartial and intelligent men, known for their probity and good understanding; two to be chosen by the disputants—each having the choice of one—and the third by those two. Which three men thus chosen, shall, unfettered by Law, or legal constructions, declare their sense of the Testators intention; and such decision is, to all intents and purposes to be as binding on the Parties as if it had been given in the Supreme Court of the United States.

In witness of all, and of each of the things herein contained, I have set my hand and Seal, this ninth day of July, in the year One thousand seven hundred and ninety [nine] and of the Independence of the United States the twenty fourth.

Source: W.W. Abbot, ed., *The Papers of George Washington, Retirement Series,* Vol. 4, *April–December 1799* (Charlottesville: University Press of Virginia, 1998–1999), 477–492.

Document 6.5   "Negroes Belonging to George Washington"

During the final months of his life, George Washington prepared a will, a list of property he owned, and a list of slaves who worked on his properties. This document details the number of slaves performing specific tasks.

Belonging to GW

| | | | Workg | | Childn | | |
Where & how Empld	Men	Women	Boys	Girls	Boys	Girls	Total
Tradesmen & others, not employed on the Farms-viz							
Smiths	2						2
Bricklayers	1						1
Carpenters	5						5
Coopers	3						3
Shoemaker	1						1
Cooks	1						1
Gardeners	2						2
Millers	1		1				2

Where & how Empld	Men	Women	Workg Boys	Workg Girls	Childn Boys	Childn Girls	Total
Tradesmen & others, not employed on the Farms-viz							
House-Servants	1						1
Distchers	4						4
Distillery							
Postilions							
Waggoners & Cartrs	1						1
Milk Maid							
Spinners & Knitrs	1						1
Mansion-Ho							
Muddy-hole	3	14	1		8	10	36
River-Farm	3	9	2	2	6	4	26
Dogue Run F.	6	7		1	7	3	24
Union-Farm	2	1				2	5
[subtotal]	36	32	4	3	21	19	115
Passed labr or that do not Work							
Muddy hole							1
River Farm	1	1					2
Dogue Run		3					3
Union Farm		1					1
Mansion Ho.	3						3
[subtotal]	40	37	4	3	21	19	124
Hired fm Mrs. French	9	9	2	4	6	10	40
Grand Total	49	46	6	7	27	29	164

Dower

Where & how Empld	Men	Women	Workg Boys	Workg Girls	Childn Boys	Childn Girls	Total
Tradesmen & others, not employed on the Farms-viz							
Smiths							
Bricklayers	1						1
Carpenters	1						1

Dower (continued)

Where & how Empld	Men	Women	Workg Boys	Workg Girls	Childn Boys	Childn Girls	Total
Tradesmen & others, not employed on the Farms-viz							
Coopers							
Shoemaker							
Cooks		1					1
Gardeners							
Millers							
House-Servants	2	4					6
Distchers	1						1
Distillery	4		1				5
Postilions	1		1				2
Waggoners & Cartrs	2						2
Milk Maid		1					1
Spinners & Knitrs	1	7					8
Mansion-Ho	3	9	3	2	8	15	40
Muddy-hole	2			2			4
River-Farm	6	9	2	1	5	5	28
Dogue Run F.		5	1		5	6	17
Union-Farm	4	6	3		8	6	27
[subtotal]	28	42	11	5	26	32	144
Muddy hole		1					1
River Farm	1	1					2
Dogue Run		1					1
Union Farm		3					3
Mansion Ho.		2					2
[subtotal]	29	50	11	5	26	32	153
Hired fm Mrs. French							
Grand Total	29	50	11	5	26	32	153

Source: W.W. Abbot, ed., *The Papers of George Washington, Retirement Series,* Vol. 4, *April–December 1799* (Charlottesville: University Press of Virginia, 1998–1999), 538–539.0

Document 6.6   Henry Lee's Funeral Oration, December 26, 1799
During the Revolutionary War, George Washington asked Henry Lee to serve
as his personal aide. Lee declined the offer, opting to enlist as a major in the
Continental army where he earned the nickname "Light-Horse Harry."
Washington maintained a close friendship with Lee through the latter's career
as governor of Virginia and as a member of Congress. Lee delivered the
following eulogy at the state funeral service for Washington held in Philadel-
phia. In it, he is addressing both houses of Congress. That service, notes
Lawrence Friedman (1975, 46), was just one of eighteen hundred memorial
services that took place in almost two hundred American towns between Wash-
ington's death and his birthday just over two months later.

In obedience to your will, I rife your humble organ, with the hope of
executing a part of the system of public mourning which you have been
pleased to adopt, commemorative of the death of the most illustrious
and most beloved personage this country has ever produced; and which,
while it transmits to posterity your sense of the awful event, faintly rep-
resents your knowledge of the consummate excellence you so cordially
honor. . . .

The founder of our federate republic—our bulwark in war, our guide in
peace, is no more! O that this were but questionable! Hope, the comforter
of the wretched, would pour into our agonizing hearts its balmy dew. But,
alas! There is no hope for us; our WASHINGTON is removed forever! Possessing the stoutest frame and purest mind, he had passed nearly to his sixty-
eighth year, in the enjoyment of high health, when, habituated by his care
of us to neglect himself, a slight cold, disregarded, became inconvenient on
Friday, oppressive on Saturday, and, defying every medical interposition,
before the morning of Sunday put an end to the best of men. . . .

How, my fellow-citizens, shall I single to your grateful hearts his pre-
eminent worth? Where shall I begin, in opening to your view a character
though sublime? Shall I speak of his warlike achievements, all springing
from obedience to his country's will, all directed to his country's good?

Will you go with me to the banks of the Monongahela, to see your
youthful WASHINGTON supporting, in the dismal hour of Indian victory, the ill-fated Braddock, and saving, by his judgement and by his valour, the remains of a defeated army, pressed by the conquering savage foe?
Or when, oppressed America nobly resolving to risk her all in defense of

her violated rights, he was elevated by the unanimous voice of Congress to the command of her armies? Will you follow him to the high grounds of Boston, where, to an undisciplined, courageous and virtuous yeomanry, his presence gave the stability of system, and infused the invincibility of love of country? Or shall I carry you to the painful scenes of Long-Island, York-Island, and New Jersey, when combating superior and gallant armies, aided by powerful fleets, and led by chiefs high in the roll of fame, he stood the bulwark of our safety undismayed by disaster, unchanged by change of fortune? Or will you view him in the precarious fields of Trenton, where deep gloom, unnerving every arm, reigned triumphant through our thinned, worn down, unaided ranks—himself unmoved? Dreadful was the night. It was about this time of winter. The storm raged. The Delaware, rolling furiously with floating ice, forbid the approach of man. WASH-INGTON, self-collected, viewed, the tremendous scene. His country called. Unappalled by surrounding dangers, he passed to the hostile shore; he fought; he conquered. The morning sun cheered the American world. Our country rose on the even; and her dauntless Chief, pursuing his blow, completed in the lawns of Princeton, what his vast soul had conceived on the shores of Delaware. . . .

To the horrid din of battle sweet peace succeeded; and our virtuous Chief, mindful only of the common good, in a moment tempting personal aggrandizement, hushed the discontents of growing sedition, and, sur-rendering his power into the hands from which he had received it, con-verted his sword into a ploughshare; teaching an admiring world, that to be truly great you must be truly good.

Were I to stop here, the picture would be incomplete, and the talk imposed unfinished. Great as was our WASHINGTON in war, and as much as did that greatness contribute to produce the American republic, it is not in war alone his pre-eminence stands conspicuous. His various tal-ents, combining all the capacities of a statesman with those of a soldier, fit-ted him alike to guide the councils and the armies of our nation. Scarcely had he rested from his martial toils, while his invaluable parental advice was still sounding in our ears, when he, who had been our shield and our sword, was called forth to act a less splendid, but more important part.

Possessing a clear and penetrating mind, a strong and sound judgement, calmness and temper for deliberation, with invincible firmness and perse-verance in resolutions maturely formed; drawing information from all; act-ing from himself, with incorruptible integrity and unvarying patriotism;

his own superiority and the public confidence alike marked him as the man designed by Heaven to lead in the great political as well as military events which have distinguished the era of his life.

The finger of an over-ruling Providence, pointing at WASHINGTON, was neither mistaken nor unobserved, when, to realize the vast hopes to which our revolution had given birth, a change of political system became indispensable.

How novel, how grand the spectacle! Independent States stretched over an immense territory, and known only by common difficulty, clinging to their union as the rock of their safety; deciding, by frank comparison of their relative condition, to rear on that rock, under the guidance of reason, a common government, through whose commanding protection, liberty and order, with their long train of blessings, should be safe to themselves, and the sure inheritance of their posterity.

This arduous task devolved on citizens selected by the people, from knowledge of their wisdom and confidence in their virtue. In this august assembly of sages and of patriots, WASHINGTON of course was found; and, as if acknowledged to be the most wise where all were wise, with one voice he was declared their Chief. How well he merited this rare distinction, how faithful were the labors of himself and his compatriots, the work of their hands, and our union, strength and prosperity, the fruits of that work, best attest. . . .

The presidential term expiring, his solicitude to exchange exaltation for humility returned with a force increased with increase of age; and he had prepared his Farewell Address to his countrymen, proclaiming his intention, when the united interposition of all around him, enforced by the eventful prospects of the epoch, produced a further sacrifice of inclination to duty. The election of President followed; and WASHINGTON, by the unanimous vote of the nation, was called to resume the Chief Magistracy. What a wonderful fixture of confidence! Which attracts most our administration, a people so correct, or a citizen combining an assemblage of talents forbidding rivalry, and stifling even envy itself? Such a nation ought to be happy; such a Chief must be for ever revered.

War, long menaced by the Indian tribes, now broke out; and the terrible conflict, deluging Europe with blood, began to shed its baneful influence over our happy land. To the first, out-stretching his invincible arm, under the order of the gallant Wayne, the American eagle soared triumphant through distance forests. Peace followed victory; and the melioration of the condition of the enemy followed peace. Godlike virtue! Which uplifts even the subdued savage. . . .

First in war, first in peace and first in the hearts of his countrymen, he was second to none in the humble and endearing scenes of private life. Pious, just, humane, temperate and sincere—uniform, dignified and commanding—his example was as edifying to all around him as were the effects of that example lasting.

To his equals he was condescending, to his inferiors kind, and to the dear object of his affections exemplarily tender. Correct throughout, vice shuddered in his preference, and virtue always felt his fosterous hand. The purity of his private character gave effulgence to his public virtues.

His last scene comported with the whole tenor of his life. Although in extreme pain, not a sigh, not a groan escaped him; and with undisturbed serenity he eloped his well-spent life. Such was the man America has lost! Such was the man for whom our nation mourns! . . .

Source: Eulogies and Orations on the Life and Death of General George Washington, First President of the United States of America (Boston: Manning and Loring, 1800), 9–18.

Document 6.7   Parson Weems's Washington

By means of a hackneyed but heartfelt compendium of myths and fables in the form of a biography, Mason Locke "Parson" Weems educated generations of Americans about George Washington. Weems's biography of Washington, which he published in 1800, was a tremendous commercial success. By 1825 it had been reprinted forty times. This excerpt from The Life of Washington *recounts a parable of the young Washington's attachment to the truth.*

Never did the wise Ulysses take more pains with his beloved Telemachus, than did Mr. Washington with George, to inspire him with an early love of truth. "Truth, George" (said he) "is the loveliest quality of youth. I would ride fifty miles, my son, to see the little boy whose heart is so honest, and his lips so pure, that we may depend on every word he says. O how lovely does such a child appear in the eyes of every body! His parents dote on him; his relations glory in him; they are constantly praising him to their children, whom they beg to imitate him. They are often sending for him, to visit them; and receive him, when he comes, with as much joy as if he were a little angel, come to set pretty examples to their children."

"But, Oh! how different, George, is the case with the boy who is so given to lying, that nobody can believe a word he says! He is looked at with aversion wherever he goes, and parents dread to see him come among their children. Oh, George! My son! Rather than see you come to this pass, dear as you are to my heart, gladly would I assist to nail you up in your little coffin, and follow you to your grave. Hard, indeed, would it be to me to give up my son, whose little feet are always so ready to run about with me, and whose fondly looking eyes and sweet prattle make so large a part of my happiness: but still I would give him up, rather than see him a common liar."

"Pa, (said George very seriously) do I ever tell lies?"

"No, George, I thank God you do not, my son; and I rejoice in the hope you never will. At least, you shall never, from me, have cause to be guilty of so shameful a thing. Many parents, indeed, even compel their children to this vile practice, by barbarously beating them for every little fault; hence, on the next offence, the little terrified creature slips out a lie! just to escape the rod. But as to yourself, George, you know I have always told you, and now tell you again, that, whenever by accident you do any thing wrong, which must often be the case, as you are but a poor little boy yet, without experience or knowledge, never tell a falsehood to conceal it; but come bravely up, my son, like a little man, and tell me of it: and instead of beating you, George, I will but the more honor and love you for it, my dear."

This, you'll say, was sowing good seed!—Yes, it was: and the crop, thank God, was, as I believe it ever will be, where a man acts the true parent, that is, the Guardian Angel, by his child.

The following anecdote is a case in point. It is too valuable to be lost, and too true to be doubted; for it was communicated to me by the same excellent lady to whom I am indebted for the last.

"When George," said she, "was about six years old, he was made the wealthy master of a hatchet! of which, like most little boys, he was immoderately fond, and was constantly going about chopping every thing that came in his way. One day, in the garden, where he often amused himself hacking his mother's pea-sticks, he unluckily tried the edge of his hatchet on the body of a beautiful young English cherry-tree, which he barked so terribly, that I don't believe the tree ever got the better of it. The next morning the old gentleman finding out what had befallen his tree, which, by the by, was a great favorite, came into the house, and with much warmth asked for the mischievous author, declaring at the same time, that he would not have taken five guineas for his tree. Nobody could tell him any thing about it. Presently George and his hatchet made their appearance. George, said his father, do you know who killed that beautiful little cherry-tree yonder in the garden? This was a tough question; and George staggered under it for a moment; but quickly recovered himself: and looking at his father, with the sweet face of youth brightened with the inexpressible charm of all-conquering truth, he bravely cried out, "I can't tell a lie, Pa; you know I can't tell a lie. I did cut it with my hatchet."—Run to my arms, you dearest boy, cried his father in transports, run to my arms; glad am I, George, that you killed my tree; for you have paid me for it a thousand fold. Such an act of heroism in my son, is more worth than a thousand trees, though blossomed with silver, and their fruits of purest gold.

Source: Mason Locke Weems, *The Life of Washington* (New edition with primary documents and introduction by Peter S. Onuf), (Armonk, N.Y. and London: M. E. Sharpe, 1996), 8–10.

Appendix A

Notable Figures of the Washington Presidency

Adams, John (1735–1826, b. Braintree, Massachusetts)
Vice president of the United States, 1789–1797

John Adams's intellectual abilities were recognized by his father, who arranged for his eldest son, alone among his children, to be college-educated. After graduating from Harvard College in 1755, Adams taught school in Worcester, Massachusetts, while saving money to study law. After admission to the bar, Adams rose to prominence as an attorney. In 1768, four years after marrying Abigail Smith, he moved his family to Boston to advance his legal career.

In the controversies surrounding British colonial policy, Adams opposed violence but supported colonial rights. At the Second Continental Congress in 1775, he nominated George Washington to serve as commander of the Continental army, and was a vigorous supporter of full and complete independence. Adams spent almost all of the years 1778–1788 representing the United States in Europe, and was one of the American signatories to the Peace of Paris that concluded the Revolutionary War. Shortly after his return to America, he was selected for the vice presidency, in part to achieve geographic balance in the government. But like many vice presidents to follow, he was frequently bored with his position in government. Moreover, he was never a confidant of the president he served, and was assigned no share of executive duties. His only influence was exerted in the Senate, where as vice president he cast more tie-breaking votes than any other vice president in U.S. history. He was, in the exercise of this duty, loyal always to the administration. As the candidate of the Federalist Party, he succeeded Washington in the presidency.

Bradford, William (1755–1795, b. Philadelphia, Pennsylvania)
Attorney general, 1794–1795

After graduating from the College of New Jersey (Princeton), William Bradford studied theology and law before joining the Continental army. Ailing health cut short his military career, permitting him to return to the law. Bradford was appointed attorney general of Pennsylvania in 1780, and served in that position for eleven years. In 1791 Bradford was appointed to the Pennsylvania Supreme Court, a post he held until Washington appointed him U.S. attorney general in 1794. During Bradford's tenure, Timothy Pickering and Oliver Wolcott sought his advice in drafting a communication to Washington about an intercepted message between

Secretary of State Edmund Randolph and French minister Joseph Fauchet that implicated Randolph in an attempt to incite violence against the government in the Whiskey Rebellion. The controversy that led to Randolph's resignation worsened Bradford's already ill health. He never recovered and died in office.

Carmichael, William (?–1795, b. Queen Anne's County, Maryland)
U.S. minister to Spain, 1790–1794
His family's financial privilege allowed William Carmichael to complete his education at the University of Edinburgh and to set up residence in London, where he was living when the Revolutionary War began in 1775. Resolved to assist in the Revolution, Carmichael served as secretary to the American commission in Paris during the early years of the war and took the lead in recruiting the Marquis de Lafayette to sail to America to aid the cause. He returned to America in 1778 and became a member of the Continental Congress from 1778 to 1779. He then returned to Europe as secretary to John Jay, who represented the United States in Spain. After Jay left for Paris in 1782, Carmichael stayed in Madrid as acting chargé d'affaires, a position to which he was finally commissioned in 1790. Because of poor health, he asked to be recalled the next year, but Secretary of State Thomas Jefferson denied his request. In 1792 he was appointed joint commissioner with William Short to negotiate a treaty with Spain. After two years, their efforts were largely successful, and Carmichael's request for recall was accepted. Carmichael died, however, before he could return to America, and was buried in Madrid.

Ellsworth, Oliver (1745–1807, b. Windsor, Connecticut)
Chief justice of the United States, 1796–1800
Oliver Ellsworth entered Yale College, but disciplinary problems during his sophomore year forced a transfer to the College of New Jersey (Princeton). After college, he returned to Connecticut and built one of the state's largest law practices. Ellsworth was among the first colonists to advocate independence, and when the Revolutionary War began, he held several leadership positions, including delegate to the Continental Congress. In Congress, Ellsworth served on the Committee of Appeals, the nation's first federal court. In 1787 Ellsworth attended the Constitutional Convention, representing Connecticut. Later, as one of Connecticut's first senators, he drafted the Judiciary Act of 1789 which organized the federal court into a three-tier system. Upon Chief Justice John Jay's resignation from the Supreme Court in 1795, Washington appointed John Rutledge to that position during a Senate recess. When the body reconvened, Rutledge's nomination was rejected. Washington then nominated Associate Justice William Cushing, but he declined the nomination. Ellsworth was Washington's third choice. On the Court, Ellsworth introduced the practice of *per curiam* opinions, in which a single opinion is released by the Court without identifying its author. He resigned from the Court in 1800.

Freneau, Philip (1752–1832, b. New York, New York)
Poet, newspaper editor, harsh critic of President Washington

Born to moderate wealth, Philip Freneau entered no profession upon graduation from the College of New Jersey (Princeton), but continued his lifelong passion, which was writing. Although he spent most of the Revolutionary War employed as secretary to a planter in the British West Indies, he earned the title "poet of the American Revolution" for vigorous verses published largely in New York newspapers. In August 1791, he accepted a sinecure at the State Department as a part-time translator so that he might devote his time and talents to the defense of his employer, Secretary of State Thomas Jefferson, and the censure of Jefferson's rival, Treasury Secretary Alexander Hamilton. On October 31, 1791, Freneau issued in Philadelphia the first edition of the pro-Jeffersonian *National Gazette,* designed to counter the pro-Hamiltonian *Gazette of the United States,* published by John Fenno. Washington, a frequent target of ridicule in Freneau's paper, was infuriated by "that rascal Freneau" and pleaded with Jefferson to restrain him if he would not fire him. Jefferson declined to do either, because he believed the editor and poet had "saved our Constitution which was galloping fast into monarchy" (Pattee 1928). Freneau followed his patron, Jefferson, into retirement from government after about two years as editor of the *National Gazette.*

Genêt, Edmond Charles (1763–1834, b. Versailles, France)
French minister to the United States, 1792–1793

Born into the French aristocracy, Edmond Genêt, like his father, joined the French Foreign Ministry. Genêt was dispatched throughout Europe for over a decade, avoiding the dangers of Paris during the start of the French Revolution. Known as an iconoclastic and free-thinking diplomat, Genêt continued to hold his position after the overthrow of the French monarchy in 1792. His first assignment for revolutionary France brought him to the United States in 1793, where as "Citizen Genêt" he sought American support for the French Republic and American aid in France's war with Britain. The announcement of Genêt's mission to America caused controversy within Washington's cabinet and among citizens generally. With the rise of the "democratic societies" that formed to welcome Genêt as he traveled around the United States, many Americans became accustomed to partisan behavior. Such societies also had a hand in promoting the establishment of the distinctive American two-party system.

Genêt acted with little regard for American sovereignty. He commissioned American merchant vessels as privateers, so they might raid British merchant vessels off the coast of America and in the Caribbean. To distribute the loot that privateers captured, Genêt established prize courts in American ports, in contravention of President Washington's proclaimed policy of neutrality in the war between Britain and France. Because Genêt was popular with pro-French Americans, President Washington was at first reluctant to act against him, but at last, in 1793,

Washington insisted that France recall Genêt. During the ensuing domestic political conflict, Genêt insulted the president as an unworthy leader of a free people. The result was a backlash against the minister and much needed support for the president's policy of neutrality. Fearing that he would be put to death if he were to return to France in disgrace, Genêt asked the president for political asylum. Washington, typically magnanimous, permitted Genêt to remain in America, where he married the daughter of New York governor George Clinton and eventually became a citizen.

Habersham, Joseph (1751–1815, b. Savannah, Georgia)
Postmaster general, 1795–1801
Despite his father's loyalty to Britain, Joseph Habersham took a leading role in mobilizing public protest in Georgia against Britain in 1774 and 1775. During the war, he became a colonel in the Continental army. After service in the Georgia Assembly, in the Continental Congress, and at the state convention that ratified the Constitution in Georgia, he was appointed by Washington to serve as U.S. postmaster general. He held the position through Washington's second term and through the term of John Adams.

Hamilton, Alexander (1755–1804, b. Nevis, British West Indies)
Secretary of the Treasury, 1789–1795
Alexander Hamilton was the illegitimate son of a working-class couple in the West Indies. His aunts, his employer, and a minister, recognizing the boy's talents, sponsored his emigration to the mainland in 1772. After studying at King's College (Columbia), he entered the war as a captain of militia and made his reputation at the Battle of Trenton in 1776. General Washington took Hamilton into his staff family and relied heavily on the young man in maintaining his official correspondence. Contrary to popular myth, however, the commander and his aide were not intimates. In part, this was the result of Hamilton's determination to keep the relationship on a business-like footing, because he did not wish it to be said that he rose in life merely through the good graces of George Washington. Hamilton ultimately received a battle command and had the satisfaction of leading a bayonet assault at Yorktown in 1781.

During the war, Hamilton married Elizabeth Schuyler, from one of the wealthiest and most prominent families in the colonies. After the war, Hamilton became a leading attorney in New York, participated in the establishment of the Bank of New York, and was elected a delegate to the Annapolis Convention of 1786. At the Constitutional Convention the next year, he delivered a five-hour speech in which he set forth a plan for a quasi-monarchical executive. His most consequential work in behalf of the new government was the fifty-one essays he contributed to *The Federalist Papers,* the series of eighty-five newspaper articles that he, James Madison, and John Jay wrote to persuade New York voters to ratify the Constitution.

After Washington's first choice, Robert Morris, turned down the post, the president nominated Hamilton to be the first secretary of the Treasury. Hamilton's 1791 "Report on Manufactures" articulated a vision of the United States as an industrializing nation with a strong government to ensure sound credit, bind the wealthy to the government, and encourage national self-sufficiency. Hamilton's plan for the federal assumption of state debts and the establishment of a national bank split the government and spurred the creation of the American two-party system. When President Washington decided to support Hamilton's plans, anti-Hamiltonians, led by Secretary of State Thomas Jefferson, gradually took on the role of an opposition party. Hamilton also took the lead in urging the imposition of an excise tax on whiskey, which Congress approved in 1791. He then accompanied the president when the latter led a military force to quell the Whiskey Rebellion in 1794. Finally, although lacking any formal authority in foreign affairs, Hamilton played a major role in Chief Justice John Jay's mission to negotiate a treaty with Britain in 1794.

Hamilton left office on January 31, 1795, but continued to lend his considerable talents and energy to the Federalist cause. Hamilton also continued to assist the president, as he did in the drafting of Washington's Farewell Address. During the threat of war with France under the John Adams administration, Washington and Hamilton were again allied in the army that the former president reluctantly raised to meet the threat. Under Washington, Hamilton served as inspector general with the rank of major general.

In the contested presidential election of 1800, Hamilton threw his influence behind Jefferson, leaving Aaron Burr with the vice presidency. In the New York gubernatorial campaign of 1804, in which Vice President Burr was a candidate, Hamilton was reported in the press as having said that Burr was not to be trusted with power. In a duel on July 11, 1804, Burr mortally wounded Hamilton, who died the next day. Three years earlier, Hamilton's oldest son had been killed in a duel with a supporter of Burr.

Harmar, Josiah (1753–1813, b. Philadelphia, Pennsylvania)
Army general

During the Revolutionary War, Josiah Harmar worked his way slowly through the military ranks, from captain to lieutenant colonel. After the war, Thomas Mifflin, a fellow Pennsylvanian serving as president of the Continental Congress, hired Harmar as his secretary. Mifflin next secured for his protégé command of the decimated peacetime American army. For several years, Harmar, who had been promoted to brevet brigadier general in 1787, managed well with meager resources, negotiating with Indian tribes for land cessions, constructing forts along the frontier, and attempting to restrict white settlement on Native American lands. White encroachment and Indian reprisals, however, led to border warfare between settlers and Indians, which Harmar could not control. To quell the fighting, he was ordered to conduct a punitive expedition against Little Turtle and his Miami Indians. In

1790 Harmar's expedition, heavily dependent on militiamen from Kentucky and western Pennsylvania, was soundly defeated. Harmar's losses were made worse by the actions of his ill-disciplined militia, who deserted the battlefield. A court of inquiry formally exonerated Harmar in this defeat, but he was replaced nonetheless by Maj. Gen. Arthur St. Clair.

Humphreys, David (1752–1818, b. Derby, Connecticut)
Assistant to the president, diplomat, poet

The son of a clergyman, Humphreys was known for his poetry and oratory at Yale College. A dedicated and skillful officer, at twenty-eight he became a lieutenant colonel and aide-de-camp to General Washington during the Revolutionary War. In that position he earned the unofficial title he would carry throughout his life, "belov'd of Washington" (Williams 1928). Humphreys lived at Mount Vernon from 1787 until the president's election as president. He then followed Washington to New York. In the capital, he was often at the president's side, serving along with Tobias Lear as staff aide and secretary to the man he revered. In 1790 Washington sent him to Europe as a secret agent for the United States in London, Lisbon, and Madrid. Washington then appointed him to a succession of diplomatic posts: minister resident to the court at Portugal, 1791–1793; commissioner of Algerine affairs, 1793–1796; and minister plenipotentiary to the court at Madrid, 1796. Humphreys was relieved from this last position after the election of Thomas Jefferson. As a poet, he participated in the writing of the famous satire "The Anarchiad: A Poem on the Restoration of Chaos and Substantial Night" (1786–1787), which mocked the anti-Federalist campaign against ratification of the Constitution.

Jay, John (1745–1829, b. New York, New York)
Chief justice of the United States, 1789–1795; special envoy to Britain, 1794–1795

John Jay, a native New Yorker and graduate of King's College (Columbia), gained prominence in the 1770s in New York by organizing protests against the British through the Committee of Fifty-One. He was among the first to advocate armed resistance and served on a secret committee of the Continental Congress in 1775 charged with securing support from abroad for a war against Britain. Jay became president of the Continental Congress on December 10, 1778. A year later, he was appointed minister to Spain. In that post he negotiated for access to the Mississippi River and recognition of American independence. Negotiations ended when Jay was asked to join Benjamin Franklin in Paris to negotiate the peace that would end the Revolutionary War. Once the preliminary articles of the Peace of Paris (often referred to as the Preliminary Treaty of Paris) were signed on November 30, 1782, Jay returned to the United States to learn that Congress had appointed him secretary of foreign affairs. He held that position until 1790 when Thomas Jefferson assumed the role as Washington's appointee under the newly refashioned national government.

In 1789 President Washington appointed Jay the first chief justice of the United States. The Court heard few cases during Jay's tenure, but established several important precedents. Chief among them, the Court under Jay's tenure as chief justice refused to provide Washington with advice on treaty law and foreign affairs, citing the separation of powers in the Constitution.

In 1794 Washington sent Jay on a critical diplomatic mission to England. Jay's Treaty kept the United States from a possibly disastrous return to war against Britain, but was fiercely opposed at home by Americans who favored a pro-French foreign policy. Jay retired from the Supreme Court in 1795 to serve as governor of New York.

Jefferson, Thomas (1743–1826, b. Shadwell, Virginia)
Secretary of state, 1790–1793
A graduate of the College of William and Mary and a wealthy planter, Thomas Jefferson served alongside Washington as a member of the Virginia House of Burgesses and the Continental Congress, where he drafted the Declaration of Independence. As governor of Virginia during the Revolutionary War, Jefferson was compelled to flee from British forces several times, at one point moving the seat of government from Richmond to Charlottesville. Jefferson returned to the Continental Congress in 1783, and in 1784 succeeded Benjamin Franklin as minister to France, where his primary mission was to increase trade between the countries. Returning to America in 1789, he reluctantly accepted the position of secretary of state in 1790.

In the president's cabinet, Jefferson clashed frequently with Treasury Secretary Alexander Hamilton. For example, Jefferson advocated a system of free trade in which America would build its commercial ties with European nations, especially France. Hamilton's plan, Jefferson contended, focused on regulated trade with Britain that would enrich few Americans at the expense of the masses. Generally, Jefferson allied himself with anti-administration members of Congress in opposing Hamilton's plans even after they became Washington's settled policy. Although he helped to forge the compromise that established the Bank of the United States and permitted the national government to assume the debts of the states, he later regretted having done so and blamed Hamilton for misleading him. In foreign affairs, Jefferson was just as skeptical of British intentions as Hamilton was skeptical of French ones. Meanwhile, President Washington worked hard to keep both men in his government. Although Jefferson was critical of Washington's policies to strengthen the national government and to forge closer relations with Britain, he appraised Washington's critical importance to public support of national unity and urged him to serve for a second term.

The revelation after Jefferson's retirement from the cabinet that he had privately referred to the president as an apostate to the American cause of liberty caused a breach in the two men's relationship that was not healed before Washington's death. Jefferson went on to serve two influential terms as the nation's third president. He and his supporters characterized their victory in the elections of 1800 as a revolution to restore the government to its original principles.

King, Rufus (1755–1827, b. Scarboro, Maine [part of Massachusetts])
U.S. ambassador to Britain, 1796–1803
Rufus King graduated from Harvard College in the class of 1777, and thereafter studied law and served briefly in the Revolutionary War. Respected for his oratory and his knowledge of business and the law, he entered politics as the representative of Newburyport to the Massachusetts General Court (the legislative body of the state). As a delegate to the Constitutional Convention of 1787, he supported the new framework of government. King moved to New York in 1787 after marrying the only daughter of a wealthy New York merchant, and retired from the practice of law. He was chosen by the New York legislature to represent the state in the U.S. Senate in 1789, and was reelected in 1795. In the Senate, he was an advocate of the policies of Alexander Hamilton. In the controversy over the Jay Treaty, he joined with Hamilton and John Jay in writing articles in favor of the treaty under the pen name "Camillus." At Hamilton's suggestion, President Washington appointed King to represent the United States in Britain in 1796. He was recalled at his own request in 1803, but continued to be active in Federalist politics into the decade of his death.

Knox, Henry (1750–1806, b. Boston, Massachusetts)
Secretary of war, 1789–1794
As a young man, the Scots-Irish Knox supported his widowed mother and his siblings by working at a bookstore, and pursued his passion for military science by training in artillery as a captain of the Boston Grenadier Corps. At twenty-one, he opened "The London Bookstore" in Boston. Despite the urging of his wife's family who remained loyal to Britain, he and his family fled from the British soldiers who occupied Boston at the outbreak of the Revolutionary War. His military knowledge helped him to achieve considerable success in the war. And Knox was with Washington when he made his famous crossing of the Delaware River in 1776. After directing the artillery at the Battle of Yorktown in 1781, Knox left the army with the rank of major general.

After the war, Knox organized the Society of the Cincinnati, a society for officers of the Continental army and their male descendants, which continues to this day. He accepted the post of secretary of war under the Articles of Confederation, and was confirmed by the Senate as the first secretary of war under the Constitution in 1789. He and the president repeatedly urged Congress to enlarge and improve the army, reform the militia, and establish an adequate naval force.

Knox was lampooned by the republican press for his extravagant tastes and corpulence, but he and Mrs. Knox were among the Washington's closest friends in government. After resigning from the cabinet, he retired to Montpelier, his mansion in Maine.

Lafayette, Marquis de (1757–1834, b. Chavagniac, France)
Revolutionary War hero
Marie-Joseph-Paul-Yves-Roch-Gilbert du Motier entered court life at Versailles in 1773. Motivated by the quest for military glory, he requested a commission from the king to aid the Americans in their war against Britain. Denied, he nevertheless crossed the Pyrenees, purchased a French ship in a Spanish port, and sailed to America. Gratified that such an eminent French nobleman wished to aid the American cause, Congress granted him a commission as a major general. Lafayette became a member of General Washington's staff "family," and quickly established an informal father-son relationship with Washington. He was, writes Washington's major modern biographer, "the man, who of all men, was closest to his heart" (Flexner 1972, 110). During the war, Lafayette returned to France to advance the American cause. After being briefly jailed for having disobeyed the king, he lobbied his government for an open alliance with the revolutionaries in North America. He returned with French reinforcements and was given responsibility for the defense of Virginia.

After the French-American defeat of Lord Cornwallis at Yorktown in 1781, Lafayette returned to France and was made a brigadier general in the French army. When the French Revolution became unforgiving of aristocracy, he fled to Austria, where he was held as a prisoner for five years. During Lafayette's imprisonment, President Washington was gravely concerned for his safety, but felt proscribed by honor and the delicate state of U.S.-French relations from using his position to seek his friend's release. The Washingtons were, however, able to ensure the safety of Lafayette's only son, Georges Washington, who traveled incognito to America and lived at Mount Vernon during part of his father's imprisonment. When changes in French politics made it possible for Austria to release its famous prisoner, Lafayette returned to Paris, but avoided politics and military service during the reign of Napoleon Bonaparte. In 1824, at the invitation of President James Monroe, Lafayette made a triumphal tour of the United States. Celebrated as "the hero of two worlds," he died in Paris on May 20, 1834.

Lear, Tobias (1762–1816, b. Portsmouth, New Hampshire)
Secretary to George Washington, 1785–1792, 1798–1799
When George Washington retired to Mount Vernon after the Revolutionary War to rehabilitate his plantation, he hired Tobias Lear, a well-traveled Harvard graduate, to serve as his private secretary. Lear managed Washington's correspondence, and tutored Martha Washington's children from her first marriage. For years, the young secretary traveled by Washington's side, becoming a lifelong friend. During Washington's first term as president, Lear and his wife were the frequent dinner guests of Philadelphia's elite families.

After the president's first term, Lear resigned and went into business as Lear and Company. The short-lived venture, which speculated in land in Washington, D.C., dissolved when a key investor went bankrupt. Lear also served as president of the Potomac River Canal Company, a business venture Washington had organized in 1785 to open the river to trade from the interior. The possibility of war with France, which brought Washington back into public service as commander of the army during the John Adams administration, returned Lear to his former job as Washington's secretary in 1798. During the final days of the former president's life, Lear was by his side, and even documented his death in detail. At Washington's request, Lear took on a final task: organizing the late president's papers. As per Washington's will, the Lears maintained a residence on the Washingtons' property for the remainder of their lives.

Lee, Charles (1758–1815, b. Virginia)
Attorney general, 1795–1801
Charles Lee was a member of Virginia's most celebrated family. Charles' older brother, Henry "Light-Horse Harry" Lee, earned acclaim as a captain in the Continental army who carried out devastating attacks on British supply lines. His youngest brother, Richard Bland Lee, distinguished himself as a member of the first Congress organized under the U.S. Constitution. Charles graduated from the College of New Jersey (Princeton), and served twelve years as a naval officer. From 1789–1793, he held the highly desirable executive post of customs collector for the port of Alexandria, Virginia. In 1795 President Washington appointed him U.S. attorney general.

Maclay, William (1737–1804, b. New Garden, Pennsylvania)
U.S. senator, 1789–1791
William Maclay was elected senator from Pennsylvania in the first congressional elections held under the new U.S. Constitution. He quickly gained prominence as an outspoken critic of the Washington administration. An advocate for the common man, Maclay opposed Hamilton's financial plans, disparaged the president as a friend to the wealthy, and shunned capital society. To ensure that a third of the Senate was elected every two years, the first Senate conducted a random drawing. Maclay drew a two-year term. Despite the brevity of his service in the Senate, he is well remembered for the copious and sarcastic notes he kept in his private journal. Because the Senate's activities were closed to the public during its first six years and senators decided not to keep an official record of their debates, Maclay's journal, published in 1880, provides the only more or less complete account of that body's debates during its first two years.

Madison, James (1751–1836, b. Port Conway, Virginia)
U.S. representative, 1789–1797
After graduating from the College of New Jersey (Princeton), James Madison returned home to Virginia to participate in the American War of Independence. As

a delegate to the Constitutional Convention, Madison wrote the Virginia Plan, which formed the basic structure for the new government. Meanwhile, at the convention Madison kept valuable notes, and coauthored the influential *Federalist Papers* advocating ratification of the Constitution. Madison was then elected to the First Congress and emerged as one of President Washington's closest advisers. Though history better recalls Madison as a protégé of Thomas Jefferson, he was at this point in his career quite close to his good friend and supporter President Washington. He wrote an influential draft of the president's first inaugural address, assisted the president in making appointments, and advised the administration on its relationship with Congress. Yet Madison opposed the financial and foreign policies of the Washington administration, and emerged eventually as a leader of the pro-Jeffersonian Democratic-Republicans. Indeed, he followed Thomas Jefferson into the presidency, and served as the nation's fourth president.

McHenry, James (1753–1816, b. Ballymena, County Antrim, Ireland)
Secretary of war, 1796–1800

James McHenry reported for service in the Revolutionary War at Cambridge, Massachusetts, with a recently acquired knowledge of medicine and a long-standing hatred of Britain acquired during his childhood in Ireland. He left his first post at the Cambridge military hospital with decorations and joined the 5th Pennsylvania Battalion as its surgeon where he was captured during the fall of Fort Washington in November 1776. Released in an exchange of prisoners after a few months' imprisonment, McHenry abandoned his medical career to become secretary to George Washington. His postwar political career included service in the Maryland Senate, Maryland Assembly, Continental Congress, and as a delegate to the Constitutional Convention. Washington appointed McHenry secretary of war in 1796, in large part to restore geographic balance to his cabinet and to bring into government late in his second term at least one man with whom he had a long acquaintance. McHenry maintained his position through the John Adams administration. At the beginning of the Quasi War with France in 1798, he worked with President Adams to negotiate Washington's return to service as commander of an enlarged military force.

Monroe, James (1758 –1831, b. Westmoreland County, Virginia)
U.S. senator, 1790–1794; minister to France, 1794–1796

James Monroe interrupted his studies at the College of William and Mary to join the Continental army. After the war, he read law with Thomas Jefferson. Even though he opposed the Constitution of 1787 at Virginia's ratification convention, in the first elections for the new government Monroe ran for Congress, unsuccessfully, against George Washington's friend James Madison. A year later, Monroe was selected by Virginia's legislature to fill a vacated Virginia seat in the U.S. Senate. In June 1794, President Washington stunned Monroe, a consistent critic of Washington's foreign policy, by appointing him minister to France. Monroe's undiplomatic condemnation of British policy and open support for some of the more radical figures in the French Revolution made him a controversial minister. When the Jay Treaty was announced between the United States and Britain, Monroe was again openly critical of his president's foreign policy. In 1796, within a climate of little support from the Washington administration and strained relations with the French government, Monroe was recalled by Secretary of State Timothy Pickering. Monroe served later as the fifth president of the United States.

Morris, Gouverneur (1752–1816, b. Morrisania, New York)
Special envoy to Britain, 1790–1791, minister to the French Republic, 1792–1794
Born at the family's 1,400-acre manor, Morrisania, in what is now the Bronx, New York, Morris was elected from Westchester County to the New York Assembly, and became a leading figure in the legislature through his oratory. As a delegate to the Continental Congress of 1777, he favored nationalist measures, such as the elimination of state currencies in favor of a single currency and state cession of western lands to the national government. The New York Assembly, annoyed that its representative would give away New York's claim to the future state of Vermont, removed him from Congress in October 1779. Morris then moved to Philadelphia.

A success in finance and business after the war, he was elected from Pennsylvania against his wishes to represent his state at the Constitutional Convention of 1787. At the convention, he spoke on "the political depravity of men, and the necessity of checking one vice and interest" against another (Mintz 1999, 15:897). He contributed substantially to the compromises that settled the nature of executive power and the electoral college system. He also was responsible for the Constitution's famous opening line, which asserts that the purpose of the newly constituted government is "to form a more perfect Union, establish Justice, . . ."

Washington appointed Morris special envoy to Britain in 1790. In 1792 he was confirmed as American minister to France. An open partisan of the monarchy, he was an unpopular choice among Democratic-Republicans at home, and when the United States at last demanded the recall of Citizen Genêt in 1793, the French retaliated by requesting that the Americans recall Morris.

Morris, Robert (1734–1806, b. Liverpool, England)
U.S. senator, 1789–1795
Robert Morris came to America at age thirteen and, after a brief education in Philadelphia, joined the shipping and banking firm of Thomas and Charles Willing. He later became a partner and director of the firm. The renamed company, Willing and Morris, contracted with the Continental Congress in September 1775 to secretly import arms and ammunition to prepare for a war with Britain. Although Morris was initially opposed to such a war, after some hesitation he signed the Declaration of Independence. Morris's dual service during the war as a member of the Pennsylvania Assembly and contractor to the government led to a

public investigation. After the investigation cleared him of wrongdoing, in 1781 the Continental Congress appointed him superintendent of finance, a position he took only after negotiations that protected his ability to engage in private commerce and gave him almost absolute power to carry out his mission.

Morris revised accounting procedures, obtained funding and supplies from states, secured a loan from France, established a federal budget, and chartered the Bank of North America, a precursor of the Bank of the United States. Once the war ended, he focused on business, but kept his hand in national politics by attending the 1786 Annapolis Convention and the 1787 Constitutional Convention. Washington offered Morris the position of secretary of the Treasury, but Morris declined in favor of a seat in the Senate. While in Congress, he worked closely with Treasury Secretary Alexander Hamilton.

Muhlenberg, Frederick Augustus Conrad (1750–1801, b. Trappe, Pennsylvania)

U.S. representative, 1789–1797; Speaker of the House, 1789–1791 (First Congress) and 1793–1795 (Third Congress)

The son of the founder of American Lutheranism, Frederick Muhlenberg was himself ordained a Lutheran minister at Reading, Pennsylvania, in 1770. He served in the Continental Congress from 1779 to 1780, and as Speaker of the Pennsylvania General Assembly from 1780 to 1783. Elected to the First Congress as a Federalist, he was chosen by his peers in the House on April 1, 1789, to serve as its first Speaker. His duties in this position were largely ceremonial. Displaced as Speaker in the Second Congress by Jonathan Trumbull, Muhlenberg was returned to leadership in the Third Congress with votes from both Federalists and Democratic-Republicans. He cast the deciding vote in 1796 to quash the House's effort to sabotage the recently ratified Jay's Treaty. This act was greatly unpopular among his constituents, one of whom (his brother-in-law) stabbed him in fury at his action. Muhlenberg changed parties two years before his death.

Osgood, Samuel (1747–1813, b. Andover, Massachusetts)

Postmaster general, 1789–1791

A Harvard graduate, Samuel Osgood served during the American War of Independence in the Continental army as well as in Congress. He opposed the Constitution of 1787, but "became sufficiently reconciled to the new government to seek an appointment under it," and was thus made the nation's first postmaster general in 1789 (Burnett 1928). When he took office, America had seventy-six post offices and fewer than 2,400 miles of post roads. Osgood prepared a plan, funded after his own term in the cabinet had ended, which systematically sought to link major cities on the east coast with smaller towns on the perimeter of the country. Upon the transfer of the government to Philadelphia, he resigned, wishing to remain in New York, where he had developed strong ties of family, business, and politics after his marriage to Maria (Bowne) Franklin of New York.

Pickering, Timothy (1745–1829, b. Salem, Massachusetts)
Postmaster general, 1791–1795; secretary of war, 1795; secretary of state ad interim, 1795; secretary of state, 1795–1800

A Harvard graduate, Timothy Pickering studied law and drilled militia in Essex, Massachusetts. His military acumen earned national recognition when he led a contingent of the Massachusetts militia to fight alongside Washington during the 1776–1777 winter campaign in New York and New Jersey. After the campaign, Pickering became adjutant general of the Continental army. The president sent him on a mission in 1790 to prevent the Seneca Indians from joining the attack on the western frontier. Upon his return after a successful trip, Washington appointed him postmaster general in 1791. In that position, Pickering established protocol for the infant agency, and his administrative success earned him an appointment as secretary of war in 1795. Pickering encouraged Washington to investigate intercepted communications between Secretary of State Edmund Randolph and French minister Joseph Fauchet that implicated Randolph in an attempt to incite violence in the Whiskey Rebellion. Upon Randolph's resignation, Pickering assumed the duties of acting secretary of state. Unable to secure for the permanent position any of the men he truly wanted, the president reluctantly asked Pickering, a trustworthy but grim figure for whom the president felt no warmth, to remain in service.

Pinckney, Charles Cotesworth (1746–1828, b. Charleston, South Carolina)
Minister to France, 1796–1797

Charles Cotesworth Pinckney and his brother, Thomas, were sent to England for schooling in 1753. Charles became active in colonial politics upon his return to America in 1769, and he assumed command of a regiment of the Continental army. An influential delegate at the 1787 Constitutional Convention, Pinckney declined to join Washington's cabinet several times. At last, however, he accepted appointment as minister to France in the wake of James Monroe's recall from that post. Unlike Monroe, who had been honored upon his arrival in France with an invitation to address the French National Convention, Pinckney did not have his legitimacy as a U.S. minister acknowledged. Therefore, he left Paris after three months of vain attempts to have the revolutionary French government do so. When President John Adams sent Pinckney back to France, his mission led to the infamous XYZ affair and America's Quasi War with France. As part of Washington's preparations for a possible return to war, he recalled Pinckney to active service with the rank of major general.

Pinckney, Thomas (1750–1828, b. Charleston, South Carolina)
American diplomat

Thomas Pinckney received a colonial aristocrat's education in English schools and universities, and studied military science in France. After returning to South

Carolina, he became a lawyer and planter. A patriot, he joined the war as a lieu-tenant in a ranger company, and served on the staff of Gen. Horatio Gates. After the war, he served two consecutive single-year terms as governor of South Car-olina, in 1787 and 1788. In 1792, with the backing of Treasury Secretary Alexander Hamilton, Pinckney was appointed by President Washington as U.S. ambassador to Britain. In early 1794, Washington bypassed Pinckney by send-ing John Jay to Britain in a final effort to avoid war through diplomacy. Pinck-ney's greatest success as a diplomat came when Washington sent him from Britain to Spain in midsummer 1795. Spain, fearing a U.S.-Britain alliance, proved will-ing to negotiate its differences with the United States. The Treaty of San Lorenzo, or Pinckney's Treaty, signed in October 1795, memorialized the U.S. right of access to the Mississippi River, and defined the border of Spanish Florida with the United States.

Randolph, Edmund (1753–1813, b. Williamsburg, Virginia)
Attorney general, 1789–1794; secretary of state, 1794–1795
Although his father returned to England at the start of the Revolutionary War and urged his son to join him, Edmund Randolph joined the rebels and was the youngest member of Virginia's constitutional convention. During the war, he served as aide-de-camp to General Washington, and in 1786 was elected gover-nor of Virginia. The same year, he attended the Annapolis Convention. At the 1787 Constitutional Convention, Randolph orally presented to his fellow delegates the famous Virginia Plan, authored primarily by James Madison. Favored by populous states, it called for three branches of government with checks and balances. The bicameral legislature, with its members elected proportionately, would choose a chief executive and members of the judiciary. In the end, Randolph refused to sign the final draft of the Constitution because he believed the chief executive possessed too much power. Later, however, he advocated its ratification.

Washington appointed Randolph as the newly constituted government's first attorney general, and he had an uneventful term. Upon Thomas Jefferson's resig-nation as secretary of state in 1793, Washington chose Randolph for the position. Randolph had the president's trust, but was handicapped by his lack of support from either of the major factions within the early government. His cousin Thomas Jefferson thought him a weak and unprincipled person. Treasury Secretary Alexan-der Hamilton held him in contempt, and suspected him of attempting to lead Washington into war with Britain. During the negotiation of Jay's Treaty, Ran-dolph complained that Jay refused to take instructions from him. (Jay was secretly directed by Alexander Hamilton.)

Randolph resigned as secretary of state in 1795 amid a scandal arising from inter-cepted French diplomatic correspondence. The documents, captured by the British and shown to the president by his other cabinet members, all supporters of Hamil-ton, suggested that Randolph had asked the French for a bribe to quell the Whiskey

Rebellion in 1794. Had the French been willing to pay Randolph's price, or so the documents suggested, he would have used his influence among Democratic-Republicans to bring a halt to the Whiskey Rebellion, which conservatives, including the president, came to believe was incited by radical Republicans bent on revolution. In 1795 Randolph published a lengthy *Vindication* proclaiming his innocence and accusing Washington of ingratitude and senility. Later, however, shortly before his death, he apologized for his intemperate remarks in a letter to Bushrod Washington, a Supreme Court Justice and nephew of George Washington.

Rutledge, John (1739–1800, b. Charleston, South Carolina)
Associate justice, U.S. Supreme Court, 1790–1791; chief justice of the United States, 1795
John Rutledge was admitted to the bar in 1760. Four years later, he was named attorney general of South Carolina. He also served as a delegate to the Continental Congress and the Constitutional Convention and governor of South Carolina during the Revolutionary War. Later, Rutledge lobbied President Washington to be appointed chief justice of the United States, but Washington instead appointed Rutledge associate justice with the second highest level of seniority. In 1791 Rutledge resigned from the Supreme Court to become chief justice of South Carolina's Supreme Court. Upon Chief Justice John Jay's resignation from the U.S. Supreme Court in 1795 to become governor of New York, Washington used his power under Article II, Section 2, of the Constitution to appoint Rutledge to Jay's former position during a Senate recess. When the Senate returned four months later, Rutledge was rejected by a 10–14 vote, possibly because of his vocal opposition to the Jay Treaty, which the Senate had recently ratified. It also was said that the nominee was insane. Rutledge attempted suicide upon learning of his rejection, and never held public office again.

Short, William (1759–1849, b. "Spring Garden," Surrey County, Virginia)
Acting minister to France, 1790–1792; ambassador to the Netherlands, 1792–1794; commissioner to Spain, 1794–1795
William Short was a founder of Phi Beta Kappa, the nation's most prestigious undergraduate honors society, as a student at the College of William and Mary in 1776. After graduation, he sat on the Governor's Council of Virginia, from 1783 to 1784, until he left Virginia to accompany Thomas Jefferson to Paris. Upon Jefferson's return to the United States to assume his cabinet post as secretary of state, Short represented the United States in Paris as acting minister. After Gouverneur Morris was appointed minister to France in 1792, Short reluctantly took the less prestigious position of U.S. ambassador to the Netherlands. From that post, he reported critically on the Terror, the period of the French Revolution from September 5, 1793, to July 27, 1794, during which hundreds of thousands of political enemies were arrested and seventeen thousand were officially put to death. Short's criticisms provoked a famous rebuke from Jefferson: rather than witness

the failure of a revolution for liberty, Jefferson wrote, "I would have seen half the earth desolated. Were there but an Adam and Eve left in every country, and left free, it would be better than as it now is" (Flexner 1970, 389).

In 1795 Washington ordered Short to Madrid to help negotiate a treaty with Spain on that empire's holdings in North America. Short served at first as joint commissioner with William Carmichael, then as sole representative of the United States when Carmichael was relieved of his duties because of ill health in the spring of 1794. As a pretext for delay during the negotiations, the Spanish government objected to continuing the negotiations with Short on the grounds that his credentials were not of sufficient rank. Before Short's successor, U.S. Ambassador Thomas Pinckney, could arrive from London, however, the Spanish decided to negotiate in earnest, and Short deserves much of the credit for the final form of the treaty that bears Pinckney's name.

St. Clair, Arthur (1736–1818, b. Thurso, Scotland)
Governor of the Northwest Territory, 1787–1802; army general

Arthur St. Clair came to America as part of the British force that wrested Canada from France in the Seven Years' War. He stayed to marry the niece of the Massachusetts colonial governor, and settled in western Pennsylvania. Under General Washington, he fought with distinction at Trenton and Princeton in the winter of 1776–1777. Advanced to major general, he became the highest-ranking Pennsylvanian of the war. After the war, St. Clair served as a delegate to the Continental Congress, under the Articles of Confederation, and was appointed first governor of the Northwest Territory in 1787. To promote white settlement in the Territory, St. Clair worked to secure land from native tribes. At the same time, he strove to prevent settlers from provoking the tribes. When the Miami Indian chief, Little Turtle, and his Shawnee subordinate, Blue Jacket, led native warriors against settlers in disputed lands, Col. Josiah Harmar was ordered to lead a punitive expedition. But the campaign failed, and St. Clair was called back to active duty as a major general (while continuing to serve as governor of the Northwest Territory) to lead a second expedition against the Indians. On the morning of November 4, 1791, Little Turtle's troops launched a devastating surprise attack on St. Clair's troops. In response, the thousand or so militiamen in St. Clair's army panicked and fled, leaving about half that number of regular soldiers to defend the camp. The result was the single greatest defeat native forces ever inflicted on U.S. troops. President Washington stood by his Federalist friend, however, who was cleared of wrongdoing in the first congressional investigation under the new Constitution.

Stuart, Gilbert (1755–1828, b. North Kingston, Rhode Island)
American portrait painter

American-born Gilbert Stuart was the first assistant of the American expatriate history painter Benjamin West. He established his reputation with the display of a full-length portrait, now known as "The Skater," at the Royal Academy in London in 1782. A profligate spender who cultivated an image of aristocratic disdain for bourgeois conventions, Stuart returned to the United States in 1793 to avoid his many creditors. He intended to make a fortune selling the portraits he planned to paint of George Washington to the president's admirers.

Washington sat for Stuart three times in 1795 and 1796. These sittings produced three distinctive images: the "Vaughn type," the "Lansdowne type," and the iconic "Athenaeum Head." After each sitting, Stuart would paint numerous canvases of each "type." After considerable practice, he reportedly was able to produce an "Athenaeum" portrait of Washington in two hours. So that he would never have to part with the original from which he made each copy, he never finished it, to the great frustration of Mrs. Washington who had commissioned the painting.

Washington, Martha (1731–1802, b. New Kent County, Virginia)
Wife of George Washington

In 1757 Martha Dandridge's husband, Daniel Parke Custis, died. At twenty-six, then, Martha was a wealthy widow with two children, John "Jack" Custis (b. 1754) and Martha "Patsy" Custis (b. 1756).

After a brief courtship, Martha married one of Virginia's most eligible bachelors, Col. George Washington, on January 6, 1759. At Mount Vernon, Martha performed the traditional duties of a plantation wife, directing the household servants and slaves, entertaining the many guests, and guiding her children to maturity. Martha and George had no children of their own, perhaps because of complications during the birth of her last child by her first husband.

After her daughter, Patsy, died suddenly in June 1773, her son, Jack, returned from college to be with his grieving mother. Early the next year, he married Eleanor Calvert from a prominent Maryland family.

During her husband's tenure as commander of the Continental army, Martha joined him in winter quarters, and spent the spring and summer at Mount Vernon. In 1781, Jack, aide-de-camp to his stepfather, contracted camp fever at Yorktown and died. The Washingtons took into their home Jack's two youngest children, Eleanor "Nelly" Parke Custis (b. 1779) and George Washington Parke Custis (b. 1781), known as Wash or Washington. Before Nelly's marriage in 1799, George Washington formally adopted his stepgranddaughter.

As the president's wife, Mrs. Washington was obliged to devote herself to entertaining political guests. Because the president announced in New York that he would accept no social invitations nor return any visits, Mrs. Washington felt trapped at home.

But after the government relocated from New York to Philadelphia, the Washingtons found themselves surrounded by the nation's true social elite. To the satisfaction of Mrs. Washington and the horror of the opposition press, the president began to relax his rule against private socializing, and the Washingtons enjoyed the company of Philadelphian high society in their rented mansion.

Upon their return to Mount Vernon in March 1797, Mrs. Washington resumed her former duties and pleasures, running the household, entertaining an endless stream of guests, and tending to her grandchildren. Martha survived George by two and a half years. Before her death, she destroyed all personal correspondence with her husband.

Wayne, Anthony (1745–1796, b. Waynesborough, Pennsylvania)
Army general

Anthony Wayne was a figure of some note in Philadelphia society when he became a colonel in the Continental army in January 1776. He participated in most of the major campaigns of the Revolutionary War. In 1779 a force of light infantry under his command stormed a hilltop British garrison on the Hudson River, at Stony Point. With bayonets alone, his soldiers captured the northernmost British post on the strategically critical Hudson, took hundreds of enemy troops prisoner, and captured valuable ordnance. Personally brave, Anthony also was mercurial and vain, and the nickname "Mad Anthony" clung to him after the war.

After two expeditions against a Native American uprising along the frontier had been badly defeated, President Washington was reluctant in 1791 to give the command of the newly reorganized and expanded American army to Wayne, because he was reputed to be a drunkard. Washington knew, however, that Wayne was experienced, physically able, and eager for the opportunity. Through strict discipline, ample training, and the appointment of competent subordinate officers, Wayne forged "the first reliable national army after independence" (Kohn 1984, 3:1169). In 1793 Secretary of War Henry Knox ordered his commander "to make those audacious savages feel our superiority in Arms" (Millett and Maslowski 1994, 97). Wayne's army won a decisive battle at Fallen Timbers on August 20, 1794. In the 1975 Treaty of Greenville, which Wayne negotiated on behalf of the United States, he won enormous Indian land cessions in the Great Lakes region, and compelled the British at long last to abandon forts in U.S. territory. Wayne died of an illness while on a tour to inspect abandoned British forts at Detroit.

Wolcott Jr., Oliver (1760–1833, b. Litchfield, Connecticut)
Secretary of the Treasury, 1795–1800

After graduating from Yale and studying law, Oliver Wolcott declined a commission as an ensign in the Continental army for a post with the quartermaster's department keeping track of military supplies. After the war, he and Oliver Ellsworth were charged with settling Connecticut's claims against the United States. Several years later, Wolcott joined Connecticut's office of the comptroller of public accounts where he drafted a plan to reorganize the state's finances. When the Assembly adopted it, Wolcott was selected by the president to serve under Treasury Secretary Alexander Hamilton as auditor of the federal Treasury. While Hamilton involved himself in various domestic and foreign affairs, Wolcott was left to establish procedures and policies for the Treasury. On Hamilton's recommendation, Wolcott was appointed comptroller of the United States in June 1791. That same year, he was offered the presidency of the Bank of the United States, but he declined. Wolcott became secretary of the Treasury when his mentor resigned. Wolcott's tenure in that position was complicated by a growing federal budget, a fluctuating level of foreign commerce, and a European recession.

BIBLIOGRAPHIC ESSAY

The single most useful biographical source for political figures from this time and place is the *Dictionary of American Biography, under the Auspices of the American Council of Learned Societies,* 20 vols. (New York: C. Scribner's Sons, 1928–1958). This resource is reproduced in: Biography Resource Center, Gale Group, 2002 (*www.galenet.com/servlet/BioRC*). The online version is not paginated, nor does it provide precise copyright dates. The American Council of Learned Societies has since updated that biography. Some of the essays in the updated edition are less detailed than those in the original, but they contain updated bibliographical annotations and sometimes reflect changes in scholarly evaluations of events and personalities. See John A. Garraty and Mark C. Carnes, gen. eds., *American National Biography, under the Auspices of the American Council of Learned Societies,* 24 vols. (New York: Oxford University Press, 1999).

On military figures, see Robert J. Spiller, ed.; Joseph G. Dawson, III assoc. ed.; and T. Harry Williams, consulting ed., *Dictionary of American Military Biography,* 3 vols. (Westport, Conn.: Greenwood Press, 1984). Biographies of cabinet members, along with historical essays on each cabinet office, are available in Mark Grossman, ed., *Encyclopedia of the United States Cabinet,* 3 vols. (Santa Barbara, Calif.: ABC-CLIO, 2000). Supreme Court justices also are the subject of a specialized biographical resource: Melvin I. Urofsky, ed., *The Supreme Court Justices: A Biographical Dictionary* (New York: Garland, 1994). On Martha Washington, consult Patricia Brady, "Martha Dandridge Custis Washington," in *American First Ladies, Their Lives and Their Legacy,* 2d ed., ed. Lewis L. Gould (New York: Routledge, 2001), 1–10.

Appendix B

Key Events in Washington's Life

1732

February 22 George Washington is born on Wakefield Farm, his family's estate located on the south bank of the Potomac River near Pope's Creek in Westmoreland County, Virginia. He is the first child of Augustine Washington and his second wife, Mary Ball Washington. (Note: George Washington celebrated his birthday on February 11, the date he was born using the Julian calendar. The British switched to the Gregorian calendar in 1752; on that calendar Washington's birthday fell on February 22.)

1743

April 12 Augustine Washington, George's father, dies in King George County, Virginia. He is forty-nine years old.

July 19 George Washington becomes in-laws with the family of Thomas, Lord Fairfax, when his half-brother Lawrence marries Anne Fairfax, the daughter of William Fairfax.

1748

March Lord Fairfax commissions Washington to assist his son George William Fairfax and James Genn, surveyor of Prince William County, Virginia, on a surveying expedition to the Shenandoah Valley.

1749

July 20 With the aid of Lord Fairfax, Washington secures the prestigious and well-paying position of surveyor of Culpeper County, Virginia; he works in this position for one year.

1750

Washington buys 1,459 acres of land in the Shenandoah Valley; this is his first western land purchase.

May The British Board of Trade recommends to Parliament that ten laws recently codified in Virginia be overruled.

1751

April The Virginia House of Burgesses rejects the idea that Parliament can overrule laws created by colonial assemblies pertaining strictly to colonial affairs.

November Washington accompanies his half-brother Lawrence to Barbados, where Lawrence hopes to recover from tuberculosis. During the trip, which was Washington's only travel outside the American colonies or the United States, he contracts smallpox. The immunity he gains from this disease in 1751 protects him during the Revolutionary War when smallpox kills a significant number of soldiers.

1752

July 26 Lawrence Washington dies. Mount Vernon, named in honor of a British general, is left to Lawrence's wife and children, but George Washington manages the plantation's affairs on their behalf.

November 6 Washington is appointed adjutant of the militia for the Southern District of Virginia. The Virginia Council gives him the rank of major.

1753

November The royal governor of Virginia, Robert Dinwiddie, gives Washington a critical job. He is to lead an expedition to the Allegheny River Valley to gather intelligence on the French military presence, to establish ties to Indian leaders in the area, and to instruct the commander of the French force in the territory to vacate British lands. To arouse English pride, Dinwiddie sees that Washington's diary of his trip is published. It becomes a best-seller in Virginia and wins the young military leader acclaim throughout the colonies.

1754

March 15 Washington is appointed lieutenant colonel of the Virginia Regiment, an army of Virginia volunteers.

April 18 Washington sets out on an expedition to occupy the Forks of the Ohio, but upon his arrival he sees that the French have already taken control of that position.

May 27–28 Washington defeats a small French scouting party in what would, in retrospect, be recognized as the first battle of the French and Indian War. He establishes Fort Necessity at what was then Great Meadows (now Farmington), Pennsylvania. The French protest that Washington's force has attacked and killed Coulon de Jumonville, a diplomat on a mission similar to the one that Washington himself had undertaken the previous year. Washington dismisses the allegation.

June 5 Washington possibly promoted Colonel of the Virginia Regiment after the June 5 death of his superior. [The governor's original commission was apparently lost in transmittal, and no direct evidence of this promotion survives. Indirect evidence exists in the correspondence of the governor with Washington.]

July 3 French and Indian forces attack Washington's troops at Fort Necessity. After a long battle, Washington signs a surrender that seems to acknowledge French claims about the death of Jumonville.

October By order of Governor Dinwiddie the Virginia military is divided into several autonomous groups. To avoid a demotion caused by this reorganization, Washington resigns his military commission.

1755

May 10 Washington accepts an appointment as aide-de-camp to Gen. Edward Braddock, commander in chief of the British troops in North America. He takes a staff position with the rank of colonel, rather than a place in the "line," because, as a mere colonial officer, he had to submit to orders from British soldiers of inferior rank, which caused him great frustration.

July 9 The 1,450 troops under Braddock's control are defeated by nine hundred French and Indian soldiers at the Monongahela River. Washington directs a retreat of the troops and is honored for bravery under fire.

August 14 Washington receives a commission as commander of the restored Virginia Regiment, with the rank of colonel. He is in charge of protecting the 350-mile frontier.

December Washington loses his first bid for election to the Virginia House of Burgesses as a representative from Frederick County. He is absent during the election because of his military obligations.

1756

February Washington travels to Boston to lobby Massachusetts governor William Shirley for a "regular" royal commission. Shirley, who at the time is commander of all British troops in North America, denies the request.

1757

Summer Washington launches a second, but unsuccessful, bid for election to the Virginia House of Burgesses from Frederick County.

1758

July 24 After two unsuccessful attempts, Washington is elected as a delegate from Frederick County to the Virginia House of Burgesses.

September 1 Washington writes to John Robinson, Speaker of the House of Burgesses, that his troops on the frontier are receiving inadequate provisions and goods from Robert Dinwiddie. He also complains of inefficient military orders.

November Washington leads seven hundred Virginia soldiers to challenge the French at Fort Duquesne. The French abandon the fort. After this successful expedition, Washington resigns his commission and returns to Mount Vernon for his wedding and to begin amassing wealth and status through land acquisitions and plantation management, or "farming."

1759

January 6 Washington marries Martha Dandridge Custis at her estate on the Pamunkey River northwest of Williamsburg, Virginia, in Kent County.

1760

October 26 George III assumes the throne of England and Ireland.

1761

Washington inherits Mount Vernon after Anne Fairfax Lee, the wife of his late half-brother Lawrence, dies.

1763

February 10 The Peace of Paris ends the French and Indian War. In the treaty, France cedes Canada to England.

1765

March 22 Parliament passes the Stamp Act. The tax requires citizens of the American colonies to pay a duty on items such as newspapers, legal forms, playing cards, and pamphlets.

March 24 Parliament passes the Quartering Act, which requires citizens of the American colonies to house and feed British troops.

August 14 Riots protesting the Stamp Act begin in Boston and climax on August 26 when rioters destroy the house of Lt. Gov. Thomas Hutchinson.

October 7 The Stamp Act Congress convenes in New York. The group is composed of delegates from nine colonies.

November 1 The Stamp Act takes effect, but because no stamps are available for shipping documents, all colonial ports close.

November 2 Virginia defies the Stamp Act by illegally opening its port without any stamps.

1766

March 17 Parliament repeals the Stamp Act.

March 18 Parliament passes the Declaratory Act detailing its authority to pass laws binding on the colonies.

1767

June 29 Parliament passes the Townshend Duties, requiring colonists to pay a duty on imported items, including tea, glass, paper, and oil.

1769

May 17 Washington serves on an extralegal committee convened by Virginia delegates after the formal session of the House of Burgesses has been dissolved. The committee drafts a Nonimportation Association as a protest to the Townshend Duties.

1770

March 5 Five Americans are killed and six are wounded in the so-called Boston Massacre. The shots are fired by British soldiers who had been assaulted by American men and boys while defending the customhouse. Massachusetts lawyer John Adams defends the British soldiers involved in the massacre.

April 12 Parliament repeals the Townshend Duties on all products except tea.

1773

May 10 Parliament passes the Tea Act, allowing the East Indian Tea Company to sell tea directly to the public without paying duties.

December 16 American colonists board three tea ships docked in Boston harbor and dump the tea overboard. It is later known as the Boston Tea Party.

1774

March 31 Parliament passes the first of the "Intolerable Acts," closing Boston harbor until colonists pay for the tea destroyed during the Boston Tea Party.

May 20 Parliament passes two additional "Intolerable Acts," prohibiting public meetings in Massachusetts and prohibiting the trials of British officials in Massachusetts who are charged with capital offenses.

May 26 Washington joins delegates from colonial assemblies around the country in calling for a general meeting to discuss the "Intolerable Acts."

June 2 Parliament passes a fourth "Intolerable Act," requiring Massachusetts residents to house and feed British troops.

July 18 Washington convenes a meeting at the Fairfax County Courthouse where the freeholders of Fairfax endorse the Fairfax Resolves, a document calling for self-taxation only and a boycott on British goods.

August Washington attends the First Provincial Congress of Virginia, where he is elected a delegate to the First Continental Congress.

September 5 Washington attends the First Continental Congress in Philadelphia. At the Congress, all colonies but Georgia are represented.

September 17 The Continental Congress passes the Suffolk Resolves, which proclaim the "Intolerable Acts" void, urge Massachusetts residents to establish a free state until Parliament repeals the acts, and urge all colonists to arm themselves.

1775

March 25 Washington attends the Second Provincial Congress of Virginia and is selected as a delegate to the Second Continental Congress.

April 19 The Battles of Lexington and Concord signal the beginning of the Revolutionary War.

May 10 Washington attends the Second Continental Congress as a delegate from Virginia. He appears in military uniform.

June 15 The Continental Congress selects George Washington to be commander in chief of the Continental army.

June 15–16 American militia astonish British regulars by inflicting heavy casualties on the British at the Battle of Bunker Hill, which takes place on Breed's Hill.

July 3 Washington assumes control of the colonial soldiers who have gathered at Cambridge, Massachusetts. His first order declares that all troops are part of the United Provinces of North America Army and no longer belong to individual colonies.

August 23 King George III announces that all thirteen colonies are in revolt.

1776

January 10 Thomas Paine publishes *Common Sense*, and over 100,000 copies of the pamphlet are sold in three months.

March 27 The British army leaves Boston. Washington plans to move troops to New York for the next major battle.

June 6 Delegate Richard Henry Lee of Virginia introduces a resolution at the Second Continental Congress declaring independence from Britain.

July 4 The Second Continental Congress passes the Declaration of Independence.

July 9 Washington holds an independence celebration among his troops in New York; the Declaration of Independence is read to all soldiers.

August 20 Washington assembles the Continental army's 20,000 soldiers in New York to prepare for an attack from British general William Howe's 32,000 troops.

August 27 The British launch the first large-scale attack of the American Revolution, forcing an American retreat from Long Island back to Manhattan.

October 16 Washington orders a retreat from New York.

December 26 Washington orders troops to cross the Delaware River in the midst of a winter freeze and launches a surprise attack on a British outpost at Trenton, New Jersey. The attack yields nine hundred British and Hessian prisoners of war and renews the confidence of the army.

December 27 Congress grants Washington the power to appoint officers, enlist troops, and raise money from the colonies without further consent from Congress.

1777

January 3 Washington leads the Continental army in a march on Princeton and seizes control of a British fort. He spends the remainder of the winter training the army at the Morristown, New Jersey, Continental army headquarters.

June 14 Congress commissions a flag with thirteen red and white stripes and thirteen white stars on a blue field.

July 2 Vermont becomes the first colony to abolish slavery. (Georgia was the only colony to forbid slavery at its inception.)

September 26 Congress leaves Philadelphia before the British occupy the city.

November 15 The Articles of Confederation are submitted to the states for ratification.

December 21 Washington leads the Continental army to Valley Forge, Pennsylvania, and establishes winter quarters.

1778

February 6 The Franco-American Treaty of Amity and Commerce is signed in Paris. In it the French recognize American independence and pledge support against Britain.

December 29 The British invade the South, seizing Savannah, Georgia.

1779

June 21 Spain declares war against Britain, but does not recognize American independence.

July 16 Washington orders Gen. Anthony Wayne to attack the British at Stony Point; the successful mission is a morale booster for the Continental army.

1780

May 12 British general Henry Clinton leads a devastating attack on the Continental army, seizing Charleston, South Carolina, and taking five thousand prisoners of war.

1781

January 1 Continental army soldiers from Pennsylvania mutiny and threaten to march on Philadelphia. Washington crafts a plan, and Congress acquiesces, to end the mutiny one week later by guaranteeing additional pay to the soldiers.

January 5 Benedict Arnold, controlling a faction of the British military, invades Richmond, Virginia, forcing the government of that state to flee.

January 20 Continental army soldiers from New Jersey mutiny. Fearing a growing trend, Washington orders the execution of the leaders and successfully ends the mutiny.

March 1 Maryland becomes the last state to adopt the Articles of Confederation.

October 14 French reinforcements arrive from the West Indies; Washington coordinates an attack between the French force and the Continental army on Yorktown, Virginia.

October 19 Eight thousand soldiers under the leadership of Lord Cornwallis surrender at Yorktown, Virginia. This decisive victory ends British hopes of defeating the combined American and French armies in North America.

October 25 Washington orders any slaves who fought against the British at Yorktown freed and any who fought for the British returned to their owners.

November 5 John Parke Custis, Washington's stepson, dies of camp fever after aiding Washington in the Battle of Yorktown. Two of Custis's children grow up at Mount Vernon under the care of George and Martha Washington.

November 26 The Continental army establishes winter quarters at Newburgh, New York, and remains there until a peace treaty is signed in Paris nearly two years later.

1782

March 31 Col. Lewis Nicola recommends the army seize control of America and crown Washington; Washington scolds Nicola.

August 19 The final battles of the Revolutionary War take place when the British and Indians attack Daniel Boone and the Kentucky militia.

1783

March 12–15 Officers of the Continental army are stationed in Newburgh, New York, awaiting the Paris peace treaty that will officially end the Revolutionary War. Citing Congress's inability to meet the military payroll and refusal to enact a promised pension for officers, the officers threaten to march on the capital. Washington averts a possibly disastrous turn of events by forcefully reminding the veterans of the significance of their victory against the British.

June 19 Washington is elected president-general of the Society of the Cincinnati, a hereditary military society founded by officers of the Revolution.

September 3 The Treaty of Paris is concluded, formally ending the Revolutionary War and establishing boundaries for the United States but leaving several issues unresolved.

November 2 Washington issues his farewell orders urging his comrades to become good citizens and aid their fellow citizens in strengthening the federal government.

December 24 Washington returns to Mount Vernon after relinquishing command of the disbanded Continental army.

1785

March 25–28 Washington hosts a conference on navigation of waterways at Mount Vernon, attended by representatives of several states.

May 17 Washington becomes president of the Potomac River Canal Company, a business venture that seeks to make the Potomac the commercial gateway to the American interior.

1786

December 4 Washington declines election as a delegate from Virginia to a Philadelphia convention designed to address weaknesses in the Articles of Confederation.

1787

January 25 A group of Massachusetts farmers led by Daniel Shays seize the Springfield arsenal and the courthouses in western Massachusetts. The event later became known as Shays's Rebellion. The rebellion alarms property owners, creditors, and law-and-order conservatives throughout the colonies.

March 28 After being lobbied by James Madison, governor of Virginia, Washington agrees to serve as a delegate from Virginia to the Philadelphia convention that will address weaknesses in the Articles of Confederation.

May 14 Washington presides over the Constitutional Convention in Philadelphia. He is unanimously elected president on May 25 when a quorum is reached.

July 13 The Northwest Ordinance is approved, establishing a policy for governing the region; slavery is banned in the Northwest Territory.

September 15 The Philadelphia convention votes to adopt the Constitution, and the document is signed two days later.

1788

June 21 The U.S. Constitution takes effect when New Hampshire becomes the ninth state to ratify the document.

1789

February 4 Members of the electoral college meet in New York to cast ballots in the first presidential election. Washington receives the unanimous support of the electors.

April 14 Charles Thomson, secretary of the Continental Congress, informs George Washington that he has been elected president of the United States.

April 30 Washington delivers his inaugural address and takes the oath of office as America's first president.

June 1 Congress approves its first act, which establishes procedures to administer oaths of office.

July 4 Congress passes a tariff act, which levies taxes on imports to protect domestic industries, to raise revenue, and to assert the power of the federal government.

July 14 Twenty thousand French protestors storm the Bastille; they free the infamous prison's seven inmates.

July 20 Congress passes a federal navigation act, taxing vessels based on weight.

July 27 Congress creates the Department of State. John Jay, secretary of foreign affairs under the Articles of Confederation, continues in his position until Washington's appointee, Thomas Jefferson, assumes office on March 22, 1790.

August 4 A federal bond is authorized to recover the war debt of the federal government.

August 7 Congress creates the Department of War. Henry Knox serves as its first secretary, beginning on September 12, 1789.

August 25 Mary Ball Washington, George's mother, dies near Fredericksburg, Virginia, at the age of eighty-one. During her life, she publicly (and falsely) charged her famous son with neglecting her material needs.

August 27 The French National Assembly proclaims the Declaration of the Rights of Man, modeled after the Declaration of Independence. The document calls for freedom of speech, assembly, religion, and the press, as well as equality for all French citizens.

September 2 Congress creates the Treasury Department. Alexander Hamilton serves as its first secretary.

September 13 The United States takes out its first loan from a New York bank.

September 22 Congress creates the Post Office. Samuel Osgood assumes office as the first postmaster general on September 26. (For the next one hundred years, the overwhelming majority of federal employees will work in peacetime for this single agency.)

September 24 Congress passes the Judiciary Act and creates the Office of the Attorney General. Edmund Randolph takes office as the first attorney general on September 26.

September 29 Congress adjourns.

1790

February 2 The Supreme Court opens its first session at the Royal Exchange building in New York.

July 16 Washington signs a bill selecting a permanent site for the capital on the banks of the Potomac River.

October 22 Gen. Josiah Harmar orders a retreat of the American military after Little Turtle, chief of the Miami tribe, carries out an ambush that kills fifty of Harmar's men. Harmar was on a mission to defend settlers in the Northwest Territory.

1791

February 25 The first Bank of the United States is chartered.

March 3 Congress passes a tax on distilled spirits and establishes the District of Columbia.

March 4 Maj. Gen. Arthur St. Clair is appointed commander in chief of the U.S. military.

November 4 An organized force of Indians under the leadership of Little Turtle overwhelms an American force under the leadership of Maj. Gen. St. Clair.

December 15 The Bill of Rights is ratified.

1792

April 2 Congress establishes the U.S. Mint.

April 5 Washington issues the first presidential veto, turning down an apportionment bill on constitutional grounds.

November 6 Washington is unanimously reelected president by electors chosen as each state sees fit, mostly by members of each state's legislature.

1793

March 4 Washington delivers his second inaugural address in Philadelphia.

April 22 Washington issues the Neutrality Proclamation to avoid entering war between revolutionary France and its enemies, in particular Britain.

July 18 Secretary of State Jefferson asks the Supreme Court for an opinion on questions pertaining to foreign policy, neutrality, and treaty law on behalf of President Washington. The Court declines to give advisory opinions.

October 28 Eli Whitney invents the cotton gin.

1794

July–November In what will be called the Whiskey Rebellion, farmers in western Pennsylvania attack excise agents whose duty it is to collect the excise tax on whiskey.

August 20 Maj. Gen. "Mad" Anthony Wayne decisively wins the Battle of Fallen Timbers against an army of Indians from several tribes. This victory marks the end of British military aid to the Indians and forces them farther westward.

November 19 John Jay successfully negotiates a treaty with Britain, and its terms are transmitted under seal to Washington to avoid immediate public backlash.

1795

March 3 In the Treaty of San Lorenzo, Spain opens the Mississippi River to American navigation.

August 18 Washington signs the Jay Treaty, a highly controversial document that keeps America and Britain from war but sacrifices American rights to freedom from British harassment at sea.

1796

May 31 The United States concludes a treaty with the Native American tribes known as the Six Nations (Seneca, Cayuga, Oneida, Onondaga, Mohawk, and Tuscarora).

September 19 Washington's historic Farewell Address is printed in the *American Daily Advertiser,* a Philadelphia newspaper.

1797

February 28 Washington issues a second veto, rejecting a law concerning the army, on policy grounds.

March 3 Washington's second term as president ends.

May 31 The XYZ affair begins when three French agents identified as X, Y, and Z, demand a $10 million bribe before their country will negotiate with America.

1798

July 11 Fearing imminent war with France, President John Adams appoints Washington lieutenant general and commander in chief of the U.S. military.

1799

December 14 George Washington dies at Mount Vernon.

Appendix C

Cabinet and Key Administration Officials, Washington Administration

C.1 Principal Executive Officers

George Washington wrote, "It is infinitely better to have a few good men than many indifferent ones" (Washington to James McHenry, August 10, 1798, in George Washington Papers at the Library of Congress, 1741–1799: Series 4, General Correspondence, 1697–1799). Washington's original choices for the major departments reflected this philosophy. He was not always able, however, to get those people he wanted for the posts available. Indeed, it is a myth that no one says "no" to a president.

In April 1793, Washington first used the term *cabinet* to refer to the heads of the major departments and the attorney general. In the table that follows, the date for the beginning of each officeholder's service indicates when he actually assumed office. For some, such as Thomas Jefferson, commissioned secretary of state on September 26, 1789, there was a considerable gap between the commission and the onset of service. (John Jay served as secretary *ad interim* in this instance until Jefferson took the post.)

Position	Officeholder	Term of service
President	George Washington	April 30, 1789–March 3, 1797
Vice president	John Adams	April 30, 1789–March 3, 1797
Secretary of state	Thomas Jefferson	March 22, 1790–December 31, 1793
	Edmund Randolph	January 2, 1794–August 20, 1795
	Timothy Pickering	August 20, 1795–May 12, 1800
Secretary of the Treasury	Alexander Hamilton	September 11, 1789–January 31, 1795
	Oliver Wolcott Jr.	February 2, 1795–December 31, 1800
Secretary of war	Henry Knox	September 12, 1789–December 31, 1794
	Timothy Pickering	January 2, 1795–February 5, 1796
	James McHenry	February 6, 1796–May 31, 1800
Attorney general	Edmund Randolph	February 2, 1790–January 2, 1794
	William Bradford	January 27, 1794–August 23, 1795
	Charles Lee	December 10, 1795–March 3, 1801

Position	Officeholder	Term of service
Postmaster general	Samuel Osgood	September 26, 1789–August 19, 1791
	Timothy Pickering	August 19, 1791–January 2, 1795
	Joseph Habersham	February 25, 1795–November 2, 1801
Minister to Britain	Thomas Pinckney	January 12, 1792–July 27, 1796
	Rufus King	May 20, 1796 to beyond end of term
Minister to France	Gouverneur Morris	January 12, 1792–April 9, 1794
	James Monroe	May 28, 1794–December 9, 1796
	Charles Cotesworth Pinckney	September 9, 1796, to end of term (credentials as ambassador rejected by France; served as envoy extraordinary)

Source: Adapted from "Principal Executive Officers during Washington's Administration," Papers of George Washington, 2002 (*gwpapers.virginia.edu/presidency/officers.html*).

C.2 Socioeconomic Status of Major Officeholders in Washington Administration

The Washington administration was one of the most elite in American history, pulling together members of prominent families from all regions of the country. As in today's administrations, lawyers were well represented among the president's top appointees.

Office and officeholder	College	Primary non-governmental occupation	Prior government experience	Important secondary economic affiliations	Family and other ties	Other
President						
George Washington	None	Planter	Commander in chief, Continental army (1775–1783); delegate, Continental Congress (1774–1775); Va. colonial legislator (1758–1774); other	President, Potomac Co. (1785–1789)	Devoted protégé of Lord Fairfax of Va.; wed wealthy widow of Daniel Custis	Popular hero of French and Indian War
Secretary of state						
Thomas Jefferson	William and Mary College	Planter, lawyer (to 1774)	Minister to France (1784–1789); member of Congress (1783–1784); governor of Va. (1779–1781); colonial legislator (1769–1775)	None	Mother a Randolph; married into another notable family (Wayles)	Author of Declaration of Independence; founder of University of Virginia
Edmund Randolph	William and Mary College (attended)	Planter, lawyer	U.S. attorney general (1789–1794); delegate, Constitutional Convention (one of leaders); governor of Va. (1786–1788); attorney general of Va. (1776–1782)	Board member, James River Canal Co. (1784–?)	Member of most socially prominent family of Va.; wed daughter of Robert Nicholas, a granddaughter of famous "King" Carter of Va.	Aide-de-camp to General Washington

Name	Education	Occupation	Government experience	Business/financial connections	Family connections	Military experience
Timothy Pickering	Harvard	Farmer and land speculator, business investor	U.S. postmaster general (1791–1795); secretary of war (1795); local government figure in Pa. (1786–1791)	None	Pickering's sister wed a prominent merchant, John Gardner	Minor Revolutionary War figure in Mass.
Secretary of the Treasury						
Alexander Hamilton	Kings College (Columbia; attended)	Lawyer, investor	Member of Congress (1782–1783, 1787–1788); N.Y. state legislator; major figure at Constitutional Convention (1787)	Board member, Bank of New York	Married daughter of Philip Schuyler, major N.Y. political and financial figure; brother-in-law of Stephen Van Rensselaer, major landholder, and John Church, banker; protégé of Elias Boudinot, Edward Livingston, Gouverneur Morris, and Robert Morris	Prominent Revolutionary War figure
Oliver Wolcott Jr.	Yale	Lawyer	U.S. Treasury Department posts (1789–1795); state fiscal posts in Conn.	None	Father a wealthy landowner and lawyer	Minor Revolutionary War figure
Secretary of war						
Henry Knox	None	Boston bookstore proprietor	Secretary of war under Articles of Confederation (1785–1789)		Substantial landholdings through wife's family	Major Revolutionary War figure

Office and officeholder	College	Primary non-governmental occupation	Prior government experience	Important secondary economic affiliations	Family and other ties	Other
Timothy Pickering	*See entry under secretary of state*					
James McHenry	Educated abroad	Physician	Member of Congress (1783–1786); Md. state legislator (1781–1786)	None	Father and brother had substantial Baltimore importing business	Secretary to General Washington during War of Independence
Attorney general Edmund Randolph	*See entry under secretary of state*					
William Bradford	College of New Jersey (Princeton)	Lawyer	Justice, Pa. Supreme Court (1791–1794); attorney general of Pa. (1780–1791)		Wed daughter of Mr. and Mrs. Elias Boudinot (he was a major N.J. landowner and she was the sister of Richard Stockton, a member of a prominent N.J. family)	Revolutionary War figure
Charles Lee	None	Planter, lawyer	Va. state legislator (1793–1795); collector, Port of Alexandria (1789–1793)	None	Son of Henry Lee, head of famous and wealthy Lee family; sister-in-law, wife of George Washington's brother John	

Source: Adapted from Philip H. Burch Jr., *Elites in American History, The Federalist Years to the Civil War* (New York: Holmes and Meier, 1981), 252–256.

Appendix D
Election Results

D.1 Electoral College Results, 1789

Eleven states had joined the Union in time to take part in the first presidential election. Of those eleven, ten selected electoral college delegates (see Table D.2, entry on New York). The ten states' sixty-nine electors who voted in 1789 were entitled to select two candidates on the presidential ballot. The person who received the greatest number of votes would become president, provided he secured a majority. Washington received one vote from all sixty-nine electors, becoming the only president in U.S. history to win unanimously in the electoral college. The person who received the next greatest number of votes would become vice president. With thirty-four electoral votes, John Adams became the first vice president of the United States.

	State										
Candidate	Conn.	Del.	Ga.	Md.	Mass.	N.H.	N.J.	Pa.	S.C.	Va.	Total
George Washington	7	3	5	6	10	5	6	10	7	10	69
John Adams	5				10	5	1	8		5	34
John Jay		3					5			1	9
R. H. Harrison				6							6
John Rutledge									6		6
John Hancock							2	1	1		4
George Clinton										3	3
Samuel Huntington	2										2
John Milton			2								2
James Armstrong			1								1
Benjamin Lincoln			1								1
Edward Telfair			1								1

Source: Compiled from information in *Presidential Elections, 1789–2000* (Washington, D.C.: CQ Press, 2003).

D.2 Selection of Electors, 1789

Congress permitted each state legislature to choose how it would select its electors. Most states used an appointment system in which the legislature picked electors. Four states used direct popular election of electors, while others used a combination of the two. The following table details the methods used to pick electors for the presidential election of 1789.

State	Method
Connecticut	State legislature chose seven electors on January 7, 1789.
Delaware	One elector was chosen by the voters in each of three districts on January 7, 1789.
Georgia	State legislature chose five electors on January 7, 1789.
Maryland	Eight electors were chosen at large in a popular election that took place between January 7 and January 10. Two electors were absent when voting took place on February 4. Therefore, four votes were not cast.
Massachusetts	Voters in each of eight districts chose two electors to send to the state legislature for approval on December 17, 1788. The legislature chose one of those electors for each of the eight districts as well as two additional electors at a meeting on January 7, 1789.
New Hampshire	Popular election was held on December 15, 1788, but no elector received a majority of the vote. On January 7, 1789, the state legislature chose five electors from the top ten candidates in the popular election.
New Jersey	Governor of New Jersey and Privy Council chose seven electors on January 7, 1789.
New York	The two houses of the New York legislature could not agree on a procedure to select electors. As a result, New York did not participate in the presidential election of 1789.
North Carolina	Because North Carolina had not yet ratified the Constitution, it did not participate in the presidential election of 1789.
Pennsylvania	Ten electors were chosen through a popular election on January 7, 1789.
Rhode Island	Because Rhode Island had not yet ratified the Constitution, it did not participate in the presidential election of 1789.
South Carolina	State legislature chose seven electors on January 7, 1789.
Virginia	A popular election was held in each of twelve districts in Virginia on January 7, 1789. One district did not properly report the returns, and one elector failed to vote on February 4. Therefore, four votes were not cast.

Source: Compiled from information in *Presidential Elections, 1789–2000* (Washington, D.C.: CQ Press, 2003).

D.3 Electoral College Results, 1792

In 1792 Washington again secured the unanimous support of electors, but the battle for the vice presidency was significantly closer than in 1789. The Democratic-Republican Party backed New York governor George Clinton, but John Adams was able to preserve his position for another term because he was supported by all the other northern states.

State

Candidate	Conn.	Del.	Ga.	Ky	Md.	Mass.	N.H.	N.J.	NY	N.C.	Pa.	RI	S.C.	VT	Va.	Total
George Washington	9	3	4	4	8	16	6	7	12	12	15	4	8	3	21	132
John Adams	9	3			8	16	6	7			14	4	7	3		77
George Clinton			4						12	12	1				21	50
Thomas Jefferson				4												4
Aaron Burr													1			1

Source: Compiled from information in *Presidential Elections, 1789–2000* (Washington, D.C.: CQ Press, 2003).

D.4 Selection of Electors, 1792

By the election of 1792, fifteen states had ratified the Constitution. The majority of states still relied on their legislatures to pick electors. Six states, however, used some form of popular election to pick electors.

State	Method
Connecticut	State legislature chose electors.
Delaware	State legislature chose electors.
Georgia	State legislature chose electors.
Kentucky	A popular election was held, with two electors being chosen in each of two districts.
Maryland	Electors were chosen at large in a popular election. Four votes were not cast.
Massachusetts	Thirteen electors who received a majority of the popular vote in their district were selected. The remaining three electors were chosen by the state legislature.
New Hampshire	Electors were chosen through a popular election.
New Jersey	State legislature chose electors.
New York	State legislature chose electors.
North Carolina	State legislature chose electors.
Pennsylvania	Electors were chosen through a popular election.
Rhode Island	State legislature chose electors.
South Carolina	State legislature chose electors.
Vermont	State legislature chose electors. Two votes were not cast.
Virginia	Electors were selected through a popular vote in each of Virginia's twenty-one districts.

Source: Compiled from information in *Presidential Elections, 1789–2000* (Washington, D.C.: CQ Press, 2003).

Works Cited

Adair, Douglass. 1974. *Fame and the Founding Fathers* (essays). Edited by Trevor Colbourn. New York: Norton, for the Institute of Early American History and Culture, Williamsburg, Virginia.

Allen, W. B., ed. 1988. *George Washington: A Collection.* Indianapolis: Liberty Classics.

Avalon Project, Yale Law School (*www.yale.edu/lawweb/avalon*).

Boller, Paul F., Jr. 1985. *Presidential Campaigns.* New York: Oxford University Press.

Bowen, Clarence Winthrop. 1889. "The Centennial Celebration of the Inauguration of George Washington as the First President of the United States—Monday, Tuesday, and Wednesday, April 29th, 30th, and May 1st, 1889: Official Program with Historical Sketches." Committee on the Centennial of Washington's Inauguration.

Bryan, William Alfred. 1952. *George Washington in American Literature, 1775–1865.* New York: Columbia University Press.

Burnett, Edmund C. 1928. "Samuel Osgood." In *Dictionary of American Biography, under the Auspices of the American Council of Learned Societies.* 20 vols. New York: Scribner's, 1928–1958.

Calliope Film Resources. 2000. "Shays' Rebellion" (*www.calliope.org/shays/shays2.html*).

Combs, Jerald A. 1970. *The Jay Treaty: Political Battleground of the Founding Fathers.* Berkeley: University of California Press.

Cunliffe, Marcus. 1971. "Elections of 1789 and 1792." In *History of American Presidential Elections, 1789–1969,* edited by Arthur M. Schlesinger Jr. New York: McGraw Hill.

Cunningham, Noble E., Jr. 2000. *Jefferson vs. Hamilton: Confrontations that Shaped a Nation.* Boston: Bedford/St. Martin's.

Custis, G. W. Parke. 1859. *Recollections and Private Memoirs of George Washington.* Washington, D.C.: W. H. Moore.

Degregorio, William A. 1993. *The Complete Book of U.S. Presidents, From George Washington to Bill Clinton.* New York: Wings Books.

Ferling, John. 2000. *Setting the World Ablaze: Washington, Adams, Jefferson and the American Revolution.* New York: Oxford University Press.

Fisher, Louis. 1995. *Presidential War Power.* Lawrence: University Press of Kansas.

Fitzpatrick, John C., ed. 1931–1944. *The Writings of George Washington from the Original Manuscript Sources, 1745–1799.* 39 vols. Washington, D.C.: Government Printing Office.

Flexner, James Thomas. 1965. *George Washington, the Forge of Experience, 1732–1775*. Boston: Little, Brown.

———. 1970. *George Washington and the New Nation*. Boston: Little, Brown.

———. 1972. *George Washington: Anguish and Farewell*. Boston: Little, Brown.

———. 1974. *Washington: The Indispensable Man*. Boston: Little, Brown.

Freeman, Douglass Southall. 1948. *George Washington: A Biography*. Vol. 2, *Young Washington*. New York: Scribner's.

———. 1951. *George Washington: A Biography*. Vol. 3, *Planter and Patriot*. New York: Scribner's.

Friedman, Lawrence. 1975. *Inventors of the Promised Land*. New York: Knopf.

Furtwangler, Albert. 1987. *American Silhouettes: Rhetorical Identities of the Founders*. New Haven: Yale University Press.

Greenfeld, Liah. 1992. *Nationalism: Five Roads to Modernity*. Cambridge, Mass.: Harvard University Press.

Griswold, Rufus Wilmot. 1854. *The Republican Court, or American Society in the Days of Washington*. New York: Appleton.

Heitman, Francis B. 1903. *Historical Register and Dictionary of The United States Army, from its Organization, September 29, 1789, to March 2, 1903*. 2 vols. Washington, D.C.: Government Printing Office.

Henriques, Peter R. 2001. "The Final Struggle between George Washington and the Grim King: Washington's Attitude toward Death and an Afterlife." In *George Washington Reconsidered*. Edited by Don Higginbotham. Charlottesville: University Press of Virginia.

Higginbotham, Don. 2001. "George Washington and Revolutionary Asceticism." In *George Washington Reconsidered*, edited by Don Higginbotham. Charlottesville: University Press of Virginia.

Hirschfeld, Fritz. 1997. *George Washington and Slavery: A Documentary Portrayal*. Columbia: University of Missouri Press.

Hofstadter, Richard. 1969. *The Idea of a Party System: The Rise of Legitimate Opposition in the United States, 1780–1840*. Berkeley: University of California Press.

Humphrey, Carol Sue. 1996. *The Press of the Young Republic, 1783–1833*. Westport, Conn.: Greenwood Press.

Hutchison, William T., and William M. E. Rachal, eds. 1960. *The Papers of James Madison*. 17 vols. Chicago: University of Chicago Press.

Jackson, Donald, ed., and Dorothy Twohig, assoc. ed. 1976–1979. *The Diaries of George Washington*. 6 vols. Charlottesville: University Press of Virginia.

Johnston, Henry P. 1890–1893. *The Correspondence and Public Papers of John Jay*. 4 vols. New York: Putnam's Sons.

Kohn, Richard H. 1984. "Anthony Wayne." In *Dictionary of American Military Biography*. 3 vols. Edited by Robert J. Spiller; Joseph G. Dawson III, Associate

Editor; T. Harry Williams, Consulting Editor. Westport, Conn.: Greenwood Press.

———. 1986. "The Inside History of the Newburgh Conspiracy: America and the Coup d'Etat." In *The Military in America: From the Colonial Era to the Present*. Rev. ed. Edited by Peter Karsten. New York: Free Press.

Landy, Marc, and Sidney M. Milkis. 2000. *Presidential Greatness*. Lawrence: University Press of Kansas.

Longmore, Paul K. 1988. *The Invention of George Washington*. Berkeley: University of California Press.

Lowi, Theodore J. 1985. *The Personal President: Power Invested, Promise Unfulfilled*. Ithaca: Cornell University Press.

Maas, David E. 2001. "The Founding Father of the American Presidency." In *George Washington In and As Culture*, edited by Kevin L. Cope. New York: AMS Press.

Maclay, Edgar S., ed. 1890. *Journal of William Maclay, United States Senator from Pennsylvania, 1789–1791*. New York: Appleton.

Malone, Dumas. 1948–1981. *Jefferson and His Time*. 6 vols. Boston: Little Brown.

Mastromarino, Mark A., and Jack D. Warren, eds. 2000. *The Papers of George Washington, Presidential Series*. Vol. 9, *September 1791–February 1792*. Charlottesville: University Press of Virginia.

McDonald, Forrest. 1974. *Presidency of George Washington*. Lawrence: University Press of Kansas.

———. 1979. *Alexander Hamilton: A Biography*. New York: Norton.

———. 1992. "Washington, Cato, and Honor: A Model for Revolutionary Leadership." In *American Models of Revolutionary Leadership*, edited by Daniel K. Elazar and Ellis Katz. Lanham, Md.: University Press of America.

———. 1994. *The American Presidency: An Intellectual History*. Lawrence: University Press of Kansas.

Meinig, D. W. 1986. *The Shaping of America: A Geographical Perspective on 500 Years of History*. Vol. 1, *Atlantic America, 1492–1800*. New Haven: Yale University Press.

Millett, Allan R., and Peter Maslowski. 1994. *For the Common Defense: A Military History of the United States of America*. Rev. and exp. New York: Free Press.

Mintz, Max M. 1999. "Gouverneur Morris." In *American National Biography, under the Auspices of the American Council of Learned Societies*. 24 vols. Rev. ed. Edited by John A. Garraty and Mark C. Carnes. New York: Oxford University Press.

Mitnick, Barbara J., gen. ed. 1999. *George Washington, American Symbol*. Stony Brook, N.Y.: Hudson Hills Press.

Nelson, Michael, ed. 1999. *The Evolving Presidency: Addresses, Cases, Essays, Letters, Reports, Resolutions, Transcripts, and Other Landmark Documents, 1787–1998*. Washington, D.C.: CQ Press.

Palmer. Dave Richard, and James W. Stryker. 1986. *Early American Wars and Military Institutions*. Vol. 4. *The West Point Military History Series*. Edited by Thomas E. Griess, Department of Military History, U.S. Military Academy. Wayne, N.J.: Avery Publishing.

Pasley, Jeffrey L. 2001. *"The Tyranny of Printers": Newspaper Politics in the Early American Republic*. Charlottesville: University Press of Virginia.

Pattee, Fred Lewis. 1928. "Henry Knox." In *Dictionary of American Biography, under the Auspices of the American Council of Learned Societies*. 20 vols. New York: Scribner's, 1928–1958.

Perret, Geoffrey. 1989. *A Country Made by War*. New York: Vintage.

Phelps, Glenn A. 1989. "George Washington: Precedent Setter." In *Inventing the American Presidency*. Edited by Thomas E. Cronin. Lawrence: University Press of Kansas.

———. 1993. *George Washington and American Constitutionalism*. Lawrence: University Press of Kansas.

Phillips, Kevin. 1999. *The Cousins' Wars: Religion, Politics and the Triumph of Anglo-America*. New York: Basic Books.

Pious, Richard M. 1979. *The American Presidency*. New York: Basic Books.

Purvis, Thomas L., ed. 1995. *Revolutionary America, 1763–1800*. New York: Facts on File.

Randall, Willard Sterne. 1997. *George Washington, A Life*. New York: Henry Holt.

Randolph, Edmund. 1855. *A Vindication of Edmund Randolph, Written by Himself and Published in 1795*. Richmond: no publisher specified.

Rasmussen, William M. S., and Robert S. Tilton. 1999. *George Washington: The Man behind the Myths*. Charlottesville: University Press of Virginia.

Rhodehamel, John, ed. 1997. *Writings / George Washington*. New York: Library of America.

Richardson, James D., comp. 1897. *Messages and Papers of the Presidents*. New York: Bureau of National Literature.

Schlesinger, Arthur M., Jr., ed. 1971. *History of American Presidential Elections, 1789–1969*. New York: McGraw Hill.

Schultz, Jeffrey D. 2000. *Presidential Scandals*. Washington, D.C.: CQ Press.

Schwartz, Barry. 1987. *George Washington: The Making of an American Symbol*. New York: Free Press.

Sharp, James Roger. 1993. *American Politics in the Early Republic: The New Nation in Crisis*. New Haven: Yale University Press.

Simmons, Wendy W. 2002. "Reagan, Kennedy and Lincoln Receive the Most Votes for 'Greatest U.S. President,'" Gallup Poll Analysis, February 19, 2001 (*www.gallup.com*).

Smith, Page. 1980. *The Shaping of America, a People's History of the Young Republic*. New York: Penguin.

Smith, Richard Norton. 1993. *Patriarch: George Washington and the New American Nation.* Boston: Houghton Mifflin.

Smith, William H. 1882. *The St. Clair Papers: The Life and Public Services of Arthur St. Clair, Soldier of the Revolutionary War; President of the Continental Congress; and Governor of the North-Western Territory, with His Correspondence and Other Papers.* Cincinnati: Robert Clarke.

Stanley, Harold W., and Richard G. Niemi. 2001. *Vital Statistics on American Politics: 2001–2002.* Washington, D.C.: CQ Press.

Stewart, Jay. 1997. *Most Humble Servants: The Advisory Role of Early Judges.* New Haven: Yale University Press.

Thach, Charles C., Jr. 1969. *The Creation of the Presidency, 1775–1789: A Study in Constitutional History.* New York: Da Capo Press.

Troy, Gil. 1991. *See How They Ran: The Changing Role of the Presidential Candidate.* New York: Free Press.

Tucker, Robert W., and David C. Hendrickson. 1990. *Empire of Liberty: The Statecraft of Thomas Jefferson.* New York: Oxford University Press.

Twohig, Dorothy. 2001. " 'That Species of Property': Washington's Role in the Controversy over Slavery." In *George Washington Reconsidered,* edited by Don Higginbotham. Charlottesville: University Press of Virginia.

Twohig, Dorothy, ed. 1987. *The Papers of George Washington, Presidential Series.* Vol. 1, *September 1788–March 1789.* Charlottesville: University Press of Virginia.

———. 1996. *The Papers of George Washington, Presidential Series.* Vol. 6, *July–November 1790.* Charlottesville: University Press of Virginia.

Wallenborn, White McKenzie, M.D. 1997. "George Washington's Terminal Illness: A Modern Medical Analysis of the Last Illness and Death of George Washington" (*www.virginia.edu/gwpapers/articles/wallenborn/index.html*).

Ward, Harry M. 1999. *The War for Independence and the Transformation of American Society.* London: University College of London.

Weigley, Russell F. 1973. *The American Way of War: A History of United States Military Strategy and Policy.* Bloomington: Indiana University Press.

Wilkins, Roger. 2001. *Jefferson's Pillow: The Founding Fathers and the Dilemma of Black Patriotism.* Boston: Beacon Press.

Williams, Stanley Thomas. 1928. "David Humphreys." In *Dictionary of American Biography, under the Auspices of the American Council of Learned Societies.* 20 vols. New York: Scribner's, 1928–1958.

Williamson, Chilton. 1960. *American Suffrage: From Property to Democracy, 1760–1860.* Princeton: Princeton University Press.

Wills, Garry. 1984. *Cincinnatus: George Washington and the Enlightenment.* Garden City, N.Y.: Doubleday.

———. 2002. *James Madison.* New York: Times Books.

Index